DIVINE CUSTODY

DIVINE CUSTODY

A HISTORY OF SINGAPORE'S OLDEST TEOCHEW TEMPLE

YEO KANG SHUA

NUS PRESS
SINGAPORE

Published with the support of the National Heritage Board

National Heritage Board

Published by:

NUS Press
National University of Singapore
AS3-01-02, 3 Arts Link
Singapore 117569

Fax: (65) 6774-0652
E-mail: nusbooks@nus.edu.sg
Website: http://nuspress.nus.edu.sg

ISBN 978-981-325-144-1 (case)

National Library Board, Singapore Cataloguing in Publication Data

Names: Yeo, Kang Shua, 1975-
Title: Divine custody : a history of Singapore's oldest Teochew temple / Yeo Kang Shua.
Description: Singapore : NUS Press, [2021] | Includes bibliographic references and index.
Identifiers: OCN 1252627218 | ISBN 978-981-325-144-1
Subjects: LCSH: Temples, Chinese--Singapore--History. | Temples, Chinese--Social aspects--Singapore. | Temples, Chinese--Singapore--Design and construction.
Classification: DDC 726.1951095957--dc23

Printed by: Markono Print Media Pte Ltd

Opposite: Wak Hai Cheng Bio's entrance gateway, and its boundary wall that was reconstructed based on archival records.
Source: Photographed by Lim Shao Bin.

Table of Contents

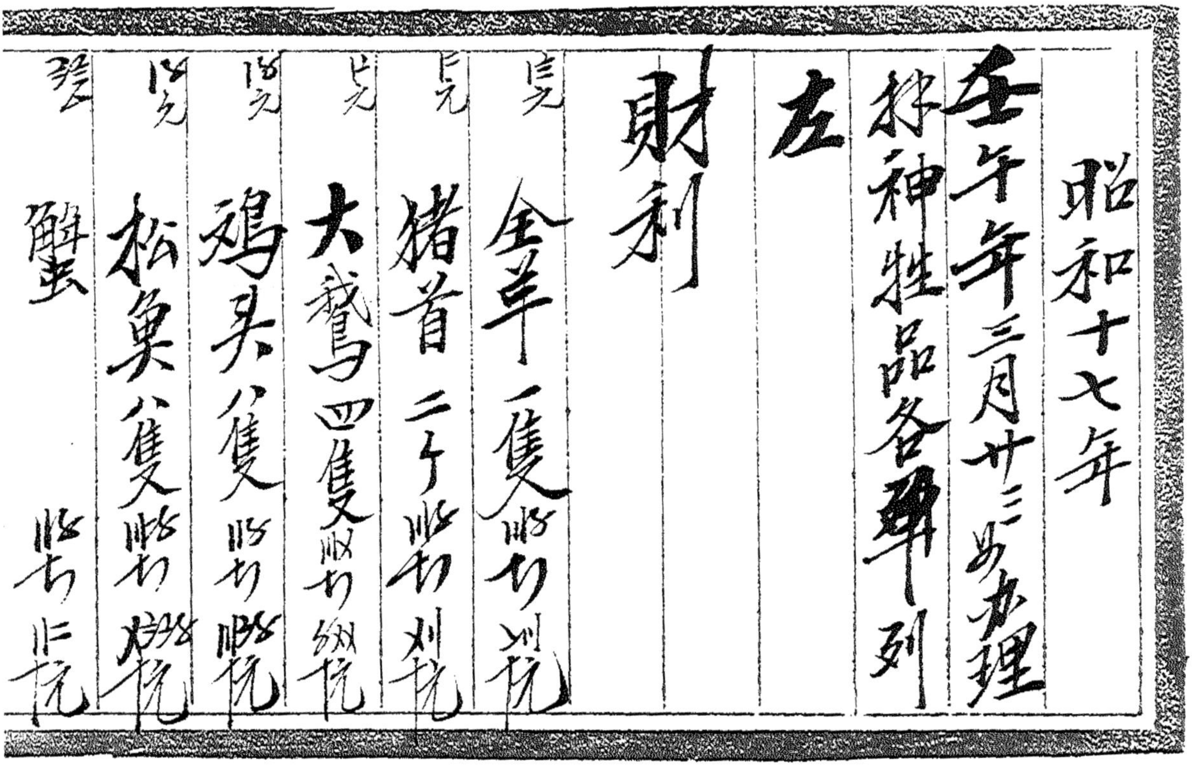
昭和十七年
壬午年三月廿三日办理
拜神牲品各單列
左
財利
全羊一隻
猪首二个
大鵞四隻
鴨头八隻
松魚八隻
蟹

Records of temple offerings on the 23rd day of the 3rd lunar month in the 17th year of the Shōwa era (1942). Source: Courtesy of the Ban See Soon Kongsi.

Note on Translation, Transliteration and Traditional Chinese Script

A number of translations have been provided throughout this research. Many texts and/or phrases have been translated or transliterated previously. In the selection and production of the translation or transliteration for this book, I have chosen to observe a few principles and conventions.

Firstly, I have attempted, wherever possible, to use existing standard translations with the original Chinese text appended in parenthesis alongside. Secondly, if there is no standard translation or, for any reason, the standard translation is not suitable, I will abide by the distinction between normative and flexible translation in my translation. In general, normative translation will serve well for technical terms or everyday objects. However, if one tries to render more complex ideas unalterably with but a single English word, then one is usually restricted to the most literal of translations. Therefore, in this book, I tend to opt for flexible translation on the principle that one should employ the English word or phrase that modern speakers would use to convey an idea. One should try to be as literal as possible, but not at the expense of intelligibility. Lastly, when working with standard translation, it has sometimes been necessary to introduce minor editorial changes to make the passage read more smoothly or intelligibly.

In the case for transliteration, firstly I will use existing popular transliteration of Chinese names. In most cases, these are rendered in the Wade-Giles romanisation system which was the preferred transliteration system used widely in the 20th century in which most of the historic materials of this book's subject are situated. The Hanyu Pinyin (漢語拼音) romanisation system, which was officially implemented in China in 1979, will be used with its diacritics, where names do not have an existing popular transliteration. In the case for Teochew (Chaozhou) romanisation, the *Diê*^{5} *Ziu*^{1} *uê*^{7} *pêng*^{1} *im*^{1} *huang*^{1} *ang*^{3} (潮州話拼音方案) or Chaozhou Dialect Romanisation Scheme issued in 1960 by the Guangdong Provincial Education Department (廣東省教育行政部門) will be used. The order of the Chinese naming system is also retained. That is, the family name (surname) comes first, followed by the given name.

The movement to promote the usage of the Chinese simplified script (簡體字) in Singapore started from the mid-1950s.[1] However, it was only in 1968 that the Ministry of Education established a committee (簡化漢字委員會) "to study and make recommendations regarding the introduction of simplified Chinese characters in schools".[2] The following year, the Ministry issued a list of simplified Chinese characters. This kickstarted the formal transition process from traditional script (繁體字) to simplified script and laid out the implementation plans starting from 1970.[3] In 1971, Chinese textbooks for primary schools began providing Hanyu Pinyin alongside the Mandarin Phonetic Symbols (注音符號).[4] And from 1974 onwards, Chinese textbooks were progressively printed in the simplified script and the layout of the text changed from vertical to horizontal.[5]

The process to switch from traditional to simplified script continued for the next decade and by the mid-1980s, the simplified script had established itself as the standard form commonly used in Singapore.[6] As most of the historic materials used in this book are rendered in the traditional script, for historical accuracy, it is decided that the traditional script will be used.

Acknowledgements

This book is the result of slightly over a decade of research. At every stage of researching and writing this book, I have enjoyed the enthusiastic support of colleagues, students, friends and family. I would like to express my gratitude to the Ngee Ann Kongsi and its Wak Hai Cheng Bio Restoration Committee, led by Mr Teo Miang Yeow. It is this restoration project that ignited the idea that a book should be written on the temple.

Research and writing are challenging but rewarding. None of this would have been possible without the assistance of many individuals. I am indebted to the many craftsmen who worked on the restoration, and who have been my teachers on traditional construction techniques. I am also grateful to the amiable Ms Tan Siew Eng and Mr Chan Chee Wai, who provided administrative and technical assistance on-site.

Special thanks are due to my remarkable wife and associate Wee Sheau Theng, who is my fiercest critic, and to my capable former research assistant Ms Martina Yeo. Both are adept at following research leads to locate important documents housed in obscure locations. I also thank another former researcher, Dr Soon-Tzu Speechley, who assisted in editing the draft manuscript.

I owe a debt of gratitude to Mr Kwa Chong Guan for his encouragement and interest in my work, and to Dr Kevin Tan for editing the manuscript. I also wish to thank the anonymous reviewers for their very lucid insights and criticisms that have improved the book, and to the team at NUS Press, namely Mr Peter Schoppert, Ms Lindsay Davis and Ms Annie Teo for the editorial and design support. I am also deeply appreciative of the kind assistance of photographers Mr Lim Shao Bin, Ms Carolyn Lim and Mr Ung Ruey Loon. My gratitude also extends to the assistance rendered by the libraries and archives from where the research materials are drawn: the library of the Singapore University of Technology and Design, the National Library Board, the National Archives of Singapore, The British Library and The National Archives of the United Kingdom.

The publication of this book is also made possible with a grant from the National Heritage Board.

粵海清廟
風調
雨順

Great Eastern
Danger

Preceding spread, left page: The main entrance of Wak Hai Cheng Bio with its Chinese name inscribed on a granite plaque.
Right page: Wak Hai Cheng Bio in Singapore's urban context.
Source: Photographed by Lim Shao Bin.

Left page: Front elevation of the Shrine of the Goddess of the Sea, or Tiānhòugōng (天后宫).
Right page: Front elevation of the Shrine of the Mysterious Supreme Emperor of Heaven, or Shàngdìgōng (上帝宫).
Source: Photographed by Lim Shao Bin.

Left page: Entrance of Shàngdìgōng with its Chinese name inscribed on a granite plaque (*top left*); detail of a corbel executed in high relief at Shàngdìgōng's prayer hall (*top right*); timber truss of Shàngdìgōng's prayer hall (*bottom*).
Right page: Ceremonial doors depicting civil officials in Shàngdìgōng.
Source: Photographed by Lim Shao Bin.

恩敷北極
澤及斯民
神功高北闕北域常沾北極恩
百千萬世佑生民祀享春秋

德沛于天
光緒念三年歲次丁酉孟春吉旦
沐恩弟子廣惠肇眾信頓首拜
曙海祥雲
赫濯聲靈
后德齊天
福海毓元靈萬派迴瀾通國
滔洲鍾瑞氣千秋發育耀新

天后宮
天后宮
天后聖母

Preceding spread, left page: Timber truss of Tiānhòugōng's front hall and calligraphy on the plastered wall.
Right page: The layering of spaces leading our gaze to the deity alcove of Tiānhòugōng (*left*); entrance of Tiānhòugōng with its Chinese name inscribed on a granite plaque (*top right*); cantilevered beam at the front elevation of Tiānhòugōng (*middle right*); tiger wall of Tiānhòugōng (*bottom right*).
Source: Photographed by Lim Shao Bin.

Left page: Dragon wall denoting the east side of the temple.
Right page: Tiger wall denoting the west side of the temple.
Source: Photographed by Lim Shao Bin.

Left page: Door Gods, Qín Qióng (秦瓊) and Yùchí Gōng (尉遲恭).
Right page: *Nídìng* (泥丁) or clay figurines panel in Shàngdìgōng (*top*); fresco panels on the front elevations of the shrines (*bottom*).
Source: Photographed by Lim Shao Bin.

Characteristic ceramic ornamentation or *qiàncí* (嵌瓷) on the temple's roof.
Source: Photographed by Lim Shao Bin.

Fig. 0.1. This is believed to be the oldest photograph of Wak Hai Cheng Bio. This photograph is thought to be taken soon after the 1895 reconstruction of the temple.
Source: Courtesy of the National Museum of Singapore (1996-00080).

Introduction

Singapore is both an island and a country, a city-state with a total land area of approximately 720 square kilometres,[1] located, one-and-a-half degrees north of the equator at the southern tip of the Malay Peninsula. Though physically small, Singapore has been an important port settlement since the 14th century due to its geographic location.[2] It was this geographic location and a deep and safe anchorage, amongst other factors, that led to the establishment of the British free port city in 1819.[3] Almost immediately, Singapore attracted the Chinese junk trade and, in 1821, "the Chinese population numbered some 1,200, up from the 30 who were mostly gambier planters".[4] In the two centuries since then, Singapore's progress and development have been remarkable. The growth of modern Singapore, however, has meant that its architectural heritage has sometimes been overshadowed. Although historical architecture that dates back to the early 19th century dots parts of the city centre, these buildings are easily overlooked.

The roots of this book lay in my time as a student. I began studying Singapore's Chinese-style buildings in my second year of architecture school in 1998. I was just beginning to gain knowledge about architecture in general, and historic architecture with its complex construction and detailing fascinated me. I had little idea of the challenges that would lie ahead. My peers and I would visit various historic sites for our sketching assignments. The eclectic style found in buildings like the Hokkien temple Thian Hock Keng (天福宫), with its cast-iron balustrades, encaustic tiles, coloured cement tiles, polychromatic glazed wall tiles purportedly imported from the United Kingdom, left a deep impression on me. Nonetheless, comments such as "adulterated", "impure" or "*rojak*" architecture were commonly heard, and buildings such as Thian Hock Keng were consequently relegated to secondary status, deemed unworthy of comparison with their supposedly more "authentic" counterparts in China. It was then that I started to think about acculturation processes and their impact on architecture in a heterogeneous society such as Singapore. Cultures intermingled and mixed in cosmopolitan Singapore, resulting in a fusion of elements in languages, arts, food, and also in architecture. I also asked myself if the predominant narrative that building materials used in Singapore's Chinese architecture were all imported from China was true.

In the years that followed, I had the opportunity to be an understudy for Mr Lim Cher See (林子施), an experienced architecture project coordinator with practical conservation knowledge. Through Mr Lim, I became acquainted with Professors Lee Chian-Lang (李乾朗) from Taiwan and Fang Yong (方擁) from China. Professor Lee's numerous publications on traditional architecture in Taiwan were the standard works students consulted in the 1990s, especially when few publications on traditional Chinese architecture were coming out of China. Through these works, I came to realise that traditional Chinese architecture was not homogeneous and that there were strong regional differences. In 2007, I wrote an article "Homogeneously Heterogeneous?: The Diversity of Traditional Chinese Architecture in Singapore" for the *Journal of Southeast Asian Architecture*[5] examining the influences different southern coastal Chinese dialects[6] had on Singapore's traditional Chinese architecture. That same year, I joined what was then the Preservation of Monuments Board at the invitation of its chairman, the well-known architect, Mr Alfred Wong (黄匡國). In the three years that I was with the Board, I had the opportunity to examine both traditional and modern Chinese architecture of Singapore and its heritage value to the nation.

In 2010, I was approached to serve as conservation consultant for the restoration of the Ngee Ann Kongsi's Wak Hai Cheng Bio (粵海清廟). I agreed without much hesitation for three reasons: first, I had been researching Singapore's traditional Chinese architecture, and this project offered me an unparalleled opportunity to study the building's material culture at close range; second, Wak Hai Cheng Bio has the highest concentration of Chinese traditional architecture crafts to be found in a single building in Singapore; and finally, the owners' sincerity and willingness to restore their building by adopting the best conservation practices was particularly inspiring.

How we think and write about history is shaped by how we study it. Many have commented that Chinese architecture in Singapore and its history has been studied extensively and there is little left to study nor is there room for new insights. Certainly, there is a wealth of literature on the subject. Scholars have used traditional archival sources and epigraphic materials to study Chinese architecture in Singapore for decades. The challenges in this regard lie in the gaps in documentation that resulted from the Second World War. There is little information on buildings from that period. It is also widely acknowledged that most Chinese organisations, fearing retribution for supporting the anti-Japanese movement and the war in China, destroyed the bulk of their historic materials prior to the Fall of Singapore in 1942 to prevent them from falling into the wrong hands.[7]

The restoration of Wak Hai Cheng Bio offered me an opportunity to adopt a different approach to studying this building and, by extension, Singapore's Chinese architecture, through a close study of the building's material culture. Such micro-observations of the temple's architectural fabric led to further questions about the aesthetics, building technologies, as well as the social and economic milieu in which it was built. How were the architectural components of this building made? Who made them and for what purpose?

In the last decade, advancements in technology – especially in the availability of databases and digital search tools have meant that archives and databases, such as the National Library Board's newspapers collection have become more accessible. These tools have proven most useful and have changed how we use archives. Other sources relating to the built environment are maps and plans. In particular, topographical maps, cadastral maps and building plans provide us with a spatial understanding of how space was ordered and used. Land records and court case files pertaining to property suits provided new insights into the temple, and how the very land it sits on has changed hands over time.

All of this made it possible to piece together a more complete narrative of Wak Hai Cheng Bio and the people behind the temple. This book is the result of this research. It is a history not just of Singapore's oldest and finest Teochew (Chaozhou) temple, but also of its community, and the patterns of migration and acculturation that have shaped the city around it.

***

Wak Hai Cheng Bio – also known as Yueh Hai Ching Temple or Twa Law Yaw Kiong (大老爺宮) to the Teochews – is Singapore's oldest surviving Teochew temple. It houses two main deities: the sea goddess Māzǔ (媽祖), also known as Tiānhòu (天后); and Xuántiān Shàngdì (玄天上帝), the Mysterious Supreme Emperor of Heaven. The temple has a twin-shrine typology, with each primary deity housed in its own shrine. It is one of the few surviving examples of traditional Teochew architecture in Southeast Asia that has remained relatively unaltered since the late 19th century. Historically serving migrants from Canton province (Guangdong), it is today an important place of worship for devotees from all dialect groups. Over the years, the temple's significance has expanded. It is now a heritage site, a tourist attraction, a National Monument, and an important repository of a wide range of traditional crafts. Given this significance, we must understand the social and architectural histories of the temple, the traditional crafts it showcases, and the techniques used in its restoration.

Despite the importance of Wak Hai Cheng Bio to Singapore's cultural and religious landscape, the temple's origins are unknown due to the absence of a historical stele and other written records. Writings on the subject have largely been uncorroborated or were based on anecdotal accounts. It is hoped that this book will provide new insights and answer questions pertaining to Chinese architecture in Singapore in general and Singapore's early Teochew organisations. This will be done through a careful study of the temple's building fabric based on first-hand knowledge acquired during the 2010 to 2014 restoration, and in-depth research into the temple's land, social and architectural histories.

Chapter One establishes the context of early Teochew migration along with the shift of the gambier and pepper trade to Singapore in the early 19th century. Wak Hai Cheng Bio was established around this time as part of the movement of the gambier economy from Riau. Without a stele and lacking in other historical documents, the temple's origins and date of establishment remain unclear. Fortunately, the re-emergence of the Bute Map and the existence of early Straits Settlements records allow us to critically review the uncorroborated accounts on the temple's origins as a plantation shrine and who founded it. A careful study of land titles and records confirms the existence of Wak Hai Cheng Bio since 1826 or earlier and the purchase of the land at the back of the temple after 1848. The temple's "territorial history" provides the basis for the tracing of its origins, and early social and architectural developments around the temple. This chapter also sheds new light on the history of real estate in early Singapore.

Chapter Two examines the changing social roles played by the temple in the 19th and 20th centuries. Besides being a spiritual focal point for devotees, Wak Hai Cheng Bio was also the Teochew community's "public property", an administrative centre, a welfare and humanitarian aid centre, a place of entertainment, and a site of inter-societal rivalry. Today, the temple no longer plays some of these roles, most of which have been rendered redundant through the passage

of time and societal change. This chapter also examines the history of early Teochew organisations in Singapore, in particular, the Ngee Ann Kongsi and its predecessors.

Chapter Three traces the temple's architectural developments from the 19th to the late 20th century. Based on an 1895 archival building plan and other textual records, we know that the temple was rebuilt in the mid-1890s to occupy its current footprint. The colour building plan confirms the existence of the twin-temple typology before the mid-1890s. In addition, the chapter details the architectural features of the mid-1890s temple after this reconstruction and traces its architectural developments in the 20th century.

Chapter Four documents the entire restoration and conservation process that was carried out from

2010 to 2014. It demonstrates how restoration and conservation of a traditional Chinese building is carried out in Asia. Most importantly, it includes the rationale for restoration decisions made and the technical details, emphasising the importance of historical research, on-site observation of extant physical fabric, using appropriate building materials, and searching for the right restoration expertise to perform the work.

Fig. 0.2. This photograph of the front elevation of Wak Hai Cheng Bio is dated 26 January 1954.
Source: Courtesy of Lim Shao Bin.

CHAPTER 1

History of the Temple's Property and Origins

The Teochews and Their Temple

The Teochews originate from Chaozhou prefecture in China's Guangdong province. The first Teochews to arrive in Singapore were generally believed to have come from the Riau Islands of Indonesia and Siam (present-day Thailand).[1] By the middle of the 18th century, gambier and pepper cultivation had already been established in Riau, with its commercial centre at Senggarang, Tanjung Pinang, and the region was well known to the Chinese from Guangdong province.[2] At Senggarang, we can find a Teochew temple group comprising of the Yuántiān Shàngdì Miào (元天上帝庙), Tiānhòu Shèngmiào (天后圣庙) and Fúdé Cí (福德祠). The origins of this temple group are obscure, but based on the oldest moveable artefact in the Tiānhòu Shèngmiào – a 1779 deity tablet of the sea goddess Māzǔ (媽祖) – they may well be the oldest Chinese temples in the Riau archipelago and date back to at least the late 18th century.[3]

Carl Trocki points out that, "by 1784, gambier cultivation and trade had become an important part of the indigenous economy of Riau"[4] and that the Chinese from the hinterland of Shantou (or Swatow) in Chaozhou prefecture "were considered to be the labourers most appropriately suited to agricultural labour".[5] It may thus be assumed that Chinese labourers working in these plantations were mainly Teochews. In 1784, the Dutch invaded Riau. The Malays and Bugis deserted the archipelago, but the Chinese who were working in the pepper and gambier plantations remained.[6] It was estimated that there were as many as 10,000 Chinese prior to the invasion of Riau.[7] As the Dutch did not return to take possession of Riau until 1818, the Chinese became "largely autonomous" and "developed their own institutions of political and economic control".[8] Constant in-fighting and factionalism between Malay chiefs in Riau meant that there was no single governing authority in the islands. As a result, the Riau gambier and pepper farmers came under the control of the Teochew Kapitan.[9]

It should be noted that Riau and Singapore island were part of the old Johor-Riau-Lingga Empire, with the Sultan based on Pulau Penyengat, off Tanjong

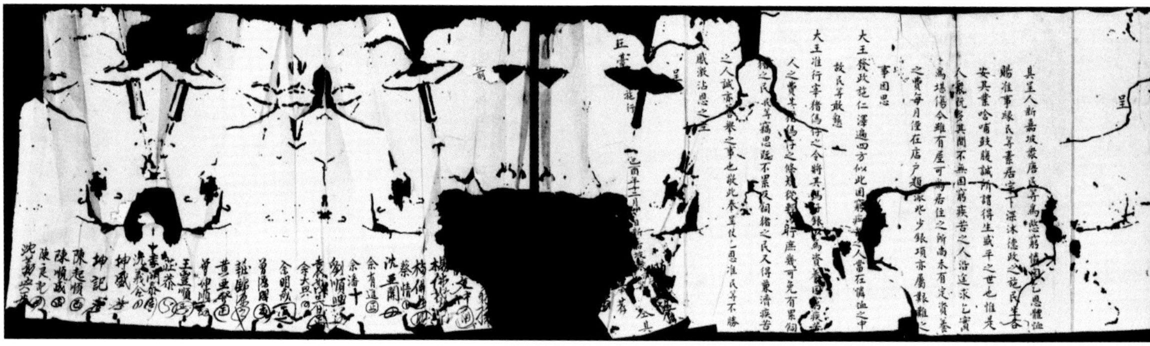

Fig. 1.1.

Pinang in Bintan.[10] In 1811, Temenggong Abdu'r Rahman supposedly moved to Singapore, and in the process, settled groups of Chinese in Singapore, including Teochew gambier planters.[11] The foothold Teochew gambier planters and traders established in Riau enabled more of them to move rapidly to Singapore when Raffles established a British "factory" (trading settlement) on the island in 1819.[12] Indeed, between 1819 and the mid-1830s, the centre of the gambier economy shifted to Singapore as merchants sought to avoid the high taxes imposed by the Dutch in Riau.[13] These lucrative cash crops (gambier and pepper) partially accounted for the rapid rise of the Teochew settlers in the Riau-Singapore region.[14] In Singapore, the Teochews settled on and near the banks of the Singapore River, especially in the present-day Boat Quay area. This area – where the Chinese Town was initially located – was marked as agricultural land on the Bute Map.[15]

As the Teochews settled in Singapore, they brought with them their two most important deities. One of them was Māzǔ, an important deity for the Teochews who came by sea. The other was Xuántiān Shàngdì (玄天上帝), or the Mysterious Supreme Emperor of Heaven, the patron deity of the Teochews. Both these deities are believed to be enshrined in a temple within the agricultural land along the Singapore River – Wak Hai Cheng Bio – Singapore's earliest Teochew temple. Given that the Teochews had established a temple group in Senggarang, Riau, and since most Teochew settlers immigrated from Riau to Singapore as gambier planters, it is possible that the deities in Wak Hai Cheng Bio arrived via the temple group in Senggarang rather than directly from Chaozhou prefecture in China.

Founding Wak Hai Cheng Bio

Wak Hai Cheng Bio is situated along Phillip Street, less than 300 metres from the Singapore River. The origins and date of the temple's establishment are unclear. Unlike other historic temples, no historical stele remains; historical documents pertaining to the temple are also lacking or unavailable. Numerous scholars who have written on the history of the temple have offered different interpretations of its founding and exactly who founded it.[16] What emerges from these accounts is, alas, both confusing and inconclusive.

Fig. 1.1. Pork Farm Petition was signed by Wáng Fēngshùn and at least 27 other Chinese residents in February 1850. Source: "From Kim Seng and 14 other Chinese Merchants, 15 February, Enclosing Petition addressed to the most noble the Marquis of Dalhousie K. T. Governor General of British India, relating to the reestablishment of the Pork Farm for the support of the Pauper Hospital at this station," 15 February 1850, Governor: Miscellaneous Letters (In), WO15, folder 61, Raffles Museum and Library. Courtesy of the National Archives of Singapore.

Two accounts attribute the founding of Wak Hai Cheng Bio to one Lín Pàn (林泮).[17] Another account lists the temple's founders as Wáng Fēngshùn (王豐順) and Wáng Qīn (王欽).[18] Goh Ngan Hong (吳彥鴻), writing in 1987, asserts that Wáng Fēngshùn and Wáng Qīnqiān (王欽千) established a plantation on 6 February 1819[19] and that an attap *shéntáng* (神堂) – a wooden and attap shrine – was built in 1820 by Lín Pàn, the founder of Ban See Soon Kongsi (萬世順公司).[20] Goh's claims are based on an undated letter held by a former Wak Hai Cheng Bio caretaker, Guō Guózhēn (郭國真).[21] Others have claimed that while it was Lín Pàn who built an attap shrine, it was Wáng Fēngshùn and Wáng Qīn who founded Ban See Soon Kongsi and rebuilt the shrine as a permanent structure.[22] Most other writers agree with Goh that Lín Pàn established the Kongsi.[23]

The identities of Lín Pàn, Wáng Fēngshùn, and Wáng Qīn or Wáng Qīnqiān remain obscure although there is mention of Wáng Fēngshùn in the historical records.[24] In February 1850, it was recorded that Wáng and at least 27 other Chinese residents in Singapore submitted a petition to the Governor-General of India, the Marquis of Dalhousie, through the Governor of the Straits Settlements, Colonel William John Butterworth to re-establish the Pork Farm, the revenue from which was to be used for the relief of the diseased and destitute at the Pauper Hospital (Tan Tock Seng Hospital) (Fig. 1.1).[25] It is further recorded that in 1857, a certificate of naturalisation was granted to one Heng Hong Soon[26] – most likely the Teochew transliteration of Wáng Fēngshùn's name. While it is possible that these two men were one and the same person, no other historical evidence has yet been found to corroborate this.

Fig. 1.2.

Fig. 1.2. One of the two carved timber couplets that date from 1826 (道光丙戌): "道本真通總攝靈源歸靜穆" and "魔憑武伏還将生氣寓威嚴" [The true way is Dao and solemn is the source of the spirit; The evil submits to the valiant and the vital majestic energy resides]. Source: Photographed by Carolyn Lim.

Establishing the Date of the Temple's Foundation

The date of establishment of Wak Hai Cheng Bio is similarly shrouded in mystery. As with the identities of its founders, there are many differing claims as to when the temple was founded. The highly improbable date of 1738 is offered by Phua Chay Long (潘醒農), who asserted that a temple had been constructed on the site and that it existed as an attap *shéntán* (神壇) around 1820[27] before being enlarged with the addition of a shrine structure dedicated to Xuántiān Shàngdì in 1826 or earlier.[28] Other writers date the founding of the temple to around 1820 or earlier.[29] Ning Ngui Ngi (林緯毅) further asserts that the *shéntán* was rebuilt in or around 1826 with the addition of a Xuántiān Shàngdì shrine.[30]

This claim is probably based on the existence of a moveable artefact in the form of a stone censer dated 1819 for Tiānēngōng (天恩公; otherwise known as Yùhuáng Dàdì玉皇大帝), or the Jade Emperor.

On the other hand, Goh, Sumiko Tan (陳澄子), and Chia Yei Yei (謝燕燕) give 1826 or earlier as the date of establishment of the temple.[31] Chia qualifies that a *shéntán* was already present at the current location of the temple in 1820.[32] The basis for the 1826 claim is the presence of another stone censer dedicated to Xuántiān Shàngdì and two pairs of couplets in the twin shrines of Wak Hai Cheng Bio. The censer was donated by Zēng Tián (曾田) or Huì Tián (會田) and the couplets were donated in the summer of 1826 by devotees from Mei County (梅邑眾治子) of Guangdong province. If the two pairs of couplets were indeed presented to the temple in 1826 at its current location, it would mean that the temple and its two main deities already existed at that time since objects such as these were usually presented to temples on significant occasions – either in the donor's life or in the temple's affairs. However, as the 1819 and the 1826 censers, as well as the 1826 couplets, are moveable artefacts, they may have been transferred from another location and thus do not provide conclusive evidence of the temple's existence at its present location either in 1819 or 1826. Documentary evidence of the temple's existence does, however, point to the temple's existence at least from 1826, if not earlier.[33]

The Temple Site

Land Titles of Wak Hai Cheng Bio

Today, the temple sits on three lots of land: TS4-98989L, TS4-98988X, and TS4-624L.[34] Two of these – TS4-98988X and TS4-98989L – are historical lots while TS4-624L (measuring 40.8 square metres) was only acquired by The Ngee Ann Kongsi (義安公司) in January 2002.[35] The twin temple and courtyard sit on TS4-98989L, while the two-storey rear building is situated on TS4-98988X. The old lot numbers for TS4-98989L and TS4-98988X are Town Subdivision IV (TS IV) Lots 428-1 and 428-2 respectively.

According to Ngee Ann Kongsi's internal records and other writers, the 14 persons listed below purchased the temple's land in the name of the Ngee Ann Kongsi.[36]

Seah Liang Seah 佘連城 (1850–1925)[37]
Low Teng Pheow 劉廷標
Teo Wee Choi 張為千
Tan Seow Kong [Kwang] 陳紹光
Seah Chin Meoy [Moey] 佘振美
Quek Num Seng 郭南盛[38]
Chan Wai Chua 曾懷泉
Heng Pang Kiat 王邦傑 (1856–1930)
Ng Yeow Quee 黃耀奎
Chua Sok Chew 蔡雪舟
Lim Chew Kwang 林秋光
Goh Teck Chue 吴竹村 (1876–1935)
Yeo Swee Keong 楊瑞恭
Sim Lye Choon 沈來春

The Kongsi's minutes give 8 April 1909 as the day on which the 14 persons – all temple trustees – received the title deed (領取呀囒) for TS IV Lot 428-1. Based on historical land records, the 999-year lease of TS IV Lot 428-1 commenced on 18 April 1909; it was issued to Seah Liang Seah, Teo Wee Choi and Quek Tye Hak as trustees of the Wan Tein Siang Tie Kongsi (元天上帝公司), a group that would later be subsumed under the Ghee Ann Koon (義安郡),[39] the predecessor of the Ngee Ann Kongsi.[40] Given that the temple had been reconstructed in 1895, it is strange that its land title was only issued to the trustees in 1909, since the land leases for the temple's immediate neighbours were issued much earlier, in 1827.

While the British East India Company established a trading post in Singapore in 1819, it did not obtain sovereignty over the island till 1824, when the island was ceded to the British by Sultan Admad Husain Muazzam Shah and Temenggong Abdu'r Rahman. It was only with the establishment of British sovereignty over the entire island that the colonialists could legitimately grant titles and leases over land in their domain. Up till the date of cession – 2 August 1824 – all land was presumed to be the possession of the Sultan.

In the 19th century, before the present land lot numbering system was used, each plot of land issued was known by its district and lease or grant numbers. The earliest existing land leases were issued between 1826 to 1828 under the form of land grants established by Singapore's second Resident, John Crawfurd. Prior to this, much of the land occupied was held without any right, title deed, or document.[41] Land held with a document before 1826 were either land grants signed by Raffles or lands held on location tickets. In total, Raffles granted some 569 plots of land, and a large number of location tickets were issued, though the exact number of these is unknown as no register was kept.[42] Location tickets entitled "the holder to a permanent grant after a proper survey, provided the land had been cleared within a specified time".[43] In 1826, it was decided that old land grants "should be recalled … [and] substituted by … [a] new form of lease", which were issued

Toponymics: Temple

Chinese: 粵海清廟
Wade–Giles from Teochew: *Wak Hai Cheng Beo, Wak Hai Cheng Bio, Watt-Hai Cheng Beo*
Wade–Giles from Mandarin: *Yueh Hai Ching* Temple
Hanyu Pinyin: *Yuè Hǎi Qīng* Temple, *Yuè Hǎi Qīng Miào*

Colloquial Names

- 大老爺宮 (Great Palace of the Deities or Palace of the Great Deity) – *Dà Lǎo Yé Gōng* (Hanyu Pinyin), *Dua^{7} Lau^{4} Ia^{5} Gêng^{2}* (Teochew).
  Teochews refer to temples in general as *Lau^{4} Ia^{5} Gêng^{2}* (*Lǎo Yé Gōng* 老爺宮) or Palace of the Deities. Wak Hai Cheng Bio is known as *Dua^{7} Lau^{4} Ia^{5} Gêng^{2}* (*Dà Lǎo Yé Gōng* 大老爺宮). This may be translated as the Great Palace of the Deities or Palace of the Great Deity; both are plausible. The former translation is possible because Wak Hai Cheng Bio is the oldest and most important temple for the Teochews in Singapore. Regarding the latter translation, Teochews refer to the Mysterious Supreme Emperor of Heaven (*Xuán Tiān Shàng Dì* 玄天上帝) as *Dua^{7} Lau^{4} Ia^{5} (Dà Lǎo Yé* 大老爺) or the Great Deity as he is the patron deity of Teochews. However, no other temple in Singapore where the Mysterious Supreme Emperor of Heaven is the main deity is referred to as *Dua^{7} Lau^{4} Ia^{5} Gêng^{2}*.
- 山仔頂大老爺宮 (Great Palace of the Deities on the Peak of a Small Hill; Palace of the Great Deity on the Peak of a Small Hill) – *Shān Zái Dǐng Dà Lǎo Yé Gōng* (Hanyu Pinyin), *Suan^{1} Gian^{2} Dêng^{2} Dua^{7} Lau^{4} Ia^{5} Gêng^{2}* (Teochew). *Suan^{1} Gian^{2} Dêng^{2}* (*Shān Zǎi Dǐng* 山仔頂) means "peak of a small hill". This hill could possibly be the one that once stood at the end of Tanjong Singapura or Singapore Point; Sir Stamford Raffles broke it up to reclaim the low marshy lands of Boat Quay, Circular Road, and the surrounding environs in 1823.[1] This colloquial name of the temple hints that it might have existed before 1823.
- 孖廟 (Twin Temple) – *Mā Miào* (Hanyu Pinyin), *Maa^{1} Miu^{6}* (Cantonese). This was a name used mainly by the Cantonese.

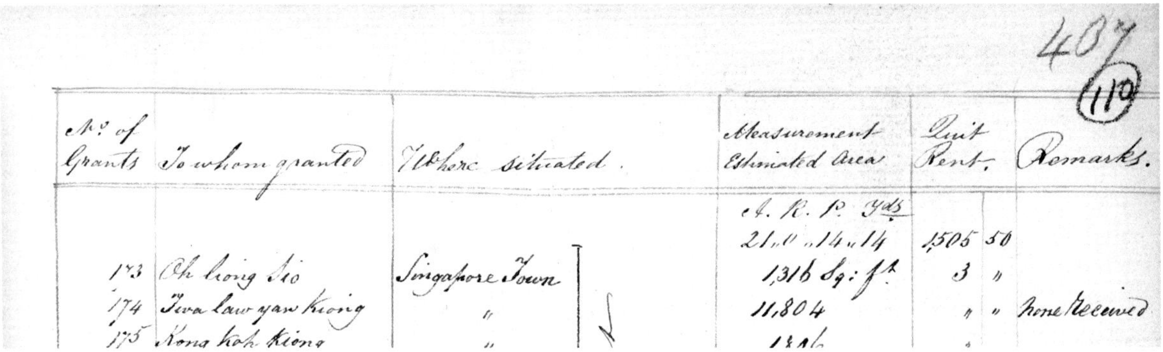

407 (119)

No. of Grants	To whom granted	Where situated	Measurement Estimated Area	Quit Rent		Remarks
			A. R. P. Yds			
			21,,0,,14,,14	1505	50	
173	Oh Kiong Sio	Singapore Town	1316 Sq: ft	3	,,	
174	Twa law yaw Kiong	,,	11,804	,,	,,	None Received
175	Kong Koh Kiong	,,	1316			

Fig. 1.3.

from 20 April 1826.[44] In addition, John Prince, who succeeded Crawfurd as Resident of Singapore, issued a Notification on 9 January 1827 in the following terms:

> The Public are hereby informed that all persons holding Lands on the Island of Singapore under signed by Sir T S Raffles Lieutenant Governor or under authority of Location Tickets received from the Resident Mr. Crawfurd and who have complied with the conditions of the same are required to redeem these documents into the Office of the Land Surveyor when they will be furnished with fresh Grants authorized and confirmed by the Right Honorable the Governor General in Council.
>
> All persons who have failed in fulfilling the terms of their original contract to clear and build on the Land so bestowed are required to complete their engagements on or before the 1st of May next in default of which the Lands of such description will be resumed by and reverted to the Honorable Company as Proprietors of the soil.
>
> It is further to be understood that no dispositions of Land will in future be made by the Resident Councillor without sanction of the Honorable the Governor in Council of Prince of Wales Island, Singapore and Malacca.
>
> By order of the Honorable the Governor in Council in Prince of Wales Island, Singapore and Malacca.
>
> (Signed) J. Prince
> Resident Councillor[45]

Existing holders of land grants and location tickets were accordingly reissued with the new form of lease provided they complied with the condition to clear and build upon the land, and if the quit rent had been fixed.[46] These were the earliest land leases in Singapore, and they were issued between April 1826 and 1828. In all, leases on 481 lots of land were reissued.[47] Land that remained unoccupied or whose occupants failed to comply with the conditions were "reassumed". A total of 217 lots of land were taken back by the East India Company.[48]

A register of lands granted between 1826 and 1828

Fig. 1.3. The entry of Grant/Lease No. 174 to Twa Law Yaw Kiong (partial), circa 1826 to 1828.
Source: "No. 2 Register of Lands held on Grants of the New Form Established by Mr. Crawfurd," Papers regarding land tenures and quit rents at Singapore, Vol. 2, 407, India Office Records and Private Papers, IOR/F/4/1042/28678. Courtesy of The British Library.

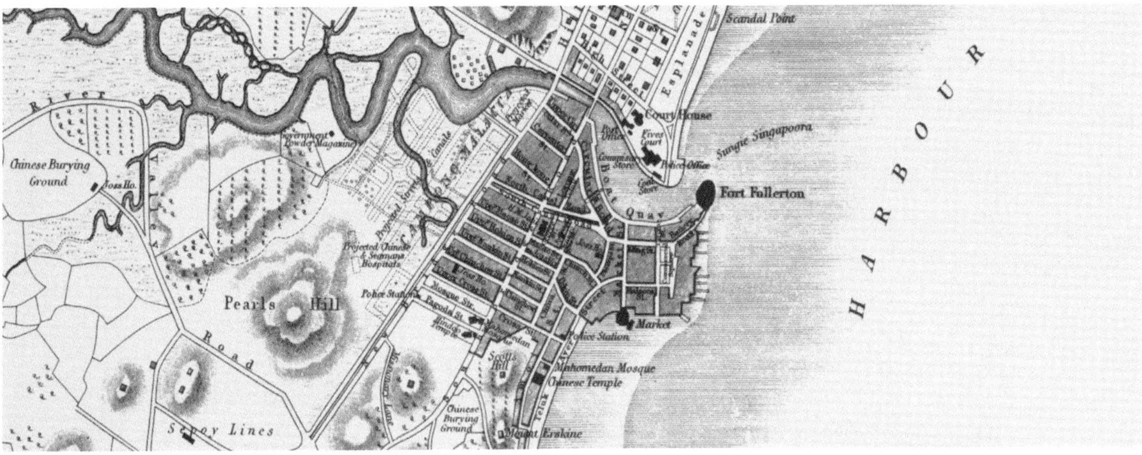

Fig. 1.4.

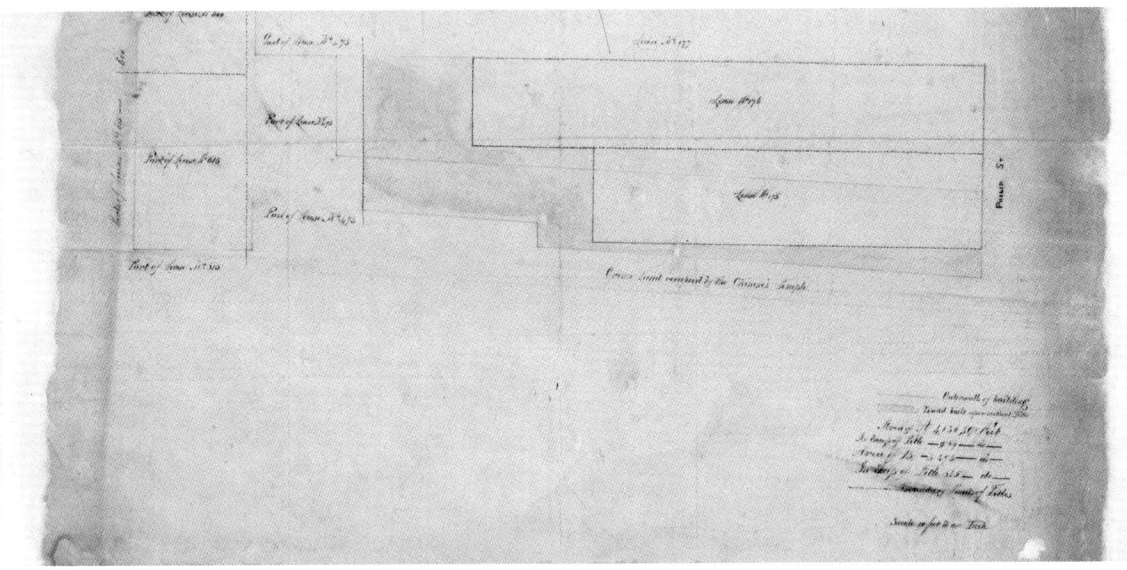

Fig. 1.5.

Fig. 1.4. "Plan of Singapore Town and Adjoining Districts from Actual Survey by John Turnbull Thomson, Govt Surveyor, Singapore" (partial), circa 1846, marked the site of Wak Hai Cheng Bio as "Joss House".
Source: Urban Redevelopment Authority Collection. Courtesy of the National Archives of Singapore (20120001620-0005).

Fig. 1.5. "Land Division at Philip Street, c. 1830–1890, SP000178" (partial), circa 1830–1890 showing the temple occupying Crown Land.
Source: Survey Department. Courtesy of the National Archives of Singapore (20050000976 - 0106_SP000178_000250-SP).

Fig. 1.6.

Fig. 1.6. "Map of Singapore around 1819–1820 (the Bute Map)." This is believed to be the earliest known landward map of Singapore.
Source: The Bute Collection at Mount Stuart, Isle of Bute, Scotland.

can be found in the India Office Records Collection of The British Library. In the "Register of Lands held on Grants of the New Form Established by Mr. Crawfurd" (Fig. 1.3), "a piece of land measuring 11,804 square feet (1096.63 square metres) at the west side of Phillip Street was granted to 'Twa Law Yaw Kiong'". This property was Lease No. 174.[49] "Twa Law Yaw Kiong" (大老爺宫) is the colloquial name of Wak Hai Cheng Bio, "Twa Law Yaw" (大老爺) being an epithet for the Mysterious Supreme Emperor of Heaven, or Xuántiān Shàngdì. This evinces the existence of the Xuántiān Shàngdì shrine at the temple's current location in 1827. And since leases were reissued to those who held an old land grant or location ticket, the temple must thus have been in existence in 1826 or earlier. The temple's land would also have had to have been cleared and built upon for it to qualify for the new lease.

The temple was required to pay an annual quit rent – which is akin to a property tax – of $3.50 in 1827 but there was "none received".[50] This probably led to the East India Company's resumption of the temple's land, even while the temple remained in situ. A map from the 1846 survey by John Turnbull Thomson shows that a "joss house" occupied the location (Fig. 1.4).[51] The land was likely reassumed only after 1848 as it was still marked out as Lease No. 174 during a survey of the adjacent Lot No. 1 of Lease No. 473 in 1848.[52] In a later map, dating from sometime between 1830 and 1890 (Fig. 1.5), "Crown Land occupied by the Chinese's Temple" is marked in the lot beside Lease No. 175, where Lease No. 174 was supposed to be.[53] Lease Nos. 175 to 177 were the land lots for 31 to 33 Phillip Street, the units formerly to the left of the temple.[54] The map was probably made only after 1848 as the temple's adjacent lots, "Part of Lease No. 473", were only issued in 1848 after Lease No. 473 was divided into three parts.[55] One of the parts, namely Lot No. 1 of Lease No. 473, forms part of Wak Hai Cheng Bio's compound today. This is the land on which the two-storey rear building now stands, corresponding to the lease number of TS IV Lot 428-2. Lot No. 1 of Lease No. 473 was issued on 25 August 1848 to William Wemyss Ker on the condition that a tiled-roofed house was built within two years, and payment of an annual quit rent of one-and-a-half Spanish dollars made.[56] The lease was for 999 years, beginning 1 October 1827 when the original Lease No. 473 was issued.[57] While it is unclear when the temple's trustees bought over this piece of land, it could not have been before 1848. It is therefore highly unlikely that the two-storey rear building would have been built before 1848. The twin shrines would thus have predated the two-storey rear building.

Even in the early 20th century, Wak Hai Cheng Bio did not seem to have had a unit number, even though the rest of the units along the street had already been numbered by the 19th century. This is evidenced by its current unit number "30B", which suggests that the temple was given the number after the adjacent units were already numbered "30" and "31". Before being numbered, the temple was simply known as the "Chinese Temple" or "Joss House" along Phillip Street. In the 1846 map mentioned above, a "joss house" is shown to be located along Phillip Street, where Wak Hai Cheng Bio is located.[58] Similarly, in a map published in 1854 as "Plan of the Town of Singapore and Its Environs Surveyed in 1842 by Government Surveyor Singapore", a "Chinese Temple" is shown to occupy the space where the temple now stands.[59]

The Temple's Pre-1826 Property and Surrounds

Early writings on Wak Hai Cheng Bio point out the temple's large land size and its location within a plantation in its early days. Phua specifically states that the temple's land was more than 130 acres (approximately 52.61 hectares or 5,662,800 square feet), which was occupied with permission granted by

Toponymics: Environs

The temple is located on a block bounded by Phillip Street, Church Street, Synagogue Street, and Chulia Street. Apart from the official English names, these streets were known by various official transliterated and colloquial non-English names. Chinese names of these streets existed in the three major dialects used locally, that is, Hokkien, Teochew and Cantonese. Where applicable, pronunciations in all three dialects and Mandarin (Hanyu Pinyin) are provided, unless the term is specifically used in only one or two of them. In most instances, the vernacular instead of literary pronunciations are used. For Hokkien, where there is more than one way of pronouncing the Chinese characters vernacularly, the two most common variants used in Singapore, that is, the Chin Chew (Quánzhōu泉州) and Amoy (Xiàmén 廈門) variants are provided.

Phillip Street

- This street was likely named after William Edward Phillips, acting governor from December 1810 to 1811 and 1816 to 1817, and lieutenant-governor from 4 June 1820 to 30 August 1824 of Prince of Wales Island (Penang).[1] In early maps of Singapore Town, the street was known as "Phillip's Street" instead of "Phillip Street".[2]

Fig. BS02.1.

- Fig. BS02.1. In this 1836 "Map of the Town and Environs of Singapore, Drawn by J. B. Tassin, from an Actual Survey by G. D. Coleman", Phillip Street is shown as Phillip's Street.
Source: Courtesy of the National Archives of Singapore (20140000101-0003-TM000037).

Transliterated Chinese:

- 披立街 – *Pī Lì Jiē* (Hanyu Pinyin), *Pi^1 Lib^8 Goi^1* (Teochew), *Phi Līp Koe* (Hokkien), *Pei^1 Laap^6 Gaai^1* (Cantonese)
- 菲立街 – *Fēi Lì Jiē* (Hanyu Pinyin)

Colloquial Chinese Names:

- 老爺宮 – *Lǎo Yé Gōng* (Hanyu Pinyin), *Lau^4 Ia^5 Gêng^2* (Teochew), *Láu Iâ Keng* (Hokkien)
- 大老爺宮頭 – *Dà Lǎo Yé Gōng Tóu* (Hanyu Pinyin), *Dua^7 Lau^4 Ia^5 Gêng^2 Tau^5* (Teochew), *Tōa Láu Iâ Keng Thâu* (Hokkien)
- 老爺宮口[3] – *Lǎo Yé Gōng Kǒu* (Hanyu Pinyin), *Lau^4 Ia^5 Gêng^2 Kau^2* (Teochew), *Láu Iâ Keng Kháu* (Hokkien)
- 孖廟街[4] – *Mā Miào Jiē* (Hanyu Pinyin), *Maa^1 Miu^6 Gaai^1* (Cantonese)

Church Street

Transliterated Chinese:

- 漆街 – *Qī Jiē* (Hanyu Pinyin), *Cag^4 Goi^1* (Teochew), *Chhat Koe* (Hokkien), *Cat^1 Gaai^1* (Cantonese)

Colloquial Chinese Names:

- 五代天宮 ("Heavenly Palace of the Five Generations"; there was a temple located along this street with this name, "in which five josses of different se^n or clan-names" were enshrined.)[5] – *Wǔ Dài Tiān Gōng* (Hanyu Pinyin), *Gōo Tāi Thien Kiong* (Hokkien)
- 五代天福宮口 ("The Junction of [the Heavenly Temple of] Five Generations and the Temple of Heavenly Bliss (that is, Thian Hock Keng)")[6] – *Wǔ Dài Tiān Fú Gōng Kǒu* (Hanyu Pinyin), *Gōo Tāi Thien Hok Keng Kháu* (Hokkien)
- 繳間口 ("The Junction of the Gambling Dens")[7] – *Jiǎo Jiān Kǒu* (Hanyu Pinyin), *Gieu^2 Goin^1 Kau^2* (Teochew)[8], *Kiáu Keng Kháu* (Hokkien)

Synagogue Street

Transliterated Chinese:

- 新那閣街 – *Xīn Nà Gé Jiē* (Hanyu Pinyin), *Sing^1 Na^2 Goh^4 Goi^1* (Teochew), *Sin Ná^n Koh Koe* (Hokkien), *San^1 Naa^5 Gok^3 Gaai^1* (Cantonese)

Colloquial Chinese Names:

- 玻璃後 ("Behind [the] Police [Station]")/保黎後第二條街 ("Second Street Behind the [Central] Police [Station]")[9] – *Bō Lí Hòu / Bǎo Lí Hòu Dì Èr Tiáo Jiē* (Hanyu Pinyin), *Bo^1 Li^5 Au^6/ Bo^2 Li^5 Au^6 Doin^6 Ri^6 Dieu^5 Goi^1* (Teochew), *Po Lê Āu/ Pó Lê Āu Tē Jī Tiâu Koe* (Hokkien), *Bo^1 Lei^4 Hau^6/ Bou^2 Lai^4 Hau^6 Dai^6 Ji^6 Tiu^4 Gaai^1* (Cantonese)

Chulia Street (formerly known as Kling Street)[10]

Transliterated Chinese:

- 吉寧街 (Kling Street)[11] – *Jí Níng Jiē* (Hanyu Pinyin), *Gig^4 Lêng Goi^1* (Teochew), *Kiet Lêng Koe* (Hokkien)
- 珠烈街 (Chulia Street) – *Zhū Liè Jiē* (Hanyu Pinyin)

Colloquial Chinese Names:

- 山仔頂 ("Small Hilltop"; this hill could possibly be the one that once stood at the end of Tanjong Singapura or Singapore Point, which was broken up by Raffles in 1823.)[12] – *Shān Zǎi Dǐng* (Hanyu Pinyin), *Suan^1 Gian^2 Dêng^2* (Teochew), *Soa^n Á Téng* (Hokkien), *Saan^1 Zai^2 Deng^2* (Cantonese)
- 萬順街[13] – *Wàn Shùn Jiē* (Hanyu Pinyin), *Bhuêng^7 Sung^6 Goi^1* (Teochew), *Bān Sūn Koe* (Hokkien), *Maan^6 Seon^6 Gaai^1* (Cantonese)
- 花園角 ("The Corner of the Garden"; "the garden" here refers to Hong Lim Green) – *Huā Yuán Jiǎo* (Hanyu Pinyin), *Huê^1 Hng^5 Gag^4* (Teochew), *Hoe Hn̂g Kak* (Hokkien), *Faa^1 Jyun^4 Gok^3* (Cantonese)
- 鐵條腳 ("The Foot of the Iron Pillars"; many iron columns were used in the building of houses along this street, the most prominent of these being two three-storey shophouses with cast-iron columns at the junction of Phillip and Chulia streets)[14] – *Tiě Tiáo Jiǎo* (Hanyu Pinyin), *Tih^4 Dieu^5 Ka^1* (Teochew), *Thih Tiâu Kha* (Hokkien)
- 鐵柱 ("Iron Pillars"; the Hokkien and Teochew pronunciations for this term is very close to the previous term and were probably used interchangeably)[15] – *Tiě Zhù* (Hanyu Pinyin), *Tih^4 Tieu^6* (Teochew), *Thih Thiāu* (Hokkien)

Malay name:

- Jalan Kedei Pisau ("Knife Shop Street")[16]

Tamil name:

- கத்திக்கடைச் சடக்கு Kathi Kadei Sadakku ("Knife Shop Street")[17]

Fig. 1.7.

native chiefs.[60] Goh also mentioned the establishment of a plantation by Wáng Fēngshùn and Wáng Qīnqiān in 1819 and the subsequent founding of the temple in 1820.[61] Although these assertions by Phua and Goh remain uncorroborated, they are highly probable as we shall see. As the city grew, the temple's surroundings were redeveloped into shophouses. By the time it obtained its 999-year leasehold land title in 1909, the temple was left with only 13,273 square feet of land.[62]

Phua's assertion that the temple's land was occupied with permission from the native chiefs is very difficult to verify since the Temenggong never kept any register of lands granted. That said, he did give permission to about 20 people to form plantations before the 1819 establishment of the British factory.[63] Permission was given verbally, with no written contract.[64] Despite the absence of a written contract and register, a more nuanced understanding of the land in the temple's locality before 1825 is made possible by the re-emergence of the Bute Map in 2012 (Fig. 1.6).[65] The Bute Map is believed to be the first landward map of Singapore, commissioned between 1819 and 1820.[66] It contains a combination of "ground truthing, depicting in reasonable detail existing topographic features, and propositions envisioned by the infant government".[67]

The southern banks of the Singapore River are shown as being the location of the "Chinese Town". Slightly upstream from this, in an area corresponding to the present location of the temple and its surrounds, was agricultural land demarcated as "Coleased Grounds".[68] This substantiates Goh's point that the locality of the temple was formerly a plantation. While it is unclear what the term "Coleased Grounds" denotes exactly, we may infer that it was either land leased out to or from more than one party. There are two possibilities: (a) William Farquhar, Singapore's first Resident, may have leased land to more than one party; or (b) the land had been leased by the Sultan and/or the Temenggong to some other party as well as to the British.

Although the 1819 Singapore Treaty signed between Raffles, Temenggong Abdu'r Rahman and Sultan Husain provided the British "no territorial cession giving a legal right of legislation", the British began issuing land leases from the inception of the British factory.[69] Existing registers of land granted under Farquhar's residency, however, show no indication of any lot of land being leased out to more than one party at a time.[70] Hence, it is unlikely that the term "Coleased Grounds" implied that the British leased out the land to two or more parties.

The second possibility is that the native chiefs leased the land out to the British and another party. From 1819 to August 1824, the British factory extended "from Tanjong Malang on the west, to Tanjong Katang

Fig. 1.7. A manuscript map (partial) dated 1825 showing gambier plantations in the areas on both sides of the Singapore River.
Source: "Part of Singapore Island, 18 June 1825," India Office Records and Private Papers, IOR/X/3346. Courtesy of The British Library.

Fig. 1.8.

Fig. 1.8. Pepper and gambier plantation scene in the 1900s. Pepper (*Piper nigrum*) and gambier (*Uncaria gambir*) have a symbiotic relationship and are typically grown together in plantations. Gambier is a shrub that grows to as high as 2 metres while pepper is a flowering vine that entwines around gambier.
Source: Courtesy of the National Museum of Singapore (2001-01562).

Fig. 1.9.

[Katong] on the east … as far as the range of cannon shot".[71] The "Coleased Grounds" were thus within the boundaries of the British factory. When the British factory was first established, it was agreed that "the gardens and plantations" would be placed "at the disposal of the Tumungong [Temenggong]" even if they were within the factory boundaries.[72] Thus, it would not be surprising if the Temenggong had granted a plot of agricultural land within the factory boundaries to another party. As the Bute Map would have been drawn from the perspective of the British, the nomenclature "Coleased Grounds" is likely to be a recognition that another party also had a lease of the land. While the Bute Map does not specify who the occupants nor lessees of the "Coleased Grounds" were, we can infer their identities from other historical materials:

> In his June 1819 "First Memo on the Administration of Singapore", Raffles directed that all the Chinese move over to the other side of the river [the Southern bank of the Singapore River], forming a campong [kampong] from the site of the large bridge down the river, towards the mouth, and all Malays, people belonging to the Tumungong [Temenggong] and others, are also to remove to the other side of the river, forming their campong [kampong] from the site of the large bridge up the river towards the source.[73]

Fig. 1.9. Map dated 1862 showing different classes of roads in the Town of Singapore.
Source: "Singapore. Reproduced from a map of 1862." Courtesy of the National Museum of Singapore (XXXX-02126).

Given that the "Coleased Grounds" were located just slightly upstream from the "Chinese Town" and Raffles' directive for the Chinese to occupy the area from the unnamed wooden bridge near the present-day Elgin Bridge downstream to the mouth of the Singapore River, it is highly probable that the "Coleased Grounds" were occupied by the Chinese. If the native chiefs – in this case, Sultan Husain and Temenggong Abdu'r Rahman – did indeed lease the land to both the British and the Chinese, Phua's assertion, that Wak Hai Cheng Bio occupied the land with the native chiefs' permission, is plausible.

Given the paucity of records and the imprecision of boundary demarcations on early cartographic references like the Bute Map, it is impossible to determine the extent of the "co-leased" area, or of the size of the actual plantation within which Wak Hai Cheng Bio was sited. What we might say with some certainty is that gambier was cultivated on the plantation where the temple was located. As mentioned earlier, the Temenggong had granted permission to Malays and Chinese for the establishment of about 20 plantations before the establishment of the British factory in Singapore in 1819, and the main crop cultivated in these plantations was gambier.

Early maps such as the 1825 British Library manuscript map of Singapore indicate the existence of gambier plantations in the areas around the Singapore River and beyond.[74] The land in the area was suitable for the cultivation of this crop. Moreover, early land transactions between Europeans and early non-European settlers show that the early pre-British settlement Chinese planters tended to cultivate gambier. Another reason it is highly likely that the "Coleased Grounds" was a gambier plantation lies in the profile of gambier planters. According to Seah Eu Chin, a prominent Teochew who made his fortune by becoming one of the largest commercial gambier

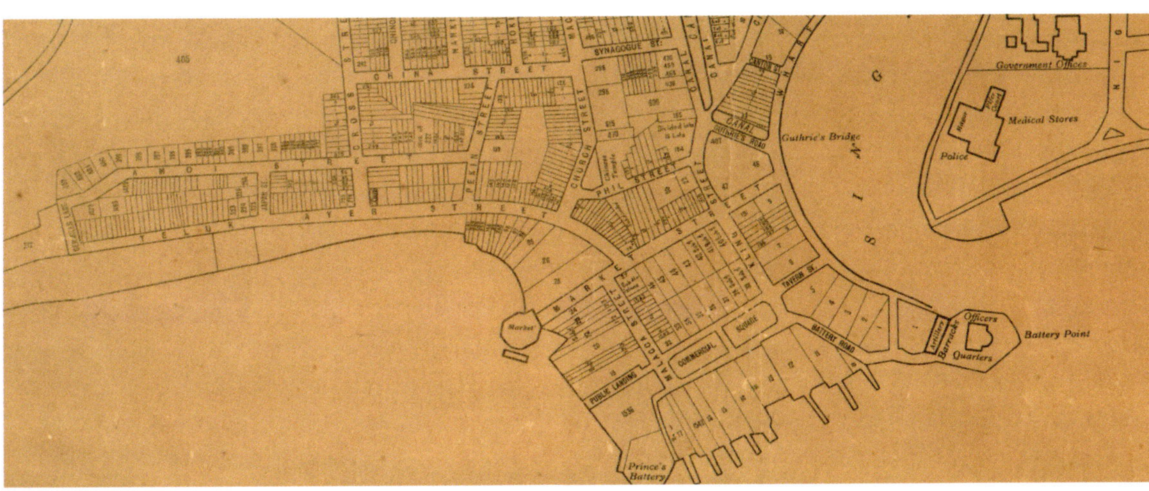

Fig. 1.10.

Fig. 1.10. This plan (partial) that was surveyed in 1842 showed the irregular land lot sizes at the block of land in which Wak Hai Cheng Bio is located.
Source: "Plan of the Town of Singapore and Its Environs Surveyed in 1842 by Government Surveyor Singapore, March 1854", Surveyor-General, Federated Malay States (F.M.S.) and Straits Settlements (S.S.). Surveyed in 1842 by government surveyor (F.M.S. Surveys No. 275, 1922). Survey Department, Singapore Collection. Courtesy of the National Archives of Singapore (20050000698 - AccNo981).

Fig. 1.11.

cultivators, 95 per cent of the Chinese engaged in the gambier trade were Teochews.[75] In addition, the majority of commercial gambier growers in Southeast Asia were reportedly Teochews.[76] Given Wak Hai Cheng Bio's early presence on former plantation grounds and its establishment by Teochews, it is highly probable that the "Coleased Grounds" were gambier plantations, and the temple originated as a gambier plantation shrine.

Early Development of Temple's Vicinity

Within a few years of the establishment of the British factory in Singapore, the area marked as "Coleased Grounds" was cleared of agriculture. An 18 June 1825 manuscript map held in The British Library shows the area being built up as part of Campong China (Chinese Town)[77] (Fig. 1.7). Wak Hai Cheng Bio thus ceased to be a plantation shrine from this point onwards. Its surrounding area became part of the Chinese Town. This is likely to be the result of Raffles' instructions to the Town Planning Committee on 4 November 1822:

> In considering the extent of ground necessary to be appropriated for the town generally, reference must be had not only to the numbers of the present inhabitants and the probability of their future increase, but to the nature and occupation of the several classes of which it is composed,

Fig. 1.11. August Sachtler's "Singapore Town from Pearl's Hill" (albumen print) circa 1867 clearly showed that land was demarcated in bigger rectilinear plots bounded by roads. Buildings, mostly shophouses, were then constructed in the smaller subdivided plots.
Source: Courtesy of the National Museum of Singapore (2009-01632).

> and the demands they may respectively have to preference in regard to advantageous sites for trade &c. and it will be a primary object to secure to the mercantile community all the facilities which the natural advantages of the port afford. At present a considerable portion of the sea and river face, which may hereafter become important for mercantile purposes, is occupied by the lower classes of Chinese [i.e. the "Chinese Town" in the Bute Map], and as might be expected many of the early settlers have occupied positions and extent of ground which are now urgently demanded by a higher and more respectable class…. The cultivators formed a third and interesting class, particularly of the Chinese population, but as no part of the ground intended to be occupied as the town can be spared for agricultural purposes [i.e. the "Coleased Grounds" in the Bute Map]…. As far as it may become necessary to exclude them.[78]

Raffles' priority was to expand the town to cater to the needs of the mercantile community. European traders were building warehouses along the north bank of the Singapore River, which Raffles intended to reserve solely for government and civic purposes. It was thus decided to allow the merchants to move their warehouses to the opposite bank, to the area already partially occupied by the Chinese.[79] The intention was to develop the land along the Singapore River for trade purposes instead of using it for agriculture. This would have included the land surrounding the temple. On the other hand, for the Chinese,

> [t]he whole therefore of that part of the town to the south west of the Singapore river (not excepted as above) is intended to be appropriated for their accommodation. They will be permitted to occupy the south west bank of the river above the intended bridge on certain conditions, and the

Overview of the Early Land Administration System in Singapore[1]

There was little change in Singapore's land allocation between the first British settlement in 1819 and the government surveyor John Turnbull Thomson's arrival in Singapore in 1841,[2] despite some reforms by the second Resident of Singapore John Crawfurd between 1826 and 1828, and Robert Fullerton the first governor of the Straits Settlements between 1826 and 1833.[3] Most of the land parcels in the Town of Singapore comprised long and narrow lots (in the form of shophouse land parcels) and were enclosed by the street and road junctions. All the land transactions in the early days of colonial Singapore could be divided into two categories: (1) acquisition of land from the government, with the government issuing a title deed with the land area written on it, and, (2) transfer of private land by landowners. In addition, prior to 1841, there were sometimes rudimentary sketches of questionable accuracy attached to a deed to indicate the limits of the said land. Moreover, prior to 1895, a land registration system had not been implemented by the government. Hence, there was neither control over nor record of private land transfers. As a result, Singapore's early colonial government did not have any record of land transfers or land mergers, nor record of land partitions. As this information was limited to both buyer and seller, land management was very difficult. Such a situation was highly unsatisfactory.

When the Straits Settlements became a British Crown Colony on 1 April 1867, and after administration was transferred from the government of British India to the Colonial Office in London, the outmoded India land law, that is, the Indian Act XIV of 1856, was found to be inapplicable in Singapore. As such, the colonial government began to gradually reform the land management system from the late 1870s and dispatched new land surveyors to Singapore to implement the reform plan.

In 1880, Surveyor-General John Frederick Adolphus McNair carried out a new cadastral survey of Singapore. In the following year, he was promoted to the post of Lieutenant-Governor of Penang and relocated there.[4] Deputy Surveyor-General Henry Edward McCallum, who was then stationed in Penang, was transferred to Singapore to serve as acting surveyor-general and continued to reform the land management system. After McCallum took over, he systematically re-recorded land records in a new format, made ground checks in conjunction with the new cadastral survey, and produced a set of cadastral maps entitled "First Series Sheets". For the first time, each cadastral map had a uniform scale and drawing dimensions. In 1881, McCallum also began to draw land property boundaries. In 1884, McCallum was promoted to colonial engineer and surveyor-general.[5] Among the various land reform measures, the government's move to encourage people to exchange their old title deeds for new property transfer deeds issued by the government was particularly significant, as it allowed the government to make records of the land held in private hands. In 1897, William Edward Maxwell, the Commissioner of Land Titles, initiated a re-survey of Singapore.[6] This reformation was finally completed in 1902 with the issuance of the first survey map of Singapore.[7]

Start of Building Plans Submission in Singapore: 1884

The earliest building plans in the collection of the National Archives of Singapore are from 1884. This is despite the Indian Act XIV of 1856 that stipulated "private persons who wished to erect houses or other buildings were required to give notice of their intention together with a plan showing the levels of foundations and lowest floor of the house".[8] In 1879, the Act was amended by Straits Settlement's Ordinance XIV prescribing rules on the "thickness of walls and the nature of foundations, and added to the plan of the levels of a new building, sections of the front wall and of all pillars".[9]

It is unknown why there are no known surviving building plans from 1856 to 1883 in the National Archives of Singapore or any other Singapore archives. Copies were perhaps sent directly to India and either there were no local copies, or they were damaged, destroyed or the requirement to submit them was simply not enforced. In The National Archives of the United Kingdom, housed in Kew, there is a limited number of building plans that were dated before 1884. These plans, dated between the mid-1860s and 1882, depicted public infrastructure buildings such as a coal store/depot, hospital, police station, post office, prison and public offices. A number of these plans were drawn by H. J. Satterthwaite, H. E. McCallum, G. C. Collyer, and J. F. A. McNair, all who held the position of colonial engineer at one point. It is believed that as these were public infrastructure works, the plans were sent directly to the Colonial Office in London, and were then deposited and maintained in The National Archives in Kew.

It is speculated that the building plans collection started in 1884 perhaps had something to do with McCallum's appointment to the post of colonial engineer and surveyor-general in the same year.

Key Chronology of Early Land Administration System[10]

1819–1825:	Land allotment via land grants and location tickets
1826–1828:	John Crawfurd's land reforms (27 October 1825) – grant occupation or location ticket, entitling ticket holder to a permanent grant after proper survey, provided land had been cleared within a specific time
1826–1833:	Robert Fullerton's Singapore Land Regulation of 1830 made provision for the appointment of a Superintendent of Lands; Registrar of Titles, Transfers, and Mortgages; and Collector of Quit Rents
1837:	Repeal of Singapore Land Regulation of 1830's provisions for land registration by the Indian Act X of 1837. However, the registration remained in force until it was superseded by the Registration of Deeds Ordinance of 1886.
1839:	Straits Land Act No. XVI of 1839 made provisions (non-compulsory) for registration and records
1841:	Arrival of John Turnbull Thomson in Singapore
1842:	New titles (existing freehold grants) are made under the Indian Act X of 1842
1856:	Indian Act XIV of 1856 (commonly called the Conservancy Act) made provision for the conservancy and improvement of Calcutta (Kolkata), Madras (Chennai), Bombay (Mumbai), Penang, Singapore and Malacca (Melaka)
1867:	Transfer of Straits Settlement to Colonial Office (Crown Colony); adoption of Indian Act XIV of 1856
1880:	J. F. A. McNair carried out a new cadastral survey of Singapore, continued by McCallum
1884:	Boundaries and Survey Maps Ordinance of 1884 paved the way for a complete resurvey of Singapore
1886:	Registration of Deeds Ordinance of 1886
1897:	Commencement of the resurvey of Singapore
1902:	Completion of land administration reform; issuance of first survey map of Singapore

> highroad leading from the bridge to the present Chinese campong, as well as the banks of the small inlet to the southward of it, will offer many advantageous situations as yet unoccupied.[80]

The temple thus found itself in a strategic location between the Chinese Town and the mercantile community at Commercial Square (later known as Raffles Place).

Before the warehouses and other masonry buildings could be built, the swampy ground had to be drained and reclaimed. The reclamation was "for the health of the Settlement" and "for securing the foundations of whatever permanent buildings may be erected thereon".[81] Before and during the reclamation,

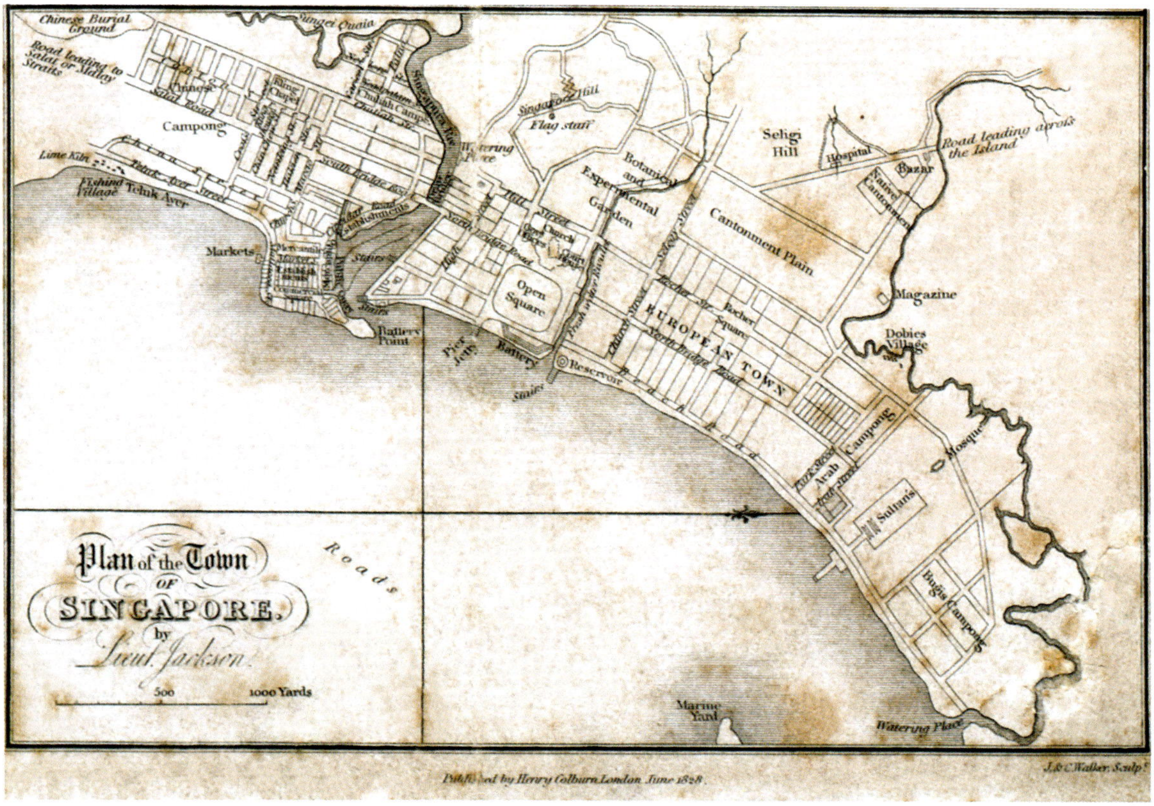

Fig. 1.12.

Fig. 1.12. The plan shown here is published by Henry Colburn, London, June 1828 and is commonly known as the 1822 Jackson Plan.
Source: "Plan of the Town of Singapore by Lieut. Jackson (London: Henry Colburn, 1822)." Courtesy of the National Museum of Singapore (XXXX-02072-002).

Fig. 1.13. This 1892 building plan entitled "Design for Proposed Brackets to Girders at Nos. 56 & 57 Kling Street [Chulia Street], Singapore" showed the metal columns, brackets, and girders that gave the street its colloquial name, i.e. "foot of the iron pillars".
Source: Building Control Division Collection. Courtesy of the National Archives of Singapore (127/1892, CBS332).

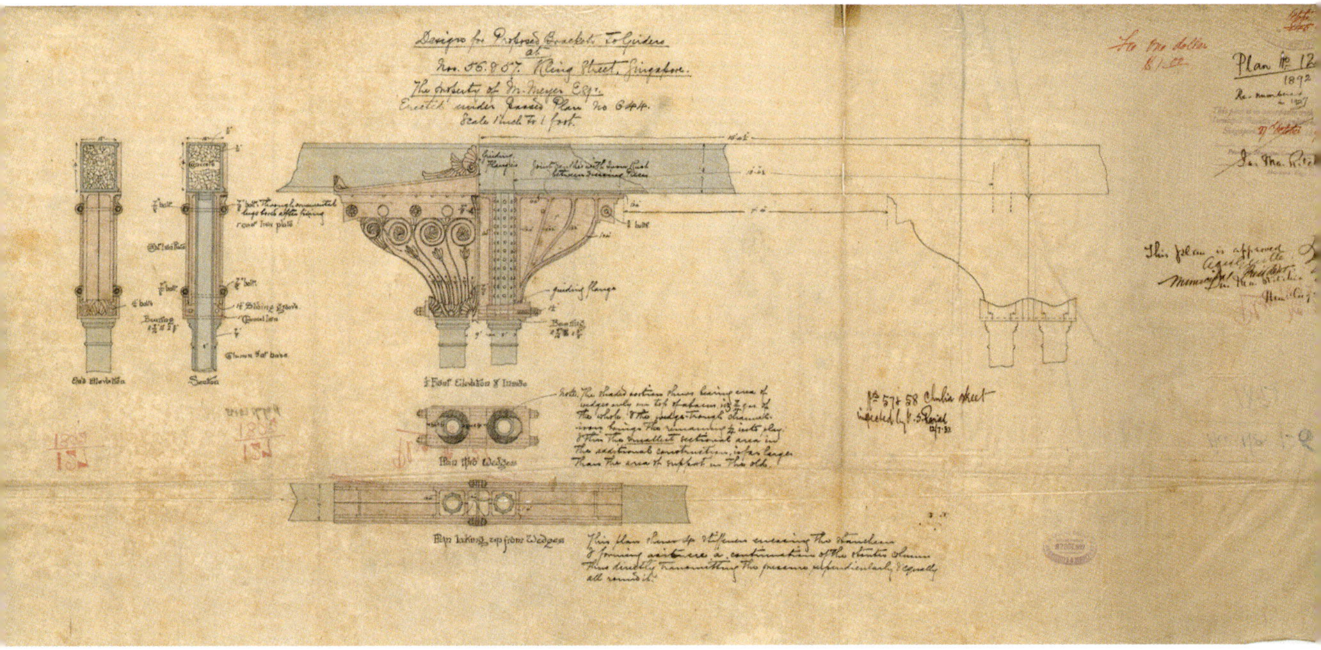

Fig. 1.13.

"temporary buildings along the banks of the river … [were to] be removed".[82] These would have been the buildings in the temple's surroundings. The buildings viewed as "temporary" might simply have been non-masonry buildings, most likely constructed out of timber and attap. While the colonial authorities may have regarded these buildings as temporary, they would have been regarded as permanent structures by non-European communities.

The southern bank of the Singapore River was partially reclaimed in 1823 with earth from a hill near Singapore Point. In addition, it was proposed in Raffles' 17 October 1823 letter to the Land Allotment Committee that an embankment is constructed "from the road opposite Ferry point [at the mouth of the Singapore River] to that which has been marked out for the intended bridge [near the present-day Elgin Bridge]" along the southern bank.[83] This was "to form an extensive crescent of about six or seven hundred yards, in the rear of which the range of the warehouses may be built on one uniform and approved plan".[84] After the ground was drained and reclaimed, it was planned to

> line out the different streets and highways, which should as far as practicable run at right angles [… and in order to] reserve uniformity and regularity hereafter, […] to class the streets according to their relative advantages of situation under the heads of 1st, 2nd and 3rd class, determining the least space along the street which shall be occupied by each house and consequently fixing the exact number of houses which each street will contain. It is proposed to fix a small ground rent on the spot occupied by each house, of one, two and three dollars for every fathom [1.829 metres] of front, according to the above classes, to be collected annually on the 1st of January and… Each street should receive some appropriate name and it will become the duty of the police to see them regularly numbered.[85]

The plan to pave roads and classify them into three different classes according to their "advantages of situation" was eventually implemented as can be seen in an 1862 map showing the various classes of roads within the Town of Singapore (Fig. 1.9).[86] Phillip Street, along which Wak Hai Cheng Bio is located, was a first-class road, probably because of its proximity to Commercial Square. If a ground rent based on the length of a building's front was collected according to the rates suggested above, Wak Hai Cheng Bio would have had to pay $41 annually with its 25 metres of frontage along a first-class road.[87] This would have been a significant sum throughout the 19th century. It is unclear if these rates were ever implemented.

By the time the first Government Surveyor, John Turnbull Thomson, surveyed the Town of Singapore in 1842 (Fig. 1.10), the land along the southern bank of the Singapore River and those in the immediate vicinity of Wak Hai Cheng Bio had already been divided into smaller rectangular lots.[88] The rectangular land lots were arranged in such a way that the shorter side of each lot fronts the road. It is clear from Raffles' 1822 letter that the intention was to maximise the number of land lots that a single road served by "determining the least space along the street which shall be occupied by each house".[89] This was significant to the development of the elongated rectangular shophouse prototype.[90] Shophouses are typically two-storey terraced buildings with repetitive façades, verandahs and windows on the upper levels, set between piers (party walls). Such urban developments were reflected in Thomson's 1846 to 1851 paintings[91] and albumen photographs taken by August Sachtler from Pearl's Hill from 1867[92] (Fig. 1.11). Some plots of land along the southern banks of the Singapore River, around Commercial Square and Wak Hai Cheng Bio appear to have been larger square plots rather than the elongated rectangular lots commonly found in the rest of Singapore Town. These larger plots tended to have smaller lease or grant numbers, suggesting that land was first issued in bigger rectilinear plots and then later subdivided into smaller plots as the town's population increased. A good example of this phenomenon is found within the block of land on which Wak Hai Cheng Bio is situated.[93] Lease number 184 is shown on an 1854 map made based on an 1842 government land survey to be "divided into 13 lots"[94] (Fig. 1.10). In addition, it may be observed from this map that Wak Hai Cheng Bio's block contained many irregular land lot sizes. The block might well have been occupied before proper roads were laid and land lots drawn out; indeed, the block is possibly the earliest occupied part of Singapore Town.

Besides the Chinese and European mercantile communities, the vicinity of Wak Hai Cheng Bio used to house a significant Jewish community. The early Jewish quarters were located on the same land block as the temple. Singapore's first synagogue was also situated here, along Synagogue Street, in a two-storey shophouse the lease of which commenced on 1 September 1841.[95] It served the Jewish population until 1878 when it was sold and relocated to Waterloo Street.[96] Besides the Jewish community, the area was also home to a significant Indian community. Kling Street, renamed Chulia Street on 1 January 1922, was named after the community.[97] The street was colloquially known in Teochew and Hokkien as *Tih*^{4} *Dieu*^{5} *Ka*^{1} (鐵條脚) or Foot of the Iron Pillars, probably because of the extensive use of cast-iron columns in many of its buildings along that street[98] (Fig. 1.13). The most prominent group of Indians in this area were the Chettys or Chettiars, who were mainly moneylenders. They played an important role in providing credit to members of the mercantile community clustered around Commercial Square.

Conclusion

In the early days of Chinese migration to Southeast Asia, Chinese temples played a crucial role in catering to the spiritual and social well-being of immigrants. The early Chinese temples were often located near rivers or by the sea since most immigrants came by boat. Wak Hai Cheng Bio was one such temple. Due to the absence of any historical stele and other written records, there is little reliable information on the origins of the temple. Nonetheless, a careful study of the land history of the temple using historical land records, old maps, early correspondence and other sources has allowed us to attain a greater understanding of the temple's convoluted origins and shed new light on its beginnings.

CHAPTER 2

Changing Social Relationships with the Temple across the Centuries

Over the course of Wak Hai Cheng Bio's nearly 200-year history, it has received countless worshippers and lay visitors. Temples were centres of communal self-governance.[1] To many, the temple was more than a place of worship. For the Teochew community, it was also "public property". It served as an administrative centre, a welfare and humanitarian aid centre, a place of entertainment, and a site of inter-societal rivalry. An individual was likely to have a complex and layered relationship with the temple, one that would have changed over time. Through an examination of how different groups of people interacted with and related to the temple, this chapter traces the changes in the temple's ownership and management structure, as well as in its social role. The activities of the temple's management, through both its trustees and organisations established to manage the site, provide insight into the Teochew community in 19th- and early 20th-century Singapore.

A Spiritual Focal Point

The primary function of a temple is to house objects of public veneration – sculptures of deities. These are generally considered to be more powerful than the effigies worshipped in private homes, and temples are thus regarded by devotees as sites of power.[2] Religious celebrations and festivities, in particular the rituals at the temple, relate to a wider network of patrons and devotees, all serving to reinforce the temple's power, both religious and secular.

Wak Hai Cheng Bio celebrated and continues to celebrate at least five festivals annually. They are Chinese New Year, the birthdays of its two main deities, the Seventh Lunar Month or Hungry Ghost Festival (中元節), and Thanksgiving (酬神) in the tenth lunar month.[3] During Chinese New Year, devotees "borrow" lanterns (借燈籠) to pray for more descendants, prosperity, and protection for their families (Fig. 2.1). Those wishing to pray for a thriving business and fortune would "borrow" a pair of sugar lions (借糖獅) made from melted white sugar poured into a lion-shaped mould (Fig. 2.2). The "borrowing" process begins with the devotee kneeling in front of the deities and asking to "borrow" a certain

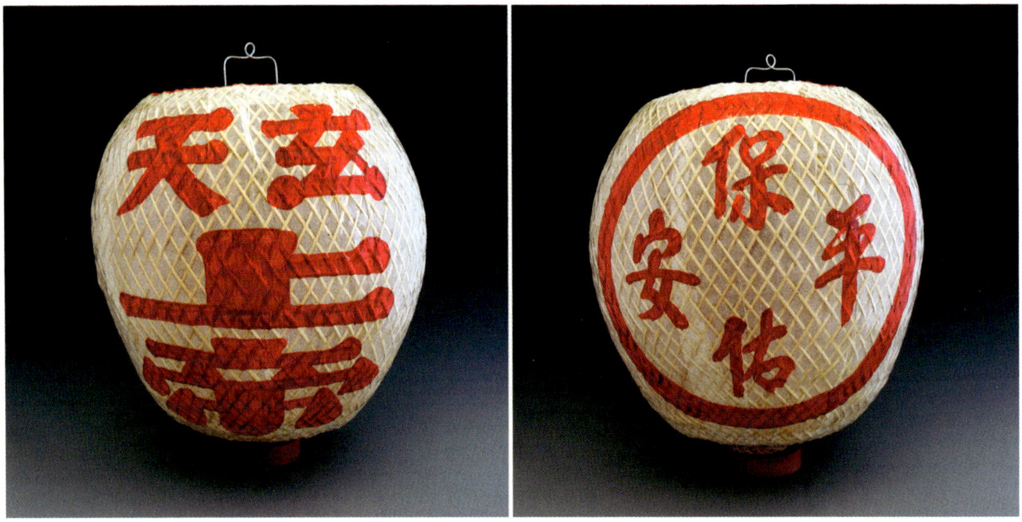

Fig. 2.1.

Fig. 2.2.

Fig. 2.1. Teochew lanterns for devotees to "borrow" are made using split bamboo as frame and wrapped with paper. The lanterns are then painted with tung oil as a waterproofing coat before the name of the deity, Xuántiān Shàngdì (玄天上帝) and *bǎoyòu píng'ān* (保佑平安) [Peace be with you] are written in red on opposing sides.
Source: Photographed by Carolyn Lim.

Fig. 2.2. A pair of Teochew sugar lions. Sugar lions are traditionally white. However, edible red dye can be added to the melted sugar to render the finished product a shade of pink.
Source: Photographed by Carolyn Lim.

quantity of an item. The devotee then casts a pair of divination blocks (筊杯). One side of each divination block is curved and resembles a crescent while the other side is flat. If both blocks landed with the same side facing upwards, the devotee has to increase his "borrowings". This usually means doubling the initial amount asked for. The process is repeated until the pair of divination blocks lands with different sides facing upwards. Devotees are required to return double what they "borrowed" the following year in cash. This practice persisted in Wak Hai Cheng Bio until 2015.[4]

The temple celebrates the birthday of the Mysterious Supreme Emperor of Heaven or Xuántiān Shàngdì (玄天上帝) on the third and fourth days of the third lunar month. Xuántiān Shàngdì is the main deity of Shàngdìgōng (上帝宫), one of the twin shrines of Wak Hai Cheng Bio. Māzǔ (媽祖), the main deity of Tiānhòugōng (天后宫), the temple's other shrine, has her birthday celebrated on the 23rd and 24th days of the third lunar month. Rituals on the first and second day of the celebration are led by the trustees of the Ngee Ann Kongsi (義安公司) and Ban See Soon Kongsi (萬世順公司) respectively. Ban See Soon Kongsi has been the customary trustee of Tiānhòugōng, even though the physical shrine is legally owned by the Ngee Ann Kongsi. The religious notices of Tiānhòugōng are still issued in the name of the Ban See Soon Kongsi. In the 1930s and 1940s, the food offerings during Māzǔ's birthday typically included peach-shaped rice cakes (紅桃粿/飯桃粿), *huêg*[4] *guê*[2] (發粿), *diem*[5] *guê*[2] (甜粿; otherwise known as *nián gāo* [年糕] in Mandarin), a whole lamb, a whole pig, pigs' heads, geese, chicken, bighead carps and crabs.[5] A two-day thanksgiving ritual is also held on the 23rd and 24th day of the 10th lunar month to thank the deities for their protection over the past year. Teochew opera is performed on all three occasions. Chinese opera is closely linked to religion. Symbolically, the opera is performed for the deities, but more importantly, it serves two roles in didactic religious rituals: it offers a discursive platform for performers to re-enact religious and popular histories for public consumption and to ward off evil spirits and bad luck.[6]

During the colonial era, the temple organised rituals popularly known as "Sumbayang Hantu" (a Malay term meaning "praying to the ghosts") to mark the seventh lunar month. This was to appease the spirits who roamed the earthly realms when the Gates of Hell opened during the Hungry Ghost Month.[7] Offerings of food would be placed on a temporary platform "twelve to fifteen feet high" (approximately 3.7 metres to 4.6 metres) in the temple's front courtyard.[8] These were known as *gūpéng* (孤棚) or *gūshān* (孤山). They were typically constructed with tables, timber columns, and bamboo poles. At midnight, on the 15th day of the seventh lunar month, the public was allowed to climb the structure and help themselves to the offerings.[9] The intention was to benefit the poor "who in former days used eagerly to assemble at the joss house and endeavour to obtain a share of the delicacies".[10]

In 1931, the issue of abolishing the practice of *gūpéng* or *gūshān* was brought up during a meeting of the temple's trustees. The trustees agreed not to erect *gūpéng* or *gūshān*; the funds for this purpose would be used to purchase offerings instead.[11] The budget was also limited to $1,000.[12] The custom of erecting *gūpéng* seems to have been revived the following year. In 1932, the temple's caretaker informed the trustees that timber columns used for this purpose were largely damaged and that an estimated $100 would be required to purchase new timber if *gūpéng* were to be erected.[13] One of the trustees, Yeo Chan Boon (楊纘文), remarked that it would be unbecoming if there was no *gūpéng*.[14] Given the cost of erecting one, he mooted limiting its height to only slightly taller than the opera stage.[15] This reduced the volume

Fig. 2.3.

of timber needed and lowered the overall cost. The matter was left to a sub-committee of four trustees to settle.[16] It is unclear if *gūpéng* was erected that year, or when the practice was finally abolished. Today, the temple continues to hold rituals on the 15th day of the seventh lunar month, though the practice of erecting *gūpéng* and the distribution of offerings has long since ceased.

The seventh lunar month rituals conducted today are relatively simple and, with the exception of some altar offerings, similar to how other dialects celebrate the occasion. It begins with the trustees of the Ngee Ann Kongsi praying to the two main deities, Xuántiān Shàngdì and Māzǔ, in their respective shrines. Thereafter, they proceed to the front courtyard of the temple, where three altars had earlier been set up. They

Fig. 2.3. Diagram of Wak Hai Cheng Bio's Chingay procession route on 15 December 1881 as reported by the *Straits Times Overland Journal* on 19 December 1881.
Source: Illustrated by Hsieh Mei-En; author's collection.

first pray at the altar dedicated to Dàshìyé (大士爺, otherwise known as Miànrán Dàshì 面燃大士), then proceed to a larger altar for adult souls, and finally an altar laid on the ground for the souls of unborn babies and children. Dàshìyé is believed to be the underworld deity governing departed souls that roam the realm of the living during the seventh lunar month. Besides paper money and flowers, food offerings to Dàshìyé include fruits (pineapples, apples, oranges, Asian pears and bananas), rice, tea, and rice wine. These foods are also offered at the altar for adult souls alongside other delicacies such as roasted piglet, a whole braised duck, a boiled chicken, two crabs, raw vegetables, bean curd, peach-shaped rice cakes, *ang ku kueh* (紅龜粿), white Teochew *huêg*[4] *guê*[2] (發粿), dried vermicelli, dried mushrooms, dried longans, dried red dates, *tau ki* (豆枝), black fungus, peanut candy (貢糖) and tea leaves.[17]

At the altar for the souls of unborn babies and children, sweets, snacks, toys, fruits (rambutans, longans, oranges, apples and Asian pears), and paper money are offered. After three rounds of rituals at each of the three altars, tea and rice wine are offered at the altars by ritualistically pouring them into cups. Finally, paper offerings are burnt. Besides food and paper offerings, male and female "toilets" for the souls are assembled using straw mats and plastic chairs. Paper basins and clogs are placed in the "toilets" and these are burnt after the ritual. In addition, a teapot and a medicinal pot are placed above charcoal stoves alongside a bag of charcoal near the altars. This mimics a kitchen where the souls may "cook" or "heat" the food offerings should they wish to do so.[18]

In the 19th century, annual Chingay processions were held in the 10th lunar month, most likely as part of the thanksgiving rituals and the return processions in the 12th lunar month.[19] These processions started from the temple and involved members of the Teochew, Cantonese, Hakka and Hainanese communities.[20] They were very elaborate affairs during which the "most gorgeous of silk banners and silk embroidered dresses and splendid processional cars were brought out".[21] Tram services were even halted in certain years so as not to interfere with the processions.[22] A Chingay procession starting from the temple would typically proceed as follows (Fig. 2.3):

> From Temple, Phillip Street, passing through Church Street, China Street, Chin Chew Street, South Bridge Road, Tanjong Pagar Road, thence back by South Bridge Road, Carpenter Street, New Bridge Road, Merchant Road, New Market Street, Ellenborough Street up Boat Quay, Coleman Bridge, River Valley Road, Back Road, Orchard Road, Tanglin Road, back by Stamford Road, Hill Street, High Street, North Bridge Road, up North Boat Quay, Coleman Bridge, New Bridge Road; up Circular Road, South Bridge Road, Boat Quay, Lorong Guthrie, Circular Road, South Bridge Road, South Canal Road, Kling Street Market Street, Teluk Ayer Street, Cross Street, Amoy Street, Pekin Street, China Street, Church Street and back to the Temple, Phillip Street.[23]

These processions were funded by subscriptions from businessmen who were grouped according to the *jiē* (街) or streets in which they conducted business or lived. The businessmen seldom donated in an individual capacity; they pooled their funds together and donated as a *jiē*. Annual processions are no longer held, and it remains unclear when the practice was discontinued, although it is believed to be in the early 1930s.[24]

It was through these celebrations and rituals that Wak Hai Cheng Bio's societal functions were amplified. These rituals enabled social cohesion by uniting people

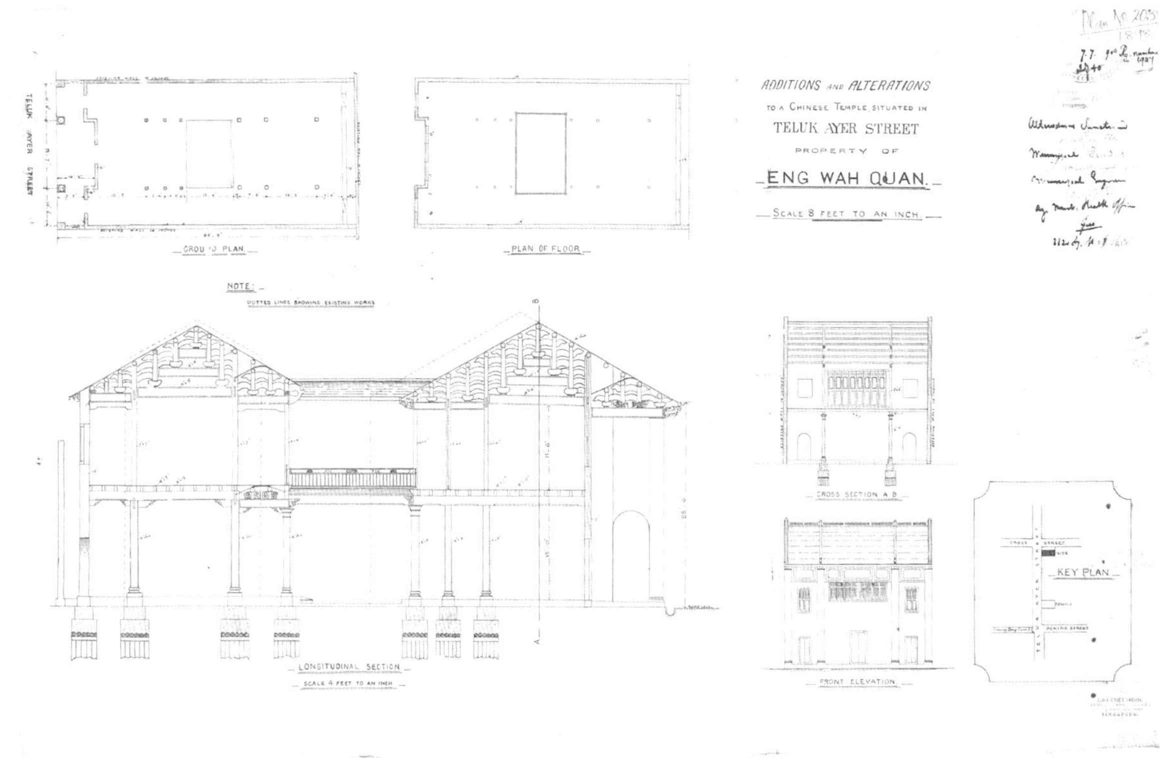

Fig. 2.4.

through shared religious and cultural symbols, values and norms; they supported social control by deploying religious rhetoric and imagery to promote conformity, and provided purpose and meaning to life through the reference to the greater schema of a God-ordained authority and traditional religious understandings of the afterlife.[25]

Site of "Secret Society" Rivalry

The 1822 "Plan of the Town of Singapore", drawn by Lieutenant Philip Jackson, segregated the main ethnic groups into different districts, and Chinese settlers were allotted the Chinese Campong (Kampong) south of the Singapore River. The pattern of early Chinese settlement in Singapore was closely connected to their dialect origins, with Chinese from the same ancestral regions in China building their temples, associations, and businesses in close proximity to each other.

The Teochew occupied the area around Wak Hai Cheng Bio next to the Singapore River. Further south, in the centre of the Telok Ayer basin stands Thian Hock Keng (天福宫), built between 1839 and 1842 by the Hokkien (Fújiàn) community from Zhāngzhōu (漳州) and Quánzhōu (泉州).[26] Nestled between the Teochew and Hokkien communities were the Cantonese from Canton (Guǎngfǔ, 廣府), Huìzhōu (惠州) and

Fig. 2.4. Architectural plans submitted by Lao Chee Hean on behalf of Eng Wah Quan (Ying Fo Fui Kun) to the municipal engineer for approval in 1898. Lao was also responsible for the drawings of Wak Hai Cheng Bio in 1895. Source: Lao Chee Hean, "Additions and Alterations to a Chinese Temple situated in Teluk Ayer Street. Property of Eng Wah Quan," 1898, 203/1898, CBS337. Courtesy of the National Archives of Singapore.

Zhàoqìng (肇慶), and the Hakka (客家) community. These communities built a common temple Fuk Tak Chi (福德祠) in 1824 on Telok Ayer Street. The Hakkas also established their clan association, the Ying Fo Fui Kun (應和會館) on Telok Ayer Street in the 1820s.[27]

Dialect group identity is seen as a subculture, practised by distinct dialect groups,[28] comprising distinctive traits and customary practices, including architectural styles. However, dialect groups can and do realign themselves under certain pressing circumstances and priorities. In the case of Chinese immigrants in Singapore, economic considerations provided strong impetus for integration. Some of these realignments were still based on ancestral origins, as in the case of the Cantonese and Hakka from Huìzhōu prefecture (惠州府). This locality affinity in China may have contributed to the joint management of Fuk Tak Chi by the Cantonese and Hakka communities. Socio-economic considerations could also have been an important factor, given that the Hakka population in late 19th- and early 20th-century Singapore made up less than 10 per cent of the Chinese population.[29] The Hokkiens were the most powerful group in terms of population size, with the Cantonese and the Teochews constituting the second- and third-largest groups respectively in the late 19th and early 20th centuries.[30]

It was thus unsurprising that the Teochews, like the Cantonese and Hakkas, would realign their associations beyond dialect lines to counteract the influence of the Hokkiens. This strategic repositioning can be interpreted from the first word of the Wak Hai Cheng Bio's name; *Wak* in Teochew or *Yuè* (粵) in Mandarin is synonymous with Guangdong province. This suggests that the temple was meant to cater to a wider community of devotees who had originated in Guangdong province and not just the Teochews. This area included the Cantonese, Hakka and Hainanese communities.[31] This is evident in the plaques and couplets within the temple,[32] which were contributed by all the major Chinese dialect groups in Singapore with the noticeable exception of the Hokkiens. Hence, Wak Hai Cheng Bio served as a spiritual focal point for devotees who were mainly from the Teochew, Cantonese, Hakka and Hainanese communities.[33] Another realignment may be observed in the use of Teochew architect, Lao Chee Hean (who was the architect for Wak Hai Cheng Bio in 1895) for the building works on the Hakka Ying Fo Fui Kun (Eng Wah Quan) in 1898[34] (Fig. 2.4).

In the last quarter of the 19th century, Wak Hai Cheng Bio and its surroundings was a site of contention between members of different clan groups or "secret societies". In 1871, the *gūpéng* food offerings went not to the poor but fell

> to the ruffians and blackguards allied to the Secret Societies as "samsengs," or fighting men. The strongest party usually carries away the lion's share, if not the whole. On Wednesday night, a crowd of Ghee Hok[35] men got inside the joss house, and at the hour for distribution some of their number took possession of a fine fat pig from the table, which thus became, according to custom, their property. A party of the Seh Tan "samsengs",[36] however, rushed upon and overpowered them, and carried off the pig in triumph. The Ghee Hoks were highly indignant, and would have inflicted summary vengeance had not Head Inspector Hayward ran and shut the doors of the temple, keeping them prisoners inside, until their more influential members persuaded them that the affair was not worth quarrelling about. The Seh Tans, however, have several times of late sought to provoke the Ghee Hoks to a quarrel,[37] and though the latter society has for some years past earned a reputation for

The First Chinese Imperial Plaque in Singapore

After the successful completion of the 1895 rebuilding of the temple, the concentration of high-level craftsmanship must have rendered it one of the most exquisite temples in Singapore, and even the region. A plaque bestowed by the Emperor of China would have been the crowning glory for this ornate temple. In 1899, the Teochews were given just this honour when the temple received the first imperial plaque in Singapore inscribed with the calligraphic text "Light of the Seas and Auspicious Clouds" (曙海祥雲), bestowed by Emperor Guāngxù (光緒皇帝).

There has been some controversy over the dating of this plaque. Phua Chay Long (潘醒農) dates it to the 22nd year in the reign of Emperor Guāngxù (光緒二十二年), or 1896.[1] Gretchen Liu and Lee Geok Boi dated the plaque to 1907.[2] Both Liu and Lee may have mistaken the date of the imperial plaque at Thian Hock Keng for the one at Wak Hai Cheng Bio.[3] Ning Ngui Ngi (林緯毅) pointed out that after the 1994 to 1997 restoration, the date on the plaque had been changed to the 30th year of Emperor Guāngxù's reign (光緒三十年) or 1904.[4] Indeed, in the article by Han Tan Juan, there was a photograph showing the plaque bearing this date.[5] However, in two separate publications by the Ngee Ann Kongsi and Teochew Poit Ip Huay Kuan respectively, both have a photograph showing the plaque dated the 5th month of the 35th year in the reign of Emperor Guāngxù (光緒三十五年五月吉立).[6] It should be noted that Emperor Guāngxù only reigned for 34 years; ending with his death in 1908. As such, the 35th year of his reign as reflected on the plaque never occurred and therefore cannot be correct.

Close examination of the two photographs reveal a gap before the character *nián* (年) and after the characters *sānshí* (三十) where the character *wǔ* (五) should have been in the photograph from Han's article. It seems plausible that the character *wǔ* (五) was missing from the plaque due to deterioration. However, according to the *Dézōng jǐnghuángdì shílù* (德宗景皇帝實錄) or Factual Record of Qing Emperor Dézōng, the plaque should be dated to the 25th year of Emperor Guāngxù's reign (光緒二十五年) or 1899.[7] A 1994 photograph of the imperial plaque taken before the 1994 to 1997 restoration shows an incomplete inscription of the date, with the remaining characters *Guāngxù … shíwǔ … wǔ … rì* (光緒 … 十五 … 五 … 日). It is highly probable that in an attempt to restore the imperial plaque during the 1994 to 1997 restoration, detailed research had not been conducted and the date on the plaque was wrongly restored to the 35th year of Emperor Guāngxù's reign. Not only were the dates confused, but the text was also rewritten in a different calligraphic style. The 1994 photograph shows the dates written in regular script (正楷), while those in the publications by the Ngee Ann Kongsi and Teochew Poit Ip Huay Kuan, and Han's article were written in the running-standard script (行楷). The spacing of the characters differs as well. In addition, a photograph taken just before the 2010 to 2014 restoration shows the month had changed from the 5th month (五月) to the 4th month (四月). Deterioration of the characters might also explain Phua's interpretation of the year as the 22nd year (二十二) instead of the 25th year (二十五), due to missing vertical strokes.

How did the Teochews in Singapore obtain this prestigious imperial gift? According to a 2014 article, without citation, by Wáng Míngguāng (王明光), in the summer of 1898, the price of rice in the provinces of Guangdong and Fujian increased sharply. The Teochew merchants of Singapore sent $30,000 to Swatow to stabilise rice prices and ended up with approximately 6,000 taels left over. They decided to donate the remaining sum for flood relief in Shandong province through a former Qing military officer, Huáng Jīnfú (統帶信勇營、前廣東南韶連鎮總兵 黃金福).[8] In return, they hoped to obtain an imperial bestowal of calligraphy for the Goddess of the Sea shrine in Singapore. Huáng reported this matter to Tán Zhōnglín (譚鐘麟), Viceroy of Guangdong and Guangxi, and Lù Chuánlín (鹿傳霖), Provincial Governor of Guangdong.[9]

Fig. BS04.1.

Fig. BS04.2.

- Fig. BS04.1. The imperial plaque blackened by incense soot. This photograph was taken on 22 March 1994 in preparation for the 1994 to 1997 renovation works. Note the gaps in between characters of the date inscription: *Guāngxù* ... *shíwǔ* ... *wǔ* ... *rì* 光緒 ... 十五 ... 五 ... 日.
  Source: Pre-Restoration Photographic Records, The Ngee Ann Kongsi 1994. Courtesy of The Ngee Ann Kongsi.

- Fig. BS04.2. The imperial plaque with the inscription date of *Guāngxù èrshíwǔ nián sìyuè jílì* 光緒二十五年四月吉立 [The 4th lunar month of the 25th year of Emperor Guāngxù's reign].
  Source: Photographed by Carolyn Lim.

According to the records of the State Council (軍機處), Viceroy Tán and Provincial Governor Lù submitted a joint petition to the Emperor and Empress Dowager on 24 May 1899 (光緒二十五年四月十五日).[10] The petition was recorded on 7 June 1899 (光緒二十五年四月二十九日). Before this, Emperor Guāngxù had approved the request on 24 May 1899 (四月十五日) and instructed the Southern Study Imperial Academician (南书房翰林) to pen a calligraphic text to be handed over to Viceroy Tán.[11] The full text of the petition can be seen to the right.

According to Wáng's uncited account, the State Council handed the inscribed calligraphic text (曙海祥雲) to the Ministry of War (兵部) on 7 July 1899 (己亥年五月三十日). This was to be handed over to Viceroy Tán and Provincial Governor Lù.[12] On 26 September 1899, the calligraphic text arrived in Singapore and was temporarily kept in the shop of Seah Liang Seah (Chop Chin Heng 振興號).[13] After the text was carved onto a timber plaque, it was hung in the temple on an auspicious date. It is not known if the arrival of the imperial calligraphy or the ceremony during which the plaque was hung in the temple was reported in the local newspapers.

拾伍
奏 谭鐘麟为 商民助賑請頒神廟匾額由
□□
四月二十九日
太子少保頭品頂戴兩廣總督 臣 譚鐘麟
跪
頭品頂戴 廣东巡撫 臣 鹿傳霖
奏為商民捐助东賑不敢請奨 籲懇
天恩賞給
天后廟匾額以答神庥恭折仰祈
聖鑒事窃據廣东潮州府屬商民貿易於新嘉
坡者聯名稟称商等係潮屬民人貿易外洋
聞山东水災饑民甚眾屡荷
聖朝發帑散賑商等同為內地子民具有天良莫不
感奮滋湊集銀六千兩請轉解山东助賑力
薄貲微不敢仰邀奨叙惟往來海上恆賴
天后默佑風波無驚敬懇
奏請
恩頒匾額於新嘉坡
天后廟敬謹懸掛以酬
神貺等情前來 臣 等查該商民懋遷重洋捐
助东賑不敢請奨自屬出於至誠除將賑艮匯
解東省外合無仰懇
天恩俯准
頒賜匾額一方以順輿情是否有当 臣 等謹合詞
缮折具陈伏乞

皇太后
皇上聖鑒訓示謹
奏
光绪二十五年四月二十九日奏
硃批著南書房翰林缮寫匾額一方交譚鐘麟等
轉行給領懸掛欽此
四月十五日[14]

> being peaceable, it would not be surprising if their tormentors should shortly succeed in rousing them to retaliate.[38]

The temple's vicinity was well known as one of the rowdiest parts of the town at the time. From 1871 to 1873, a series of serious Chinese riots "between the Hokien [Hokkien] and Teo Chew [Teochew] Chinese" broke out, and though this was a long-standing feud, "a quarrel between these two factions is a serious affair and their hatred of each other is so intense that when they once break out into open riot they are not easily pacified."[39] One of the flogging triangles for punishing rioters was set up at Wak Hai Cheng Bio.[40] To maximise the impact of this punishment as a deterrent, it needed to be carried out in a public place to draw as large a crowd as possible.[41] The temple was chosen as the site of public punishment as it was a place where many people, especially potential troublemakers, gathered.

A Humanitarian and Administrative Centre during the Japanese Occupation

Besides giving away the *gūpéng* food offerings to benefit the poor, the temple also served the welfare and humanitarian needs of the broader community during times of hardship. While the Chinese Charitable Institutions Union (中華慈善機構聯合會),[42] formed during the Japanese Occupation, and the temple were separate entities, the front courtyard of the temple was used to house the headquarters of the Union and served as an administrative centre for humanitarian aid.[43]

Being one of the charitable, religious and welfare organisations permitted to continue its operations during the Occupation, the Union provided humanitarian relief to those in need, regardless of their nationality, ethnicity, or religion. The Union's members were popularly known as the Blue Cross workers (藍十字),[44] probably due to the association with the Union's insignia – "a Blue Cross in a Red Circle".[45] In 1945, the Japanese authorities even openly supported the operations of the Blue Cross workers by contributing $3,000 to its funds. Mamoru Shinozaki (篠崎護), the head of the Kosei-ka Cho (厚生科) or Welfare Department was the Blue Cross's patron.[46] With increased casualties resulting from more frequent Allied bombings and food shortages, the Blue Cross sought to expand its operations. It held meetings with other charitable organisations on the temple's premises and coordinated relief efforts,[47] which resulted in its amalgamation with two other relief bodies, the Black Cross Association (黑十字)[48] and the Nanyang Sacred Union (南洋聖教總會), working with the Syonan Buddhist Association (昭南佛教協會) and the World Red Swastika Society (世界卍字會) for more effective relief work in April 1945.[49]

It also provided free meals to the destitute twice daily, medical aid to the sick, shelter for the homeless, and collected dead bodies from the streets and buried them. Those who wanted to receive aid had to apply for registration cards[50] at the courtyard of Wak Hai Cheng Bio.[51]

Apart from providing humanitarian aid, Wak Hai Cheng Bio continued to be an administrative centre for the Teochew community in general. It served as the Teochew sectional sub-office throughout the Occupation and was an intermediary between the Japanese authorities, the Oversea Chinese Association (昭南島華僑協會), and ordinary Teochews.[52] For instance, Teochews who wanted to join the Gunpo (軍捕, Auxiliary Service) could apply either at the sub-office at Wak Hai Cheng Bio or the Oversea Chinese Association (Singapore Chinese Chamber of Commerce) at 47 Hill Street.[53] The Gunpo performed miscellaneous duties under the Japanese Military and were given basic military training.[54] Successful Chinese applicants were awarded $100 by the Oversea Chinese Association, and received a testimonial from the Japanese authorities "for the protection of his family".[55] When the Oversea Chinese Association began its Endau Development Scheme (興樓新村) in late 1943 to solve food shortage problems in Singapore by encouraging the Chinese to resettle in Endau, Johor, where they could farm and be self-sufficient, Wak Hai Cheng Bio similarly served as an application centre for the Teochew community.[56] Likewise, the temple was the Teochew application centre for the recruitment of Chinese policemen[57] when the Chinese were being recruited for the purpose of maintaining peace and order in the city after they were trained by the Keimubu (警務部, Police Affairs Department).[58]

A Place for Entertainment

During temple festivities, Wak Hai Cheng Bio served as a place of entertainment for the deities, those living in the vicinity, and the general public. Traditional Teochew opera performances would usually be staged in the evening within the courtyard of the temple. These performances were free and open to all, and were originally meant for the entertainment of the deities and to show appreciation to them. Before the television set became commonplace, these Teochew operas were so popular that many brought along wooden crates and chairs to reserve the best spots in the daytime, hours ahead of the shows. Latecomers would sometimes have difficulty even catching a glimpse of the stage as the courtyard became too crowded. As a child, Chua Kian Thye (蔡建泰) who lived at 7 Church Street until 1976 recalled his parents going to the temple for the performances even though their family was Hokkien. He would play with his friends under the stage, which was built on stilts, as he did not understand Teochew. Even on non-festival days, he and his friends would play tag in the front courtyard of the temple.[59]

Temple festivities were not unlike carnivals. Each festival was accompanied by other peripheral activities, which provided entertainment to the public. During these festivities, mobile food and games stalls lined the entire length of Phillip Street and the front courtyard of the temple. Street hawkers sold food such as *ngoh hiang* (五香), cuttlefish, *tau pok* (豆卜), cockles and snails.[60] Others sold toys or set up game stations featuring pastimes such as *tikam*, a game of chance. Crowds thronged the street leading up to the temple.[61] They came to immerse themselves in the atmosphere of the festivals as much as they came to pray.

"Public Property" of the Teochew Community

From its early days, Wak Hai Cheng Bio has been regarded as a "public property" (公共產業) of the Teochew community. Rather than being owned by private individuals, it was and remains held and managed by a group of trustees on behalf of a larger pan-Teochew community. At first, the temple was managed by small, informal groups of trustees formed primarily to manage the affairs of the temple. The temple's trustees eventually joined forces with trustees of other Teochew "public properties", an alliance of temples and burial grounds, under an umbrella organisation known as the Ghee Ann Koon (義安郡) although each property remained officially vested under different trustees. This allowed for better management of resources amongst these small and scattered groups established to look after the welfare of the Teochew community.

The Ghee Ann Koon did not adopt any definite rules and the administration of its affairs was often left to the discretion of individual trustees. This arrangement was found to be unsatisfactory and two major attempts were made to reform the society's management structure, first between 1914 and 1916, and subsequently between 1927 and 1933. This eventually led to the promulgation of the

1933 Ordinance to incorporate the society as the Ngee Ann Kongsi. For the remaining portions of this section, we examine how Wak Hai Cheng Bio's management was restructured, formalised and codified in legislation to enable it to better manage the temple and other assets as "public properties" of the larger Teochew community.

Management of Wak Hai Cheng Bio prior to 1916

Before 1916, Wak Hai Cheng Bio's two lots of land – TS IV Lots 428-1 and 428-2 – were officially vested in the trustees for "Wan Tein Siang Tie"[62] and "Heang Tiang Siang Tee"[63] respectively. "Wan Tein Siang Tie" is the English transliteration of the Teochew pronunciation of Yuántiān Shàngdì (元天上帝), while "Heang Tiang Siang Tee" is that of Xuántiān Shàngdì (玄天上帝). Used interchangeably, both terms refer to the Mysterious Supreme Emperor of Heaven, one of the temple's two main deities. The "Wan Tein Siang Tie" trustees for this temple were "Seah Liang Seah [佘連城], Teo Wee Choi [張為千] and Kwek Tye Hak [郭泰合]". On the other hand, the "Heang Tiang Siang Tee" trustees were "Seah Euching [佘有進], Laow Soon Heng, Sim Ah Kie [沈亞開] and Weng Moh Thang".[64] The two groups of trustees should be understood simply as trustees of the Mysterious Supreme Emperor of Heaven. They were not separate organisations, but trustees at different points in time. The "Heang Tiang Siang Tee" group were the earlier trustees, active up till about the late 1870s or early 1880s, while the "Wan Tein Siang Tie" trustees were active from the 1880s to the late 1910s.[65]

The trustees of the Mysterious Supreme Emperor of Heaven were active from at least 1850. Besides Wak Hai Cheng Bio, they were trustees of three other shophouses down the road (Fig. 2.5). On 27 April 1850, No. 33 Phillip Street was transferred from the Estate of Choa Yen Ding to the trustees of "Wun Yien Seang Tie Kongsi," comprising Seah Eu Chin, Sim Ah Kie, Tay Ah Bock and Wan Mong Sun.[66] Notably, Seah Eu Chin and Sim Ah Kie were consistently listed as the "Mysterious Supreme Emperor of Heaven" trustees of both Wak Hai Cheng Bio and No. 33 Phillip Street. They were also trustees of No. 32 Circular Road and No. 48 South Boat Quay, as well as a burial ground in the "District of Amokiah"[67] (Fig. 2.6). This signifies their importance as leaders of the temple and Ghee Ann Koon.

It is interesting to note that the trustees of the twin temples were specified as being trustees of the Mysterious Supreme Emperor of Heaven, while no mention was made of the other main deity, the Goddess of the Sea. This might have been because the two shrines were managed by different groups of trustees in the early days, even though they occupy the same lot of land. It is widely acknowledged through oral history that Ban See Soon Kongsi was established to manage the Shrine of the Goddess of the Sea in 1820, and the Shrine of the Mysterious Supreme Emperor of Heaven when it was established six years later.[68] According to some writers such as Ning Ngui Ngi (林緯毅), the Ban See Soon Kongsi was established by Wáng Qīn (王欽) and Wáng Fēngshùn (王豐順), both of whom came from Ampou (Ān Bù 庵埠) town in Teo Ann (Chao An 潮安) district.[69] The writers added that the management of the shrines was transferred to Ghee Ann Koon when it was established in or around 1845.[70] While this has not been verifiable against primary sources, it remains customary today for any notices of celebratory events pertaining to the Shrine of the Goddess of the Sea to be issued in the name of the Ban See Soon Kongsi.

The 1914 "Ghee Ann Society" Lawsuit

Between the mid-19th century and 1914, the management of Wak Hai Cheng Bio was transferred from the "Wan Tein Siang Tie" trustees to Ghee Ann Koon. In fact, during this period, other "public properties" of the Teochew community were gradually transferred to Ghee Ann Koon as well. In 1914, the first

Fig. 2.5.

attempt was made by the trustees of Ghee Ann Koon to legally consolidate these properties. Seah Liang Seah, President of the "Ghee Ann Society" filed a petition on behalf of 14 persons asking for the regularisation of the "society's titles to its various properties in Singapore" during the year.[71] As a result, the Straits Settlements Supreme Court issued an Order of Court on 8 February 1916 vesting a total of 14 immovable properties, including the two Wak Hai Cheng Bio lots, in the society's trustees.[72] The Order also named the following 14 petitioners and "the survivors and survivor of them" as trustees of the society:

1. Seah Liang Seah (佘連城) of "Bendemeer" Serangoon Road Singapore
2. Quek Num Seng (郭南盛) of No. 54 Circular Road Singapore[73]
3. Lim Chew Kwang (林秋光) of No. 13 Upper Circular Road Singapore
4. Low Teng Pheow (劉廷標) of No. 53 Boat Quay Singapore
5. Chan Wai Chua (曾懷泉) of No. 40 Upper Circular Road Singapore
6. Goh Teck Chue [Chng] (吴竹村) of No. 30 Boat Quay Singapore
7. Teo Wee Choi (張為千) of No. 49 North Boat Quay Singapore
8. Heng Pang Kiat (王邦傑) of No. 53 Circular Road Singapore
9. Yeo Swee Keong (楊瑞恭) of No. 14 Upper Circular Road Singapore
10. Tan Seow Kwang (陳紹光) of No. 47 North Boat Quay Singapore
11. Ng Yeow Quee (黄耀奎) of No. 201 Orchard Road Singapore
12. Sim Lye Choon (沈來春) of No. 31 Chin Nam Street Singapore
13. Seah Chin Moey [Mui] (佘振美) of No. 54 North Boat Quay Singapore
14. Chua Sok Chew (蔡雪舟) of No. 17 New Bridge Road[74]

The Court Order gave the trustees the "right to sue for and recover any chose[75] in action or any other interest, right or privilege in respect of & in connection with" 13 of the 14 immovable properties listed in the Schedule.[76]

Besides Wak Hai Cheng Bio's two lots of land, the schedule in the Order of the Court also listed the pre-1916 trustees of 12 other plots of land that formally came under the management of the society in 1916. The 12 other plots of land were mainly burial grounds,

Fig. 2.5. Properties around Wak Hai Cheng Bio owned by trustees of the Mysterious Supreme Emperor of Heaven (superimposed on a present-day road map).
Source: Illustrated by Chen Jingwen; author's collection.

Fig. 2.6 .

temples and shophouses. Amongst the trustees listed were those of the "Ghee Ann Congsee" or "Ghee Ann Society".[77] They include Tan Seng Poh (陳成寶), Heng Tek Heng (also spelt as Heng Teck Heng 王得興), Seah Cheok Sia (also spelt as Seah Cheo Seah 佘石城), Ung Ah Watt (also known as Wee Ah Watt 黃亞發) and Goh Teck Tee.[78] Other pre-1916 trustees were listed as having belonged to other informal groups set up for the purpose of managing a single property, or at most two properties. They include "Hin Tean Sang Te" (Xuántiān Shàngdì 玄天上帝), "Wan Tien Seang Tee" (Yuántiān Shàngdì 元天上帝), "Poh Seng Tye Tee" (Bǎoshēng Dàdì 保生大帝 Fig. 2.7), "Choh Soo Kong Temple" (Zǔshī Gōngmiào 祖師公廟 Figs. 2.8 & 2.9), "Teo Chew Burial Ground" and "Teo Chew Chinese Burial Ground".[79]

The Ghee Ann Koon is the predecessor of the Ngee Ann Kongsi. Despite the two names being used interchangeably by many writers, the organisation was officially known as "Ghee Ann Koon" (also spelt as "Ghee Ann Khoon"), "Ghee Ann Koon Society", "Ghee Ann Society" or "Ghee Ann Association" before the Ngee Ann Kongsi was incorporated in 1933.[80] The term "Ghee Ann Koon" is the English transliteration of the Hokkien pronunciation of Yì'ān Jùn (義安郡), the ancient name of the Teochew prefecture in China.[81] The English transliteration of the Teochew

Fig. 2.6. Location of the burial ground in the "District of Amokiah" that was part of Kwong Ngee Suah Teochew Cemetery (廣義山), located along Upper Serangoon Road (superimposed on a present-day road map).
Source: Illustrated by Chen Jingwen; author's collection.

pronunciation of the term at the time is *Ngi*[6] *Ang*[1] *Gung*[6] or "Ngee Ann Kun".[82] Despite it being a Teochew organisation, the terms "Ghee Ann Koon" and "Ghee Ann Society," instead of "Ngee Ann Kun" or "Ngee Ann Society," were used in all official matters to refer to the society. This was probably because Hokkien was the lingua franca of the local Chinese at the time. That the society was named after the ancient name of the Teochew prefecture implies that it was intended to be a pan-Teochew organisation, instead of being a society serving those originating from certain districts. It became an umbrella organisation bringing numerous smaller societies and informal groups under it. This would have given the societies an economy of scale that put them in a better position to manage both profit-making (shophouses for rent) and non-profit-making (temples and burial grounds) assets.

Prior to 1914, only two lots of land were officially under the direct management of Ghee Ann Koon. They were a piece of land situated in the District Toah Pyoh, which was "known as Lot No. 9-1 of Town Subdivision XXIX" (Fig. 2.10) and "nos. 197, 198, 199 and 200 New Bridge Road"[83] (Fig. 2.11). They were used as a burial ground and shophouses for the earning of rental income respectively. The burial ground was Kwong Eng Suah (廣恩山), located at the junction of Balestier Road and Thomson Road. It was acquired by the Ghee Ann Koon trustees in 1872 from Hoo Ah Kay (also known as Whampoa) and is the earliest property acquired in the name of the society.[84] This is significant in showing the existence of Ghee Ann Koon in 1872, if not earlier. The earlier Ghee Ann Koon establishment date of 1845 commonly stated or alluded to by other writers was based on the purchase date of Tye Swah Teng (泰山亭), a cemetery commonly accepted as the first pan-Teochew burial ground in Singapore.[85] It is worth noting that Tye Swah Teng only came under the management of Ngee Ann Kongsi later and was not officially vested in the Ghee Ann Koon until 1916. The Tye Swah Teng land was instead vested in "Seah Euchin and Choa Po Choo [蔡報之]" as "Trustees of the Chinese Burial Ground 'Tie Swah.'"[86] Hence, the year 1845 should not be taken as the year in which Ghee Ann Koon was founded if no other historical sources can be found to support this.

In 1889, the newly enacted Societies Ordinance required the registration of "any club company partnership [*sic*] or association of ten or more persons" regardless of its "nature or object".[87] However, societies formed for the purposes of recreation, charity, religion or literature could be exempted from registration by application to the Colonial Secretary.[88] Ghee Ann Koon was one such society. On 21 August 1890, "The Ghee Ann Koon Society, Singapore" was "exempted from registration by Order of the Governor in Council".[89] This was the first mention of the term "Ghee Ann Koon" in official records. The society was included in the "List of Existing Societies Exempted from Registration" up till 1933.[90] Similarly, in 1916, when Seah Liang Seah subscribed to the Federated Malay States Loan on behalf of the society, it was indicated as being "for Ghee Ann Koon Association".[91] When

Fig. 2.7. Location of "Poh Seng Tye Tee" (保生大帝) temple along the expunged Johore Road (superimposed on a present-day road map).
Source: Illustrated by Chen Jingwen; author's collection.

Fig. 2.8. "Choh Soo Kong Temple" (祖師公廟) was located along Jalan Besar Road (Town Subdivision XVII Lot No. 14) (superimposed on a present-day road map). The temple's land was first bought by Seah Liang Seah in his capacity as trustee of the Temple on 23 October 1894.
Source: Illustrated by Chen Jingwen; author's collection.

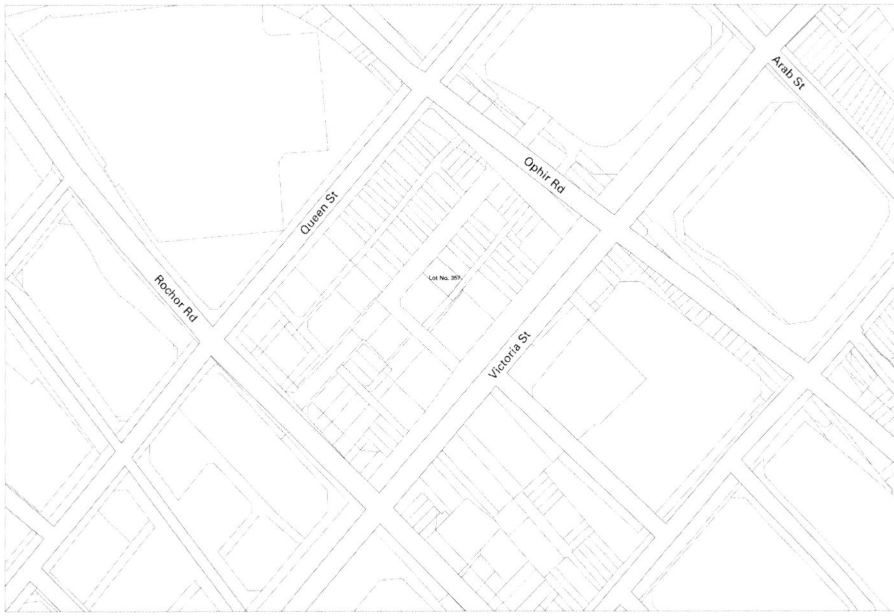
Arab St
Ophir Rd
Queen St
Lot No. 357
Rochor Rd
Victoria St

Fig. 2.7 .

Sturdee Rd
Lavendar St
Jln Besar
Lot No.14
Foch Rd
Beatty Lane
Pertain Rd
Tyrwhitt Rd
Jln Besar

Fig. 2.8 .

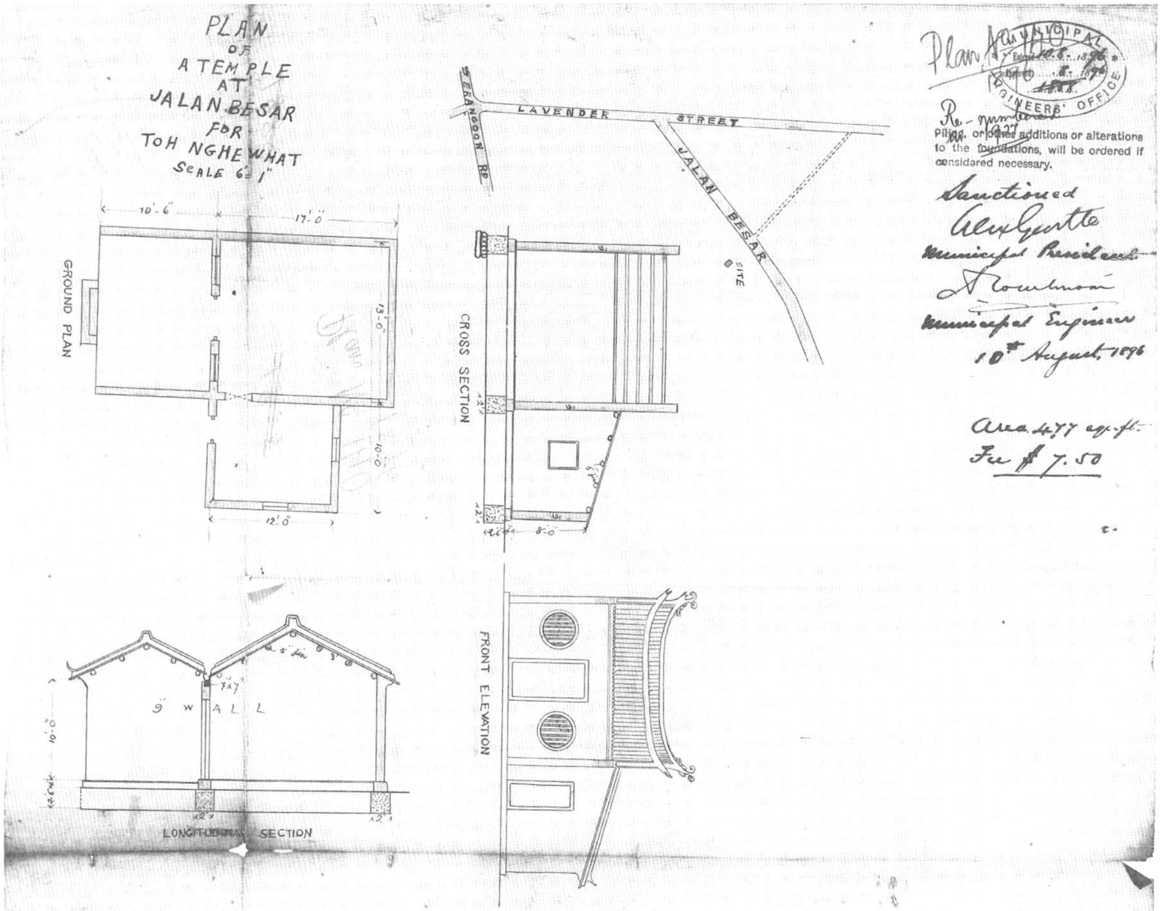

Fig. 2.9 .

the society was involved in a lawsuit with an 80-year-old pig and poultry farmer over a piece of land at the junction of Thomson and Balestier Roads, the term "Ghee Ann Society" was again used.[92]

Reforming the Society's Management Style and the 1933 Incorporation Ordinance

After the 1914 to 1916 "Ghee Ann Society" lawsuit, Seah Liang Seah strove to initiate further reforms in the society for the better management of its "public properties". He sought to move the society's management structure away from one akin to a traditional Chinese family business model towards a modern corporate structure governed by definite rules. This led to the idea of incorporating the Ghee Ann Koon, which was first considered when Seah Liang Seah held a conference with the Protector of Chinese after the 1916 Order of Court was issued.[93] To ensure that

Fig. 2.9. Architectural plans of "Choh Soo Kong Temple" (祖師公廟) temple at Jalan Besar submitted to the municipal engineer in 1896.
Source: "Plan of a Temple at Jalan Besar for Toh Nghe What," 1886, 140/1896, CBS335. Courtesy of the National Archives of Singapore.

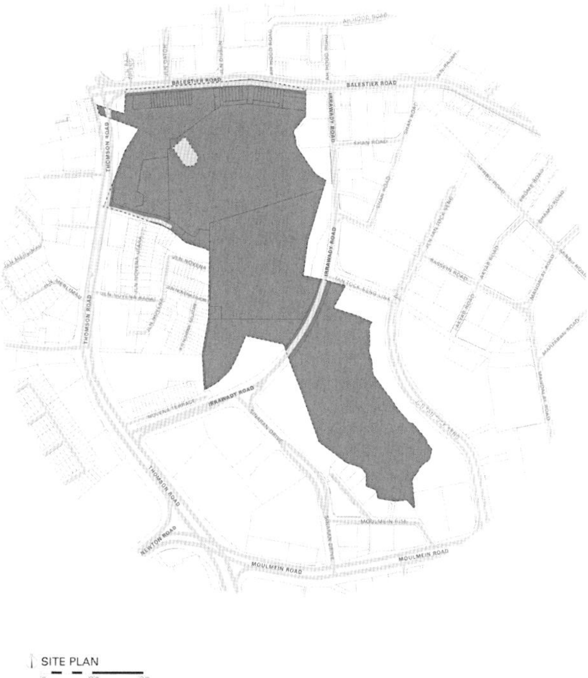

Fig. 2.10 .

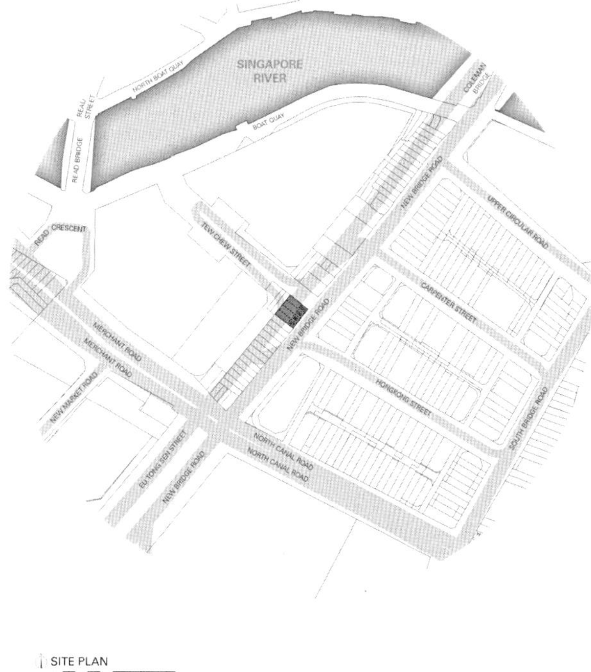

Fig. 2.11 .

a set of definite rules for managing the society was enforceable, and to make it more difficult to reverse the good management practices he sought to put in place, Seah endeavoured to have them passed as an ordinance. He approached the colonial government to obtain their support of the introduction of an incorporation bill in the Legislative Council.[94] After a few years' delay, a bill was prepared. However, with Seah's death at the age of 75 in 1925, the matter was shelved; nothing more was done in the next two years to regularise the administration and management of the society.[95]

In December 1927, Seah Liang Seah's reform initiatives were again picked up by a group of prominent Teochews led by Lim Nee Soon (林義順), many of them Straits-born Chinese businessmen with advisory positions in colonial institutions.[96] They were:

Lim Nee Soon (林義順) of Chop Thong Mui, 112 and 144 Robinson Road
Yeo Chan Boon (楊纘文) of Chop Yong Guan Seng, 60 Circular Road
Tan Chew Char (陳秋槎) of Chop Sam Lye Heng, 10 Carpenter Street

Fig. 2.10. The earliest property was acquired by the Ghee Ann Koon trustees in 1872. The property located at the junction of Balestier Road and Thomson Road was used as the Kwong Eng Suah (廣恩山) burial ground (superimposed on a present-day road map).
Source: Illustrated by Teh Xue Ting Priscilla; author's collection.

Fig. 2.11. Shophouses, Nos. 197, 198, 199 and 200 New Bridge Road, were properties of Ghee Ann Koon (superimposed on a present-day road map).
Source: Illustrated by Teh Xue Ting Priscilla; author's collection.

Lee Wee Nam (李偉南) of Chop Chye Hua Seng, 17 New Bridge Road
Goh Yang Pheng (吴揚屏) of Chop Siang Hua, 58 Boat Quay
Yeo Choo Tian (楊書典) of Chop Long Huat, 35 Circular Road,
Chew Swee Lin (周瑞麟) of Chop Nam Heng Hak Kee, 4-5 Fish Street
Tan Lip Sek (陳立植) of Chop Tan Guan Lee, 79 Boat Quay
Quek [Kwek] Theng Thong (郭廷通) of Chop Teo Siang Guan Kee, 65 Circular Road
Sim Ai Tng [Whye Cheng] (沈□□) of Chop Kheng Soon Long, 9 Circular Road
Lim Woo Ngam (林雨岩) of Chop Seng Moh, 166-5 Middle Road
Nah Wee Liat (藍偉烈) of Chop Wee Heng, 253 South Bridge Road
Tan Guan Chua (陳源泉) of Chop Chua Seng Heng, 20-14, Armenian Street
Low Chia Heng (劉正興) of Chop Low Miang Heng, 25 and 26 Circular Road

This group of Teochew leaders was concerned that the status of the Teochew community's "public properties" was being compromised, as they were being controlled solely by an exclusive group headed by the Seah family. This perception is unsurprising given that the Seah family had been in control of Ghee Ann Koon since its founding. Based on the dates of death of the various heads of the family and traditional Chinese familial hierarchy, and with the assumption that these individuals had held leadership positions in the organisation, the Seah family would have possibly provided four de facto heads of the society up to this point:[97]

Seah Eu Chin 佘有進 unknown–1883 (b. 1805–d. 1883)
Seah Cheo Seah 佘石城 1883–1885 (b. 1846–d. 1885)
Seah Liang Seah 佘連城 1885–1925 (b. 1850–d. 1925)
Seah Eng Tiong [Tong] 佘應忠 1925–1930 (b. 1880–d. 1940)[98]

In addition, when the addresses of societies were first listed in the "List of Existing Societies Exempted from Registration" in 1929, Ghee Ann Koon's address was "c/o 4 North Bridge Road",[99] the business address of the Seah family's Chop Chin Heng.[100] Moreover, the society's accounts were privately kept by the Seah family; other members of the Teochew community had no access to them. Given the lack of transparency, it is no wonder that members of the Teochew community came to regard the "public properties" status of Ghee Ann Koon's assets as being questionable. This became even more of a concern as many of the "public properties" previously under the trusteeships of various smaller Teochew groups were by the late 1920s consolidated under the charge of the Ghee Ann Koon. The Ghee Ann Koon was by this time responsible for more "public properties" than ever before.

On 29 December 1927, Lim's group sent an official letter to Seah Eng Tong and the Ghee Ann Koon's trustees; this was published in local Chinese newspapers including *Lat Pau* and *Nanyang Siang Pau*[101] (Fig. 2.12).The letter marks the start of a reform process that was to take place over more than five years. It was also the start of negotiations with the Seah family regarding increased transparency in the management of the Kongsi as a Teochew charitable organisation.[102] The letter asked that Seah's group respond to and provide details on the following six points:

(1) Are the assets of Ghee Ann Koon the public properties of the entire Teochew community

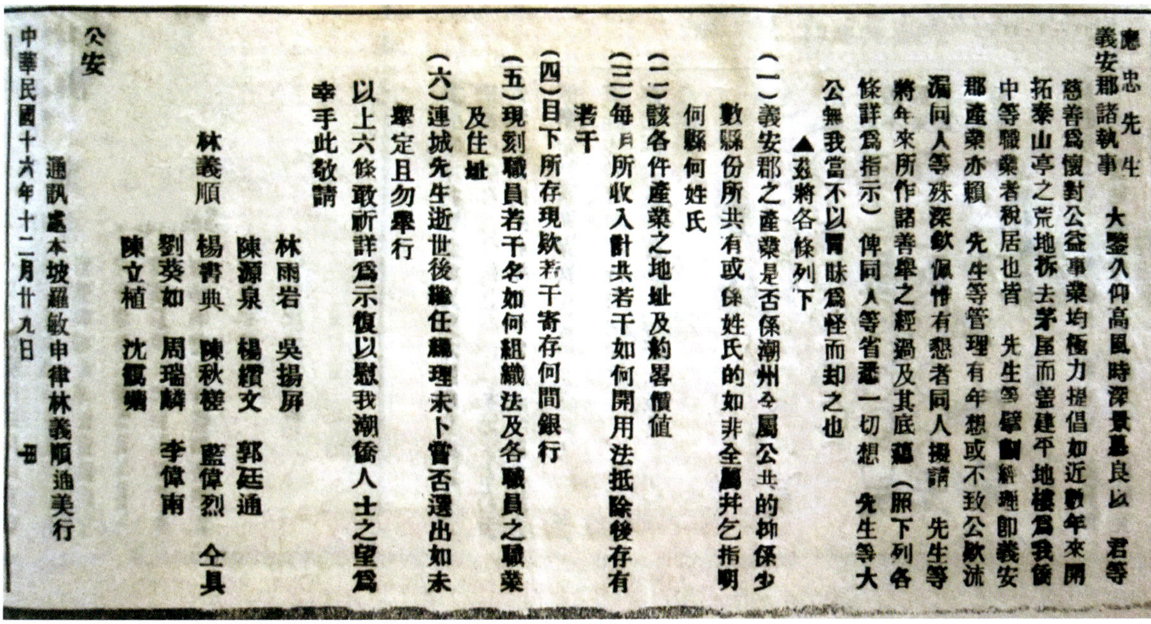
應忠先生
義安郡諸執事 大鑒久仰高風時深景慕良以 君等
慈善爲懷對公益事業均極力提倡如近數年來開
拓泰山亭之荒地拆去茅屋而蓋建平地樓爲我儕
中等職業者稅居也皆 先生等擘劃經理即義安
郡產業亦賴 先生等管理有年想或不致公欵流
漏同人等殊深欽佩惟有懇者同人擬請 先生等
將年來所作諸善舉之經過及其底蘊（照下列各
條詳爲指示） 俾同人等省悉一切想 先生等大
公無我當不以冒昧爲怪而却之也
▲茲將各條列下
（一）義安郡之產業是否係潮州全屬公共的抑係少
數縣份所共有或係姓氏的如非全屬并乞指明
何縣何姓氏
（二）該各件產業之地址及約略價值
（三）每月所收入計共若干如何開用法抵除後存有
若干
（四）目下所存現欵若干寄存何間銀行
（五）現刻職員若干名如何組織法及各職員之職業
及住址
（六）連城先生逝世後繼任總理未卜會否選出如未
舉定且勿舉行
以上六條敢祈詳爲示復以慰我潮僑人士之望爲
幸手此敬請
公安
林雨岩 吳揚屏
陳源泉 楊纘文 郭廷通
林義順 楊書典 陳秋槎 藍偉烈 仝具
劉葵如 周瑞麟 李偉南
陳立植 沈鶴鳴
通訊處本坡羅敏申律林義順通美行
中華民國十六年十二月廿九日 冊

Fig. 2.12 .

or do they belong to those from certain districts or surname groups?

(2) The address of Ghee Ann Koon's properties and their estimated value.
(3) The society's monthly revenue, expenses and profit.
(4) Ghee Ann Koon's current cash balance amount and the bank in which the cash is deposited.
(5) The names, position and address of Ghee Ann Koon's staff and its organisational structure.
(6) After the death of Mr. [Seah] Liang Seah, the succeeding president is yet to be confirmed. Has one been chosen? If it has not been fixed, please do not hold [an election].

On 4 January 1928, Lim Nee Soon wrote a letter to the Straits Settlements Secretary for Chinese Affairs, Arthur Mitchell Goodman. He asked to meet Goodman the following day together with two other Teochew leaders, Tan Chew Char (陳秋槎) and Lim Ah Woo (Lim Woo Ngam 林雨岩), to discuss two matters.[103] The first was to "explain the gross mis-management of the Association by the Committee", with the hope that Goodman might help "put the matter right".[104] The second matter was to discuss their "proposal to form a Teochew Huai [Huay] Kuan on similar lines to the Hockien Huai Kuan [Hokkien Huay Kuan]".[105] Lim pointed out that having a Huay Kuan was important for the Teochew community and for the colony as a whole as "the lack of it was reflected on [*sic*] the recent Teochew clan fighting".[106]

Fig. 2.12. Lim Nee Soon and 13 other individuals' public letter to Seah Eng Tong and trustees of Ngee Ann Kun published in *Lat Pau* on 29 December 1927.
Source: "*Yīngzhōng xiānshēng yì'ān jùn zhū zhíshì* 應忠先生 義安郡諸執事 [Mr. Eng Tong and the Various Trustees of Ngee Ann Kun]," *Lat Pau* 《叻報》, 29 December 1927.

Kwangtung Hui Kuan (*Guǎngdōng Huìguǎn* 廣東會館)

While the term *Guǎngdōng* is today mostly associated with Cantonese, the province of Guangdong in China historically consisted of four major dialect groups. They were the Cantonese, the Teochew, the Hakka, and the Hainanese.[1] The province was and is also known by the geographical term *Yuè* (粵). Although the term *Yuè yǔ* (粵語) is often used to refer to the Cantonese language and *Yuè jù* (粵劇) to Cantonese opera, the use of the term *Yuè* is not confined to the Cantonese dialect group. The first word of Wak Hai Cheng Bio's name is also the Chinese character *Yuè*. On the plaques presented by eastern Guangdong merchants to the temple, they refer to themselves as *Yuèdōng zhòng shēnshāng* (粵東眾紳商), or "elite merchants of eastern *Yuè*". Eastern Guangdong geographically refers to the Teochew prefecture (潮州府) and also the Kar Ying County (嘉應州).[2] Unsurprisingly, the Teochews identified themselves as people of eastern Yuè, given that they occupy the eastern parts of Guangdong province. By using the word *Yuè* instead of *Cháo* (潮), a term referring specifically to the Teochew community, the temple signalled that it was intended to cater to a larger community based on geographic rather than dialect lines; it served, and was meant to serve, the people whose origins lay in Guangdong province. According to anecdotal accounts, the temple was a neutral ground where those of Guangdong origin could go to resolve disputes. The presence of the deities was said to ensure a fairer resolution of disputes, and made agreements more binding at a time when there were few written contracts, and law enforcement was weak amongst Singapore's non-European communities.

Unsurprisingly then, the Kwangtung Hui Kuan (廣東會館) was first located in the premises of Wak Hai Cheng Bio.[3] The founding of the Kwangtung Hui Kuan was led by a Teochew, Lee Wee Nam (李偉南), who was then a member of the Ngee Ann Kongsi's Committee of Management and Vice-President of the Teochew Poit Ip Huay Kuan. The idea of forming the Kwangtung Hui Kuan was first mooted at a banquet hosted by Chin Kee Sun (曾紀辰) on 5 October 1936. Many at the banquet were merchants of Guangdong origin (hereafter Guangdong merchants). While discussing the development of the Hokkien Huay Kuan (another province-based organisation that catered to those of Hokkien or Fujian origin) and its achievements in providing education, these Guangdong merchants were reminded that people of Guangdong origin in Singapore lacked an equivalent organisation. This was despite the early existence of many Guangdong province-, clan-, county- and dialect-based organisations in Singapore. The Guangdong merchants were in support of forming the Kwangtung Hui Kuan. They wrote to the various Guangdong province associations, who also threw their support behind the idea.[4]

In a general meeting of the associations' representatives on 17 November 1936, a committee to prepare for the formation of the Hui Kuan was formed. The committee consisted of 27 people and was headed by Lee Wee Nam. During the second committee meeting in June 1937, the Kwangtung Hui Kuan's constitution was passed, which stated that it would accept members who were Cantonese, Teochew, Hakka and Hainanese.[5] Thereafter, the members applied to the colonial government to become a legal organisation.[6] Permission was granted on 24 September 1937, and the Hui Kuan was exempted from registration under the Societies Ordinance.[7] This was also the year in which Japan began its military campaign into China proper. Hence, immediately after the Hui Kuan was formed, its members busied themselves with gathering support for China's war effort against Japan.[8]

In 1937, the two-storey rear building of the temple played host to the newly established Kwangtung Hui Kuan. Its address was 16 Church Street. Not only was the use of the temple's premises free from rent, the Hui Kuan did not have to pay for its water, electricity or telephone bills either; these were covered by the Ngee Ann Kongsi.[9] It was only in 1960 that the Hui Kuan's administrative office moved out of the rear building, after the renovation

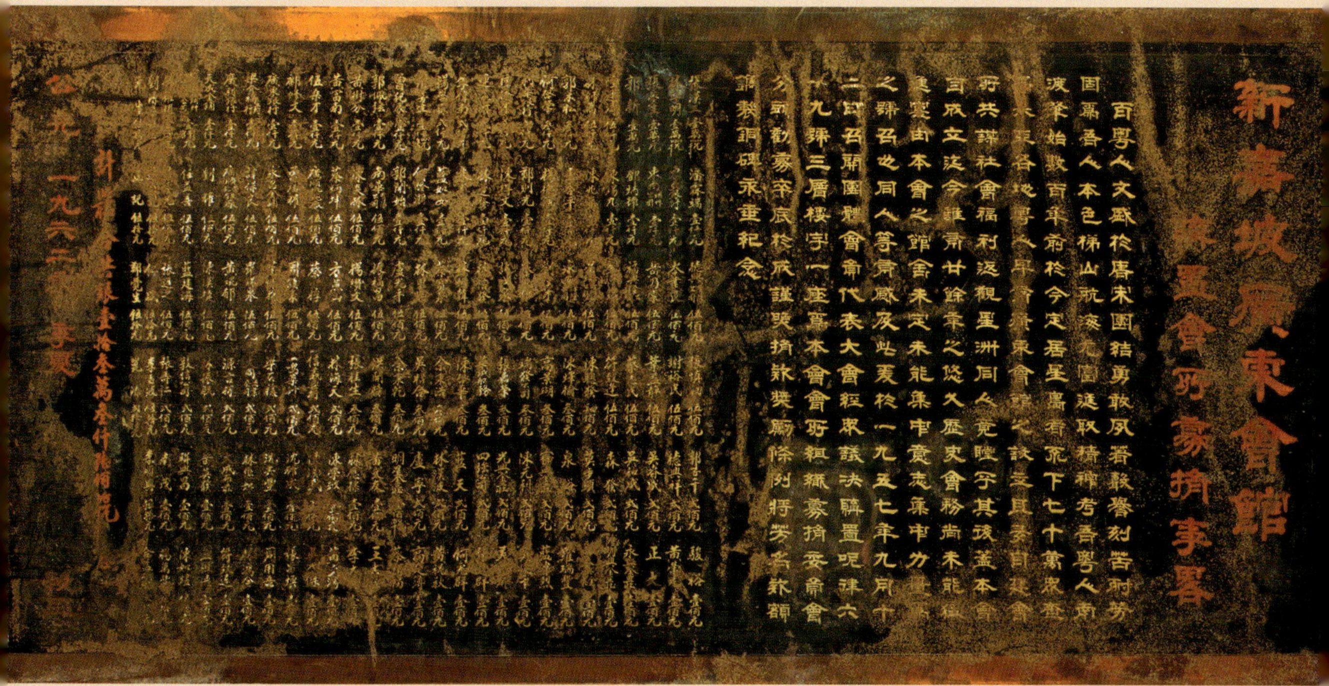

Fig. BS05.1.

of its newly acquired premises at 69 Neil Road was completed.[10] In 1984, the Kwantung Hui Kuan – which was then led by another Teochew, Yeo Siew Hua (楊紹和) – moved back to the temple's rear building when the Hui Kuan's Neil Road premises were acquired by the State for urban redevelopment. The Kwangtung Hui Kuan then occupied the rear building until 1994, when the 1994 to 1997 temple's restoration began.[11]

While clearing out Wak Hai Cheng Bio's rear block in 2013 during the 2011 to 2014 restoration, a metal plaque from 1962 was found. The plaque explains how the Hui Kuan did not have its own premises despite having been established for more than 20 years. It went on to say that in a general meeting held on 12 September 1957, it was decided to raise funds to purchase 69 Neil Road to house the Hui Kuan. The plaque also lists the names of donors and the amount they donated. It has since been returned to the Hui Kuan.

■ Fig. BS05.1. Metal plaque entitled "新嘉坡廣東會館 購置會所募捐事畧" [An account of fundraising efforts to purchase premises for Singapore Kwangtung Hui Kuan] dated 1962. Source: Photographed by Carolyn Lim.

The Secretary for Chinese Affairs agreed to facilitate a meeting between representatives of the Ghee Ann Koon's management committee led by Seah Eng Tong and Lim's group. This was held at the Chinese Protectorate at Havelock Road. Seah's group of representatives agreed to hand over Ghee Ann Koon's assets and form a new management committee to manage them. However, other members of the Seah family, led by Seah Eng Tong's cousin, attempted to prevent the handover.[107] There were apparently disagreements and disputes about control of the Ghee Ann Koon within the Seah family. As a result, no acceptable resolution came about from the drawn-out negotiations mediated by Goodman.[108]

Having failed to reach a compromise with the Seah family, a Teochew general meeting was then held at the Singapore Chinese Chamber of Commerce on 15 September 1928.[109] During the general meeting, the Teochew (Eight Districts) Public Property Preservation Association (潮州八邑公產維持會) was formed.[110] The issue of naming the new Teochew association was also brought up, the formation of which had been proposed by a group of 40 Teochew leaders led by Lim a week earlier on 8 September 1928.[111] It was decided to name the association Teochew Poit Ip Huay Kuan (潮州八邑會館), "Poit Ip" being the eight Teochew districts in the Guangdong province of China. In December 1928, a meeting was convened at 29 Tank Road, the premises of Tuan Mong School (端蒙學校), to prepare for the formation of the Huay Kuan. Eight committee members were also tasked with preparing the Huay Kuan's constitution.[112] The Singapore Teochew Poit Ip Huay Kuan was finally established in 1929 and granted exemption from registration on 18 March 1929.[113]

During the inauguration ceremony of the Teochew Poit Ip Huay Kuan's first management committee on 4 September 1929, seven of its members were tasked with negotiating with the existing Ghee Ann Koon trustees on the matter of the "public properties" of the Teochews.[114] They were Lim Nee Soon, Lim Woo Ngam, Yeo Chan Boon, Lee Wee Nam (李偉南), Tan Chew Char, Tan Guan Chua (陳源泉) and Goh Yang Pheng (吳揚屏). Recognising the futility of their opposition, the Seahs voluntarily sought to settle the matter amicably.[115] This eventually led to a restructuring of Ghee Ann Koon's management committee and a new constitution was promulgated in April 1930.[116] At a meeting on 12 April 1930 held at Tuan Mong School, Lim Nee Soon was elected the new President of Ghee Ann Koon, with Low Peng Soy (劉炳先) and Lee Wee Nam as vice-presidents, and Tan Lip Sek (陳立植) as treasurer.[117] This marked the end of the Seah's hereditary de facto leadership of and control over the society, which had lasted for almost a century.

The society's reform was completed with the passing of the Ordinance to Incorporate the Ngee Ann Kongsi (No. 5 of 1933) on 10 March 1933 by the Straits Settlements Legislative Council. This was the first ordinance passed in the Straits Settlements to incorporate a Chinese society. The Ordinance recognises the Kongsi as a charitable organisation and limits the Kongsi's membership to Teochews whose ancestors originated in one of eight specified districts in Teochew prefecture, namely Teo Ann (潮安), Theng Hai (澄海), Teo Yeonh (潮陽), Kit Yeonh (揭陽), Jeow Pheng (饒平), Phow Leng (普寧), Hui Lye (惠來) and Nam Oh (南澳). It also rules that a person who had been the president or honorary treasurer "for two years shall not be entitled to hold office as such for the next ensuing two years".[118] The committee of management should also consist of 17 to 25 members.[119] The Kongsi's office was fixed at "the Teochew Temple in Phillip Street, Singapore, or at such other place as may from time to time be decided".[120] The Ordinance also contains a schedule listing the properties of Ngee Ann Kongsi, their land areas, and the form of legal ownership of these properties. This allowed for greater transparency where the Kongsi's assets were concerned and made their details known to the public for the first time. At the same time, the Ordinance put checks and balances in place and provided for greater accountability to the general Teochew community.

Prior to the passing of the Ordinance to Incorporate the Ngee Ann Kongsi (No. 5 of 1933), the trustees were:[121]

Seah Eng Tong (佘應忠) of Bendemeer, Serangoon Road,
Seah Chin Mui [Moey] (佘振美) of No. 58 River Valley Road
Kwek Liang Choon (郭雨存) of Chop Kwek Khai Seng of No. 60 Chulia Street
Low Peng Soy (劉炳先) of Chop Low Yong Hong of No. 57 Boat Quay
Chan Kim Seng (曾□□) of Chop Chan Yong Soon of No. 561 Beach Road
Goh Tek Chng [Chue] (吳竹村) of Chop Goh Yong Buan Long of No. 51 Circular Road
Teo Keong Meng (張恭銘) of Chop Teo Nguan Hwa of No. 49 North Boat Quay
Heng Pang Keat (王邦傑) of Chop Heng Say Yee Heng of No. 7 North Canal Road
Yeo Huang Kok (楊□□) of Chop Yeo Liang Huat of No. 21 Teochew Street
Tan Miang Long (陳綿隆) of Chop Tan Liang Seng of No. 25 Hertford Road
Ng Chok Sam (吳□□) of Chop Ng Hock Seng of No. 55 River Valley Road
Sim Ka Siew (沈教授) of Chop Sim Kheng Soon Seng of No. 48 Circular Road
Chua Ngak Chew (蔡□□) of No. 21 Carpenter Street
Lim Hak Khiam (林□□) of No. 1-B River Valley Road

The 1933 Incorporation Ordinance named the following as Trustees (Committee of Management):[122]

Lim Nee Soon (林義順)
Low Peng Soy (劉炳先)
Lee Wee Nam (李偉南)
Tan Lip Sek (陳立植)
Lim Woo Ngam (林雨岩)
Yeo Choo Tian (楊書典)
Kwek Liang Choon (郭雨存)
Liau Chia Heng (廖正興)
Yeo Chan Boon (楊纘文)
Tan Chew Char (陳秋槎)
Goh Teck Chng [Chue] (吳竹村)
Tan Miang Long (陳綿隆)
Sim Ka Siew (沈教授)
Goh Yang Pheng (吳揚屏)
Kwek Soo Kow (郭斯高)
Low Chia Heng (劉正興)
Lim Soo Siam (林樹森)
Chew Swee Lin (周瑞麟)
Nah Wee Liat (藍偉烈)
Kwek [Quek] Teng Thong (郭廷通)
Low Peng Soo (劉炳思)
Lee Kim Soo (李金賜)
Lim Chong Pang (林忠邦)
Seah Eng Tong (佘應忠)

Three reasons were offered for the need for the 1933 Incorporation Ordinance. First, "to facilitate the administration of the property and affairs of the Society";[123] second, to "effect the proper constitution of the Society, and to provide for the regulation of its affairs by definite rules";[124] and, third, to allow for the properties belonging to the society to be vested "in a separate legal corporation having perpetual succession" instead of in individual trustees.[125] This last point proved very important for the Society in the long run because it eliminated "future difficulties as to the Society's title to and dealings with its immoveable property". Before the Ordinance was enacted, dealings with its immoveable properties were often hindered by changes in its trustees. In 1929, when the Singapore Improvement Trust (SIT) was acquiring parts of 33 Phillip Street for the creation of a back lane, it was found that the property was vested in the trustees named by the 1916 Court Order instead of in the Society's 1929 trustees. Many of these earlier trustees had either passed away or left the colony by that time. In the end, the decision was to have the compensation money for land acquisition paid into court because compensating the society or its present trustees would not give a good discharge to SIT.[126] Incorporating the society eliminated this problem as the "death, retirement or departure from the Colony" of individual trustees would no longer affect the society's interests.[127]

As part of the reform of Ghee Ann Koon, the new group of trustees also attempted to revise the caretakership system of Wak Hai Cheng Bio to make it more transparent. The caretakers or temple attendants were and remain responsible for running the day-to-day affairs of the temple. Caretakers are not Taoist clergy. They are closely connected with the maintenance of a temple. By virtue of their association with the temple, they are considered more knowledgeable about religious matters than the average devotee and hence are often called upon to assist devotees on religious matters.[128]

It is unclear if the caretakers before 1930 were salaried staff or if they paid a fee to operate the temple. The latter was the traditional norm, that allowed caretakers to sell incense and offerings as well as to collect donations. During a meeting on 28 October 1930, the trustees decided to discontinue the hereditary system of caretakership for all temples owned by the Society.[129] The positions were to be opened for tender and awarded to the highest bidder, who would pay a fee in return for the right to run the temple.[130] The caretakership term was set at three years.[131] The then caretaker of Wak Hai Cheng Bio, Kwek Yong Hock (郭永福), was the son of the previous caretaker.[132] By 1930, he had been in the role for more than 10 years.[133] When the term of the existing Wak Hai Cheng Bio caretakership was ending in 1931, a tender was called and nine bids were received. Although Kwek did not tender, he wrote to the Society to ask for a reconsideration of the annual tender fees, citing reasons of declining donations. Considering Kwek's familiarity with the role and his requests, the trustees of Ghee Ann Koon decided to give Kwek the privilege of continuing as the temple's caretaker for an annual fee of $670, which was $140 less than the highest bid.[134] For the next decade, Kwek continued requesting for the annual fees to be lowered, and to change the terms of fee deposits.[135] Kwek thus remained the temple's caretaker, and earlier attempts to open the position up and to be filled by tender were abandoned. Kwek's requests were considered, and the annual fee was eventually lowered to $570,[136] the rate that was maintained for many years afterwards.[137] The attempts to reform Wak Hai Cheng Bio's caretakership system in the 1930s, and make it more transparent, were therefore unsuccessful. Kwek's position was eventually taken over by his son, Qwek Wee Chew (郭維洲), who retired in 2014. It was only in the mid-1990s that the reform process was taken up again. From 1996, the caretakers drew a monthly salary and could continue to sell incense, even though donations to the temple now went to the Ngee Ann Kongsi.[138] This was further revised in 2014 when salaries were substantially increased, but caretakers were no longer allowed to sell incense; incense was instead made available to devotees for free.[139]

An Administrative Centre

As the first and oldest "public property" of the Teochew community in Singapore, Wak Hai Cheng Bio was the natural choice for housing the headquarters of a newly reformed organisation tasked with the care of the "public properties" belonging to the Teochews. In November 1930, the headquarters of Ghee Ann Koon and the newly formed Teochew Poit Ip Huay Kuan moved from their temporary premises at the Tuan Mong School on Tank Road into the rear building of the temple.[140] Administrative affairs of the two Teochew organisations were conducted from this building even though No. 29 Tank Road remained the official address of the two Teochew organisations in the "List of Existing Societies Exempted from Registration" up till the outbreak of the Second World War.[141] The Ghee Ann Koon's official address was changed from the Seah family's "c/o 4 North Bridge Road" business address to "c/o 29 Tank Road" in 1931.[142] This change in address reflects the transfer of effective control over Ghee Ann Koon from the Seah family to the new group of trustees led by Lim Nee Soon.

The rear building of the temple had a separate Church Street address. It was known as No. 16 Church Street and was accessible from both Church Street and the shrine of the Mysterious Emperor of Heaven. The former entrance provided direct access to the building without the need to walk through the temple from Phillip Street. The temple also played host to a number of societies and associations, including the relatively unknown Yit Hai Hoe Kuan (粵海會館), a society exempted from registration on 6 July 1890, and the Kwangtung Hui Kuan (廣東會館), a Guangdong province-based umbrella association led by a Teochew founding president, Lee Wee Nam, who then held executive positions in the Ngee Ann Kongsi and the Teochew Poit Ip Huay Kuan.[143] It also housed the Nantao Publishing House (南島出版社) belonging to Phua Chay Long (潘醒農), Secretary of the Ngee Ann Kongsi, Teochew Poit Ip Huay Kuan, and Kwangtung Hui Kuan.[144] This publishing house published mainly Chinese travel guides and was active from 1933 to the mid-1960s.

Conclusion

The relationships which were formed with Wak Hai Cheng Bio over the course of its history have been complex and multifaceted. Although the temple was and is primarily a place of worship, many who frequented the place related to it in more than one way. The temple was a spiritual focal point as much as it was a "public property" of the Teochew community, an administrative centre, a welfare and humanitarian aid centre, a place of entertainment, and a site of inter-societal rivalry. Over the centuries, some of these roles and functions played by the temple have become defunct. Indeed, the temple has ceased to be an administrative centre, a place of entertainment, a welfare and humanitarian centre, and a site for inter-societal rivalries. On the other hand, it continues to be an important place of worship and a symbolic site for the Teochew community in Singapore as their first "public property". The temple has also taken on new roles and functions as each generation forms new relationships with and ascribes new meaning to the place. Besides its traditional roles, Wak Hai Cheng Bio today has also taken the role of a national monument, a historical building, a heritage site, a repository of traditional crafts, and a tourist destination. In other words, it is now a sacred place to be preserved and conserved, a place of spiritual importance that extends beyond its historic communities.

CHAPTER 3

Architectural Developments in the 19th and 20th Centuries

Extension, Renovation and Restoration

The identities of the designers and builders of traditional Chinese buildings in Singapore remain largely unknown. Wak Hai Cheng Bio is no exception. While mandatory submission of building plans required an architect to sign off on building plans, it remains unclear whether the signing architect was the actual designer of many of the traditional Chinese buildings in Singapore. And while the materials used in these traditional Chinese buildings are widely thought to have been imported from China, this is questionable, given the relative abundance and accessibility of certain building materials in the region as compared to China.

Wak Hai Cheng Bio has undergone numerous rounds of extension, renovation and restoration works since the early 19th century. The most significant of these is the reconstruction of the temple that began in 1895. Unfortunately, works carried out before 1895 were unrecorded. The temple's architectural development before this date is therefore uncertain, and it is unclear when it took on its current twin-shrine typology. Accounts of the temple from before 1895 are largely anecdotal. Written evidence of the twin-shrine typology first appears in a letter to the press dated 1890, which complained about the temple's unkempt condition.[1] The temple's dilapidation would have been a major reason for its reconstruction. Building plans for the 1895 reconstruction reveal that the temple was rebuilt on its existing footprint. The plan also indicates the use of local building materials in the temple, a matter which will be examined in greater detail later in this chapter.

Minor alterations to the temple in the first three-quarters of the 20th century were also undocumented and it is not until 1979 that we find clear documentary evidence of alteration works. That year, the temple needed a new boundary wall after some neighbouring shophouses were demolished. By the early 1990s, almost a full century since the temple's last major reconstruction, it was evident that Wak Hai Cheng Bio needed a major overhaul. The temple's owners, the Ngee Ann Kongsi, therefore commissioned a series of pre-renovation measured drawings and photographic surveys. These surveys proved to be a very important record

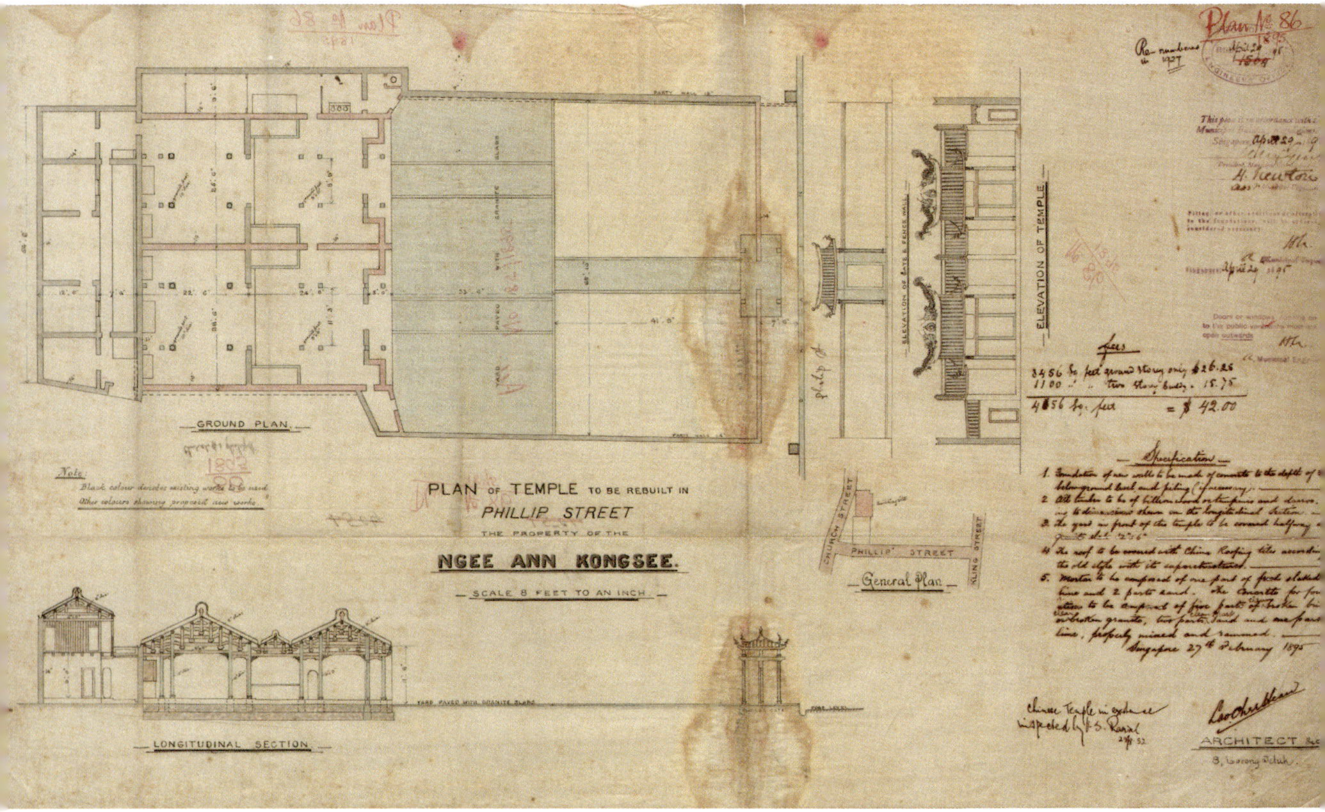

Fig. 3.1.

of the alterations that took place during the 1994 to 1997 renovation and a useful resource allowing subsequent restoration teams to understand the temple's architecture prior to this renovation.

The Temple Before 1890

Accounts of works carried out on the temple before 1895 are largely anecdotal. While other writers have briefly dealt with these works, no historical records have yet been found that corroborate these accounts. Little is known about the architecture of the temple before 1890, though it has existed at its current location since at least 1827. As we saw in Chapter One, Phua Chay Long (潘醒農), a former Secretary of the Ngee Ann Kongsi, believed that the temple existed in the 1820s as a simple attap shrine structure (神壇) dedicated to Māzǔ (媽祖), the Goddess of the Sea, but was later enlarged with the addition of another shrine structure dedicated to the Mysterious Supreme Emperor of Heaven or Xuántiān Shàngdì (玄天上帝) in 1826 or earlier.[2] Some time later, renovations were supposedly made to the temple.[3]

Fig. 3.1. Building Plan of Wak Hai Cheng Bio submitted to the municipal engineer in 1895.
Source: Lao Chee Hean, "Plan of Temple to be Rebuilt in Phillip Street," 27 February 1895, 86/1895, CBS334. Courtesy of National Archives of Singapore (20170000001-0001).

Two bronze bells were presented to the Shrine of the Goddess of the Sea, or Tiānhòugōng (天后宫), and the Shrine of the Mysterious Supreme Emperor of Heaven, or Shàngdìgōng (上帝宫), in 1837 and 1838 respectively.[4] Objects were usually commissioned for and donated to temples, to mark significant events in the temple, or to mark major events in the donor's life. To date, no records have been found to indicate why the two bronze bells were donated in the 1830s, although it is possible that the bells might have been donated to mark the completion of renovation works. Several writers including Phua also mention that between 1850 and 1855, extension works were carried out.[5] Lee Geok Boi writes that the altar in Shàngdìgōng was brought to the temple from China in 1852.[6] However, this remains unverified by historical documents.

The First Evidence of the Twin-Shrine Typology

Wak Hai Cheng Bio today consists of two shrines. Tiānhòugōng is dedicated to Māzǔ, and Shàngdìgōng to Xuántiān Shàngdì. It is unclear when the temple first came to comprise two shrines instead of one. The only evidence suggesting the existence of this feature before 1890 comes from Chinese oral history accounts. The first textual evidence of the double shrine is from early 1890. It comes in the form of a letter to *The Straits Times* complaining about the condition of the temple:

> Sir, —One of my pious friends having made a call, and requested me to call the attention of the managers and trustees to the state of the temple in Phillip Street known as the "Double Temple," one wing of which is dedicated to the Queen of Heaven, or Goddess of Sailors, and the other to the supreme ruler of the sombre heavens or Tauist God of the North Pole....[7]

The letter also mentioned the existence of a courtyard. At this time, this courtyard was probably not paved; one of the specifications in the 1895 building plan is for the courtyard to be paved halfway with granite slabs.[8] The letter also pointed out the general untidiness of the temple, and the unpleasant stench emanating from it. The poor condition of the temple – which had become a matter of public outcry – may have been one of the reasons it was reconstructed in the 1890s.

The Rebuilding of the Temple from 1895

The temple owes its current form to the reconstruction which began in 1895. A building plan was lodged with the Municipal Engineer's Office by the architect Lao Chee Hean of No. 8 Lorong Teluk on 27 February 1895 (Fig. 3.1). This plan was approved by the acting municipal engineer, Howard Newton, on 29 April 1895.[9] Like all other pre-1900 building plans submitted to the municipality, the plan was renumbered in 1927. The temple was also inspected against the plan by V. S. Raniah in 1932. The 1895 fees and specifications given on the plan were as follows:

> Fees
> 3,456 sq feet ground storey only $26.25
> 1,100 sq feet two storey building $15.75
> 4,556 sq feet = $42.00
> Specification
> 1. Foundation of new walls to be made of concrete to the depth of 3 feet below ground level, and piling (if necessary).
> 2. All timber to be of billion wood or tempanis and darroo, according to dimensions shown on the longitudinal section.[10]
> 3. The yard in front of the temple to be covered halfway with granite slabs 12"x 6".
> 4. The roof to be covered with Chinese Roofing

tiles according to the old style with its superstructures.

5. Mortar to be composed of one part of fresh slaked coral lime and 2 parts sand. The concrete for foundations to be composed of five parts of clean broken bricks, or clean broken granite, two parts clean sharp sand and one part lime, properly mixed and rammed.

Singapore 27th February 1895
Lao Chee Hean
Architect & C.
8, Lorong Teluk

Based on the given fees and specifications, it is evident that the two shrines and the bulk of the rear building were rebuilt. Fees payable are calculated based on areas of new construction or alteration. The fees paid for 3,456 square feet of new construction or alteration within the two shrines correspond approximately to the approved prayer area in the latest renovation of 2013, which measured some 3,203 square feet (397.66 square metres). Likewise, in the two-storey rear building, the 1,100 square feet altered in 1895 corresponds to the bulk of the area in the 2013 renovation, which measured 1,647 square feet (153.09 square metres).[11]

The plans state that "[b]lack colour denotes existing works to be used. Other colours showing proposed new works". The other colours used were pink and green. Comparing the colours on the building plan with the existing structures, we may infer that for the ground plan, pink denotes new brick and plaster structures, while green indicates new granite. For the longitudinal section and elevation, pink denotes new timber and green new granite. The coloured building plans show that the temple was extensively rebuilt on the old temple's existing footprint.[12] The party walls shared with neighbouring shophouses, the granite walls adjacent to the shrines' entrance doorways, the walls separating the prayer halls and main halls of each shrine, the plinths for the niches where the deities are placed (神龕), the wall between the two shrines and the rear courtyard, as well as the brick walls and internal partitions of the rear building were retained. Significantly, the positions of the plinths and the two sets of shrine doorways demonstrate the existence of the twin-shrine typology before 1895.

Similarly, the rear building's extant walls testify to its presence before 1895. Prior to that, the rear building's ground floor spanned five bays, with each bay being a room. This layout was retained till at least 1979.[13] It is unclear from the building plan if the pre-1895 layout of the upper storey was similar. This entire level, apart from the plastered brick walls abutting the neighbouring shophouses, was rebuilt in 1895. The height of the rear building's extant walls shows that there were two storeys even before 1895. The proportion of the main entrance gateway in the 1895 elevation drawing is inaccurate, and that of the dragon ornamentations on the front hall's roof ridges are exaggerated. Perhaps the signing architect did not fully understand this type of architecture, and the discrepancies between the drawings and the building suggest that it was designed and built by craftsmen following traditional Chinese practice.

The building plan dispels the popular claim that most building materials used in the temple were imported from China.[14] The timbers specified in the plan were all excellent species of tropical hardwoods, mainly billion (belian), tempanis (tempinis), and darroo (dedaru, bedaru, or daru-daru). Given Singapore's climate, the use of tropical hardwood rather than temperate woods imported from China was the most logical choice.[15] Due to the extremely hard nature of billion and tempanis, it is very difficult to carve them intricately. It is therefore unlikely that these woods were used for portions of the building featuring decorative carvings. Their extreme hardness allows them to take on heavy structural loads, and these woods were thus more likely to have been used as timber for structural frames. Darroo, on the other hand, though classified as a hardwood, is slightly softer and more abundantly available. This type of wood was usually cut into smaller pieces and used as sacrificial timber in areas exposed to weathering. It is therefore likely that darroo was used for the roof rafters in this temple.[16]

All the granite used in the temple was added or replaced during this reconstruction based on the reading of the 1895 plan. This was both locally quarried and imported.[17] Based on their petrographic characteristics, the granite floor slabs in the two shrines and the forecourt were identified by geologist Lee Kim Woon as Pulau Ubin-type granite.[18] This assessment is based on the proportions of mica, quartz, and feldspar present in the stone. In locally quarried granite, the proportion of mica to other minerals is typically higher than in granite quarried elsewhere. This gives the granite a dull, greyish appearance. Granite quarried in Singapore also tends to have a defect known as inclusion, which appears as a dark patch (Fig. 3.2). This can still be seen in some of the temple's granite floor slabs. While the granite used in Wak Hai Cheng Bio might not necessarily have been quarried from Pulau Ubin, it was sourced from local quarries. The granite floor slabs used in the temple are also petrographically similar to those used as edging slabs for shophouses and those used in Hong San See Temple.[19]

The granite walls of the main entrance gateway have a slight pinkish hue, a type of stone known as *lǒngshí* (壟石). It is the type of feldspar present in this granite which gives it its colour. The granite in the entrance gateway cannot be found naturally in Singapore. On the other hand, the granite used for the external columns and cantilever beams of the main entrance gateway is greyish with visible inclusions; it is unclear if this stone was quarried locally or imported. Although the granite walls, columns, and all other granite features of the two shrines except the floor have a greyish hue, their petrographic characteristics suggest that they are not Pulau Ubin-type granite. One possible reason for not using locally quarried granite for the more visible areas of the temple is the presence of inclusions. Inclusions within the granite in columns and other eye-level features would have been visually jarring and affected the grandeur of the architecture.

Fig. 3.2.

Fig. 3.2. Photograph of locally quarried granite with inclusion.
Source: Author's collection.

The rebuilding of the temple was not carried out by a single team. Temples were built by multiple teams, each specialising in a trade such as stone masonry, tiling, fresco painting, *dàmù* (大木), and *xiǎomù* (小木). Both *dàmù* and *xiǎomù* are timberwork trades. There is typically only one team for each trade. For timberwork, however, it was not uncommon in the Southern Chinese coastal provinces of Fujian (Hokkien) and Guangdong (Canton), including the Teochew region, to have two teams working competitively on the same building. The temple was divided along an imaginary central axis into left and right sides or front and back portions. Each team built one side of the temple using its own techniques and style. If the temple is divided into left and right sides, this is known as "competitive construction", *duìcháng* (對場) or *pīncháng* (拼場). There are relatively rare cases where the temple is divided into front and back portions. Indeed, this practice is relatively undocumented in Singapore. The winning team usually receives prize money. This competition encouraged better overall quality of work. Although there were two distinct competing teams, the master craftsmen were expected to coordinate with one another to integrate the two halves into a congruous whole.

Wak Hai Cheng Bio's timberwork was constructed using *duìcháng*. As the temple is made up of two separate shrines, it is unclear how many distinct teams were involved in the timberwork. Although there are no documentary records concerning this aspect of the 1895 reconstruction, the difference in carving techniques, styles, and proportions of the timberwork suggests that there were between two and four separate teams.

The identities of the temple's builders are not recorded on the 1895 building plan. Nevertheless, Phua and Ngow Wah (吳華) mentioned Chén Miánjié (Teochew: *Dang*[5] *Miêng*[5] *Zieb*[8]) as the supervisor responsible for overseeing construction works (督造人陳綿捷).[20] It is also unclear when the rebuilding of the temple was completed. Only Ning Ngui Ngi (林緯毅) specifically mentions 1896 as the year of completion.[21] The date inscribed on the three secondary ridge beams (*zǐsūn liáng* 子孫樑), found in the main halls of the two shrines and the rear building, corresponds with this date. The inscriptions on all three of these beams are identical. It says that between 9.00 am and 11.00 am on the 25th day of the third lunar month in the 22nd year of the reign of the Qing Emperor Guāngxù (i.e. 7 May 1896), the gentlemen and traders from eastern Yue restored the temple (旹大清光緒念二年歲次丙申三月念五日巳時 粵東眾紳商重修). *Yue* (粵) refers to Guangdong province, with eastern Yue referring geographically to Teochew prefecture (潮州府) and Kar Ying County (嘉應州).[22] Beams in temples will usually bear the date that the building's timber frame or the entire temple was completed. Traditionally, the completion of the timber frame is ritually marked with a beam-raising ceremony (*shàngliáng yíshì* 上樑儀式), during which the main ridge beam (*zhōngyíng*

同申慶賀 ○本坡粵海清廟前因破損現擬改作一新茲悉本日係該廟上樑之期潮郡各舖戶分爲六股如長興街順豐街順興街萬順街嘉興街和順街各處經已搭棚結綵偕有菊部數十班演唱以申慶賀所有粵籍之人亦無不張燈掛綵備形熱鬧云

Fig. 3.3.

Fig. 3.3. *Lat Pau* (叻報) article reported that Wak Hai Cheng Bio's beam-raising ceremony took place on 24 September 1896. This date is different from the date, 7 May 1896, inscribed on three secondary ridge beams (*zǐsūn liáng* 子孫樑) in the main halls of the two shrines and in the rear building. Hence, 7 May 1896 ought to be understood as the date for commencement of works.
Source: "*Tóngshēn qìnghè* 同申慶賀 [Universal Celebration]," *Lat Pau* 《叻報》, 24 September 1896.

Fig. 3.4.

中楹) and secondary ridge beams are installed. A *Lat Pau* (叻報) article reported that Wak Hai Cheng Bio's beam-raising ceremony took place on 24 September 1896[23] (Fig. 3.3). It was a great occasion celebrated by the Guangdong people including the Teochew, Cantonese, Hakka and Hainanese communities.[24] Many streets were decorated and there were no fewer than 10 performances staged.[25] Since the timber frame was officially completed on 24 September 1896, 7 May 1896 could only be the official construction commencement date.

To complete the timber frame within just four-and-a-half months, the teams must have worked efficiently. The main and secondary ridge beams had to be completed by the time of the beam-raising ceremony. Ideally, work on all other timber structures would have been completed before the installation, but as malleating during the assembly of the timber frame could potentially damage the timber surface finishes, it is unlikely this would have been the case. During the 2010 to 2014 restoration, when the timber structures were disassembled for repair and restoration, it was found that the mortise and tenons of the gilded and lacquered beams remained unlacquered and ungilded. This suggests that they were only finished after being fixed to the timber frame. Most of the timber members were partially worked on at ground level before installation. They would have first been shaped to fit – including the creation of mortise and tenons – and sanded smooth. Following this, an extremely thin layer of timber putty would have been applied such that the grain of the timber was no longer visible. The wood would then have been sanded once more to ensure consistency and smoothness. After dusting off the timber, the beams would have been installed. Final finishes were

Fig. 3.4. Secondary ridge beams (*zǐsūn liáng* 子孫樑) in the front hall of Shàngdìgōng. The secondary ridge beams in the front halls of the two shrines have the same two sets of inscriptions that bear the dates of the 1994 and 2014 works: "旹次甲戌年九月廿八日午時重修 公元一九九四年十一月一號" [Temple (commenced) restoration on 1 November 1994] and "旹次甲午年三月初一 公元二零一四年竣修 義安公司主持大修" [Full restoration of temple by The Ngee Ann Kongsi was completed on 31 March 2014].
Source: Photographed by Ung Ruey Loon.

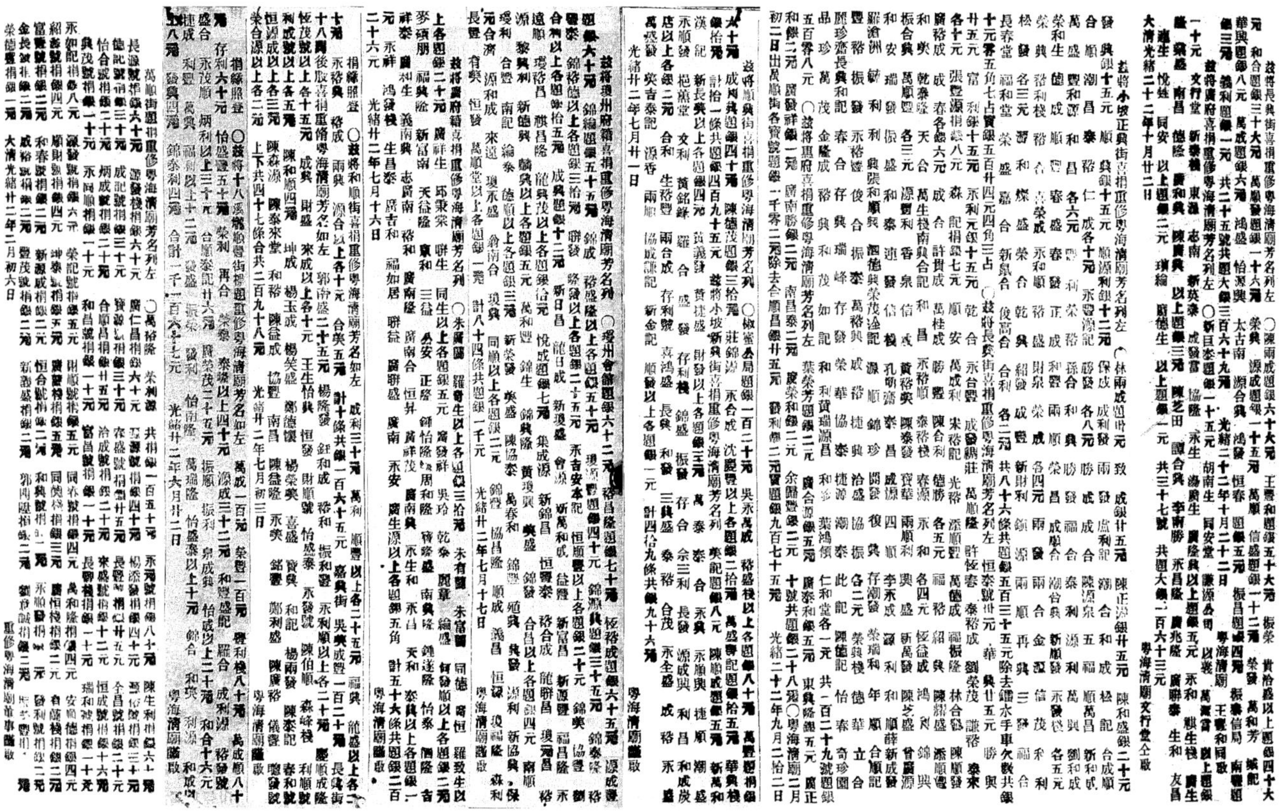

Fig. 3.5.

Fig. 3.5. Donation notices published in 1896 for the rebuilding of Wak Hai Cheng Bio: 19 March; 1, 11, 24, 25, and 29 August; 29 October; and 26 November.
Source: "*Wànshùnjiē tíjuān chóngxiū yuèhǎiqīngmiào fāngmíng lièzuǒ* 萬順街題捐重修粵海清廟芳名列左 [List of Wànshùn Street (Chulia Street) Donors for the Reconstruction of Wak Hai Cheng Bio]," *Lat Pau*《叻報》, 19 March 1896; "*Juānlù zhàodēng* 捐錄照登 [List of Donations Published Accordingly]," *Lat Pau*《叻報》, 10 August 1896; "*Juānlù zhàodēng* 捐錄照登 [List of Donations Published Accordingly]," *Lat Pau*《叻報》, 11 August 1896; "*Zījiāng guǎngfǔjí xǐjuān chóngxiū yuèhǎiqīngmiào fāngmíng liè* 茲將廣府籍喜捐重修粵海清廟芳名列 [The Names of Delightful Cantonese Donors for the Cause of Reconstructing Wak Hai Cheng Bio are hereby Listed]," *Lat Pau*《叻報》, 24 August 1896; "*Zījiāng qióngzhōu fǔjí xǐjuān chóngxiū yuèhǎiqīngmiào fāngmíng liè* 茲將瓊州府籍喜捐重修粵海清廟芳名列 [The Names of Delightful Hainanese Donors for the Cause of Reconstructing Wak Hai Cheng Bio are hereby Listed]," *Lat Pau*《叻報》, 25 August 1896; "*Zījiāng shùnxīngjiē xǐjuān chóngxiū yuèhǎiqīngmiào fāngmíng liè* 茲將順興街喜捐重修粵海清廟芳名列 [The Names of Delightful Shùnxīng Street (Boat Quay) Donors for the Cause of Reconstructing Wak Hai Cheng Bio are hereby Listed]," *Lat Pau*《叻報》, 29 August 1896; "*Zījiāng xiǎopō zhèngxīngjiē xǐjuān chóngxiū yuèhǎiqīngmiào fāngmíng lièzuǒ* 茲將小坡正興街喜捐重修粵海清廟芳名列左 [The Names of Delightful Small Town's Zhèngxīng Street (possibly the expunged Chin Hin Street that is normally known in Chinese as Zhènxīngjiē 振興街) Donors for the Cause of Reconstructing Wak Hai Cheng Bio are hereby Listed on the Left]," *Lat Pau*《叻報》, 29 October 1896; "*Zījiāng chángxīngjiē xǐjuān chóngxiū yuèhǎiqīngmiào fāngmíng liè* 茲將長興街喜捐重修粵海清廟芳名列 [The Names of Delightful Chángxīng Street (Circular Road) Donors for the Cause of Reconstructing Wak Hai Cheng Bio are hereby Listed]," *Lat Pau*《叻報》, 26 November 1896.

most likely applied in situ after the assembly of the timber frame, that is, after the beam-raising ceremony. The finishing would have included lacquering and gilding the beams. As for the purlins, an undercoat and second coat of paint would have been applied before installation. Purlins are typically installed before the beam-raising ceremony takes place.

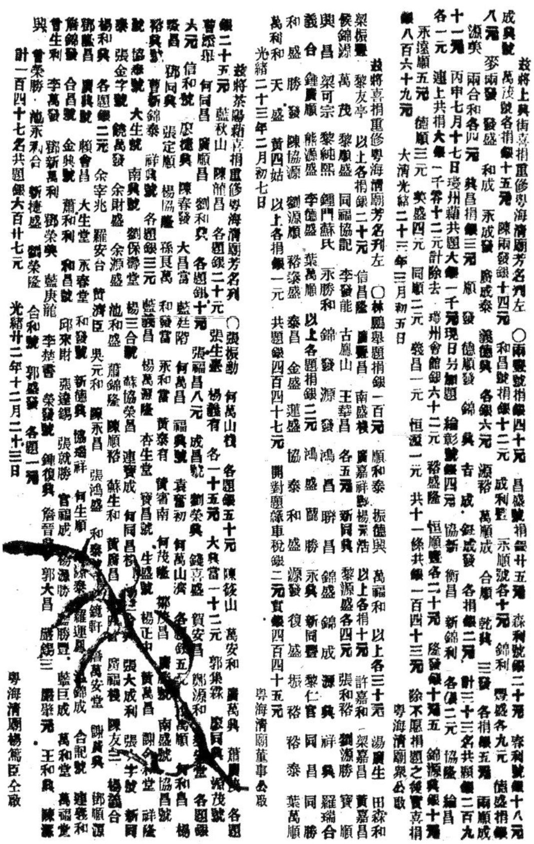

Fig. 3.6.

The roof and roof ornaments would have been added after the timber frame was completed. During this time, the teams could also work on the interior finishing and decoration. Given the amount of work left to be done after the beam-raising ceremony, it would have been impossible to conclude the rebuilding exercise in the remaining three months of 1896; the reconstruction was most likely completed in 1897. Ning probably mistook the date on the secondary ridge beams for the completion date of the 1895 reconstruction. In the meantime, the deities were likely housed in a temporary shrine within the compounds of the temple, and the temple would have carried on its normal religious functions for the duration of the rebuilding exercise. Less than two months after the beam-raising ceremony, leaders of the Teochew community drew divination lots on 19 November 1896 in the temple for a procession date.[26]

The reconstruction of the temple was funded by donations from businesses, individuals, clan associations and societies. These donations were collected by dialect groups, or by geographical divisions known as *jiē* (街), referring to the "street" on which the donor was located. These *jiē* were organised along community lines, and may not have necessarily corresponded to the entire official length of a street. The names of donors and the amount donated were then published in a local daily newspaper, *Lat Pau*, categorized by *jiē* or dialect groups (Figs. 3.5 & 3.6). Between 19 March 1896 and 6 April 1897, a total of 11

Fig. 3.6. Donation notices published in 1897 for the rebuilding of Wak Hai Cheng Bio: 25 January; 9 March and 6 April. Source: "*Zījiāng cháyángjí xǐjuān chóngxiū yuèhǎiqīngmiào fāngmíng liè* 兹將茶陽籍喜捐重修粵海清廟芳名列 [The Names of Delightful Cháyáng Donors for the Cause of Reconstructing Wak Hai Cheng Bio are hereby Listed]," *Lat Pau* 《叻報》, 25 January 1897; "*Zījiāng xǐjuān chóngxiū yuèhǎiqīngmiào fāngmíng kānzuǒ* 兹將喜捐重修粵海清廟芳名刊左 [The Names of Delightful Donors for the Cause of Reconstructing Wak Hai Cheng Bio are hereby Published on the Left]," *Lat Pau* 《叻報》, 9 March 1897; "*Zījiāng shàngxīngjiē xǐjuān chóngxiū yuèhǎiqīngmiào fāngmíng liè* 兹將上興街喜捐重修粵海清廟芳名列 [The Names of Delightful Shàngxīng Street Donors for the Cause of Reconstructing Wak Hai Cheng Bio are hereby Listed]," *Lat Pau* 《叻報》, 6 April 1897.

Teochew Architecture in Singapore

To most casual observers, Chinese architecture appears homogeneous. Visually, it is typified by large tiled roofs that are supported by a structural framework of timbers. Spatially, it is typified by the use of bilateral symmetry, enclosed open spaces, and the ordering of space through a social hierarchical logic, as well as orientation according to the cardinal cartographical directions, connecting the social order to cosmology.[1] While Chinese architecture has unifying characteristics, it is not completely homogeneous. Buildings vary depending on their function, geographic location, and even the ethnicity or dialect origin of their designers or builders; these variations appear primarily in the details of timber construction, spatial proportions, and the choice of finishes and colours.[2]

Linguistically, Teochew is a subgroup of the Min-nan language family, which also includes Hokkien. Teochew and Hokkien architecture share some similarities, but there are also subtle differences. For the lay observer, the most distinct difference is the colour preferences of the two dialect groups. The former is characterised by grey clay roof tiles, while the latter tend to use red terracotta roof tiles. The timber trusses in Teochew architecture tend to be finished with gilding on a black lacquered background, while in Hokkien architecture, the trusses are often finished with red oil-based paint.

When Teochew architecture in Singapore is discussed today, attention is drawn to several key buildings: Wak Hai Cheng Bio is regarded as the quintessential Teochew temple, while residential

Fig. BS06.1.

Fig. BS06.2.

Fig. BS06.3.

Fig. BS06.1. One of the four grand mansions, the House of Seah Eu Chin (佘有進) at North Boat Quay, circa 1913.
The entrance gateway was typical of Teochew architecture.
Source: Bels Collection. Courtesy of the National Archives of Singapore (20060001669-0009).

Fig. BS06.2. Distinctively Teochew roof forms of Kwan Im Thong Hood Cho Temple at Waterloo Street, circa 1962.
Source: Courtesy of the Urban Redevelopment Authority.

Fig. BS06.3. A Buddhist temple (良德堂) was located at 291 Victoria Street, circa 1963. This Teochew temple was demolished between the late 1980s and early 1990s.
Source: Courtesy of the Urban Redevelopment Authority.

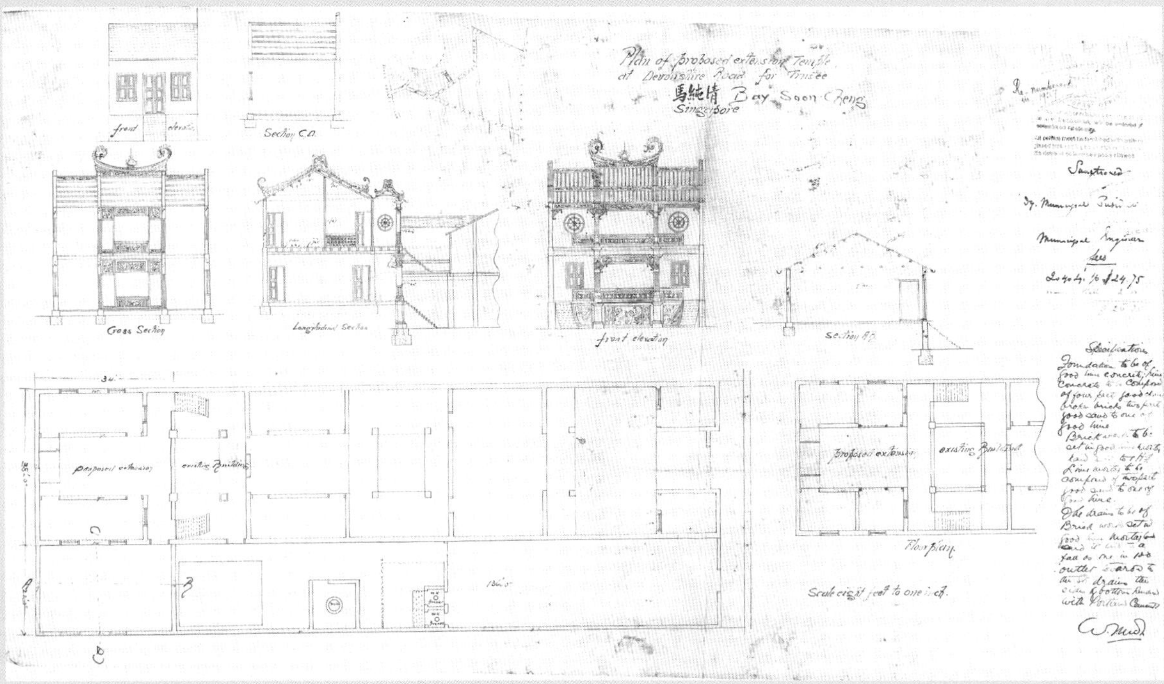

Fig. BS06.4.

architecture is exemplified by the *si*^{3} *dua*^{7} *cu*^{3} (四大厝) or four grand mansions, referring to the late 19th-century Teochew-style homes of Tan Seng Poh (陳成寶), Wee Ah Hood (黃亞佛), Seah Eu Chin (佘有進) and Tan Yeok Nee (陳旭年). These mansions were first mentioned collectively in Song Ong Siang's *One Hundred Years' History of the Chinese in Singapore* published in 1923.[3] The colloquial term *si*^{3} *dua*^{7} *cu*^{3} (四大厝) was first used by Hsu Yun Ts'iao (許云樵) in a 1961 radio broadcast[4] and the term soon caught on among the Chinese communities in Singapore. The house of Tan Yeok Nee is the only one left standing today. Our understanding of the remaining three mansions is fundamentally based on historical materials including old maps, building plans, photographs, newspapers and land records.[5] The last widely known Teochew building in Singapore is the late 19th-century River House, also known as the House of Ripples (漣漪軒), that was owned by Choa Moh Choon (蔡茂春), Lee Ah Hoey (李亞會) and Neo Ah Loy (梁亞□).[6] Apart from these, the 1895 building of Kwan Im Thong Hood Cho Temple (觀音堂佛祖廟) on Waterloo Street,[7] demolished in the late 1970s and replaced by the current reinforced concrete structure in 1984, was also distinctively Teochew.

Other extant religious buildings that have Teochew architectural influences include the 1897 Tong Sian Tng (同善堂)[8] at Devonshire Road, owned by the Teochew Bay Soon Cheng (馬純清),[9] and the 1907 Seng Wong Beo (都城隍廟) at Peck Seah Street, built for the Buddhist monk Swee Ooh (釋瑞于).[10] Both buildings are stylistically Teochew, with their characteristic ceramic ornamentations or *qiàncí* (嵌瓷) and Teochew timber carvings. Interestingly, although the Seng Wong Beo's architecture is Teochew in its layout and ornamentation, the temple's donor Khoo Seok Wan (邱菽園) and its monk Swee Ooh were both Hokkien. Although the temple underwent some works in 1917,[11] when a fair amount of contemporary ornamental accretions, out of scale with the original building,

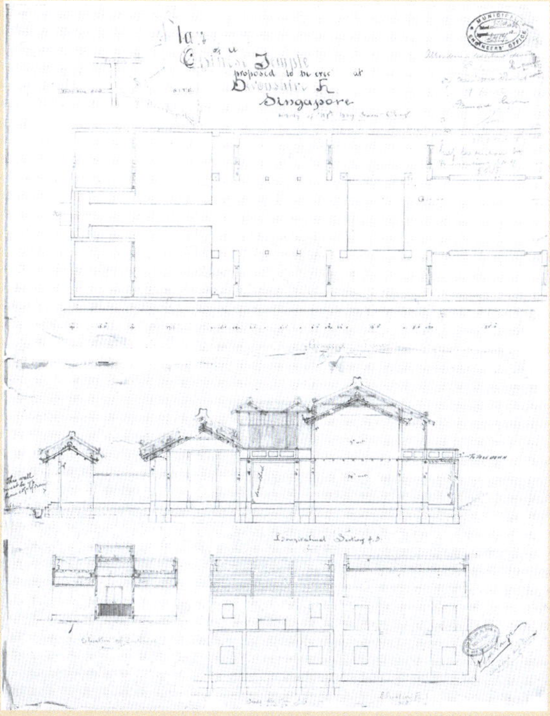

Fig. BS06.5.

Fig. BS06.4. Architectural plans of Tong Sian Tng (同善堂) at Devonshire Road, dated 1897. Source: “Plan of Proposed Extension. Temple at Devonshire Road for Trustee Bay Soon Cheng,” 1897, 141/1897, CBS336. Courtesy of the National Archives of Singapore.

Fig. BS06.5. Architectural plans of Tong Sian Tng (同善堂) at Devonshire Road, dated 1897. Source: “Plan of a Chinese Temple proposed to be Erected at Devonshire Road, Singapore. Property of Mr Bay Soon Cheng,” 1897, 304/1897, CBS336. Courtesy of the National Archives of Singapore.

Fig. BS06.6 Architectural plans of Tong Sian Tng (同善堂) at Devonshire Road, dated 1902. Source: “Plan of alterations and additions Buddhism Temple at Devonshire Road Mc No 1-C For Bay Soon Cheng (Trustee),” 1902, 5101/1902, CBS1139. Courtesy of the National Archives of Singapore.

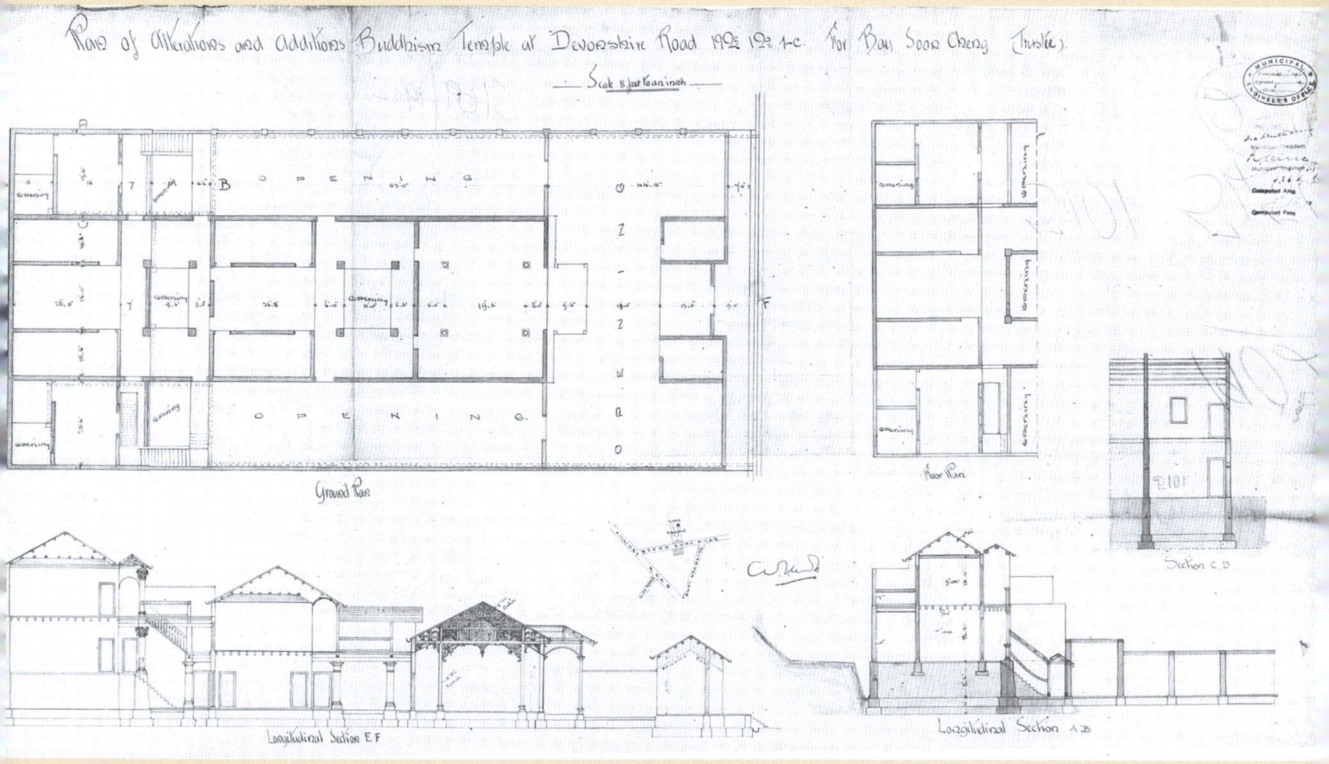

Fig. BS06.6.

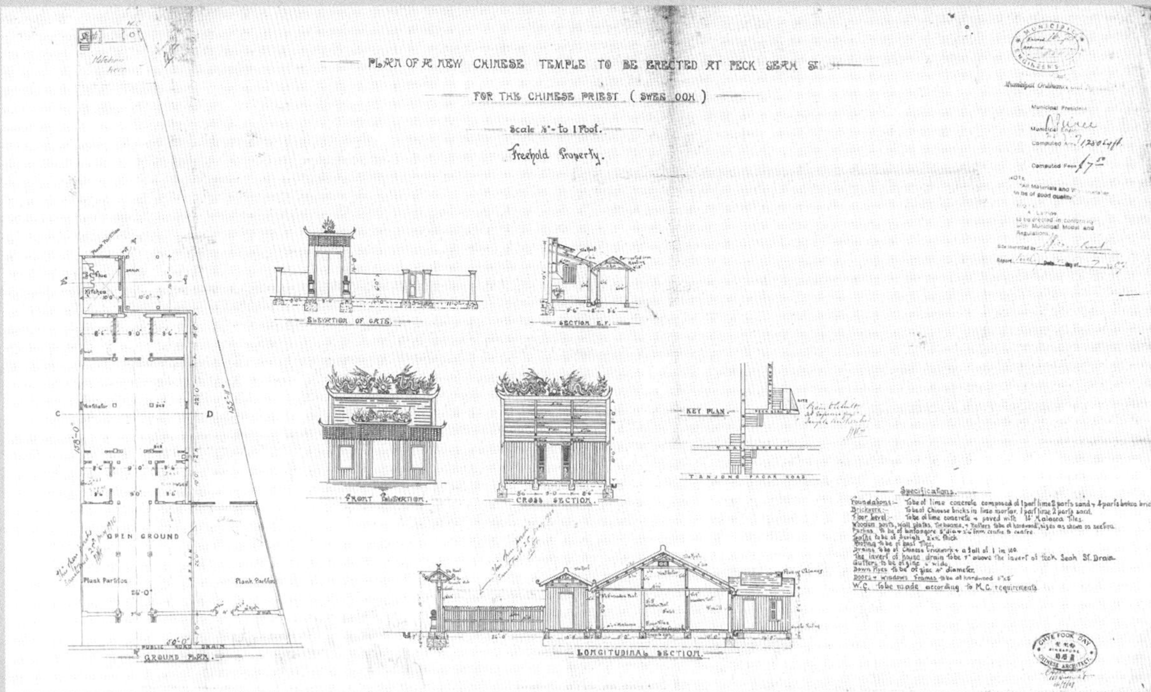

Fig. BS06.7.

were added, the temple's Teochew architecture is still discernible beneath these additions. Two buildings located on Telok Blangah Heights, Ban Siew San Temple (萬壽山觀音堂)[12] and Koon Seng Ting (埜成堂) have Teochew architectural characteristics in parts of the buildings, although it is unknown if these Teochew characteristics were a feature of the original designs or added subsequently. For Koon Seng Ting, oral account states that the builder who worked on the building in 1905 was a Teochew.[13] The building plans in the archives, however, date to 1906.[14] It is unclear from these building plans whether the building originally had a Teochew influence. Koon Seng Ting also underwent a major remodelling exercise in a few phases between 1919 to 1932.[15]

It is not surprising that the Hakka community in 19th-century Singapore adopted Teochew architecture for their buildings, as the minority group aligned itself with the Teochews to counteract the influence of the Hokkien majority. Two extant examples of Teochew-influenced Hakka buildings can be seen in the additions and alterations works carried out on the Ying Fo Fui Kun (應和會館) in 1898[16] and the Foot Tet Soo Khek Temple, also known as Hock Teck See Temple (客屬八邑福德祠 or 望海大伯公廟).[17] In 1896, the Ying Fo Fui Kun even had the architect Lao Chee Hean, who was responsible for the 1895 building plans of the Wak Hai Cheng Bio, draw up plans for the building.[18]

In the case of residential typologies, apart from the House of Tan Yeok Nee and the River House, No. 253 River Valley Road, currently owned by the Nanyang Sacred Union (南洋聖教總會), was built by Seah Song Seah (佘松城), son of Seah Eu Chin in 1896. The two-storey townhouse typology has Teochew architecture ornamentations.

Fig. BS06.7. Architectural plans of Seng Wong Beo (都城隍廟) at Peck Seah Street, dated 1907.
Source: "Plan of a New Chinese Temple to be erected at Peck Seah Street for the Chinese Priest (Swee Ooh)," 1907, 8861/1907, CBS1130. Courtesy of the National Archives of Singapore.

Fig. 3.7.

notices were published in *Lat Pau*.[27] Excluding those who eventually withdrew their donations and those who donated anonymously, the total sum collected as published in *Lat Pau* was $7,366.43.[28] Publishing the details of donations was an excellent way of ensuring accountability in an era before stringent laws and enforcement for such purposes were put in place. Announcing donation details would have also encouraged others to donate to the cause.

At least 13 plaques were presented to the temple by members of the Teochew, Cantonese, Hakka and Hainanese communities between 1896 and 1898 for the reconstruction. The only major local Chinese dialect group not represented were the Hokkiens. Unlike the other four dialect groups, the Hokkiens did not originate from Guangdong province. As the first character of Wak Hai Cheng Bio's name, *Wak* or *Yuè* (粵), suggests, the temple was meant to cater to those originating from Guangdong province. In addition, there was a strong Hokkien–Teochew rivalry at the time. It would have been unthinkable for Hokkien devotees to donate plaques to a Teochew temple or even to pray there, despite the Goddess Māzǔ originating from Fujian province. Māzǔ's Hokkien devotees would instead have worshipped at Thian Hock Keng.

Fig. 3.7. Plaques presented to Wak Hai Cheng Bio: Hèzhuó shēnglíng 赫濯聲靈 [(The god's) dynamic influence and supernatural power are well known and widespread] presented by Char Yong Association (潮郡茶陽會館眾信商敬酬) in 1897 (光緒式十三年丁酉冬月吉旦); Nìyuán tiānxià 溺援天下 [(All) those drowning in suffering will be aided (by the goddess)] presented by Ying Fo Kun (應和館眾等仝敬) in 1898 (光緒戊戌歲冬月吉旦); and Shǔhǎi xiángyún 曙海祥雲 [Auspicious clouds above the sea at dawn] bestowed by Emperor Guāngxù in 1899 (光緒二十五年四月吉旦) (*left to right*).
Source: Photographed by Lim Shao Bin.

The Architecture of the 1895 Temple

Wak Hai Cheng Bio is a twin-shrine temple housed within a walled compound that is fronted by an entrance gateway that leads to a spacious forecourt. Each of the shrines has its own entrance and is of a similar size and spatial arrangement, albeit with slightly different ornamentation. Entering through the main entrance gateway, Tiānhòugōng stands on the left and Shàngdìgōng on the right. On the extreme right, abutting Shàngdìgōng, there is a narrow shophouse-type plot which serves as the temple caretaker's quarters and storeroom. To the rear of the shrines stands a two-storey building that once housed the administrative offices of the Ngee Ann Kongsi, the Teochew Poit Ip Huay Kuan, and the Kwangtung Hui Kuan. It is separated from the two shrines by an elongated courtyard.

The temple is a fine example of traditional Teochew architecture. The most striking feature is its predominantly grey and white colour scheme. This differs from the primarily red colour scheme of Hokkien architecture, which is found widely in Singapore as a result of the island's large Hokkien population. Apart from this difference, Teochew and Hokkien buildings look alike to the untrained eye. There are, however, some major differences. Unlike Hokkien buildings, Teochew buildings, in general, do not have any windows opening to the exterior. The roof tiles are usually grey and the walls are either grey or white. On the ridges of the roof are ornamentations made of cut ceramics known as *qiàncí* (嵌瓷).[29] *Qiàncí*, which means "embedded ceramics", is also known as *jiǎnnián* (剪黏) or "cut and paste". The latter term is a recent one and its use was popularised by Taiwanese writers. *Qiàncí* is a characteristic Teochew craft. It is unclear when the craft first started, though most scholars believe that it began between the Song (960–1279 CE) and Ming (1368–1644 CE) dynasties, when the Teochew prefecture (潮州) became a centre of ceramics production. This craft later spread to the Hokkiens, and *qiàncí* is also seen on the roof ridges of Hokkien buildings, although it is generally more two dimensional and less elaborate in Hokkien architecture.

The Entrance Gateway and its Walled Compound

The visitor approaching Wak Hai Cheng Bio from Phillip Street is greeted by the entrance gateway of the temple and its boundary walls. The distinctive Teochew roof-form of the gateway and high boundary walls make the temple's presence felt from the street. With the white boundary walls as a backdrop, the entrance gateway is the centre of focus. Unlike in Hokkien architecture, where grand entrance gateways make an imposing first impression, the subtler architecture of Wak Hai Cheng Bio's entrance exudes an air of tranquillity. The high plastered brick boundary walls of the compound also block the view of what lies beyond, adding to the feeling of mystery and anticipation. The continuous white wall is punctuated only by the entrance gateway; it is only through this gateway that one can glimpse the temple's compound from the street. The axis of the entrance gateway is slightly asymmetrical, leaning slightly closer towards Tiānhòugōng.

Unlike many Chinese temples in which there are three sets of doors, the entrance gateway of Wak Hai Cheng Bio consists of just one well-proportioned doorway. The main aesthetic feature of the gateway is the gablet roof (or hip-and-gable roof) covered with thin, delicately curved grey clay tiles, approximately three to four millimetres thick. The roof ridge (屋脊) and the four hip rafter ridges (戧脊) have gentle curves terminating in ornamental ceramic spiral finials (嵌瓷卷草). At the ends of the four gablet rafter ridges (垂脊) are ceramic ornamentations known as *páitóu* (牌頭). *Qiàncí* is found on the main ridge, the gablet ridge (also known as sloping ridge), and the hip ridges; there is no

Fig. 3.8.

qiàncí on the slope of the roof. The fascia board (*yánbǎn* 檐板),[30] typical of Teochew architecture, is carved.

The roof of this gateway is supported by four octagon-shaped granite columns and a wall. The columns of the entrance gateway end where it meets the beam to form a T-shaped joint. This is unlike in Hokkien architecture where the column continues past the beam. The granite wall is punctuated by a set of plain timber doors. The temple's name, "粵海清廟", is inscribed on the granite plaque above the door, elevated by two stone lion plaque brackets or *biǎntuō* (匾托). The *biǎntuō* rest in the void between the lintel (門楣) and the granite plaque. This characteristic void is known as *tiāndì zǐsūn fèng* (天地子孫縫).[31] Between the door and plaque brackets lies a pair of door seals (*fáyuè* 閥閱)[32] with the words "合境" [Within the Boundary] and "平安" [Peace] carved onto the lintel (Peace within the boundary). Next to the door seals is a pair of eyelets or *diàoliánkǒng* (吊帘孔) carved in the shape of a dragonfish (鰲魚). A pair of incense stick holders (插香孔) decorated with scrolls and flowers are also carved into the stone jamb.

Fig. 3.8. Entrance gateway of Wak Hai Cheng Bio. The temple's gilded name "粵海清廟" is inscribed on the granite plaque. The void below this plaque is known as *tiāndì zǐsūn fèng* (天地子孫縫).
Source: Photographed by Lim Shao Bin.

Fig. 3.9.

The granite wall of the entrance gateway consists of three panels on both sides. The upper panels or *dǐngdǔ* (頂堵) are separated from the rest of the wall by a void and are elevated by stone brackets known as *shítuō* (石托). These are decorated with bas-reliefs of cranes (瑞鶴) with peaches (壽桃) on the right, and groups of deer (群鹿) with pine trees (松樹) on the left, as seen when facing the main entrance. Cranes, peaches, and pine trees symbolise longevity (壽), while the deer signify prosperity (祿). The middle panels (中堵) have a high-relief rhombus motif in the centre, with bas-relief caltrop plants and bat motifs in the four corners. Bats, a homonym of the character "福", are a symbol of good fortune. Each of the high-relief rhombus motifs is inscribed with a character in green and gold. The one on the left reads "福", and the one on the right reads "祿". The lower panels (裙堵) are simply decorated with edged mouldings. The lowest part of the granite wall is carved like the legs of a table. This is known as *guījiǎo* (圭角) or *guìtáijiǎo* (櫃台腳). Just before the threshold of the gateway lies the praying stone, or *bàishí* (拜石). It was here that devotees paid their respects before entering the temple's compound.

As mentioned earlier, this imported granite wall has a slightly pinkish tone and is known as *lǒngshí*. There are two main reasons why local granite was not used here. It is relatively dull in appearance and it contains a higher content of quartz. The latter makes the stone relatively brittle and therefore unsuitable for high-relief carvings.

The Front Courtyard (前埕)

Stepping through the entrance gateway, the visitor enters the front courtyard of the temple. The courtyard

Fig. 3.9. View towards Phillip Street of Wak Hai Cheng Bio's forecourt and entrance gateway, circa January 1954.
The photograph showed that the entire forecourt was already paved with granite slabs.
Source: Courtesy of Lim Shao Bin.

is an important area where temporary opera stages on stilts were erected during temple festivities. Holes cut into the granite pavement for the anchoring of the main posts of the opera stage and *gūpéng* (孤棚) can still be found. As is evident from the 1895 building plan, slightly less than half the courtyard was paved with granite slabs during the late 19th-century reconstruction of the temple. Only the area immediately in front of the two shrines and a pathway leading up to it was paved, with the paved area forming a T-shape. It is unclear

Fig. 3.10.

Fig. 3.10. A selection of Wak Hai Cheng Bio's religious procession regalia.
Source: Photographed by Carolyn Lim.

Fig. 3.11.

when the remaining parts were paved, but by 1954 the forecourt was entirely covered with granite slabs (Fig. 3.9). Today, one can easily distinguish the parts that were paved later as the granite slabs appear more yellowish than the earlier paving stones. Moreover, the pathway from the entrance gateway as well as the pathways leading to each shrine (御道) are bordered by edging granite slabs (丁砱).

The temple shared party walls with its neighbours prior to their demolition. Metal rings used to line these walls. They can still be seen on the gable end of the twin shrines' front elevation and were used for anchoring tentage ropes during temple festivities. From the 1980s till November 2014, the remaining rings on the twin shrines' front elevation were used to anchor ropes for the hanging of coiled incense. As incense smoke was causing rapid deterioration to the interior finishes of the twin shrines, the Ngee Ann Kongsi's committee of management sought permission from the deities in October 2013 to allow incense to be offered only in the front courtyard. This prevents the build-up of oil and tar deposits in the shrines' interiors. New stone censers were also placed in the forecourt in front of each shrine. Devotees may bring incense into the shrines to pray but can only leave them at the new stone censers outside. Coiled incense was similarly permitted only within the front courtyard. Before this, the temple's caretaker would move the coiled incense into the shrines when it rained. The practice of offering coiled incense at the temple was discontinued entirely in November 2014.

Front Elevation of the Twin Shrines

Entering the temple compound from the main gateway, it is immediately clear that the temple has two shrines rather than one. The shrines appear identical, although Tiānhòugōng is slightly bigger than Shàngdìgōng. The most striking feature of the temple is the unparalleled amount of vivid *qiàncí* ornamentation on the roof. *Qiàncí* is usually found only on the roof ridge in Teochew architecture. In Wak Hai Cheng Bio, the *qiàncí* work extends beyond the ridge to cover half the roof's front slope. This is a feature not seen elsewhere in Singapore or overseas.

Fronting each shrine is a set of timber gates (栅門) and balustrades (欄杆). The use of timber balustrades in temples originates from their use in the Yámén (衙門) or Magistrate's Office in China. Temples echo the conventions of the Magistrate's Office and parallel the traditional Chinese courtroom. These parallels extend

Fig. 3.11. Photograph showing the middle fresco painted plaster mouldings and upper *qiàncí* panels at the recessed entranceway of Shàngdìgōng.
Source: Photographed by Lim Shao Bin.

beyond architecture, influencing the ritual practices of temples too. For instance, temples were furnished with the regalia of a traditional Chinese courtroom, or symbolic objects used to demonstrate the majesty of the deities, including ceremonial arms and flags (Fig. 3.10). The adaptation of Chinese courtroom conventions in temples is not unique to the Teochews, and can be seen in the architecture of other dialect groups as well. The timber balustrades originally served to keep people out of courtrooms. Within the enclosed front courtyard of Wak Hai Cheng Bio, however, the timber balustrades serve more as symbolic markers, rather than as actual barriers.

The intricately carved fascia boards are another noticeable feature of the front elevation of the two shrines. Fascia boards are exposed to weathering and are usually seen as sacrificial components to be constantly replaced. It is therefore unsurprising that fascia boards generally remain undecorated in most forms of Chinese architecture. Teochew and Cantonese architecture, with their carved fascia boards, are an exception to the rule. Different types of timber are used for the fascia boards in Wak Hai Cheng Bio. One of them is teak, a tropical hardwood which can withstand weathering and is suitable for intricate carving.[33]

The recessed entranceway (*āodù mén* 凹肚門)[34] of each shrine is typical of Teochew architecture. With the exception of the main doors, there are no openings in the front elevation of the temple. The beams in the recessed portion of the entranceways are carved while the purlins are not. The truss system is made of gilded timber. In contrast to the main entrance gateway, the only stone features in the front elevation of the two shrines are the two pairs of columns, the floor, the

Fig. 3.12.

cantilever beams (*jītóu fāngzǎi* 屐頭方櫼)[35], and the main doorways. The lime-plastered brick walls are finished with plaster mouldings, frescoes and *qiàncí*.[36] There are six sets of panels in the recessed section and two sets in the unrecessed section of each shrine's entranceway (Fig. 3.11). As in the main gateway, the recessed entranceway to Tiānhòugōng consists of lower, middle and upper panels. There are six sets of three panels within the recess and two sets of three panels in the unrecessed portion. In Shàngdìgōng, there are four panels rather than three on each of the walls perpendicular to the shrine's doorway; the two uppermost panels are roughly half the size of the other

Fig. 3.12. Photograph showing the condition of fresco painted plaster mouldings mimicking timber trusses in the recessed entranceway of Tiānhòugōng before restoration.
Source: Photographed by Ung Ruey Loon.

panels. In the unrecessed part of the entrance, there are two sets of four panels. Most of the uppermost panels are decorated with *qiàncí*. The exceptions are the four uppermost panels perpendicular to the two shrines' doorways, which are decorated with plaster mouldings and fresco work mimicking timber trusses (Fig. 3.12). In the four-panelled section, the second panels are similarly decorated with *qiàncí*. The middle or third and lowest panels are fresco painted plaster mouldings. The middle or third panels in the recess are heavily painted and depict classical stories, while those in the unrecessed portion portray scenes from nature. The lowest panels are the simplest in terms of decoration. Auspicious motifs such as *rúyì* (如意), scrolls, brushes, and flowers are depicted on these lowest panels of the recess.

The names of the shrines – "天后宮" and "上帝宮" – are inscribed on the granite plaques above the doorways of the shrines to Māzǔ and Xuántiān Shàngdì respectively. As in the main gateway, these granite plaques are held up by stone lion brackets. Features akin to those of the main gateway include a void between the lintel and the stone plaque, a pair of door seals on the lintel, a pair of dragonfish eyelets, and a pair of incense stick holders carved with scroll and flower motifs on the stone jamb. There are also *bàishí*, or praying stones, in front of the shrines' threshold. The words on the door seals of Tiānhòugōng are "風調" [moderate winds] and "雨順" [timely rain], which together mean "favourable weather conditions", while the door seals of the Shàngdìgōng read "合境" [Within the Boundary] and "平安" [Peace], meaning "peace to all that gathered within the premises of the temple". Both pairs of lacquered wooden main doors are decorated with paintings of the door gods, Qín Qióng (秦瓊) and Yùchí Gōng (尉遲恭). They were famous generals from the early Tang dynasty (618–907 CE).

A less noticeable feature of the temple's principal elevation are the two small wooden doors adjacent to the shrines. The small door between Tiānhòugōng and the boundary wall nearest to Church Street leads to a storeroom. Above the door is a sign which reads "鳳儀" [Bearing of a phoenix]. A similar door between Shàngdìgōng and the boundary wall nearest to it leads to the temple caretaker's quarters. The sign above it reads "龍德" [Virtues of a dragon]. These two signs are made of plaster rather than stone.

Interior of the Twin Shrines

Upon entering either shrine, the visitor's eyes are drawn to the innermost hall where the main deity is the centre of focus. The sense of layered spaces is reinforced by a number of architectural devices. The two sets of doors separating the three halls within each shrine contribute greatly to this effect. There are the ceremonial doors (*píngmén* 屏門) which separate the front hall (前殿) and the prayer hall (拜亭), as well as the screen doors (*píngyè* 屏頁)[37] segregating the prayer hall and the main hall (主殿). The layout of the shrines follows a "工-shape" plan. Each shrine has three halls, with internal air wells (龍虎井) found on either side of the prayer halls.[38] Square terracotta tiles were most likely used to pave the front and main halls, while hexagonal terracotta tiles would have been used in the prayer hall. The changes in flooring patterns reinforce the impression of layered spaces. These architectural features serve to direct the devotees' gaze towards the niches that house the main deities through an enfilade.

The colour scheme within the twin shrines is like that of the front elevation. The predominant colours are gold on black, and maroon and green against a white plastered background. Green rafters rest upon maroon coloured purlins and ridge beams with the white underside of the roof tiles visible in

Fig. 3.13.

the background. The shades of red used in the temple are darker than Hokkien temples; bright vermillion is hardly utilised. The black beams are gilded with gold, and gold coloured struts sit above the grey granite columns. In the air wells, colourful figurines are set against the background of a white plastered wall. The floor is mainly paved with terracotta.

The Front Halls (前殿) of the Twin Shrines

Stepping into either of the two shrines, the visitor enters the front hall. These halls are divided into three bays (*sānjiān guò* 三間過)[39]. Each bay is equal in width to the span of a beam. A secondary ridge beam can be found in the front hall of each shrine. It is unclear if any date was inscribed upon these secondary beams before 1994. They currently bear the dates of the 1994 and 2014 restorations. Secondary ridge beams serve two main functions: they are a space for the inscription of construction dates and for hanging

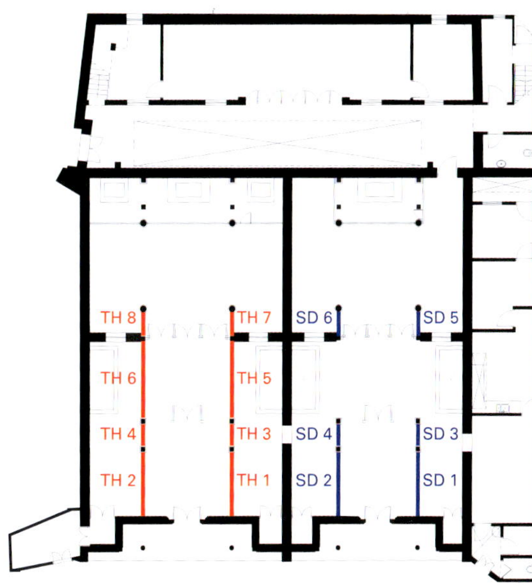

Fig. 3.14.

Fig. 3.13. Photograph of pseudo-beam panels or *zǎifù* 櫼腹 in Wak Hai Cheng Bio showing full-relief carvings or *tōngdiāo* 通雕 before surface cleaning.
Source: Photographed by Ung Ruey Loon.

Fig. 3.14. Diagram of plan showing the location of pseudo-beam panels or *zǎifù* 櫼腹within the two shrines.
Source: Illustrated by Hsieh Mei-En; author's collection.

religious or ceremonial paraphernalia such as lanterns and embroidered banners.

The roof truss structure used in the two shrines follows the *táiliáng* system (抬梁式) which consists of "successive tiers of beams and struts in a transverse direction".[40] In the front hall, gilded black lacquered beams are supported by pumpkin-shaped struts. Each triangular timber structure is made up of three beams, five pumpkin-shaped struts, and twelve carved components (*sānzài wǔguā shí'èr kuài* 三檅五瓜十二塊). This truss system is also known as the "five internal organs with twelve carved components structure" (*wǔzàng nèi shí'èr kuài huāpī* 五臟內十二塊花坯).[41] The 12 carved components, or *huāpī* (花坯), are highly intricate timber ties placed between struts to resist lateral movements. Timber elements are usually carved at ground level and then coated with red lacquer after installation. The lacquer acts as bole or ground for receiving gilding, and the visible final layer of the struts, timber ties, and other timberworks are completely gilded.

Beneath the black lacquered beams are pseudo-beam panels known as *zǎifù* 檅腹[42] which are gilded and carved (Figs. 3.13 & 3.14). The timber for these panels is from the camphor family and was probably imported from either China or Indonesia. These panels act as stiffeners by resisting bending at the beam-column joints. Timber corbels (雀替) at the beam-column joints are used as stiffeners in most timber buildings. In more elaborate buildings such as Wak Hai Cheng Bio, carved timber panels spanning the entire length of the beams are used. The temple's panels are the most technically challenging and intricate in situ carvings found in any of Singapore's historic buildings. They are full-relief carvings or *tōngdiāo* (通雕), that is, the entire length is executed in high relief with some portions entirely hollowed out. This is seen even in sections near the beam-column joints. The craftsmen who made these panels were clearly highly skilled. They mastered not only the incredibly complex craft of *tōngdiāo* but even managed to produce four-layered full-relief panels (四層通雕) without compromising the structural function of these timber members. Ten out of 14 of these four-layered panels have survived to this day.[43]

The ceremonial doors separating the front and prayer halls are meant for the deities' use. An offering table is normally placed in front of the door to prevent people from unknowingly walking through them. Based on anecdotal accounts, the pair of figures depicted on the ceremonial doors of Tiānhòugōng have always been ladies-in-waiting (宮娥). On the other hand, those in Shàngdìgōng are civil officials (文官). The floor of this hall would traditionally have been laid with terracotta tiles, which are presently laid in a diagonal diamond pattern in the hall's centre bay and a running bond pattern in the right and left bays. The diagonal diamond pattern resembles the character "人", or people, and the running bond pattern looks similar to the character "丁", or man. The two sets of tiling patterns connote a thriving temple with many devotees. While it is unclear if the floor tiles were laid in these patterns during the 1895 reconstruction, this arrangement was commonly used in many local temples and houses at the time.

The Prayer Halls (拜亭) of the Twin Shrines

Beyond the ceremonial doors of each shrine is the prayer hall. The prayer hall is where devotees pray and make offerings to the deities. Traditionally, the laity would not go beyond the prayer hall of the temple; only the temple's trustees, caretakers and esteemed guests could enter the main hall. As the prayer hall was the furthest point most could enter, it is the most ornate part of the temple.

The prayer hall has a round ridged roof or *chóngcuò* (重厝).[44] In fact, it has a triangular roof

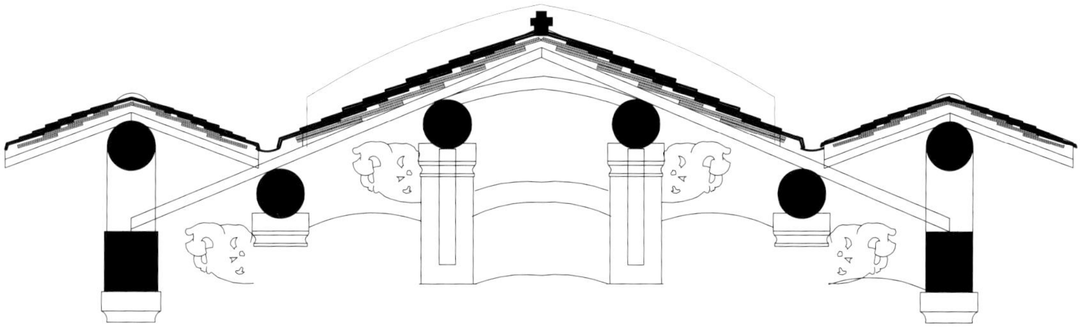

Fig. 3.15.

supported by two layers of green rafters at its apex. The top layer of rafters, on which the roof tiles rest, are flat. The bottom layer comprises rounded rafters to give the impression that the roof has a round ridge. The roof truss system in the prayer hall is also *táiliáng*. It is in this hall that timber carvings are the most elaborate. Instead of pumpkin-shaped struts, the ones holding up the beams in the prayer halls are carved in the shape of lions and crabs. At least one gilded crab strut holds a brush in its claws, while another holds an official's hat. This symbolises success in the imperial examinations (金榜題名); in Chinese, the words "golden crab" (金蟧) are phonetically similar to the "golden list" (金榜) of successful imperial examination candidates. On the other hand, the lion is an auspicious animal that can be found in many Chinese temples across different dialect groups. Lion struts in Teochew architecture tend to be longer and flatter, with rounder edges. This can be seen in Wak Hai Cheng Bio.

Intricately carved *zǎifù* panels are likewise found in the prayer hall of Tiānhòugōng. In Shàngdìgōng's prayer hall, gilded timber corbels are employed instead of *zǎifù* to resist bending moments. The corbels nearer to the dragon wall (龍堵) are in the shape of cloud-spewing dragons, while those closer to the tiger wall (虎堵) are cloud-spewing dragonfish. Screen doors separate the prayer hall from the main hall. These were kept open so that the laity could glimpse the deities placed in the main halls. Before square terracotta tiles were laid in the mid-1990s, the floor of the prayer halls was paved using hexagonal terracotta tiles (六角磚), which resemble the pattern on tortoiseshell and symbolise longevity.

The Dragon and Tiger Air Wells (龍虎井)

There are air wells on either side of each prayer hall (龍虎井). The dragon air well (龍井) is found on the right while the tiger air well (虎井) is on the left when facing the main hall. The dragon symbolises the east, while the tiger symbolises the west. These directions are symbolic rather than actual cardinal points. It is into the air wells that all the rainwater from the middle section of the temple is drained.

The gable walls along the sides of the air wells are known as the "dragon and tiger walls" (龍虎堵). The dragon and tiger motifs are executed in fresco painted high-relief plaster mouldings. Above the walls are frescos on plaster mouldings with *qiàncí* ornamentations. The ornamentations above Shàngdìgōng's dragon wall depict the classical Chinese

Fig. 3.15. Diagram showing section of the prayer hall's round-ridged roof construction or *chóngcuò* 重厝 details. Source: Illustrated by Hsieh Mei-En; author's collection.

Fig. 3.16.

story of Wǔ Sōng fighting a tiger (武松打虎). On either side of the tiger motif in Shàngdìgōng is a pair of fresco couplets with the words "思無邪皆現佛法" [Speak your mind, that is the Dharma] and "志於道便是西天" [Aspirations for the Tao, that is the heavenly realm].[45] Two vertical panels containing clay figurines or *nídīng* (泥丁) line both sides of Shàngdìgōng's dragon wall. *Nídīng* is a composite craft that comprises clay moulding or *nísù* (泥塑), plaster moulding or *huīsù* (灰塑), fresco painting (灰塑彩繪), and *qiàncí*. The *nídīng* craftsman is required to know all these different skills and very few mastered this art form. Moreover, the headgear of some of the female *nídīng* figurines are made of copper wire filigree and cut coloured glass. This means the *nídīng* craftsman would have had some knowledge of metal- and glass-work. The hem of one figure's skirt was made using glass instead of cut ceramics. This reveals the experimental nature of the craftsman, who was trying out new materials using traditional techniques. This is impressive, as glass, with its smooth surface, lacks the grip needed to adhere to the plaster moulding. In the 1980s, Taiwanese craftsmen tried a similar experiment by using sheet glass instead of cut ceramics for *qiàncí* ornamentation. Sheet glass proved to be an unsuitable material that fell off easily.

Fig. 3.16. Photograph showing the interior of Tiānhòugōng, date unknown.
Source: Courtesy of National Museum of Singapore (XXXX-13316).

A wall punctuated by a pair of ornamented fenestrations separates the air wells and main halls of the two shrines. The motif on both fenestrations in Tiānhòugōng is phoenixes. In Shàngdìgōng, the motif on the left is a phoenix and the one on the right is a dragon, as seen when facing the main hall. These ornamented fenestrations were made of moulded plaster with fresco work.

The Main Halls (主殿) of the Twin Shrines

The most sacred spaces in the entire temple are behind the screen doors. These are the main halls of the two shrines, where the deity niches are situated. In Tiānhòugōng, there are three plinths upon which the deities' niches rest. The principal deity of the shrine, Māzǔ, the Goddess of the Sea – otherwise known as Tiānhòu (天后) – sits on the central plinth. From the perspective of the devotees, the two main secondary deities, the Emperor Who Moved Heaven, or Gǎntiān Dàdì (感天大帝), and the Dragon-tailed Sage King, or Lóngwěi Shèngwáng (龍尾聖王), occupy the right and left plinths respectively. There are numerous other deities, either sharing the three principal niches or in separate niches within the main hall. In Shàngdìgōng, there is only one plinth occupied by deities. The principal deity in this shrine is Xuántiān Shàngdì, or the Mysterious Supreme Emperor of Heaven – otherwise known as Shàngdìgōng (上帝公). As in Tiānhòugōng, there are numerous secondary deities in the shrine. The secondary ridge beams bearing the 1896 date are found within the main halls.

The main halls are the largest of the three halls. It is here where the roof is the highest, giving the space a dignified feel. The *táiliáng* roof truss system is also used in this hall. Timber corbels in the shape of dragonfish instead of *zǎifù* are used to resist bending moments in the main halls. Besides *huāpī*, *wānbǎn* (彎板)[46] are also used in the main halls as timber ties for resisting lateral movements. *Wānbǎn* are less intricately carved than *huāpī* and are generally camber-shaped. The timber carving and gilding in the two main halls are also much less elaborate than the work found in the front and prayer halls. The struts in the main hall are long black timbers (斗立筒) that have been left without gilding. Apparently, unlike humans, omniscient deities are above being impressed by highly detailed decoration. The height of the main halls and their simpler ornamentation give them a more solemn atmosphere.

In one corner of Shàngdìgōng's main hall, a small set of wooden doors lead to the rear courtyard and rear building. That the rear building can only be accessed through Shàngdìgōng and not Tiānhòugōng reflects the origins and management of the shrines, as well as the social structure of the Teochew community. Tiānhòugōng is customarily seen as separate from the rest of the temple. Although the temple's land is legally owned by the Ngee Ann Kongsi, the religious management of the two shrines remains separate to this day. Tiānhòugōng is traditionally managed by the Ban See Soon Kongsi (萬世順公司), and all religious notices are still issued in its name. On the other hand, Shàngdìgōng is managed by the Ngee Ann Kongsi. It was probable that the two shrines were established by different groups of people. The rear building was held in trust by the predecessor of the Ngee Ann Kongsi before being officially vested in the latter in 1933.[47] Since Shàngdìgōng and the rear building were under the same management, access to the latter is through the former. The caretaker's counter, being under the charge of the Ngee Ann Kongsi, was and is also located in Shàngdìgōng. In addition, Xuántiān Shàngdì is the patron deity of the Teochews, and his shrine would have been viewed as a "public" space of the community. It is therefore unsurprising that access to the rear building, which served as the headquarters and offices of pan-community organisations such as the Ngee

The Land Acquisition of No. 33 Phillip Street for Singapore Improvement Trust's Provision of Back Lanes

The Singapore Improvement Trust (SIT) was initially set up on 1 July 1927[1] to implement the recommendations set out in the sanitation conditions report by Professor W. J. Simpson, who arrived in Singapore in 1906 and published his findings the following year.[2] Simpson recommended the introduction of back lanes and open spaces around the city[3] to stop the spread of diseases by facilitating the proper removal of waste as well as creating better ventilation and light.

Prior to 1929, the urban block where Wak Hai Cheng Bio is located, bounded by Phillip Street, South Canal Road/Kling Street, Synagogue Street, and Church Street, had land lots that abutted back to back. Some lots fronting the adjacent streets had depths that extended along two-thirds of Phillip Street.

In 1925, No. 33 Phillip Street, held under 999-year Government Leases Nos. 177 and 2676 dating from 25 January 1827, was to be vested in the municipal commissioners for the construction of back lanes. This property had been owned by the trustees of Wun Yien Seang Tie Kongsi (元天上帝公司), comprising Seah Eu Chin (佘有進), Sim Ah Kie (沈亞開), Tay Ah Bock (鄭□□), and Wan Mong Sun (袁茂春), since 27 April 1850.[4]

The land acquisition process was protracted and only concluded in 1933 due to legal challenges to confirm that the land compensation was to be paid out to the Ghee Ann Society. According to a SIT report, the process was complicated by the fact that "the affairs of the Ghee Ann Kongsi are in a terrible muddle, some of the Trustees appointed by the Court in 1914[5] are dead, others are missing and the remainder quarrel among themselves".[6] On 26 September 1929, five out of a total of 14 trustees, namely Heng Pang Kiat (王邦傑), Goh Tek Cher (吳竹村), Seah Chin Moey (佘振美), Quek Liang Choon (郭兩存), and Seah Eng Tong (佘應忠), resolved to accept the land acquisition compensation, and a sum of

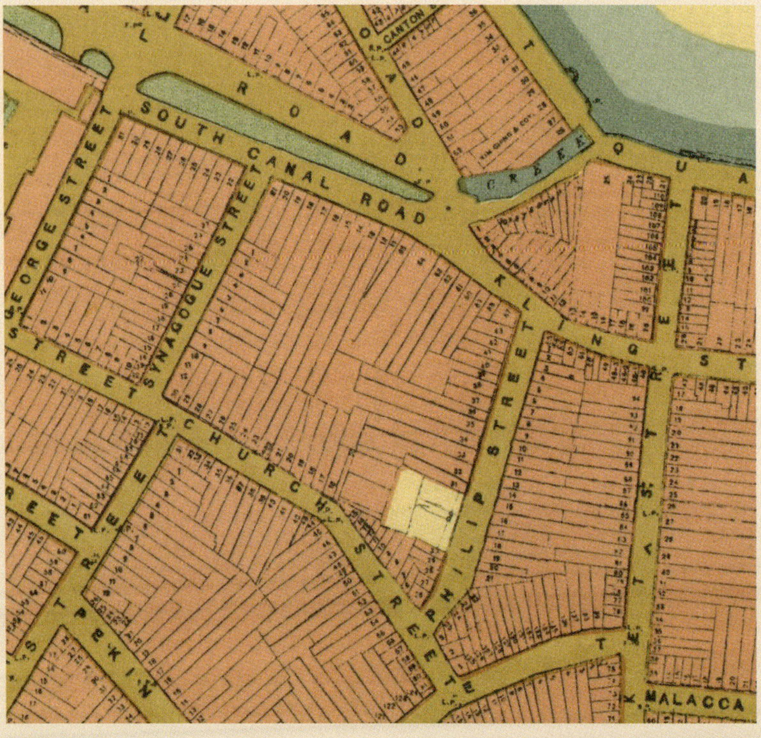

Fig. BS07.1.

Fig. BS07.1. Plan showing the land lots' boundaries around Wak Hai Cheng Bio, circa 1893.
Source: "Plan of Singapore Town Shewing Topographical Detail and Municipal Numbers. His Excellency Sir Cecil Clementi Smith, G.C.M.G. Governor of The Straits Settlements. Major H. E. McCallum, R.E.; C.M.G. Colonial Engineer and Surveyor General S.S. 1893". Courtesy of Mok Ly Yng.

$18,840 was paid into Court on 8 November 1929. Only the first three trustees listed were appointed by the Court in 1914. It was not until the legalities were sorted out through the formal incorporation of the Ghee Ann Society as the Ngee Ann Kongsi in 1933 that payment was finally released to the Kongsi.[7]

A back lane was constructed using, in part, 286 square feet of the land from No. 33 Phillip Street.[8] By 1935, the SIT managed to realise an open space surrounded by back lanes in the centre of the urban block and this can be seen in an aerial photograph taken by the British Royal Air Force on 28 January 1950.

This photograph showed a relatively unknown open space north of Wak Hai Cheng Bio and provided the lead into researching SIT's land acquisition, which led to the subsequent discovery of the existence of Wun Yien Seang Tie Kongsi.

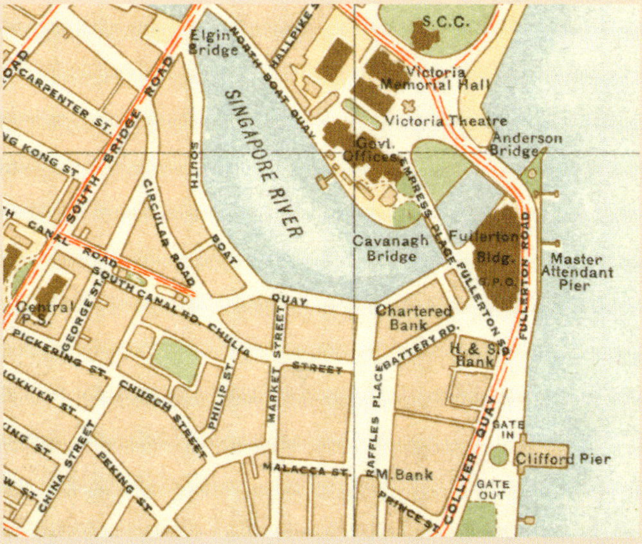

Fig. BS07.2.

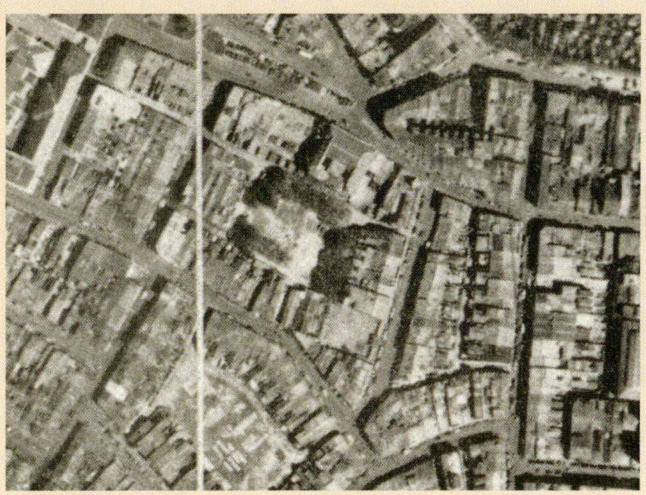
Fig. BS07.3.

Fig. BS07.2. The open space, demarcated in green, and the back lanes surrounding the open space accessible from Phillip Street, Synagogue Street, and Church Street can be seen in this map of 1935.
Source: "Gazetteer of Singapore (Federated Malay States Surveys No. 54, 1935)". Courtesy of Mok Ly Yng.

Fig. BS07.3. Detail of aerial photograph taken by the British Royal Air Force in January 1950. The photo shows the open space and the tops of the trees that grew around its perimeter.
Source: "Singapore Town. Singapore Photomap, Sheet 16 (1950)". A Collection held by the National Archives of Singapore. Crown Copyright.

Ann Kongsi, the Teochew Poit Ip Huay Kuan, and the Kwangtung Hui Kuan, was through Shàngdìgōng.

The Rear Courtyard (後埕) and Rear Building (後厝)
Stepping through the small set of wooden doors in Shàngdìgōng, the visitor enters the rear courtyard (後埕) of the temple. The rear courtyard occupies the space immediately behind the twin shrines. At the other end of the courtyard is a set of wooden doors providing direct access to Church Street. These doors are usually kept closed. The rear courtyard once had archways at either end, but these were demolished in 1995.

The two-storey rear building is historically one of the two secular parts of the temple compound, the other being the caretaker's quarters. As mentioned earlier, the rear building once housed the offices of the Ngee Ann Kongsi, the Teochew Poit Ip Huay Kuan, the Kwangtung Hui Kuan and Nantao Publishing House. The building stretches across the entire breadth of the temple and comprises five bays (五間過) on each level. On the ground floor, each bay has a room. In the late 1890s, this layout was likely to have been mirrored on the upper storey as well. The rooms on the extreme ends of the building have their own doors, but the three other rooms can only be accessed through the screen doors of the central room. Before 1980, the three rooms were segregated by internal partitions. Located at the Church Street end of the building is a timber staircase leading to the second level corridor. The corridor overlooks the rear courtyard. The floorboards separating levels one and two are composed entirely of timber. A timber plaque in the central room of the upper level indicates that the building or the hall is known as Chóngdé Táng (崇德堂). The third secondary ridge beam bearing the 1896 date of reconstruction in the temple compound is found in this room. As in the roof of the two shrines, the *táiliáng* roof truss system is used in the rear building. The only gilded timber carvings found in this building are the truss members. They are much simpler than those found in the twin shrines.

The Temple's Roofing System

The roofing system of Wak Hai Cheng Bio is typical of Teochew architecture. The roofs of the front, prayer and main halls, as well as that of the rear building, are gabled roofs (double-pitched roofs) or *pí* 埤.[48] "Inverted hull" (*fǎnbèi chuán* 反背船)[49] roofs link the gabled roofs. There are four sets of inverted hull roofs in the temple, two in each shrine. This unique roof construction system can only be found in Teochew architecture. As its name suggests, the inverted hull roof is in the shape of an overturned hull when seen from the top. Rainwater from the gabled roofs either flows directly to the ground or the inverted hull roofs. From the inverted hull roofs, water is then channelled into the two internal air wells of each shrine and removed through an underground drainage system.

In the absence of any horizontal surface on the roof, the inverted hull shape eliminates the need for a gutter (*liūmǔcáo* 霤母槽)[50] at the valley where two gabled roofs join. The use of a gutter is not ideal because leaves could choke it, causing water to pool. Before the invention of modern waterproofing technologies, it was essential to ensure rapid rainwater runoff from the roof. Gutters are graded to fall, but these gradients are often gentle, leading to water seepage in the long run. By contrast, water runs off the inverted hull roof at a much faster rate.[51]

The roof tiles used in Wak Hai Cheng Bio are Teochew clay tiles (潮州土瓦), a type of tegula, also known as *wǎbǎn* 瓦板[52] (Figs. 3.17 & 3.18). A preference for gentler roof curvatures in Teochew architecture means a high degree of overlap in tiling. Each tile overlaps another by 80 per cent such that there are five layers of tiles in a set. With two sets of tiles on Wak Hai Cheng Bio's roof, there are 10 layers of tiles at any one point. This would equate to a much larger quantity of tiles used, which increases the load of the roof significantly. To reduce this load, Teochew clay tiles are very light and thin. Each tile is merely three to four millimetres thick. The tiles are made of clay and sand, and fired at a lower temperature than that used for typical Chinese roof tiles. The high sand content of the tiles reduces their weight. The roofs of the temple are curved in two directions. While most parts of the roofs slant downwards, the four ends curve slightly upward. Rafter lengths vary slightly at the roof ends to form an upward curve. Where the direction of curvature changes, roof tiles are laid in a staggered manner (错槽).

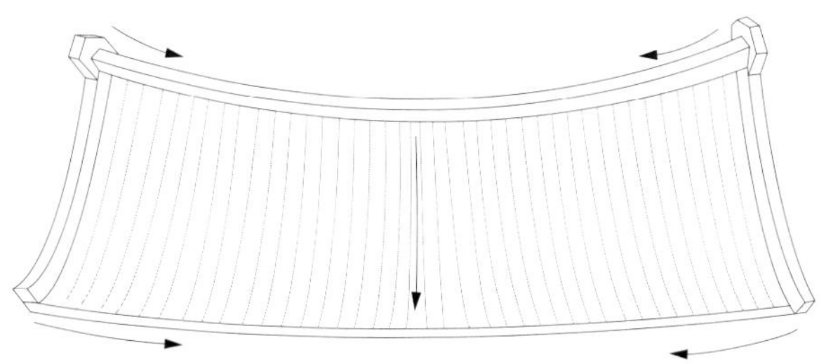

Fig. 3.17.

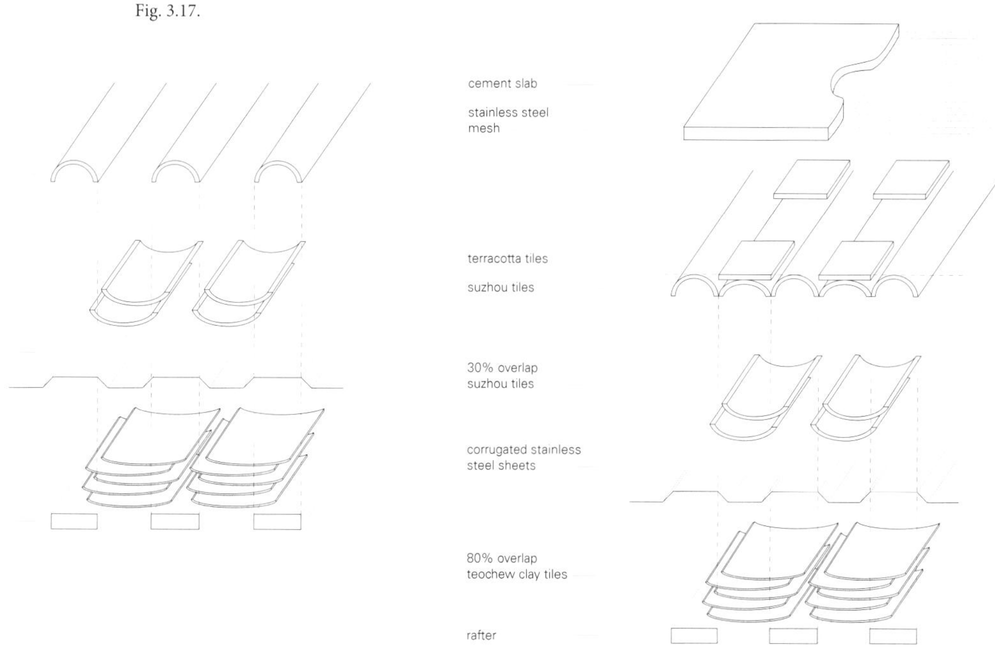

Fig. 3.18.

Fig. 3.17. Diagram showing Wak Hai Cheng Bio's roof curvatures.
Source: Illustrated by Hsieh Mei-En; author's collection.

Fig. 3.18. Exploded isometric illustrations of Wak Hai Cheng Bio's roofing system with secondary roofing (corrugated stainless steel sheets) inserted between Teochew clay tiles and Suzhou tiles.
Source: Illustrated by Hsieh Mei-En; author's collection.

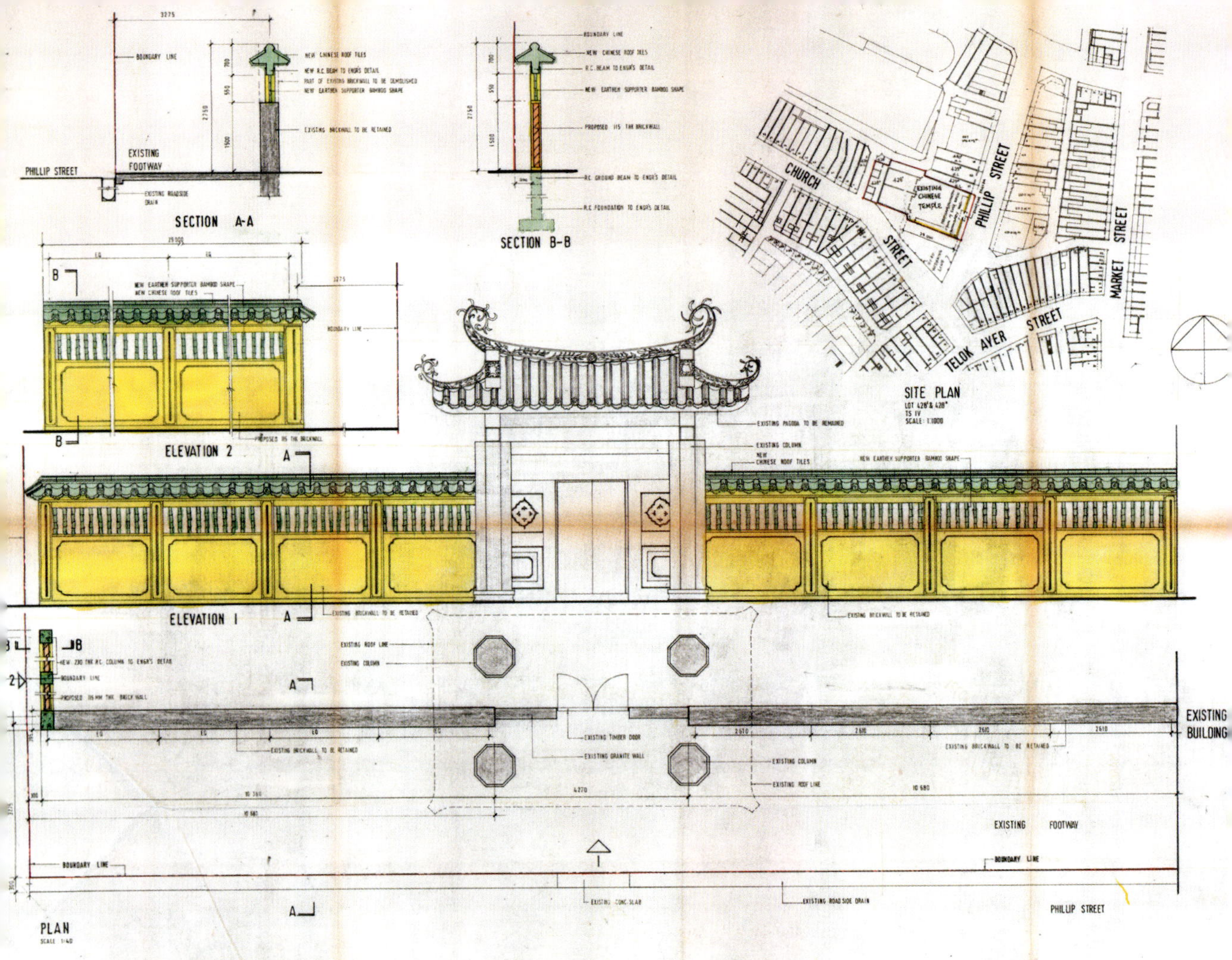

Fig. 3.19.

Architectural Changes in the Latter Half of the 20th Century

Few records of the architectural changes to the temple in the first three-quarters of the 20th century have been found. One of the very few surviving records is a brief account of the 1930 renovation and furnishing of the temple's rear building.[53] This was carried out after a new team of trustees led by Lim Nee Soon took over the management of Ghee Ann Koon (later Ngee Ann Kongsi). The renovation took place between April and November 1930 and was carried out to prepare the rear building to house the Ghee Ann Koon's office.[54] The renovations were likely minor ones as no alteration plans were filed with the municipal authorities. Within a few years of renovation, however, the building experienced water leakage problems. A craftsman was engaged in March 1933 to resolve this issue.[55]

Between 1933 and 1976, evidence of alteration and repair works carried out on the temple comes largely from anecdotal accounts. These works included the

Fig. 3.19. Building plan for new boundary wall designed by Ang Kheng Leng & Associates.
Source: "Proposed Reconstruction of Existing Brick Boundary Wall on Lots 428-1 & 428-2 T.S. IV at Phillip Street for M/S The Ngee Ann Kongsi," 12 November 1979, 3299/1979. Courtesy of The Ngee Ann Kongsi.

Fig. 3.20.

repainting of the Door Gods in 1962–1963,[56] the electrification of the building, the removal of internal partition doors in the main halls, and the tiling of the walls and floor with ceramic tiles and terracotta respectively.[57] Most of the major alterations done after 1895 only took place in the last quarter of the 20th century.

In 1979, a well-known local Teochew architect, Ang Kheng Leng (洪慶龍)[58], was asked to design new boundary walls for the temple (Fig. 3.19). The new boundary walls were to run along Phillip Street and one side of the front courtyard abutting what was 30 Phillip Street. The demolition of neighbouring shophouses necessitated this reconstruction. Between late 1976 and early 1977, the shophouses on the triangular plot of land bounded by the temple to the north, Church Street to the south, and Phillip Street to the east were acquired by the state[59] (Fig. 3.21). They were demolished by 1979. The party wall shared with 30 Phillip Street was torn down, leaving the temple's front courtyard with no boundary wall on this side. This created the need for new boundary walls (Fig. 3.22). Although the Church Street shophouses' rear walls

Fig. 3.20. The entrance gateway and its boundary wall along Phillip Street. One side of the temple courtyard abuts the gable wall of the neighbouring shophouse. This is believed to be the original boundary wall that was replaced by Ang Kheng Leng's design.
Source: Courtesy of National Museum of Singapore (XXXX-15924).

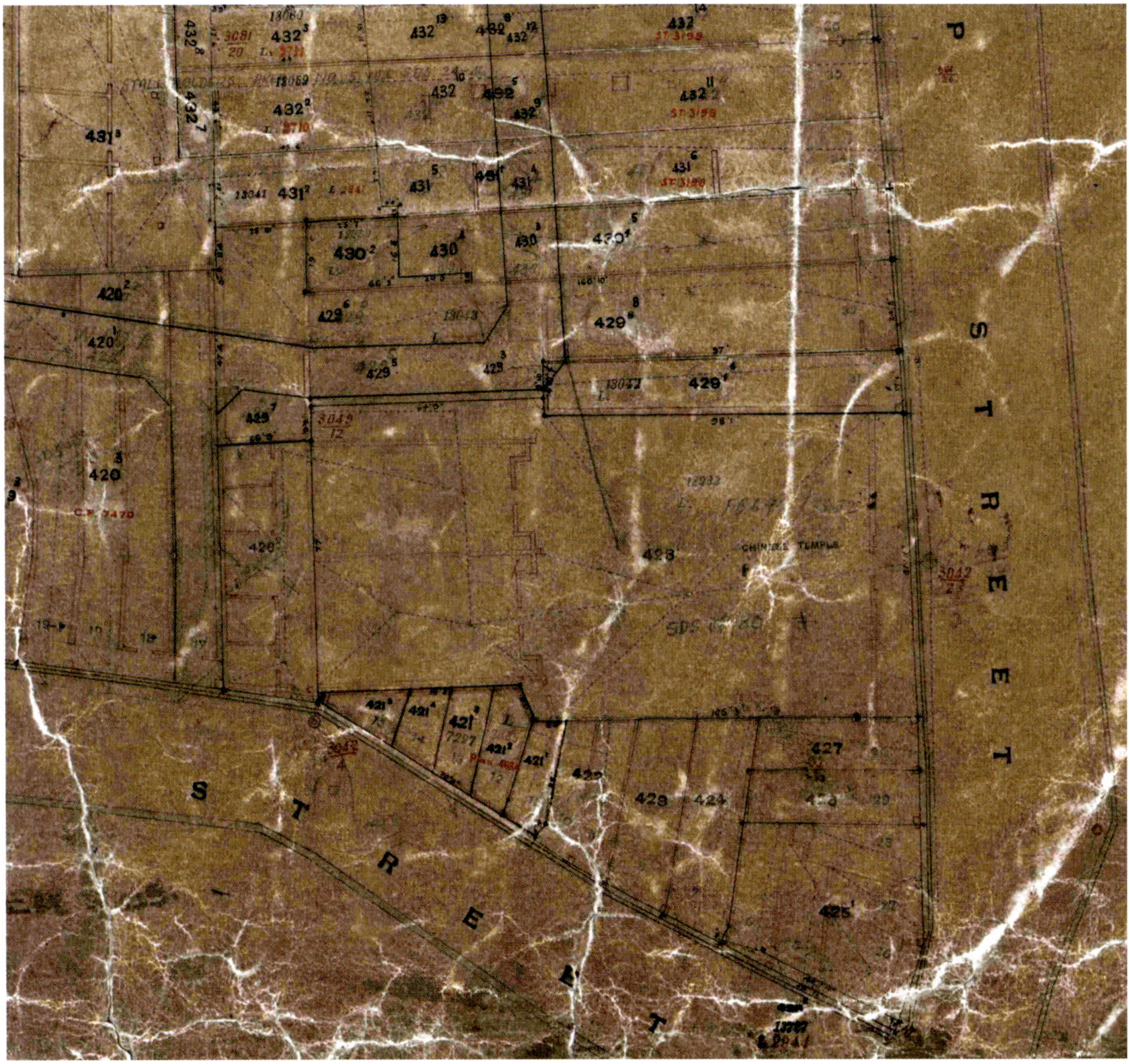

Fig. 3.21.

Fig. 3.21. Map of Phillip Street showing Wak Hai Cheng Bio and adjacent shophouse lots in the triangular plot of land before their demolition in thc 1970s.
Source: "Singapore. Resurvey Town Sub-Division No. 4. Block No. 3," circa 1910s. Courtesy of Lim Shao Bin.

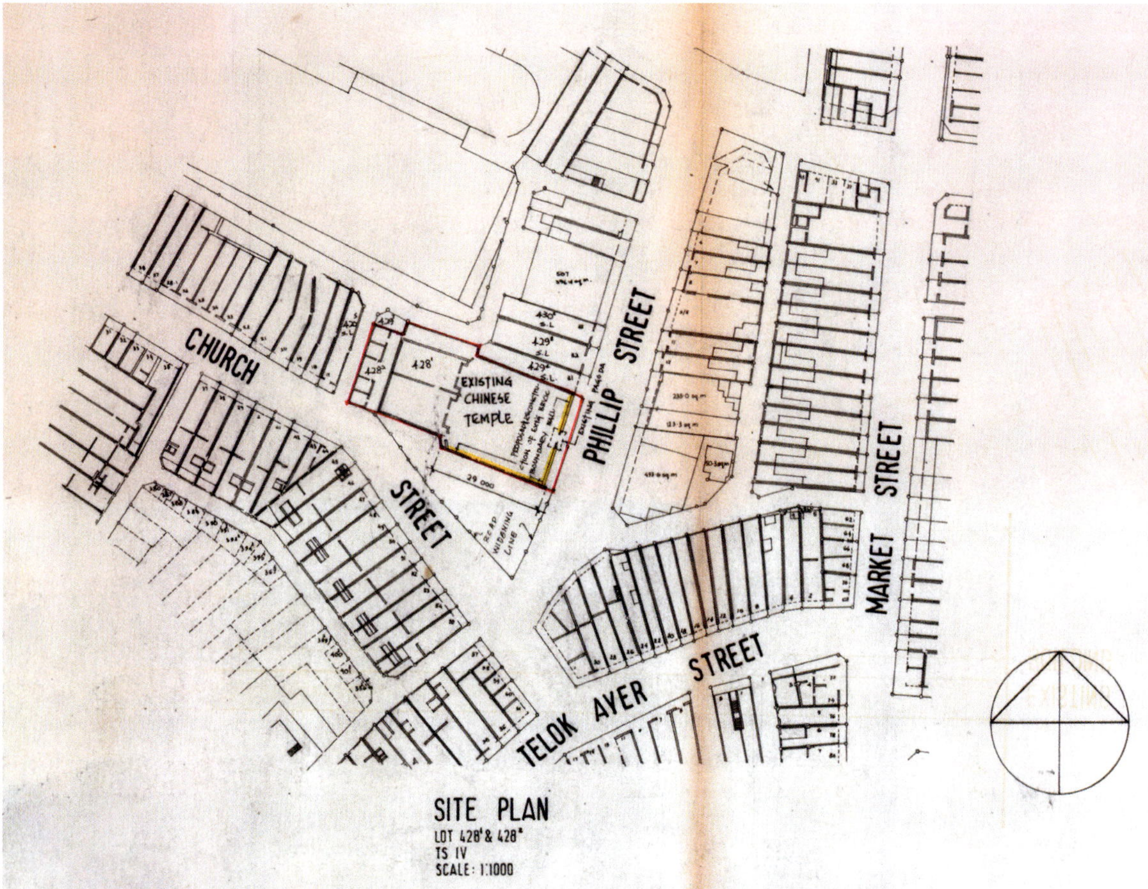

Fig. 3.22.

abutting Tiānhòugōng were also knocked down, the load-bearing gable wall of Tiānhòugōng was retained as it was not a party wall shared with the neighbouring shophouses. The Tiānhòugōng wall was entirely rebuilt in 1895 on the temple's land.[60] Actual boundary wall reconstruction works were carried out by Chong Tong Huat & Sons Construction Co. (莊東發父子建築公司), probably in early 1980.[61] The boundary wall abutting the 31 Phillip Street lot was not altered.[62] This shophouse was yet to be demolished at this stage, even though it was acquired by the state in January 1977.[63]

Ang had already gained fame for his modernist Chinese architectural style by 1979. He designed Nanyang University with Ng Keng Siang (黄慶祥) between 1954 and 1958, and the House of Tang (later C. K. Tang) in 1958. These buildings were all designed

Fig. 3.22. The site plan of the 1979 building plan by Ang Kheng Leng & Associates showing the location of the new boundary wall (coloured in yellow).
Source: "Proposed Reconstruction of Existing Brick Boundary Wall on Lots 428-1 & 428-2 T.S. IV at Phillip Street for M/S The Ngee Ann Kongsi," 12 November 1979, 3299/1979. Courtesy of The Ngee Ann Kongsi.

in a similar style; they are all reinforced concrete structures with glazed Chinese roofs, in what is sometimes known as the Chinese "Traditional Eclectic Style".[64] Wak Hai Cheng Bio's new boundary walls were built in this same style, constructed using reinforced concrete with glazed tiles and cylindrical "bamboo" grilles. Such designs were thought to be representative of Chinese-ness. There was, however, no consideration of Teochew architectural typology or style in the design.

Despite several minor alterations and renovations over the course of the 20th century, the temple's built fabric had deteriorated significantly by the early 1990s. Besides natural degeneration, the construction of neighbouring high-rise structures would have impacted the historic building. This included the construction of the Oversea-Chinese Banking Corporation

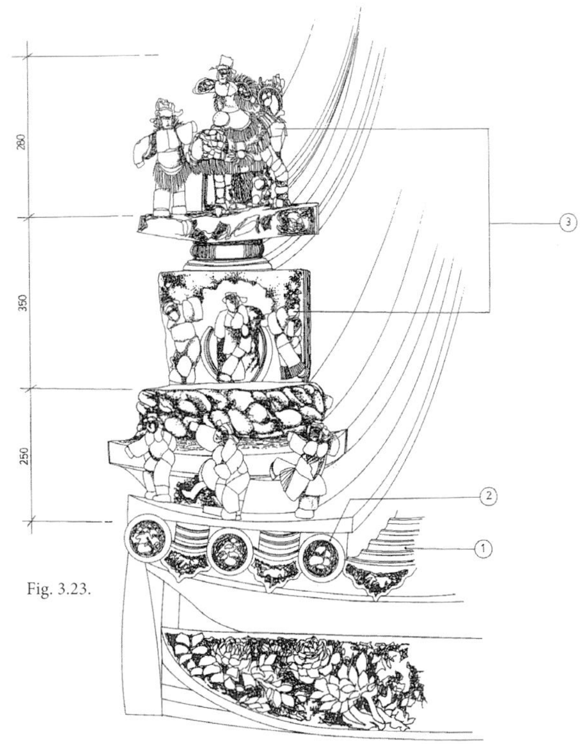

Fig. 3.23.

Fig. 3.24.

Fig. 3.23. Tiānhòugōng gable roof ornamentation measured drawings of 1992.
Source: Chia & Associates Architects, "Wak Hai Cheng Bio Chinese Temple: Measured and Record Drawings of Existing Structure," September 1992. Courtesy of The Ngee Ann Kongsi.

Fig. 3.24. Tiānhòugōng roof ridge dragon ornamentation measured drawings of 1992.
Source: Chia & Associates Architects, "Wak Hai Cheng Bio Chinese Temple: Measured and Record Drawings of Existing Structure," September 1992. Courtesy of The Ngee Ann Kongsi.

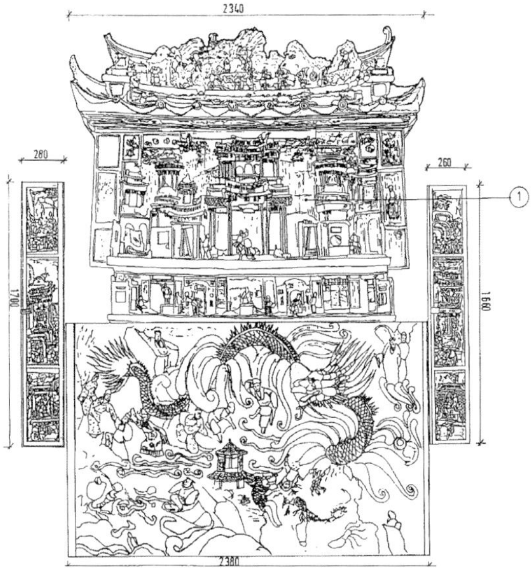

Fig. 3.25.

Centre or OCBC Centre (completed in 1976) and OCBC Centre South between 1980 and 1985.[65] When it became clear that the temple was in need of a major revamp, the Ngee Ann Kongsi commissioned a measured drawing survey in preparation. The survey was conducted by Chia & Associates Architects between 1991 and 1992.[66] In addition to measured drawings, a photographic survey was undertaken in March 1994.[67] This set of photographs proved very important for understanding the alterations carried out during the 1994 to 1997 renovation.

The first and only major renovation of the temple in the 20th century took place between November

Fig. 3.26.

Fig. 3.25. Shàngdìgōng dragon wall measured drawings of 1992.
Source: Chia & Associates Architects, "Wak Hai Cheng Bio Chinese Temple: Measured and Record Drawings of Existing Structure," September 1992. Courtesy of The Ngee Ann Kongsi.

Fig. 3.26. Shàngdìgōng front elevation upper panels ornamentation measured drawings of 1992.
Source: Chia & Associates Architects, "Wak Hai Cheng Bio Chinese Temple: Measured and Record Drawings of Existing Structure," September 1992. Courtesy of The Ngee Ann Kongsi.

Fig. 3.27.

Fig. 3.28.

1994 and early 1997. Based on an interview with *qiàncí* master craftsman Lú Zhīgāo (盧芝高), the artisan was invited from China to work on a portion of the temple's roof in 1993 or 1994.[68] This was meant to be a demonstration piece to ascertain his skills as a *qiàncí* craftsman.[69] Lú did not eventually work on the renovation project. His demonstration piece was likely the *qiàncí* on the roof of the main entrance gateway, as these were more intricate than the repairs made to the ceramic ornamentations above the twin shrines. Portland cement was heavily used in the latter. Since Lú would have only used lime plaster and not Portland cement, it is unlikely that he worked on the *qiàncí* of the twin shrines. Moreover, terracotta tiles were not removed from the repaired *qiàncí* above the twin shrines after installation. These tiles would have been used to hold *qiàncí* in position during fabrication. This approach suggests that the people who worked on the repairs to the *qiàncí* of the twin shrines in the 1990s were not from the trade.

Fig. 3.29.

Fig. 3.30.

Fig. 3.27. The front elevation of Tiānhòugōng had its timber balustrades and casement gates removed during the 1994 to 1997 renovation works. The same was carried out at Shàngdìgōng.
Source: Author's collection.

Fig. 3.28. Door Gods of Shàngdìgōng repainted during 1994 to 1997 renovation works. The same was carried out at Tiānhòugōng.
Source: Photographed by Ung Ruey Loon.

Fig. 3.29. *Qīngshí* (青石) granite tiger and dragon wall panels replaced original panels during the 1994 to 1997 renovation works.
Source: Photographed by Ung Ruey Loon.

Fig. 3.30. Circular *qīngshí* (青石) granite phoenix and dragon fenestrations replaced the original deteriorated fenestrations during the 1994 to 1997 renovation works.
Source: Photographed by Ung Ruey Loon.

Fig. 3.31.

The 1990s renovation was undertaken by a Singapore company, Malacca (Wah Kee) Handicraft Co. (馬六甲[華記]工藝品公司), for a contract sum of more than $2 million.[70] It was led by Zhèng Hànkǎi (鄭漢凱) who was a timber craftsman and building contractor.[71] Malacca (Wah Kee) Handicraft Co. was very active in the 1980s and 1990s within the temple construction industry. One of the temples it renovated in 1999 was the Thong Teck Sian Tong Lian Sin Sia (同德善堂念心社) located at 1A Boon Teck Road.[72] The architect who signed and submitted the building plans for the 1994 to 1997 Wak Hai Cheng Bio renovation was Raymond Woo. The temple was gazetted as a National Monument during the renovation on 28 June 1996. Interestingly,

Fig. 3.31. The longitudinal timber beams (black base paint) were painted over in Suzhou style during the 1994 to 1997 renovation works. The walls were tiled in homogeneous tiles.
Source: Photographed by Ung Ruey Loon.

Fig. 3.32. The rear courtyard archway, probably tiled in the 1980s with gradated orange coloured ceramic tiles, was demolished during the 1994 to 1997 renovation works. There was a corresponding archway on the other end of the rear courtyard.
Source: Rear Hall – Pre-Restoration Photographic Records, The Ngee Ann Kongsi 1994. Courtesy of The Ngee Ann Kongsi.

Fig. 3.32.

the Preservation Guidelines were only produced in September 1997, after the completion of the renovation.[73]

A comparison between the 1994 pre-renovation photographs and existing features of the temple prior to the 2010 to 2014 restoration shows that the following works were carried out during the 1994 to 1997 renovation:

1. Repairs were carried out to the *qiàncí* on the roofs.
2. A layer of waterproofing chemicals was applied to the roofs without retiling the entire roof; it is likely that only localised re-roofing was carried out, with visibly damaged tiles replaced.
3. The timber balustrades and two sets of timber casement gates were removed from the entrance gateways of the twin shrines (Fig. 3.27).
4. All timber doors were repainted (Fig. 3.28).
5. Mosaic floor tiles, probably added during the 1960s or 1970s, were replaced with square terracotta tiles.
6. White, off-white, and maroon ceramic wall tiles (5 x 5 inches), popular during the 1960s or 1970s and likely added at the time, were replaced with light maroon tiles (18 x 18 inches).[74]
7. The dragon and tiger walls made of plaster with fresco work and *qiàncí* were entirely replaced with newly fashioned *qīngshí* (青石) granite ones (Fig. 3.29).
8. The circular plaster phoenix and dragon fenestrations separating the main and prayer halls were replaced with *qīngshí* (青石) granite ones (Fig. 3.30).
9. The gilded black longitudinal timber beams were repainted in a poorly executed Suzhou style[75] (Fig. 3.31).
10. The two archways within the rear courtyard were removed (Fig. 3.32).

Conclusion

Within a few years of the 1994 to 1997 renovation, ceramic shards began falling off the newly repaired *qiàncí*. This was due to the extensive use of Portland cement to hold the ceramic shards and plaster moulding together. The great difference between the rates of thermal movements of Portland cement and ceramic resulted in the latter falling off within a short span of time. By contrast, lime plaster is a more compatible binder for ceramic work. In 2005, less than 10 years after the 1990s renovation was completed, serious issues began to surface. A severe rising damp problem resulted in moisture and salt damage to untiled sections of the temple's walls and its plaster bas-relief.[76] In addition, the roof leaked in several places and became infested with termites. Parts of the gilded fascia boards in the two shrines were also devoured by termites and plagued with wet rot. These mounting issues prompted the Ngee Ann Kongsi to take action, undertaking another restoration commencing in 2010.

CHAPTER 4

The 2010 to 2014 Restoration

A full-scale restoration and conservation of Wak Hai Cheng Bio was carried out between 2010 and 2014. This chapter documents the entire process of this restoration project. It outlines why this restoration was needed and shows how a full-scale restoration of a historic building may be devised based on historical research and technical surveys of the building, its artefacts, and the requirements of its stakeholders. This project was guided by a set of objectives, philosophy, and methodology that was grounded in the principles of global conservation and preservation charters. The chapter further shows the importance and feasibility of engaging a team of restorers or craftsmen with the necessary expertise and in-depth knowledge of historical construction methods to carry out restoration and conservation works. Finally, it demonstrates how specific decisions in the restoration process are made by considering the conditions of the particular situation, the feasibility of the various options, and the broader objectives of the restoration.

Rationale of Restoration

A few years after the 1994 to 1997 renovations, the deterioration of the physical fabric of Wak Hai Cheng Bio became evident. Over the next decade, the owner of the temple commissioned a series of localised repairs in an attempt to address this deterioration. These localised repairs, however, did not seem to have tackled the root of the problem and the degradation of the building's physical appearance persisted. Two major areas of deterioration prompted the Ngee Ann Kongsi to consider another full-scale restoration of the temple.

The first area of deterioration was in the carved pseudo-beam panels (*zǎifù* 橚腹) below the beams in the two shrines. The panels had previously been damaged by termite infestation and faced moisture-related degradation issues. The problem was dramatically brought to the attention of the Kongsi when one of the panels came crashing down. This led to consolidation works being carried out on the panels between 2008 and 2010 with the assistance of an artefact conservator.[1]

During the consolidation process, L-shaped brackets were added to provide additional support to these panels. Besides the panels, some sections of the rafters (*jué* 桷)[2] and purlins (*yíng* 楹)[3] were also affected by termite attacks and damaged by wet rot, a result of water penetrating through broken roof tiles. Localised repairs to the roof in 2008 did not resolve the issue. Some fascia boards (*yánbǎn* 檐板) similarly faced moisture issues due to exposure to the elements. In a moist environment, timber becomes "softer" and more attractive to termites. Since many visible parts of the timber roof structure were affected by termite attacks and wet rot issues, it was feared that other non-visible structural elements of the building, such as the timber mortises and tenons, were likewise damaged. Without taking the roof and timber structures apart, it was impossible to determine the condition of these non-visible structural elements.

The temple was also plagued by severe rising damp problems. The decorative plaster-relief panels on the front elevation of the twin shrines had delaminated and the fresco work on the panels was damaged by salt efflorescence. During the 1994 to 1997 renovation, the interior walls of both shrines were tiled, and the lowest panels on the front elevation were recast in Portland cement. This use of inappropriate materials resulted in moisture being trapped within the walls. With capillary action, moisture rose to the lower part of the middle panels, causing salt efflorescence and subsequent plaster delamination. By 2008, the rising damp was beginning to affect the uppermost panels on the front elevation. The moist environment caused by water penetration and rising damp not only risked exacerbating the termite issue but also had the potential to weaken the structure of the building over time. It was apparent that the building was deteriorating rapidly, and this made it even more pressing to address the root of the problem.

The two major forms of deterioration were strikingly visible and manifested themselves in many different parts of the temple. The owner of the temple recognised that the severity of the building's deterioration went beyond localised damage. They therefore decided to embark upon a major restoration to resolve the problem at its source. On 12 April 2010, then Secretary-General of the Ngee Ann Kongsi, Baey Theng Mong (馬廷茂), and Lee Ee Khim (李燕琴) approached Yeo Kang Shua (楊茳善) to act as consultant for the restoration of Wak Hai Cheng Bio.[4] Yeo went on to conduct a preliminary study in preparation for the restoration between April and May 2010; photographic documentation of the moveable artefacts in the temple was carried out during the study.

Objectives, Philosophy and Methodology

Conservation Philosophy

Architectural conservation is grounded in the belief that buildings can communicate values, traditions and culture, as well as inspire the general public. It recognises and respects the integral nature of a building, including its architectural design and spatial relationships, its construction technology, its creators and stewards over time, and the objects and documents associated with it, as well as the effects of age on the visual appearance of the building. The building's history, as evidenced by renovations and modifications over time, is valued as a testament to its continuous occupancy and use; it serves as a reflection of broader social and cultural changes.

Conservation work was undertaken to preserve Wak Hai Cheng Bio in perpetuity, safeguard the building for continued use, and provide a new generation with opportunities to engage with the building. To achieve this, it was necessary to have a clear and collective understanding of the changes that could be made to the building. As the owner of the temple and one of its main stakeholders, the Ngee Ann Kongsi wanted the temple to maintain its original function as a place of worship and to be a showcase of traditional Teochew craftsmanship.

The conservation project was guided by two basic principles widely recommended by conservation and preservation charters globally: first, minimal intervention, and second, reversibility of interventions. Every attempt was made to keep as much of the original material (timber, granite, clay roof tiles, and surrounding masonry) as possible with minimal intervention. Where intervention was inevitable, it had to be reversible. Departures from these two basic principles were required to be justified and documented.

As Wak Hai Cheng Bio was gazetted as a National Monument on 28 June 1996, it was subject to the regulatory requirements of the National Heritage Board's Preservation of Sites and Monuments (PSM) division as well as the standard regulatory framework governing building works. The PSM issues Preservation Guidelines that document the historical and architectural merits of the monument to ensure that restoration works meet the stipulated standards by acting as a control document for future audits of the building and its contents. Besides the two basic principles of minimal intervention and reversibility of interventions, the restoration of Wak Hai Cheng Bio had to also adhere to these Preservation Guidelines.

Objectives of the Restoration Project

Before the start of the restoration project, it was highly important to lay out the objectives, philosophy, and methodology of the restoration. This would then guide subsequent decision-making processes. This also meant that if and when differing views arose during decision-making for the restoration process, a common consensus could be obtained with reference to the objectives, philosophy and methodology set out at the very beginning of the project. For the 2010 to 2014 restoration of Wak Hai Cheng Bio, the objectives were as follows:

1. To preserve the temple as a living monument, along with its contents including artefacts and documents, which reflects the history of the building and its stakeholders;
2. To present, through conservation, the temple as a fine example of Teochew architecture and showcase its traditions of ornamentation and craftsmanship; and
3. To function for a diverse audience, both religious and non-religious, providing a window into the broader context of Chinese art, architecture and culture.

Methodology

The restoration team referred closely to two globally recognised conservation charters when preparing the methodology to be used in the Wak Hai Cheng Bio restoration project. The first was the Australia International Council on Monuments and Sites (ICOMOS) *The Burra Charter* and special attention was paid to Article 4 concerning knowledge, skills and techniques of conservation, Article 15.2 on the reversibility of change, Article 21 on adaptation, and Article 22 regarding new works to buildings.[5] The second charter used was the 2004 *Principles for the Conservation of Heritage Sites in China* 《中國文物古跡保護准則》 issued by ICOMOS China. The parts most relevant to the Wak Hai Cheng Bio restoration project were Article 19 on minimal intervention, commentary paragraph 4.4.3 on the reversibility of interventions, and commentary paragraphs 12.3 and 12.4 on major restorations.[6] The availability of the two documents online enabled all parties involved in the restoration project to learn more about conservation principles and the work involved in such projects.

The owner of Wak Hai Cheng Bio was determined to conserve the temple both as a place of worship and as a heritage site. The conservation and restoration methodology adopted to achieve this were as follows:

a. **Retention of Original Elements and Components**
Every attempt was made to retain as many of the original 1895 elements and components as possible. Damaged elements and components were consolidated and conserved, restored, or repaired if possible; they were reused instead of being replaced by new ones. Elements and components that were exceptionally old, or were the result of an atypical or unusual construction technique, were retained unless they posed structural danger. They were consolidated and repaired where necessary.

b. **Removal of Unsafe Elements and Components**
During assembly and reassembly, all structural issues were rectified through the removal of unsafe and insensitive elements and components. This was to ensure that all structural consolidation, conservation, restoration, and repairs were robust, compatible in material, and stylistically sensitive, such that no further treatment may be required for an extended period of time.

c. **Reinstatement of Missing Parts**
Restoration of the building's elements to historical conditions was based on extant physical fabric or remains; no conjecture established solely with documentary records was permitted. A missing element or component was reinstated using only the same materials and construction technology and with reference to examples of the same typology, vintage, and origin. This newly reinstated fabric was labelled or documented with the date of replacement. For timber components, damaged carvings were consolidated to prevent further degradation and reinstated, if necessary, with the reinstatement dates carved in an inconspicuous location. Ornamentation that was rare and valuable because of its age or design was consolidated without reinstatement. In the interest of authenticity, there was no requirement to strive for uniformity in style or appearance.

d. **Observation of Appropriate Aesthetic Criteria**
The aesthetic value of a structure is derived from its historical authenticity. No modification of the historical conditions solely for cosmetic purposes or to achieve visual completeness was permitted. This restoration project respected the building's patina-of-age and did not attempt to return the temple to its newly completed state.

e. **Use of Techniques and Materials**
Restoration techniques and materials used were selected based on conservation requirements and the benefits of using them. While traditional techniques were preferred, new materials and techniques could also be used if they had been tried and tested. This was to ensure that no damage was caused to the physical fabric. Distinctive traditional techniques, craftsmanship, and materials of special value were retained.

f. **Documentation**
All conservation decisions and interventions were documented. These included both

elements that were removed and those which were newly added. Samples of removed elements and components were kept and recorded in the project archives. This serves an important purpose for future restoration teams to understand the building's original fabric.

Pre-Restoration Investigations and Documentation

An understanding of the building's extant fabric is critical for deciding what to retain, remove, consolidate, reconstruct, and add in a manner sensitive to its architecture, history, and function. Before restoration

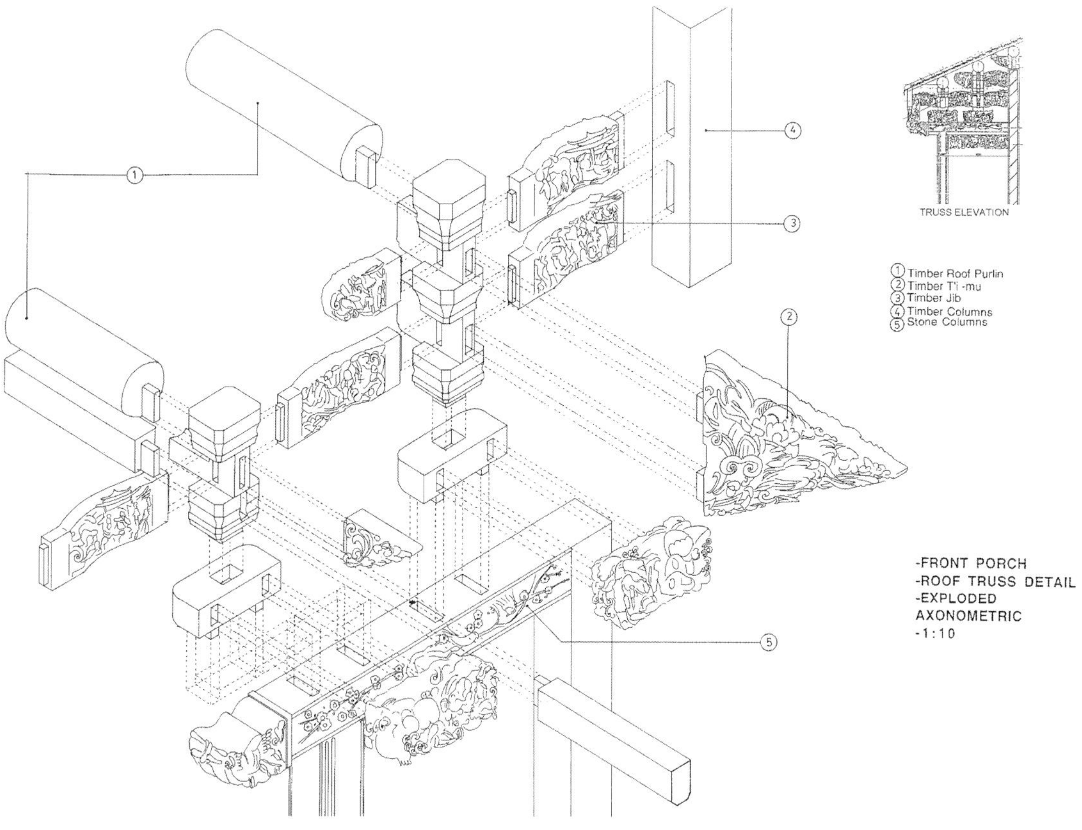

Fig. 4.1.

Fig. 4.1. An exploded axonometric measured drawing dated September 1992 commissioned by The Ngee Ann Kongsi prior to the 1994 to 1997 renovation. This set of drawings was incorporated into the 1997 Urban Redevelopment Authority's *Yueh Hai Ching Temple Preservation Guidelines*, prepared for the Preservation of Monuments Board. Source: Chia & Associates Architects, "Wak Hai Cheng Bio Chinese Temple: Measured and Record Drawings of Existing Structure," September 1992. Courtesy of the Ngee Ann Kongsi.

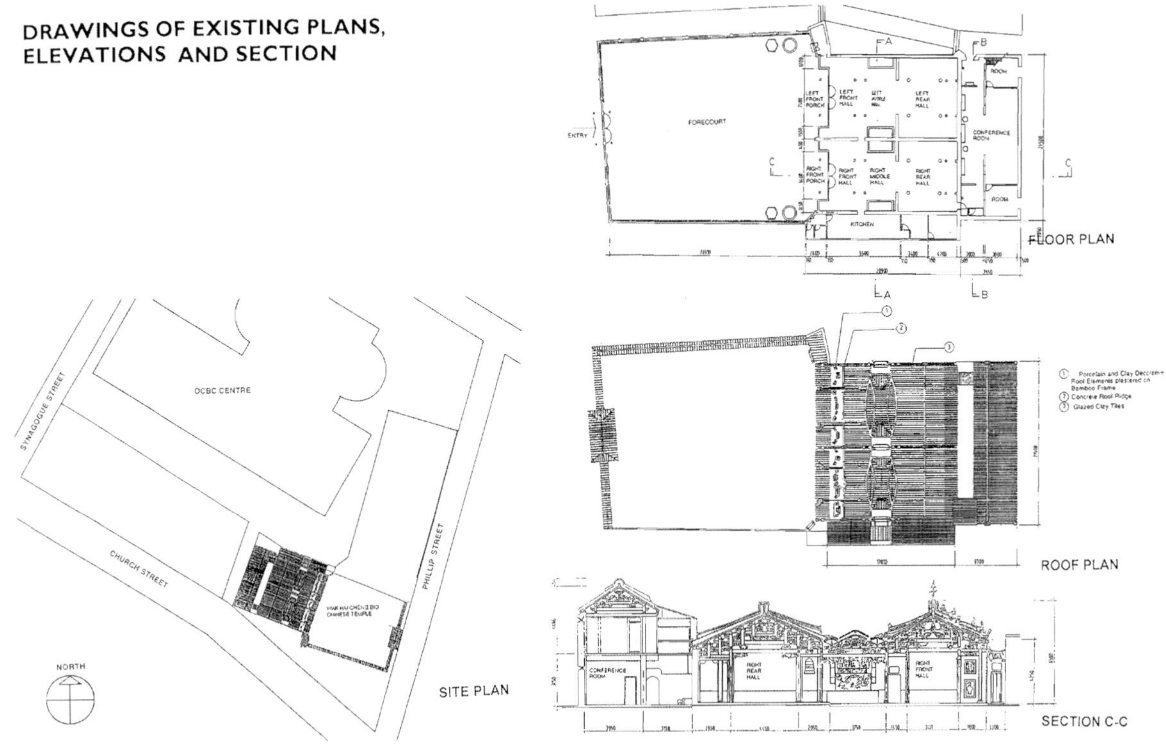

Fig. 4.2.

work begins, it is important to know in detail the current state and elements of the building. This includes a knowledge of the original fabric and more recent elements, insensitive additions, missing components, the types of crafts required in restoring or reconstructing the building, the materials used, and the periods during which different elements were added. The restoration team conducted pre-restoration investigations and documentation to aid their understanding of the temple's physical fabric for decision-making in planning the restoration. This included a series of technical surveys and historical research.

Technical Surveys

Between April and May 2010, a detailed photographic condition survey of both the interior and exterior of the temple was conducted. Photography of the ceramic ornamentations or *qiàncí* (嵌瓷) on the temple's roofs was carried out in areas accessible with a ladder. These photographs were compared against three different

Fig. 4.2. Drawings of existing plans and section dated 1994 commissioned by The Ngee Ann Kongsi for the 1994 to 1997 renovation works.
Source: Raymond Woo & Associates Architects, Chin Jian Ping, and Lee Zhi Gao, "Proposed Additions & Alterations and Preservation to the Existing Yueh Hai Ching Temple on Lot 428-1 and 428-2 TS 4 at 30B Phillip Street," (Raymond Woo & Associates Architects; Construction and Planning Institute, Guangdong Province, Teochew City, June 1994). Courtesy of The Ngee Ann Kongsi.

sets of records commissioned by the Ngee Ann Kongsi before the 1994 to 1997 renovation. The first was a set of detailed photographs of the temple taken in 1994. Another record used in the technical investigations was a set of measured drawings completed in September 1992 by Chia & Associates Architects. The final record used was the "Proposed Additions & Alterations and Preservation to the Existing Yueh Hai Ching Temple on Lot 428-1 and 428-2 TS 4 at 30B Phillip Street" drawings prepared by Raymond Woo & Associates Architects in June 1994. The comparisons between the various sets of drawings and photographs allowed the team to have a better grasp of the alterations performed since 1994.

Historical Research

Very targeted research into the temple's architectural history was conducted before restoration began. This aided the understanding of the building's style and the existence of various building elements at different points in time. The restoration team also surveyed various writings on the temple's architecture, found an 1895 building plan of Wak Hai Cheng Bio, and a few old photographs from the early 1900s. Some of this research is now part of Chapter Three.

Conclusions of Pre-Restoration Investigations

From the pre-restoration investigations, documentation, and research, the restoration team formed the following preliminary conclusions:[7]

1. The current temple retained its original 1890s spatial layout as depicted on the 1895 building plan.
2. The boundary wall had been altered between 1979 and the early 1980s.
3. Repairs were carried out to some of the *qiàncí* above the roofs during the 1994 to 1997 renovation.
4. The timber balustrades and two sets of timber casement gates were removed from the entrance gateways of the twin shrines during the 1994 to 1997 renovation.
5. All timber doors were repainted.
6. Mosaic floor tiles, probably added during the 1960s or 1970s, were changed to square terracotta tiles.
7. White, off-white, and maroon ceramic wall tiles (5 x 5 inches), probably added during the 1960s or 1970s as these were popular at the time, were replaced with light maroon ones (18 x 18 inches) during the 1994 to 1997 renovation.[8]
8. The frescoed plaster and *qiàncí* dragon and tiger walls (*lónghǔ dǔ* 龍虎堵) were entirely replaced with newly fashioned granite ones during the 1994 to 1997 renovation.
9. Circular plaster phoenix and dragon fenestrations separating the main and prayer halls were replaced with granite ones during the 1994 to 1997 renovation.
10. The gilded black longitudinal timber beams were repainted in a poorly executed Suzhou style during the 1994 to 1997 renovation.[9]
11. The two archways at either end of the rear courtyard were removed.

These preliminary conclusions helped the team formulate the restoration approach, which is detailed in the restoration proposal in the following section. Since Wak Hai Cheng Bio retained much of its mid-1890s physical fabric, the restoration team decided to restore the temple based on the mid-1890s temple. The approach taken was to disassemble and reassemble the building (*luòjià dàxiū* 落架大修). The pre-restoration investigations confirmed the view that previous works carried out to the temple were mainly minor repairs to

[B] The plaster ornamentation and fresco [灰塑與彩繪] on the front elevation of the shrines retained much of the historic colour scheme despite suffering from previous insensitive repair (especially for loss of figurines' heads).

[C] The ceramic ornamentation [嵌瓷] on the roof was restored during the last renovation between 1994 and 1997. It was apparent that this figurine was restored ex situ and installed by a person unfamiliar with this craft. The terracotta tile behind the figurine has to be removed during installation, but this was not carried out.

[D] This dragon ceramic ornamentation [嵌瓷] was restored between 1994 and 1997 using inappropriate binder, i.e. Portland cement, which resulted in loss of ceramic shards due to incompatability of adhesion materials.

[E] Overall view of the temple's roof. Much of the intricacies of ceramic ornamentation [嵌瓷] have been lost over the years.

[A] Boundary wall with green glazed coping tiles, eaves tiles and bamboo-shaped grilles was constructed in 1979 in the style that is incongruous with Teochew architecture.

Fig. 4.3.

[F] The longitudinal beams were painted over in the Suzhou style during the last restoration between 1994-97. This was a major change that is incongruous with Teochew architecture. There is also loss of gold-gilded surfaces on many of the carvings.

[G] The composite ceramic, clay and plaster ornamentation [泥丁] as well as fresco located in Shàngdìgōng [上帝宫] was badly degraded. However, it is fortunate that there was minimal intervention on these ornamentation during the last restoration.

Fig. 4.3. Axonometric cutaway illustration of Wak Hai Cheng Bio showing degradation, insensitive repairs, and/or additions prior to 2010–2014 restoration works.
Source: Illustrated by author; base illustration adapted from Efren Mendoza's illustration for Lee Geok Boi's *The Religious Monuments of Singapore: Faiths of Our Forefathers* (Singapore: Landmark Books, 2002).

[D] The Door Gods were altered during the last restoration between 1994 and 1997. Fortunately, the cartoons of the pre-1994 restoration Door Gods were found. They were reinstated with the assistance of these cartoons and archival photographs.

[E] The ceramic ornamentation [嵌瓷] on the roof has been meticulously restored. Helming this restoration is master craftsman Xǔ Shàoxióng [許少雄], a fourth-generation master craftman working on traditional Teochew ceramic ornamentation.

[F] The main hall's rear ridge is decorated with plaster and ceramic ornamentation as well as frescos. Master craftsman Xǔ (ceramic [嵌瓷]) and master craftsman Lín Mùkūn [林慕坤] (plaster and fresco [泥塑與彩繪]) collaborated to restore the ridge.

[B] The timber balustrade and gate [木欄杆與欄杆門] were removed during the last restoration of 1994–1997 for unknown reasons. The two sets of gates were found in the storeroom and reinstated to their rightful positions.

[C] It is unknown when the screen doors were removed. They were reinstated during this restoration.

Fig. 4.4.

[A] Plain white boundary walls with moulded copings are reinstated using archival photographs.

There is no change to the roof form, timber truss, ornamentation, spatial layout and form of the temple. These were retained with conservation treatment and cleaning.

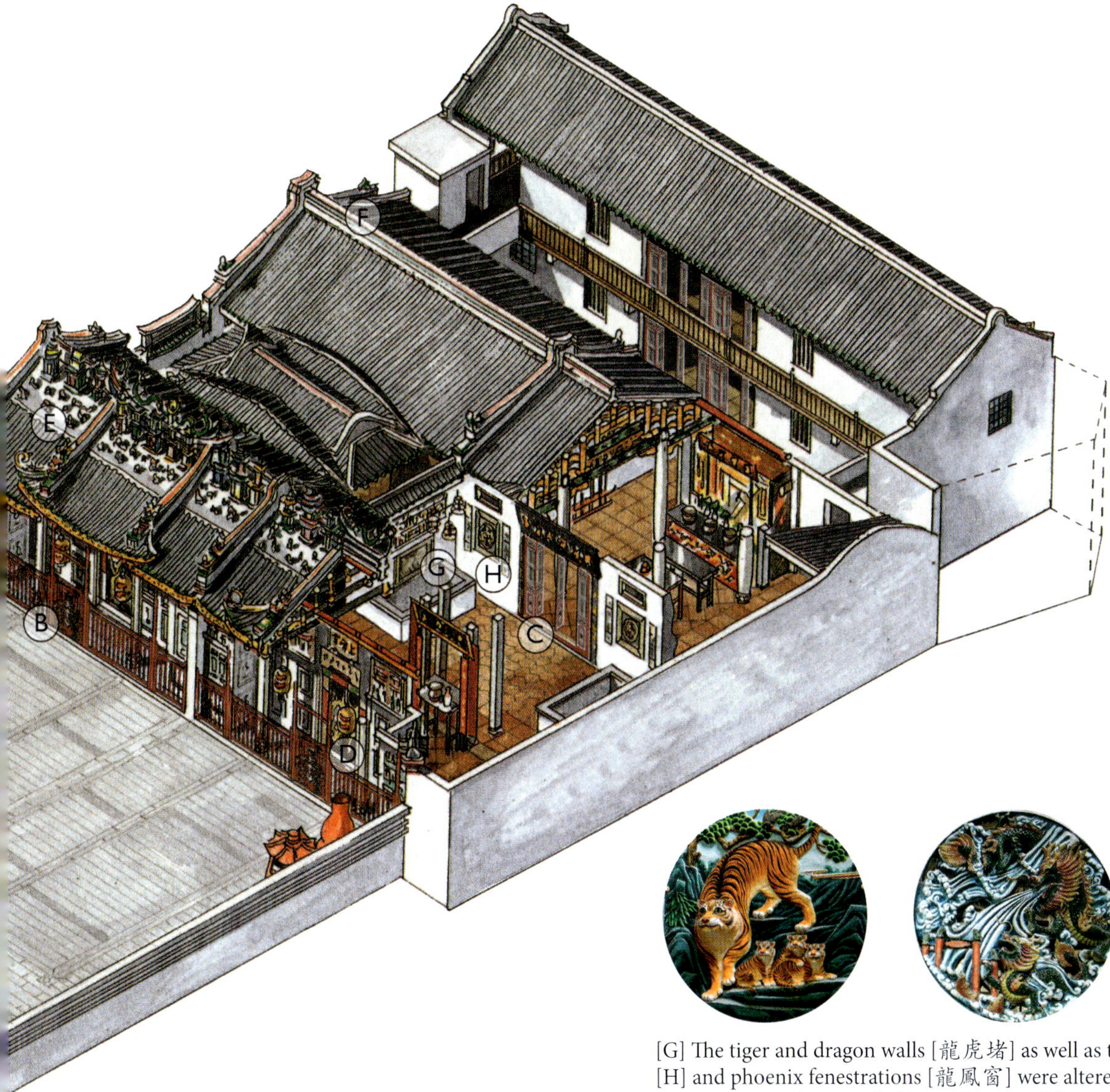

[G] The tiger and dragon walls [龍虎堵] as well as the dragon [H] and phoenix fenestrations [龍鳳窗] were altered both in composition and materials (from plaster and fresco to granite) during the last restoration. These were reinstated using archival photographic documentation.

Fig. 4.4. Axonometric cutaway illustration of Wak Hai Cheng Bio after 2010–2014 restoration works.
Source: Illustrated by author; base illustration adapted from Efren Mendoza's illustration for Lee Geok Boi's *The Religious Monuments of Singapore: Faiths of Our Forefathers* (Singapore: Landmark Books, 2002).

architectural finishing; it appears there were no repairs or checks done to structural members between the mid-1890s and 2010. It was thus recommended that a thorough check of the building be conducted. This was only possible through disassembly and reassembly. This would also ensure that the building's ongoing termite issue was fully and properly treated.

Proposal for Restoration

Once the restoration approach had been fixed, the next step was to prepare a restoration proposal. This would encompass a full restoration of Wak Hai Cheng Bio including its entrance gateway, front and rear courtyards, twin shrines, and rear building.

Restoration Proposal

Floor levels:	Professional engineer to determine if soil or ground strengthening work is required.
Internal floorings:	All terracotta tiles are to be removed and reinstated after chemical waterproofing, termite soil treatment and, if necessary, ground or soil strengthening works. The flooring pattern of the twin shrines' prayer halls is to be reinstated with the original hexagonal terracotta tiles. All terracotta tiles are to be sealed with boiled linseed oil or tung oil after cleaning and before being finished with wax. All floor levels are to be graded to fall.
External floorings:	All terracotta tiles at the rear courtyard are to be removed and reinstated to the original level after chemical waterproofing, termite soil treatment and, if necessary, ground or soil strengthening works.[10] All terracotta tiles are to be sealed with boiled linseed oil or tung oil after cleaning and before being waxed to finish. If necessary, all external granite slabs are to be numbered and removed section by section for soil strengthening works. The substrate is then to be re-graded and granite slabs cleaned with a neutral or slightly alkaline cleaning agent before reinstatement. Crack lines of broken slabs are to be filled with lime-based mortar (coloured to match granite).
Internal walls:	All ceramic tiles are to be removed and the wall treated with chemical waterproofing. In the absence of evidence suggesting that the dado was given decorative treatment before it was tiled with light maroon ceramic tiles during the 1994 to 1997 renovation, the entire length of the wall is to be finished with plain plaster and potassium silicate paint.

Fig. 4.5.

Fig. 4.5. The boundary wall along Phillip Street was a solid wall without any fenestrations as shown in this 1960s photograph.
Source: Courtesy of the National Archives of Singapore (KF Wong 1960: 19990003439_0029).

Fig. 4.6.

Fig. 4.6. The entrance gateway and its boundary wall at night, possibly on the eve of the Lunar New Year.
Source: Courtesy of the National Archives of Singapore and Singapore Press Holdings (SPH 1971: PCD 0385-0012).

Fig. 4.7. The crowds along Phillip Street entering and leaving via the entrance gateway. Many were seen holding lanterns and joss sticks, possibly after "borrowing" lanterns on the eve of the Lunar New Year.
Source: Courtesy of the National Archives of Singapore and Singapore Press Holdings (SPH 1971: PCD 0385-0013).

Fig. 4.7.

External walls:	All plain walls are to be stripped of plaster, treated with chemical waterproofing, replastered, and refinished with potassium silicate paint. On the front elevation of the twin shrines, pigmented plaster reliefs on the middle panels are to be consolidated before restoration. Insensitively repaired geometric reliefs on the lowest panels are to be removed. The wall is to be treated with chemical waterproofing before the reinstatement of reliefs using traditional techniques and mineral pigments. The granite wall of the entrance gateway is to be cleaned with a neutral or slightly alkaline cleaning agent before realignment.
Boundary walls:	Existing boundary walls with green glazed roof tiles are to be demolished and walls reinstated based on historical photographs.
Timber truss:	All non-ornamented timber components suffering from wet rot or termite infestation are to be repaired with traditional splicing techniques or replaced with newly treated timber components if repairs are not feasible. All replaced timber components are to be disposed of immediately after documentation to prevent other timber from being infested. Attention is to be paid to the joints between new and old timber such that there is room for thermal expansion to prevent warping. The "L-shaped" brackets supporting consolidated carved pseudo-beam panels or *zǎifù* 櫼腹 are to be removed and the panels spliced with new tenons.
Stone cantilever beams and columns:	Stone beams and columns are to be cleaned with a neutral or slightly alkaline cleaning agent. Beams and columns that are broken are to be cleaned before being repaired with embedded stainless-steel rebar and epoxy grouting as per professional engineer's specifications or equivalent. A pair of rear courtyard granite columns that has been painted with white enamel paint to be reinstated to bare granite.
Roof:	Green glazed roof eaves tiles to be consolidated and reinstated. Missing or broken eaves tiles to be replicated. Clay roof tiles to be replaced and laid under secondary corrugated stainless steel sheets profiled to suit the clay tiles. Ceramic ornamentations are to be reinstated using traditional techniques and materials.

Fenestrations and stone carvings:	Carved circular granite fenestrations to be removed and reinstated based on historical photographs. Paintings of Door Gods and female attendants are to be repainted in traditional techniques and materials. Door decorations of the entrance gateway are to be reinstated in solid timber. Two pairs of granite panels at the dragon and tiger walls (龍虎堵) are to be removed and reinstated based on historical photographs.
Surface finishes:	Plaster-moulded wall calligraphy and painting in the prayer hall of Tiānhòugōng are to be re-executed using fresco technique and mineral pigments. Gold gilded timber components are to be cleaned and consolidated. New timber components are to be finished in Chinese lacquer before gilding; the new gilding is to match the gold colour tone of existing gilding.
Mechanical and electrical services:	To install an underfloor trunking system for electrical, telephony and computer network services to minimise the amount of exposed trunking in the temple. Underfloor water-supply piping should likewise be installed, where possible. To remove existing ventilation and its awnings at the main halls of both shrines. This is to be replaced with a unidirectional ventilation system.
Additions of new toilet facility:	New toilet facility at the rear of the temple (northern corner) to be designed in a new architecture language to distinguish its vintage from that of the temple. The structure should preferably be set slightly away from the temple.
Removal of previously added toilet facility:	The existing toilet at the rear courtyard is to be demolished and the rear courtyard reinstated to the original. The existing toilet at level two of the rear building is to be removed. It is located above a granite plaque engraved with the temple's name, "粵海清廟" over the side entrance. This insensitive addition is not in line with the Chinese practice of avoiding a profane space above an important architectural element.
Storage space:	To cater for sufficient storage space for religious paraphernalia; there is currently insufficient room for such purposes.
Environs:	To work with relevant authorities to redesign pedestrian pavement and drainage around the temple. Streetside planting should be set some distance away from the temple.

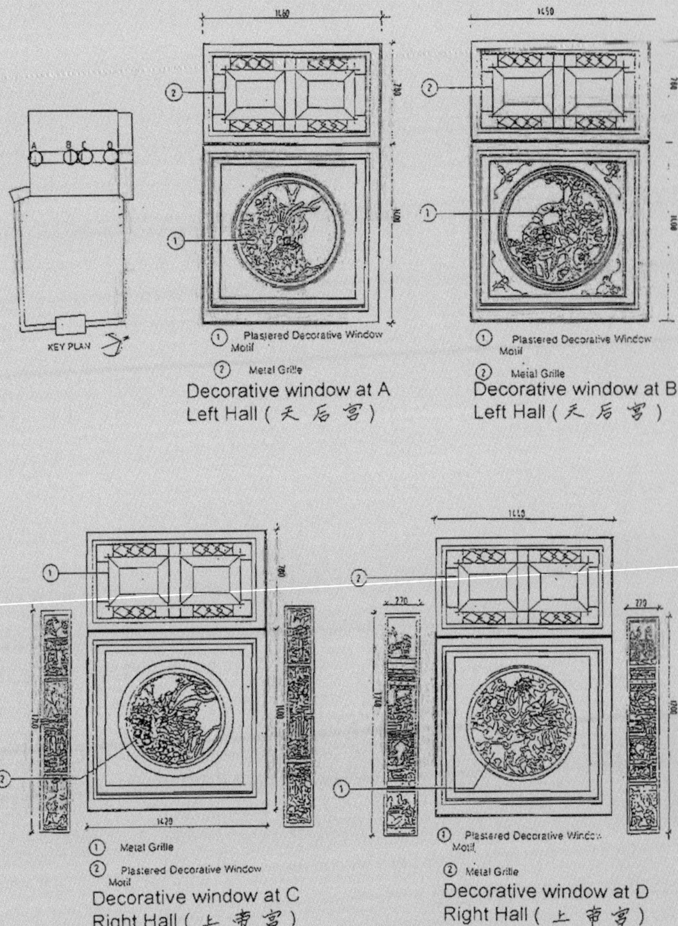

Fig. 4.8.

Fig. 4.9.

Fig. 4.8. Line drawing documentations of the circular fresco painted plaster fenestrations prior to the 1994 to 1997 renovation. Source: Raymond Woo & Associates Architects, Chin Jian Ping, and Lee Zhi Gao, "Proposed Additions & Alterations and Preservation to the Existing Yueh Hai Ching Temple on Lot 428-1 and 428-2 TS 4 at 30B Phillip Street," (Raymond Woo & Associates Architects; Construction and Planning Institute, Guangdong Province, Teochew City, June 1994), 14. Courtesy of The Ngee Ann Kongsi.

Fig. 4.9. Shàngdìgōng circular fresco painted plaster fenestrations prior to the 1994 to 1997 renovation. Source: Shàngdìgōng – Pre-Restoration Photographic Records, The Ngee Ann Kongsi 1994. Courtesy of The Ngee Ann Kongsi.

Fig. 4.10. The rear view of the circular fresco painted plaster fenestration looking from the main hall toward the entrance. The walls were finished in ceramic tiles while the floor was finished in mosaic tiles in 1994. Source: Tiānhòugōng – Pre-Restoration Photographic Records, The Ngee Ann Kongsi 1994. Courtesy of The Ngee Ann Kongsi.

Fig. 4.11. Tiānhòugōng circular fresco painted plaster fenestrations prior to the 1994 to 1997 renovation.
Source: Tiānhòugōng – Pre-Restoration Photographic Records, The Ngee Ann Kongsi 1994. Courtesy of The Ngee Ann Kongsi.

Fig. 4.12. Tiānhòugōng (*left*) and Shàngdìgōng (*right*) Door Gods prior to the 1994 to 1997 renovation. These Door Gods were possibly painted by Liáng Zhōng (梁忠) circa 1962–1963. Source: Tiānhòugōng (*left*) and Shàngdìgōng (*right*) Door Gods – Pre-Restoration Photographic Records, The Ngee Ann Kongsi 1994. Courtesy of The Ngee Ann Kongsi.

Fig. 4.10.

Fig. 4.11.

Fig. 4.12.

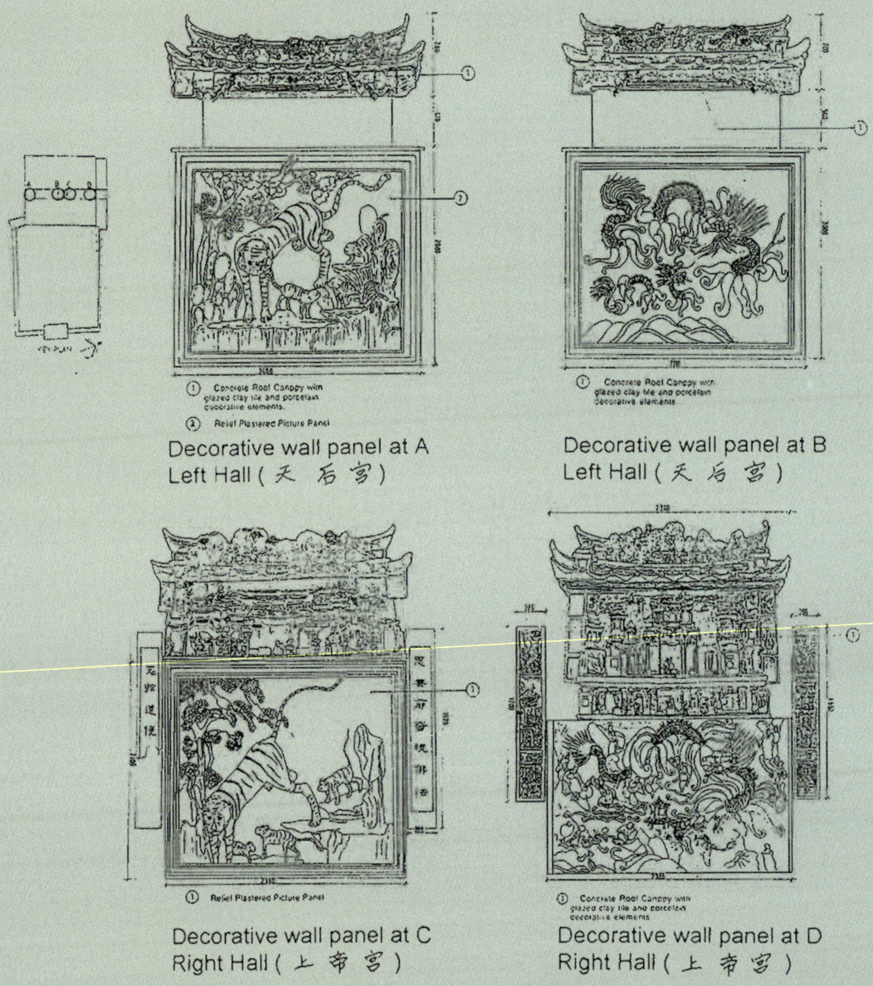

Fig. 4.13.

Fig. 4.13. Line drawing documentations of the fresco painted plaster dragon and tiger walls prior to the 1994 to 1997 renovation.
Source: Raymond Woo & Associates Architects, Chin Jian Ping, and Lee Zhi Gao, "Proposed Additions & Alterations and Preservation to the Existing Yueh Hai Ching Temple on Lot 428-1 and 428-2 TS 4 at 30B Phillip Street," (Raymond Woo & Associates Architects; Construction and Planning Institute, Guangdong Province, Teochew City, June 1994), 13. Courtesy of The Ngee Ann Kongsi.

Fig. 4.14. Tiānhòugōng fresco painted plaster dragon and tiger walls prior to the 1994 to 1997 renovation.
Source: Tiānhòugōng – Pre-Restoration Photographic Records, The Ngee Ann Kongsi 1994. Courtesy of The Ngee Ann Kongsi.

Fig. 4.15. Shàngdìgōng fresco painted plaster dragon and tiger walls prior to the 1994 to 1997 renovation.
Source: Shàngdìgōng – Pre-Restoration Photographic Records, The Ngee Ann Kongsi 1994. Courtesy of The Ngee Ann Kongsi.

Fig. 4.14.

Fig. 4.15.

Fig. 4.16.

Restoration Proposal

This restoration proposal was submitted to the Ngee Ann Kongsi's Restoration Sub-committee in July 2010. The architect, Raymond Woo, then went on to provide annotated architectural drawings between August and December 2010. In the meantime, the structural engineers and mechanical and electrical engineers gave their inputs, while the quantity surveyor did a preliminary costing for the project based on the recommendations of the various consultants.

Search for Restoration Craft Expertise

After the restoration proposal was approved, the next step was to look for a team with the necessary skills to execute the restoration works. As no craftsmen in Singapore had the requisite expertise, a team would have to be engaged from abroad. As Wak Hai Cheng Bio's architecture is Teochew, the restoration team would ideally be composed of craftsmen trained in the Teochew style. Although craftsmen specialising in the various trades could be found elsewhere, subtle regional differences in the various trades exist. To maintain the stylistic and material authenticity of the building, the restoration team, therefore, sought Teochew craftsmen. The craftsmen would preferably work under a single specialist contractor to simplify logistical matters. The prospective specialist contractor would need to have both the capacity and capability to carry out the restoration works; he should be a craftsman in his own right and be familiar with the various trades.

Two specialist contractors were identified as potential candidates for the job. They were Cháo'ān xiàn jīnhú jiànzhú gōngchéng yǒuxiàn gōngsī 潮安縣金湖建築工程有限公司 and Shāntóu Jì Chuányīng Ancient Construction and Decoration Designing Co. Ltd. (Shāntóu shì Jǐ Chuányīng gǔ jiànzhù zhuāngshì shèjì yǒuxiàn gōngsī 山頭市紀傳英古建築裝飾設計有限公司). Both companies were based in the Teochew region of China. The secretary of the Restoration Sub-committee, Tan Siew Eng (陳秀英), corresponded with the companies, and the restoration team decided to pay a visit to China to observe their works.[11]

The trip to China took place between 19 and 22 January 2011.[12] During the trip, the team visited the restoration sites that the two specialist contractors had worked on, and enquired about the methodology employed for these restorations. In addition, the specialist contractors discussed preliminary costs with the Ngee Ann Kongsi's Restoration Sub-committee members, namely Jamie Teo Miang Yeow (張綿耀) and Richard Lee Sew-Iam (李秀炎). The Shāntóu Jì Chuányīng Ancient Construction and Decoration Designing Co. Ltd. was headed by Jì Chuányīng

Fig. 4.16. *Qiàncí* master craftsman, Xǔ Shàoxióng (許少雄), working on the roof ridge of Wak Hai Cheng Bio's entrance gateway.
Source: Photographed by Lim Shao Bin.

(紀傳英) and employed a core group of craftsmen from different trades. The company had workshops capable of milling timber and Ji was experienced in project management. The restoration team was convinced that Ji's company had the capability and the capacity to execute the restoration works under the guidance of the appointed restoration consultants. The only considerations were that the company's *qiàncí* craftsmanship could be improved and Ji's restoration methodology required guidance.

On the last day of the trip, the team travelled past Cúnxīn Shàntáng (存心善堂) where there were *qiàncí* restoration works being undertaken on its gable walls. After getting off the bus to speak to the *qiàncí* master craftsman, Xǔ Shàoxióng (許少雄),[13] three members from the team were allowed to climb the scaffolding to observe the ongoing works.[14] They were impressed with the work of Xu's team and asked for his contact details. On returning to Singapore, more research was conducted and the team discovered that Xu was well known in the trade and descended from a family of prominent *qiàncí* craftsmen. The team decided to appoint Shāntóu Jì Chuányīng Ancient Construction and Decoration Designing Co. Ltd. as the specialist contractor of the project, on the condition that Xu's team was engaged as the *qiàncí* craftsmen for the project. The Chinese specialist contractor was novated under the Singapore main contractor.

General and Structural Works

Floor levels:	No soil strengthening work was carried out as there were no active settlement issues.
Internal floorings:	Works were carried out as per the Restoration Proposal.
External floorings:	Only the granite floor slabs at the recessed entranceway of the twin shrines were removed for ground levelling. These were cleaned and reinstated. All other granite floor slabs were untouched as no soil strengthening work was required.
Internal walls:	Works were carried out as per the Restoration Proposal.
External walls:	Works were carried out as per the Restoration Proposal.
Boundary walls:	Works were carried out as per the Restoration Proposal.
Stone cantilever beams and columns:	Works were carried out as per the Restoration Proposal.
Mechanical and electrical services:	Works were carried out as per the Restoration Proposal.
Additions of new toilet facility:	Works were carried out as per the Restoration Proposal.
Removal of previously added toilet facility:	Works were carried out as per the Restoration Proposal.
Storage space:	Works were carried out as per the Restoration Proposal.
Environs:	Works were carried out as per the Restoration Proposal.

Execution of Restoration

The restoration craftsmen and general labourers worked primarily in teams according to their trades. The specialist contractor and master craftsmen were then responsible for coordinating between the different trades to ensure a seamless restoration. A registered technical officer in turn acted as the coordinator between the contractors and restoration consultants. In the rest of this section, we shall see how the restoration of Wak Hai Cheng Bio was executed by the craftsmen of the various trades.

Roof Tiling (瓦作)

The disassembly of the building began with the removal of the roof tiles. Before this, a Light Detection and Ranging (LiDAR) scan of the roof was conducted to understand the complex geometry of the inverted-hull roof. LiDAR is a surveying method that uses a laser to create a three-dimensional representation of the object. The main and sloping ridges were secured in position with scaffolding supports before the roof tiles were removed. This was to ensure that the positioning of the roof and the entire building would not be altered.

As explained in Chapter Three, there were originally two layers of Teochew clay tiles (潮州土瓦) on the roof of Wak Hai Cheng Bio. In this restoration project, the top-most layer of Teochew clay tiles was replaced with Suzhou tiles (蘇州瓦)[15], while the Teochew clay tiles were still used for the soffit. Compared to Teochew clay tiles (which are only about three to four millimetres thick), Suzhou tiles are thicker and less susceptible to breakage. In Singapore, there is a lack of skilled craftsmen to maintain the roofs of Chinese buildings. Untrained general workers would very likely damage the thin Teochew clay tiles if they do not know how to move around the roof appropriately.[16] Broken roof tiles would allow moisture into the building, and this would affect the timber structures. Since the timber trusses of the temple are highly finished, the decision was made to prioritise the prevention of moisture from reaching the timber trusses over the retention of Teochew clay tiles as the top layer of the roof. The use of the thicker Suzhou tiles did not alter the curvature or aesthetics of the temple's roof.

During this restoration, a secondary roofing system was added. Corrugated stainless steel sheets were placed between the first and second layer of roof tiles to prevent water leakage, an issue that the temple faced before the 2010 to 2014 restoration. This approach has been widely used in Singapore since the 1980s, particularly in the restoration of shophouses. It was also used in the restoration of the House of Tan Yeok Nee, a Teochew-style residential building. This secondary roofing system has been tried and tested locally and has proven to be effective in preventing water leakage, a major problem in Singapore's tropical climate.

Fig. 4.17. Light Detection and Ranging (LiDAR) scan of Wak Hai Cheng Bio's roof from the multi-storey carpark of OCBC Bank Building.
Source: Author's collection.

Fig. 4.18. Disassembly works: After the masonry roof ridge was secured in place, the roof tiles were removed before the timber trusses could be disassembled for close inspection and repairs.
Source: Author's collection.

Fig. 4.19. Tiler Wú Chǔzhāng (吳楚章) (*left*) and tiler Yáng Xīzhōu (楊錫洲) (*right*) working on the inverted hull roof at Shàngdìgōng.
Source: Author's collection.

Timberworks (木作)

There are generally two types of timber craftsmen in Chinese architecture, namely *dàmù* (大木) or carpenters and *xiǎomù* (小木) or joiners. In traditional Chinese construction, timber craftsmen were accorded a high status as buildings were essentially timber structures. The *dàmù* craftsmen worked on the structural timber components and were indispensable to the restoration of Wak Hai Cheng Bio. Their expertise was essential for the disassembly and reassembly of the building. On the other hand, the *xiǎomù* craftsmen worked on the carvings and decorative timberwork. Fewer *xiǎomù* craftsmen were employed in this restoration project as the decorative members of the temple were for the most part in reasonably good condition.

While the structural principles of *dàmù* are similar throughout Chinese architecture, different aesthetic preferences mean that the proportions of buildings are distinctive to the various regions of China. This has an impact on structural strategies, and it was, therefore, preferable to engage Teochew timber craftsmen for the restoration of this Teochew building. Teochew *xiǎomù* carving, otherwise known as gilded woodcarving (*jīnqī mùdiāo* 金漆木雕), is one of the four famous regional timber carving styles of China.[17]

One of the main concerns with regard to structural timber is the type of wood used. The 1895 building plan of Wak Hai Cheng Bio specified three types of timber, namely belian, tempanis and daru. These timbers are no longer available commercially. Since tropical hardwood was already being used in the temple, it was decided to replace damaged structural components with tropical hardwood. Therefore, the restoration's specialist contractor would need to be familiar with sourcing and processing tropical timber. The prospective specialist contractors were asked about the types of wood they used for the replacement of both structural and non-

Fig. 4.17.

Fig. 4.18.

Fig. 4.19.

Fig. 4.20.

structural components during the 2011 visit to China. Three main types of tropical timber were considered for this restoration, namely chengal, teak (柚木), and merbau (菠蘿格). Merbau was eventually chosen for the replacement of structural members, where necessary, as chengal and teak are extremely expensive. In fact, merbau has been a popular choice of timber for restoration in the Teochew region of China over the past decade. It was used in the restoration of Xiāngzi Qiáo (湘子橋; otherwise known as Guǎngjì Qiáo 廣濟橋), one of the four historic bridges of China. Merbau for the Wak Hai Cheng Bio restoration project was sourced from Indonesia and treated in China before being sent to Singapore.

For the replacement of non-structural decorative components, the restoration team was initially undecided about the type of wood to use. Hardwood except for teak is generally not suitable for fine carving. It is therefore not recommended that hardwood be used for the replacement of decorative components. While teak was a possible choice, it was not historically used in this temple. The only teakwood architectural element employed were the fascia boards, which had been newly replaced in the early 21st century. When the *xiǎomù* craftsmen arrived in Singapore, they observed that the non-structural timbers used in the temple were mainly from the camphor family (樟木). As a result, camphorwood was selected for use in the repair and replacement of non-structural timber carvings.

After the temple's timber structures were disassembled, the *dàmù* craftsmen sanded down the beams to remove the inappropriate Suzhou style paintings from the 1994 to 1997 renovation. They also checked the structural members for wet rot and termite infestation. Affected timbers were disposed of immediately after documentation to prevent the spread of termites. Original timbers that were still in good condition, including smaller members such as the rafters and purlins, were retained and reused. The craftsmen then went on to shape the entire length of the log to the desired shape, as well as construct mortises and tenons for structural timber members requiring replacement. In the Restoration Proposal, it was originally recommended to remove the "L-shaped" brackets supporting the newly consolidated pseudo-beam panels. After the *xiǎomù* and *dàmù* craftsmen consulted with the structural engineer, it was decided to keep the "L-shaped" brackets instead of creating new tenons at both ends of each panel. This was to ensure the structural strength of the panels, which act as stiffeners to resist bending moments in the beam-column joints. The extant historical panels in Wak Hai Cheng Bio were so finely carved that full-relief carvings extended all the way to the edge of the panels

Fig. 4.20. Carpenter Lǐ Xiánzhōng (李鹹忠) (*left*) and carpenter Wú Zhàoxīn (吳兆新) (*right*) chiseling merbau logs to create mortises.
Source: Author's collection.

and were extremely close to the tenon position; there was no way new tenons could be constructed without weakening the panels.

In the meantime, the *xiǎomù* craftsmen were busy with a number of tasks. They cleaned up the existing timber and worked on decorative timber ornamentations in need of replacement or repair, including one of the lion-shaped struts (*shīzuò* 獅座)[18]. During this process, there were differing opinions over the repair or replacement of some of the deteriorated timber components. An example of this was the four "hanging baskets" strut or *huātǒng* (花筒)[19] at the front elevation of the twin shrines, which were found to have different degrees of wet rot and termite infestation in their mortise portions. *Huātǒng* is a form of hanging strut. The restoration strategy for this temple was to retain the original building fabric unless structural integrity was compromised. However, the degree of deterioration of the *huātǒng* was unclear. The craftsmen believed that they could be repaired by removing and replacing the rotten parts with new timber; the old and new timber could be connected using splice joints. On the other hand, the site supervisor suspected the structural integrity of the *huātǒng* would be compromised if too much of the original timber was removed. The restoration team thus decided to engage an arborist, Derek Yap of Camphora Pte. Ltd., to conduct a resistograph® test to determine the density of the timber. A drill needle 1.5 millimetres in diameter was driven into the *huātǒng* to establish the density of the timber at various depths. It was concluded that the original timber was strong enough for the *huātǒng* to be repaired using the method suggested by the craftsmen.

Fig. 4.21.

Non-Decorative Rendering and Plastering (圬作)

The *wūzuò* (圬作) craftsmen were responsible for the non-decorative rendering and plaster works (*mǒhuīgōng* 抹灰工) in Wak Hai Cheng Bio. Firstly, the wall tiles in the interiors of the twin shrines and the cement concrete rendering added during the 1994 to 1997 renovation were removed, but earlier pure or hydraulic lime renders and plasters were kept. This was followed by the application of chemical waterproofing, which is highly essential for historic buildings without a damp-proof course such as Wak Hai Cheng Bio. The temple also had a serious rising damp issue. All vertical walls were therefore treated with chemical waterproofing to prevent rising damp. This was achieved by drilling holes at approximately 300 millimetres above ground level on both sides of the wall at a downward angle of 30 to 45 degrees. The waterproofing chemical was then introduced into the walls through these holes. For this treatment to be effective, the chemical needed to cover the entire

Fig. 4.21. Joiner Zhèng Kǎilín (鄭凱霖) carving a lion-shaped strut in camphorwood to replace a badly deteriorated strut.
Source: Author's collection.

Fig. 4.22.

Fig. 4.23.

length of the wall such that moisture could not travel up from any part of the structure.

After the waterproofing works had been completed, the craftsmen began plastering and rendering the non-decorative walls of the temple with a lime-based plaster or render. Historically, the source of lime in Teochew and Hokkien architecture has been seashells. This is due to the proximity of the two regions to the sea, and hence the abundance of seashells. Oyster shells are used to produce oyster lime (*bèihuī* 貝灰). For the restoration of Wak Hai Cheng Bio, the specialist contractor ordered a batch of specially manufactured oyster shell lime powder.[20] This was to ensure the purity of the lime powder, as most ready-made oyster lime currently on the market contains a large amount of additives. The form of oyster lime imported into Singapore for this restoration was hydrated lime, that is, lime that has already been slaked with water.

Bricklaying, Brick Masonry and Floor Tiling (磚作)

Based on old photographs, the front and main halls of the temple were historically paved with square terracotta floor tiles, while the prayer halls were paved with hexagonal ones. These were replaced by mosaic tiles probably in the 1960s or 1970s given the popularity of these tiles at the time. During the 1994 to 1997 renovation, square terracotta floor tiles were reinstated within the twin shrines. During the 2010 to 2014 restoration, the square terracotta tiles were removed to waterproof the floor of the twin shrines. Waterproofing works were necessary to address the rising damp issues.

Fig. 4.22. Interiors of Tiānhòugōng before the 2010–2014 restoration. The floor was finished in square terracotta tiles.
Source: Author's collection.

Fig. 4.23. Interiors of Tiānhòugōng after the 2010–2014 restoration. The floor at the front hall was finished in diagonal terracotta tiling pattern while the prayer hall was finished in hexagonal terracotta tiles.
Source: Photographed by Ung Ruey Loon.

Some of the tiles were already found to be chipped before the removal. Hence, it was decided to replace all floor tiles within the shrines with newly fabricated ones. Handmade square and hexagonal terracotta floor tiles were specially ordered and reinstated according to their historical state. The hexagonal tiles were made based on an early hexagonal tile sample found in the temple's storeroom. The decision was to order handmade tiles instead of machine-made ones as the latter are too cleanly cut and finished. Since the restoration approach was to restore the temple based on its mid-1890s state, handmade tiles were deemed more appropriate.

Stone Masonry (石作)

The stone masonry in Wak Hai Cheng Bio was generally in very good shape and did not require any repair or replacement. The only works done were a minor realignment of the granite wall at the main entrance gateway and the granite floor slabs at the recessed entranceway of Shàngdìgōng. Both realignments were performed to address the differential settlement of the temple; the structure had since settled and stabilised. At the recessed entranceway of Shàngdìgōng, the granite slabs were removed, and the ground compacted before the slabs were replaced. Minor cleaning of all the masonry within the temple using water and a neutral pH detergent was also undertaken.

Decorative Plastering and Pargeting (灰塑)

During this restoration, the lowest panels on the recessed entranceways on the front elevation of the twin

Fig. 4.24.

Fig. 4.25.

Fig. 4.24. Fresco master craftsman Lín Mùkūn (林慕坤) painting a lower panel after pargetting master craftsman Xiè Qìngshēng (謝慶升) finished the vase with auspicious motifs parget.
Source: Photographed by Lim Shao Bin.

Fig. 4.25. Fresco master craftsman Lín Mùkūn (林慕坤) painting on the middle panel after conservation treatment.
Source: Photographed by Lim Shao Bin.

shrines were reconstructed. These panels were painted over in white between the 1950s and the mid-1990s and were remade during the 1994 to 1997 renovation. It was decided not to keep these panels as the proportions and aesthetics of the decorative elements were incorrect. Moreover, the panels were cast in cement concrete, contributing to the rising damp problem by locking moisture in the walls. Hence, it was deemed better to reconstruct the panels. The reconstruction was carried out by craftsmen from the *huīsù* (灰塑) or pargeting trade. Using historical photographs, it was determined that the motifs depicted in the lowest panels were a vase, flowers, brushes and other auspicious motifs. These motifs were similarly present in the panels from the mid-1990s renovation, albeit with different workmanship. During this restoration, the same motifs were retained, but the proportions and style employed during the mid-1990s renovation were abandoned. The craftsmen were given the artistic license to re-interpret the proportions and colour of these panels. They drew out the life-size cartoons of the motifs based on their knowledge of the Teochew decorative plastering tradition. These were then transferred to the panels after they were approved by the restoration consultant. The vase and borders of the panels were decorated in a geometric style known as *bógǔwén* (博古紋).

The middle panels at the recessed entranceways on the front elevation of the twin shrines are historical figurative works. The whitewashing of the lowest panels, done some time between the 1950s and mid-1990s, did not affect the middle panels. During this restoration, these panels were restored rather than reconstructed as they were relatively intact, with the exception of a few portions that had been badly restored earlier or damaged by the rising damp. The original pargeting and painting were superb, even though the panels had been weathered by dust and incense stains, and the colours appeared duller due to deterioration. The lime plaster substrate had also degenerated due to the age of the panels. This was exacerbated by the rising damp problem, which resulted in a friable substrate.

To resolve these issues, the surface of the fresco was first cleaned with distilled water and cotton swabs. The entire middle panels were then consolidated chemically, and the badly restored panel borders removed. Following this, the missing figurine heads and the panel borders were reinstated. At this point, the restoration team had to decide how best to restore and treat the old and new fresco paintings of the middle panels. One option was to keep the old and new work distinct from each other such that the difference between them would be obvious to the untrained eye. This approach, while in keeping with the principles of many heritage conservation charters, was eventually not adopted since one of the restoration objectives was to preserve the temple as a living monument. Both the owner of the temple and its devotees would have deemed this approach unworthy of honouring their deities. The second option was to paint over the panels. This would, however, not retain the material authenticity of the panels as the original painting would be covered by the new. The solution adopted ultimately was to partially repaint the panels. A layer of reversible protective coating was first applied to the entire panels.[21] The foreground and the figurines in the midground were then repainted over the protective coating. The largely intact background was left untouched so that the original brushwork and craftsmanship were visible. Due to the application of the protective coating, the traditional method of fresco painting could not be used to repaint the foreground and the midground. The secco method, in which painting was done on dry plaster, was used instead. In addition, the borders of the middle panels were all newly reconstructed. Each panel took one month to restore. The uppermost pargeted pseudo-truss panels were cleaned and repainted.

The panels in the non-recessed portions of the front elevation of the twin shrines were mainly conserved and refinished. While removing the cracked plaster at the borders of the middle panels in this area of the Shàngdìgōng, it was discovered that this portion of the building had previously been decorated with plaster fish motifs. The original fish motifs that remained in good condition were kept and consolidated, while the missing ones were reinstated.

Besides this, the *huīsù* craftsmen also worked on the gable mouldings (*shānqiáng zhuāngshì* 山牆裝飾) of Wak Hai Cheng Bio. The temple was previously surrounded by shophouses, which were subsequently redeveloped into skyscrapers. As its party walls once abutted these shophouses, there were originally no exposed exterior gable walls. As such, the temple did not have any exterior gable mouldings. With the demolition of the abutting shophouses, the gable ends had become visible. The undecorated gable walls made them appear incomplete. As one of the restoration objectives was to restore the temple as a living monument, it was important that the temple looked complete and worthy of its status as a house of the deities for the devotees. It was therefore decided to create the gable mouldings to complete the building. Before the internal walls of the twin shrines were tiled, there were internal gable mouldings where the purlins meet the gable walls. These were reinstated during this restoration. Both the internal and external gable mouldings were kept simple so that it would be obvious that they are new and not architectural survivors from the mid-1890s.

The materials used for the pargeting works were a lime-based mixture similar to the one used for the non-decorative plastering and rendering works. Besides the oyster shell lime, the craftsmen added sand, hide glue (*niújiāo* 牛膠), alum (*míngfán* 明礬), water and paper fibre to form the pargeting mixture for the surface render finish. This mixture is otherwise known as paper fibre lime or *zhǐjīnhuī* (紙筋灰). Natural plant fibres, which are typically long and strong, are added to provide tensile strength and to prevent cracking. The paper fibre made from the bark of the mulberry tree is preferred for its long fibre and high tensile strength. For finer pargeting works such as the faces of the figurines, cigarette paper, which has more delicate cellulose fibres, was used in place of mulberry paper. Hide glue was added as a binding agent, while alum acted as a paint fixative and a preservative for the hide glue.[22] In addition, the craftsmen added a small amount of sugar to the mixture to improve its workability. Sugar is a plasticiser that delays the curing of lime such that the craftsmen would have more time to work with the material. A small amount of Portland cement was also added to the mixture used to create the dragon and tiger wall mouldings.[23]

A new boundary wall was also reconstructed during this restoration to suit the overall Teochew architectural style of the temple. The extant boundary wall from 1979 was insensitive to the overall architectural style of the building. In contrast to the solid white walls, which completely segregated the temple's interiors from the outside world in the traditional Teochew building, the 1979 wall was punctuated with openings through which the temple could be seen. In addition, green glazed tiles and green bamboo grilles were used. This was in stark contrast to the plain white boundary walls of the mid-1890s temple. It was therefore decided to reinstate plain walls during this restoration in the interests of stylistic unity and historical fidelity. Besides other decorative plastering works, the *huīsù* craftsmen were also responsible for creating the mouldings on the boundary walls. An oyster shell lime-based mixture was also used here. The new mouldings were made simpler than the ones shown in historical photographs so that the reconstructed boundary walls would not be mistaken for the original

Fig. 4.26.

structure. This was especially important given that parts of the reconstructed boundary walls did not exist historically, as there were once shophouses abutting the temple.

Clay Moulding (泥塑)

The *nídīng* (泥丁)[24] or clay figurines in the temple were the product of a composite craft. Although the craft is closely related to *nísù* (泥塑) or clay moulding, it also encompasses the trades of plaster moulding or *huīsù* (灰塑) and fresco painting (灰塑彩繪). Yet it is different as it may involve *qiàncí* (嵌瓷) and copper filigree works. Each figurine demonstrates a combination of these crafts. *Nídīng* can be found in the vertical panels beside the dragon wall (龍堵) and dragon fenestrations of Shàngdìgōng. The figurines were relatively intact thanks to their location within niches. The missing figurines were mostly in the more accessible areas, suggesting that their loss was likely a result of vandalism. According to the previous temple caretaker, this was the reason for the installation of anodised aluminium-framed glass to protect the niches.[25] The presence of the glass caused a lack of ventilation, which resulted in the degradation of the *nídīng*. The lack of ventilation triggered the build-up of moisture and subsequent salt crystallisation within the recessed shelves. The plasterworks thus became friable, which affected the fresco paintings and resulted in pieces of *qiàncí* work falling off.

For this restoration, the extant figurines were restored by the fresco master craftsman. He first brushed off the salt crystals and applied some weak lime plaster onto the affected figurines. The weak lime plaster absorbed the remaining salt in this process of consolidation. The weak lime plaster was then removed and the necessary parts replastered. Following this, the craftsman touched up the fresco painting, reattached the detached *qiàncí* pieces, and redid all the copper filigree. The old copper filigree had corroded beyond salvageability.

Based on the existing gaps in the composition and oral accounts of the temple caretaker, it was clear that there were missing figurines. The caretaker was unfortunately unable to provide more details regarding the missing figurines. As the gaps were obvious, it was decided to recreate figurines to fill them. The fresco craftsmen were not confident of doing the work and a *nísù* master craftsman from Dàwú (大吳), a Teochew town famous for the *nísù* craft, was therefore engaged. After a visit to Wak Hai Cheng Bio, the *nísù* master craftsman moulded the maquettes on-site and recreated the figurines in his Dàwú workshop. The maquettes had to be slightly bigger than the intended figurine as they would shrink after firing. The newly recreated figurines were fired clay figurines without any *qiàncí*, fresco, or filigree work. This was mainly

Fig. 4.26. Fresco craftsman Chéng Péiguāng (程培光) putting final finishes to a restored *nídīng* (泥丁) panel.
Source: Photographed by Lim Shao Bin.

Fig. 4.27.

because the master craftsman was not confident in his ability to create composite figurines. Moreover, this served to make the differences between the newly added figurines and historical *nídīng* obvious.

After the restoration and recreation of the *nídīng* figurines, the decision was made to continue covering the recessed shelves with glass. This was to reduce the risk of damage through vandalism. This time, frameless glass was used so that there would be ventilation gaps to prevent moisture from being trapped in the recesses. The lack of frame also allowed visitors to better appreciate the figurines.

Qiàncí (嵌瓷)

The overall state of the *qiàncí* was highly deteriorated and it was obvious that the repairs from the mid-1990s were of low quality. The deterioration was partly caused by age, but more significant damage had been caused by previous inappropriate repairs using Portland cement. Before restoration works began, the *qiàncí* craftsmen measured and documented the dimensions and positions of the extant *qiàncí* relative to the ridge and sloping roofs.[26] At the same time, the *qiàncí* were labelled. This was followed by the removal of the *qiàncí* from the roof slopes and sloping ridges. The pieces were wrapped, labelled, and put into storage. The *qiàncí* on the main ridge remained in situ.

The restoration of all the existing *qiàncí* was briefly considered. However, this option was quickly abandoned after considering the practicality of implementing it. This process would also have entailed the removal of the extant Portland cement repairs, which were rather extensive. Little original material would remain after the Portland cement repairs were removed. Furthermore, there would be adhesion issues between the old and the new plasters. This would be exacerbated by huge diurnal temperature differences, which cause substantial thermal movement of plaster, resulting in plaster drop-off. In addition, it would have been very costly and difficult to match the colour of the new *qiàncí* shards with the old ones. Hence, the decision was made to completely replicate most of the *qiàncí* instead of restoring them.

The *qiàncí* craftsmen replicated the *qiàncí* figurines and towers based on documentation data from the mid-1990s, as well as data collected before the restoration began. However, there was missing information due to the deteriorated condition of the *qiàncí* at the time of documentation. The missing information included the details of the heads and hands of figurines, the streamers on the flags carried by the warrior figurines, and paintings on individual ceramic pieces. Some

Fig. 4.27. Clay figurines made by Wú Déxiáng (吴德祥), a *nísù* master craftsman from Dàwú (大吴).
Source: Photographed by Lim Shao Bin.

Competitive Timberwork Construction in Wak Hai Cheng Bio

Competitive construction, also known as *duìchǎng zuò* 對場作 or *pīnchǎng zuò* 拼場作 in Chinese, refers to the construction of a single building by two different teams of craftsmen. The building is divided along a central line, with each team working on corresponding mirrored components of the building. The imaginary line dividing the building can be either along the north–south axis (split into left and right sides) or the east–west axis (split into front and back). While the building must come together in the middle, each team is free to use differing forms, styles and even techniques in their half of the building. While this style of construction is by no means limited to timberwork, it is most commonly found in the work of carpenters and joiners. The resulting building will showcase a variety of architectural expressions in the details of its components and yet maintain a coherent architectural language at the building scale.[1]

This form of cooperative competition is prevalent in southern China, particularly in the Minnan (閩南) and Chaozhou (潮州) regions, and was brought to Southeast Asia, including Singapore, by Teochew and Hokkien migrants.[2] While such construction arrangement exists in other parts of China, it is known differently from that of southern China. In Jiangsu and Zhejiang, it is known as *pīzuò zuò* 劈作做.

The origin of this unusual system of construction is not known. However, there are two plausible reasons as to how it may have evolved. The first of which is that time constraints may have rendered it impossible for a single construction team to complete a project on time, necessitating the introduction of an additional team to the site. In such a case, the degree of cooperation would be higher than the degree of competition. The division of the building into mirroring halves on the left and right along the north–south axis is perhaps suggestive of the second reason, which is a competitive arrangement that aims to foster a better-finished building with a higher degree of craftsmanship.[3] The division of the building down the north–south axis renders it easier for onlookers to compare the techniques and craftsmanship of the two different teams and decide which team's craftmanship was superior. Typically, there would be a cash reward for the winning team. In Singapore, the results of this competitive construction arrangement can be seen in Thian Hock Keng, Hong San See and Wak Hai Cheng Bio.

In the case of Wak Hai Cheng Bio, evidence of this can be observed at the Shrine of the Goddess of the Sea or Tiānhòugōng (天后宫), the Shrine of the Mysterious Supreme Emperor of Heaven or Shàngdìgōng (上帝宫), and the entrance gateway or *ménlóu* (門樓). As there are no surviving documentary records detailing the temple's reconstruction, it is unknown how many teams were involved in the project. Were two teams responsible for the entire temple, or were there two teams competing within each shrine and the entrance gateway? Alternatively, could there have been some form of competitive elimination in which two teams competed on one building, with the winner moving on to construct another building with another team?

A close inspection of the buildings provides some clues. Within Tiānhòugōng, there are no perceivable differences in craftsmanship, style and technique

Fig. BS08.1. Carved timber cantilever arms in the form of phoenixes (*fèngtuō* 鳳托) supporting circular transverse purlins on the western side of the prayer hall in the Shrine of the Mysterious Supreme Emperor of Heaven, or Shàngdìgōng (上帝宫). The wings of the phoenixes have bas-relief feathers.
Source: Photographed by Lim Shao Bin.

Fig. BS08.2. Carved timber phoenix cantilever arms on the eastern side of the prayer hall of the Shrine of the Mysterious Supreme Emperor of Heaven, or Shàngdìgōng (上帝宫). These phoenixes have filigree-type wings and carry baskets in their beaks.
Source: Photographed by Lim Shao Bin.

Fig. BS08.1.

Fig. BS08.2.

Fig. BS08.3.

in the timberworks. However, in Shàngdìgōng, differences can be seen, especially in the roof truss of the prayer hall or *bàitíng* (拜亭). For example, there are four sets of carved timber cantilever arms supporting four circular transverse purlins on either side of the prayer hall. On the western side, the four cantilever arms are carved as phoenixes (*fèngtuō* 鳳托).[4] On the eastern side, two cantilever arms are carved as phoenixes carrying baskets in their beaks while the other two cantilever arms have highly carved brackets placed on top of the arms in the longitudinal direction. The phoenixes' wings on both sides are also executed differently, with those on the eastern side having filigree-type wings. These differences in the execution of the timberwork can also be seen in the four phoenix cantilever arms at the entrance gateway. The truss at the entrance gateway is physically separated into front and back portions by the stone doorway. Interestingly, the differences between the two halves are only perceivable at the rear truss. While the two phoenixes on the front truss are similar in form and style, the eastern and western phoenixes on the rear truss are carved differently. It is, therefore, possible that the competition in the entrance gateway began with the rear truss, with the winner being awarded the task of completing the front truss.

Two fundamental conditions must be met before such an arrangement is possible. The building owner(s) must have the necessary financial means to employ two groups of craftsmen. The cost of this endeavour is not related to the total number of craftsmen on site but rather in employing two master craftsmen who are capable of coordinating the sizing and joining details of critical components, rather than just one. There must have been a sizeable number of master craftsmen and their teams working in the region to make this competitive construction feasible.

Fig. BS08.3. The cantilever arms on the eastern and western sides at the front hall of the Shrine of the Mysterious Supreme Emperor of Heaven, or Shàngdìgōng (上帝宮) are distinctively different.
Source: Photographed by Lim Shao Bin.

of these problems were more pressing than others. The craftsmen were able to easily recreate the streamers based on the few remnant samples found on site. Missing figurine heads posed a greater challenge as each figurine's head was orientated differently and featured different expressions, headgear and facial features. The craftsmen would need to rely on their expertise and the traditions of the craft to recreate these missing parts. They were able to postulate the orientation of the various figurines' heads based on the posture of their bodies. The headgear and facial expressions of the figures were also extrapolated from their clothing.

The recreation of the temple's *qiàncí* was separated into two main parts, namely in situ and off-site replication. All *qiàncí* located on the main ridge and sloping ridges were replicated in situ. There are in total four dragons on the two main ridges of the front hall of the twin shrines. The Portland cement from an earlier repair was removed but the form of the dragons was kept without any remoulding performed. Originally, only one side of the dragons was covered with ceramic shards, on the front elevation of the building. The other side of the dragons were simply painted over as they were not visible to the public before the surrounding shophouses were demolished. During this restoration, both sides of the dragons were covered with ceramic shards because the rear sides were now visible from Church Street and the surrounding skyscrapers. Since the building was to continue to serve as a living temple, it was deemed best to make the dragon *qiàncí* and the building look complete.

The other figurines were replicated off-site before being installed on the roof. The craftsmen first used

Fig. 4.28.

metal wires to create the overall frames of the figurine. They then created the forms of the figurine using lime plaster and pieces of fired clay made from Teochew clay tiles cut with pliers. The lime plaster mixture used contained mulberry paper fibre. A terracotta tile was placed behind the figurines to act as a support so that they could remain upright while the craftsmen worked on the rest of the parts; this step was necessary as the legs of the figurines were unable to support their weight. The heads of the figurines were moulded separately out of cigarette paper lime plaster and painted using the fresco method. Following this, the craftsmen cut ceramic shards from specially fired bowls using pliers. These bowls are glazed only on the outside, with the insides remaining unglazed. The porous and rough surface of the inner side provides the grip necessary for the adhesion of the ceramic shards to the lime plaster forms of the figurines. These specially fired bowls are made as such because they have three different curvatures, allowing for myriad

Fig. 4.28. *Qiàncí* craftsman Mǎ Gěngzhōng (馬耿忠), the cousin of Xǔ Shàoxióng, working on the dragon *qiàncí* on the roof ridge.
Source: Photographed by Lim Shao Bin.

Fig. 4.29.

shapes to be cut from them. The different curvatures are found at the rim, the body, and the base of the bowl. After the ceramic shards are cut out, they are adhered to the figurines to create their clothing. Up to this point, the works were carried out in the workshop of the master craftsman, Xǔ Shàoxióng, in China before being shipped to Singapore. The figurines were secured in padded timber crates for shipment. The *qiàncí* figurines were partially replicated off-site as there was a lack of space on-site in Singapore for a workshop. This off-site replication could only be carried out as there was good documentation data available including the dimensions and visual representations of the *qiàncí*. After the figurines arrived in Singapore, the craftsmen worked on the finer parts. These included the streamers on the figurines, the hems of their clothing, and motif paintings on the ceramic shards. For some of these finer parts, such as the streamers and the command tokens (*lìngpái* 令牌), white porcelain teacups were used in place of ceramic shards from bowls. During installation, the craftsman removed the terracotta backing tiles from the figurine with a skilful strike of the mallet. Following this, the figurines were installed onto the roof of the temple using lime plaster.

A small portion of the extant *qiàncí* was restored instead of being replicated. These were located on the main ridges of the main halls of both shrines and were found to be in good condition; most ceramic shards on these portions remained intact. This was probably because this part of the roof had less exposure to direct sunlight; the rear building provided the area with some shade during parts of the day. Moreover, there was no interference caused by inappropriate materials as no repairs with Portland cement were carried out at this location. The oldest *qiàncí* work in the temple can therefore be found here. This *qiàncí* is visible from level two of the rear building. Since they were highly intact, they could be conserved in situ without the need for replication. Minor missing parts were replaced with old ceramic shards salvaged from the roofs of the front halls of the twin shrines, where the *qiàncí* were to be replicated.

Architectural Surface Finishing

Architectural surface finishing generally refers to the painting and gilding of building surfaces. In Wak Hai Cheng Bio, three main types of surface finishing were applied:

1. Non-decorative painting
2. Fresco painting
3. Lacquering and gilding

Fig. 4.29. Warrior figurine *qiàncí* made by Xǔ Shàoxióng. Source: Photographed by Lim Shao Bin.

Non-Decorative Water-Based Painting ("灰水"粉刷)

The plastered wall surfaces of buildings constructed before the 20th century would have been generally rendered in limewash. Such plastered wall surfaces historically constituted the bulk of the wall finishes within Wak Hai Cheng Bio. This is based on the understanding that plastered walls in traditional Teochew architecture are rendered in white limewash; historical black-and-white photographs showing the temple's plastered walls in a light tone and an on-site paint sampling conducted in 2010 similarly suggested that the plain plastered walls of the temple were white.

Limewash is made up of slaked lime diluted with water. In the course of Wak Hai Cheng Bio's architectural history, emulsion paint was used instead of limewash when the former became more readily available. Emulsion paint was generally preferred over limewash as the latter had to be slaked and its consistency is difficult to control. As previously mentioned, the wall tiles within the shrines were removed and white plastered walls were reinstated. It was decided not to use emulsion paint as the high polymer content in contemporary emulsion paints causes the paint to coalesce, forming a continuous polymer film. This gives the paint a waterproofing quality. Although this prevents rainwater from entering the walls, it also traps moisture within the wall. If the wall is not allowed to "breathe", it will eventually result in deterioration of the building fabric. This is especially the case with historic buildings. It is thus desirable to have a paint system that allows moisture to escape.

While the restoration team initially considered using the traditional limewash, this option was eventually not adopted due to the difficulty in controlling the quality and consistency of the limewash, factors that are essential for ensuring uniform coverage. In addition, limewash needs to be refreshed frequently, that is, once every few years. It was finally decided to use potassium silicate paint. Silicate paint is petrified by binding to any silicate (sand) within the substrate, forming a micro-crystalline structure and resulting in a breathable finish. This chemical process makes the paint integral to the substrate, rather than being a coating. Silicate paint was used on all plain plastered surfaces in Wak Hai Cheng Bio during this round of restoration.

Non-Decorative Oil-Based Painting (油漆)

Oil-based paint was mainly applied to timber and metal surfaces. This included the timber rafters, purlins, beams, window frames, casement screen doors and metal window grilles at the rear building. In the past, the craftsmen would have mixed their own tung oil-based paint. Alkyd resin paint was used in place of a self-mixed blend in this restoration to ensure uniformity.

Fresco Painting (灰塑彩繪)

Fresco paintings were historically found at the dragon and tiger walls and the dragon and phoenix fenestrations of both shrines. During the 1994 to 1997 renovation, these were replaced with newly fabricated granite panels. The bodies of the tiger and the dragon are conventionally orientated to face the main entrance of the shrine, while their heads turn to face one another or the deities. However, the new granite tiger motifs were incorrectly orientated. Since both the materials and orientation of the tiger motifs were not historically accurate, it was decided to remove the granite walls and fenestrations and to reinstate the fresco painted plaster mouldings. This reinstatement was to be informed by historical photographs taken just before the mid-1990s renovation. These photographs showed the plaster mouldings in a deteriorated state with a recent colour scheme. For the most recent restoration, the craftsmen were instructed to keep the form of the

Fig. 4.30.

plaster mouldings as shown in the photographs but use their artistic license with a traditional colour palette to complete the work.

Another part of the temple that was historically decorated with fresco work was the middle panels of the non-recessed portion of the twin shrines' front elevation. These frescos were whitewashed at some point between the 1950s and the early 1990s and painted with floral and landscape motifs during the 1994 to 1997 renovation. By 2010, these paintings were in a highly deteriorated state. This made it impossible to decipher the types of flowers and landscapes painted during the mid-1990s. It was similarly unclear from historical photographs what the original mid-1890s motifs were. Considering these circumstances, it was decided to continue painting the panels in floral and landscape themes. The four panels at Tiānhòugōng were fresco painted with plum blossoms, orchids, bamboo and chrysanthemums (*méilán zhújú* 梅蘭竹菊) respectively. The four flowers are known as the "four gentlemen (*sì jūnzǐ* 四君子)" and they signify the virtues of a gentleman. On the other hand, the Shàngdìgōng panels were fresco painted with landscape scenes from the four seasons of spring, summer, autumn and winter (*chūnxià qiūdōng* 春夏秋冬). The two sets of motifs were chosen as they are common themes in Chinese iconography.

Lacquering and Gilding (髹漆貼金)

After the timber beams were sanded down to remove the Suzhou-style paintings that were done in the 1994 to 1997 restoration and to smoothen the surfaces, they were painted with at least two layers of black lacquer. Following this, the craftsmen laid their cartoon patterns on the beams, punctured the cartoons with a needle, and chalked them to transfer the patterns onto the beams. These cartoons were drawn out earlier by the craftsmen and approved by the restoration consultant. With the desired patterns on the beam, a gilding adhesive known as size was then applied to parts that were to be gilded. Gold leaf was then applied to the

Fig. 4.30. The granite tiger wall (*top*) in Tiānhòugōng with the incorrect tiger orientation was replaced with the fresco painted plaster tiger wall (*bottom*) during the 2010–2014 restoration.
Source: Photographed by Ung Ruey Loon (*top*) and Lim Shao Bin (*bottom*).

Fig. 4.31.

Fig. 4.32.

Fig. 4.33.

beams. The parts without the adhesive beneath were removed with a brush. The craftsmen were instructed not to perform perfect gilding work and to leave the gilt unburnished. This was to blend the old and new gilding, minimising the contrast between them. The extant decorative timber carvings that remained in good condition were cleaned. Lost areas were then regilded. Previously ungilded areas remained so.

The main doors of both shrines and the ceremonial doors between their respective front and prayer halls were made of wooden planks joined by tongues and grooves. The joint lines were covered using a technique known as *dìzhàng* (地丈). A layer of hemp (*mábù* 麻布) was first wrapped around the joined planks and a thin layer of lime plaster was applied. Following this, the doors were dried and smoothened by sanding. After the dust had been cleaned off, three layers of lacquer were applied in a hot and humid environment. The lacquer was left to dry, after which the lacquered doors were polished with a very fine grade of sandpaper. For this restoration project and other important Teochew architecture, the craftsmen used their hands instead of sandpaper to perform this final round of polishing. The

Fig. 4.31. Cartoon of the beams' gilding motif painted on vellum paper.
Source: Author's collection.

Fig. 4.32. Painter Chén Yuèqún (陳躍群) drawing the cartoon of a Door God.
Source: Photographed by Lim Shao Bin.

Fig. 4.33. Painter Chén Yuèqún (陳躍群) adding the final touches to his Door God painting.
Source: Photographed by Lim Shao Bin.

Fig. 4.34.

craftsmen would first rub the Teochew clay tiles with their palms to transfer some of the very fine powdery clay dust from the tiles to their hands. They then used their dust-covered palms to polish the lacquered surface. Thereafter, the lacquered surface was polished using a cloth and tung oil. The doors were then ready to receive further decorative works.

As the proportions of the Door Gods on the main doors of the twin shrines painted during the 1994 to 1997 renovation were inaccurate, it was decided to repaint them during this restoration. The Door Gods were created through a mixture of gilding and polychromatic oil-based painting. The craftsmen first sketched out a cartoon of the Door Gods on paper, taking care to ensure the correct proportions. The pattern was then transferred to the doors. The gilding techniques used here were the same as the ones used for the beams.

According to the memories of the trustees and devotees who frequented the temple, the ceremonial doors between the front and main halls of Shàngdìgōng and Tiānhòugōng depicted civil officials and ladies-in-waiting respectively. No pre-1990s photographs of the ceremonial doors were found. There was thus no documentary evidence for this tradition. In the absence of other evidence, the restoration team decided to retain these figures, supported by oral accounts. After some discussion with the craftsmen, the restoration team opted to use a traditional Teochew technique known as incised gilding (*tiěxiànmiáo* 鐵線描). Firstly, chalk was

Fig. 4.35.

Fig. 4.34. Painter Qiū Jǐnbō (邱錦波) using a metal stylus to incise patterns on the gilding.
Source: Photographed by Lim Shao Bin.

Fig. 4.35. Details of the Door God (*top*) and civil official (*bottom*) door paintings.
Source: Photographed by Lim Shao Bin.

mixed with animal glue to draw the outlines of the figures. The craftsman then applied gold leaf to the door with an oil-based size. Following this, a metal stylus was used to draw out the patterns on the gold leaf, creating a slight incision on the surface of the gold. A variation of the technique where the metal stylus creates incisions on the lacquered surface prior to gilding was also used. Black paint was then applied to the incised parts. Finally, the craftsman used a burnishing tool to polish the surface of the gilding.

Fig. 4.36.

Modern Mechanical and Electrical (M&E) Additions

Just prior to the 2010 to 2014 restoration, surface wiring was visible throughout the temple. This is unsurprising given that the temple did not originally have electricity. The twin shrines of the temple were rebuilt in the mid-1890s before the first regular supply of electricity to consumers in Singapore began in March 1906.[27] Electricity was introduced into the temple only later. Before this restoration, fluorescent lighting tubes were hung from the timber trusses with their wires exposed. There was thus a challenge in lighting the temple without exposed wiring, especially given that the building was not originally designed for electrification. Six rounds of lighting mock-ups were carried out to determine the type of luminaires to use, the location of lights, the angle of illumination, the lux level, the wiring paths, and other technical decisions.

Since this was going to be a full-scale restoration, the decision was made to holistically consider the lighting scheme of the building, that is, from both aesthetic and functional viewpoints. The overall strategy was to create a lighting scheme that mimicked the lighting conditions of lanterns and candles. A warm colour temperature was therefore favoured over the cool light of fluorescent tubes. The lux level was also kept low to mimic candle lighting. The highest lux level in the temple was employed in the alcoves of the deities such that one's eyes are naturally drawn to the deities upon entering the relatively dark shrines.

Cylindrical light-emitting diode (LED) downlights were hung at various locations within the shrines to provide functional lighting. Along the walls in the front and main halls, LED wall-washers were installed on the floor. They illuminate the white walls with light, thereby providing reflected light for the shrines; reflected light is important in creating a certain ambience within the shrines. One of the highlights of the Wak Hai Cheng Bio is the excellent craftsmanship of its decorative ornamentations, especially its timber carvings. LED spotlights and LED strip lights were thus installed to

Fig. 4.36. The night lighting scheme of Shàngdìgōng.
Source: Photographed by Lim Shao Bin.

highlight portions of the timber truss carvings; these light fittings were hidden in the trusses.

All fittings chosen were black in colour and simple in shape. This helped ensure that they blended in aesthetically in places where it was impossible to conceal them entirely. Wires were generally lined on the top surfaces of timber beams and trusses. Where technically feasible and not damaging to the historical fabric, the wires were also concealed within plain plastered walls and under terracotta floor tiles. The same principle was adopted for the temple's water supply and management, with pipes largely concealed underground.

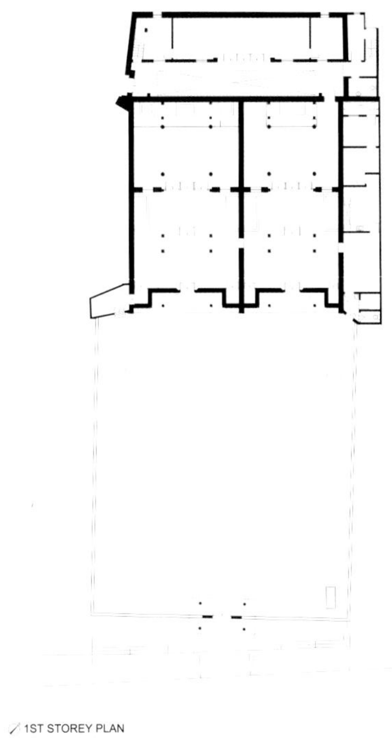

Fig. 4.37.

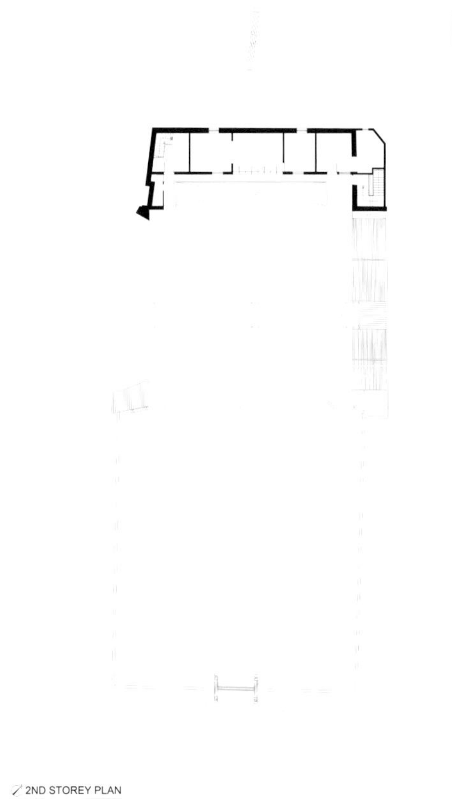

Fig. 4.38.

Fig. 4.37. First storey plan of Wak Hai Cheng Bio.
Source: Illustrated by Hsieh Mei-En; base illustration adapted from restoration drawings by Shāntóu Jì Chuányīng Ancient Construction and Decoration Designing Co. Ltd (山頭市紀傳英古建築裝飾設計有限公司); author's collection.

Fig. 4.38. Second storey plan of Wak Hai Cheng Bio's rear block and roof plan.
Source: Illustrated by Hsieh Mei-En; base illustration adapted from restoration drawings by Shāntóu Jì Chuányīng Ancient Construction and Decoration Designing Co. Ltd (山頭市紀傳英古建築裝飾設計有限公司); author's collection.

Conclusion

The 2010 to 2014 restoration served to rectify major issues which had arisen in Wak Hai Cheng Bio over the course of more than a century, problems which had been exacerbated by the use of inappropriate materials in more recent repairs. This major restoration also provided the restoration team with the opportunity to learn more about the temple's historic fabric and how it had evolved since the 1890s. The most recent restoration has reinstated a certain stylistic unity to the temple that had been lost over the course of the 20th century, rectified insensitive additions, and harmonised the building with its changing setting. The restoration also highlighted traditional Teochew

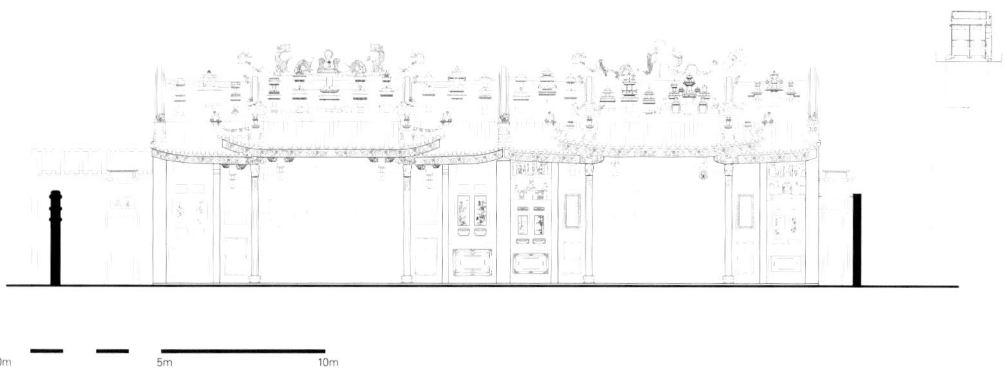

Fig. 4.39.

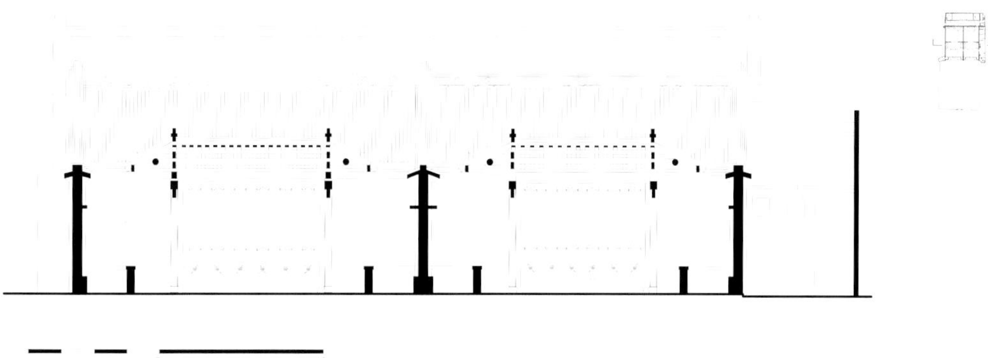

Fig. 4.40.

Fig. 4.39. Front elevation of Wak Hai Cheng Bio.
Source: Illustrated by Hsieh Mei-En; base illustration adapted from restoration drawings by Shāntóu Jì Chuányīng Ancient Construction and Decoration Designing Co. Ltd (山頭市紀傳英古建築裝飾設計有限公司); author's collection.

Fig. 4.40. Transverse section of Wak Hai Cheng Bio at prayer hall.
Source: Illustrated by Hsieh Mei-En; base illustration adapted from restoration drawings by Shāntóu Jì Chuányīng Ancient Construction and Decoration Designing Co. Ltd (山頭市紀傳英古建築裝飾設計有限公司); author's collection.

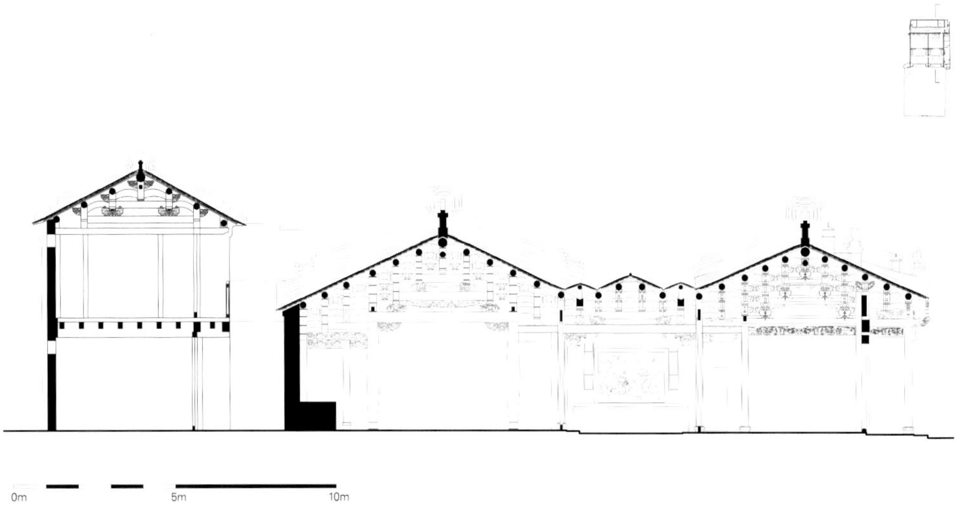

Fig. 4.41.

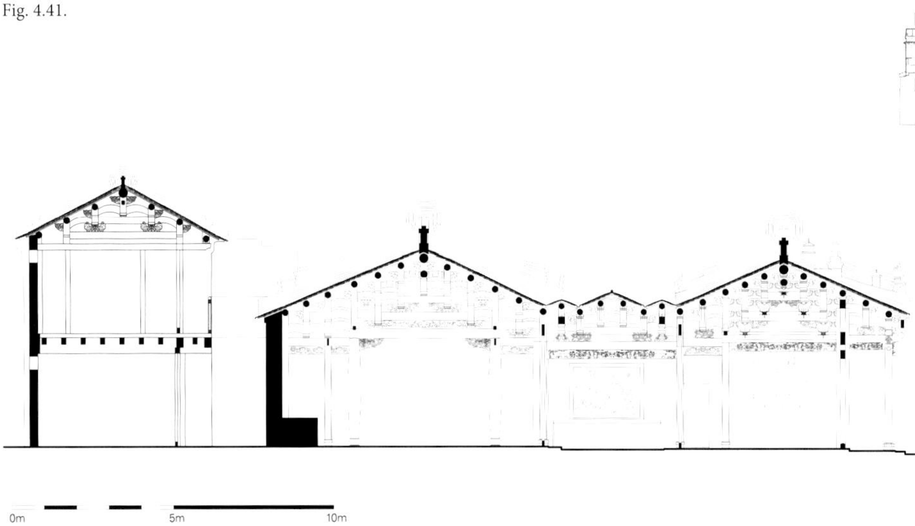

Fig. 4.42.

Fig. 4.41. Longitudinal section of Wak Hai Cheng Bio at Shàngdìgōng.
Source: Illustrated by Hsieh Mei-En; base illustration adapted from restoration drawings by Shāntóu Jì Chuányīng Ancient Construction and Decoration Designing Co. Ltd (山頭市紀傳英古建築裝飾設計有限公司); author's collection.

Fig. 4.42. Longitudinal section of Wak Hai Cheng Bio at Tiānhòugōng.
Source: Illustrated by Hsieh Mei-En; base illustration adapted from restoration drawings by Shāntóu Jì Chuányīng Ancient Construction and Decoration Designing Co. Ltd (山頭市紀傳英古建築裝飾設計有限公司); author's collection.

architectural crafts through the repair, restoration, and replication of architectural elements through traditional crafts, reaffirming the value of these traditions in the 21st century. Wak Hai Cheng Bio's restoration has helped underline the building's importance as a living monument, both as a house of worship and a valuable part of Singapore's architectural heritage.

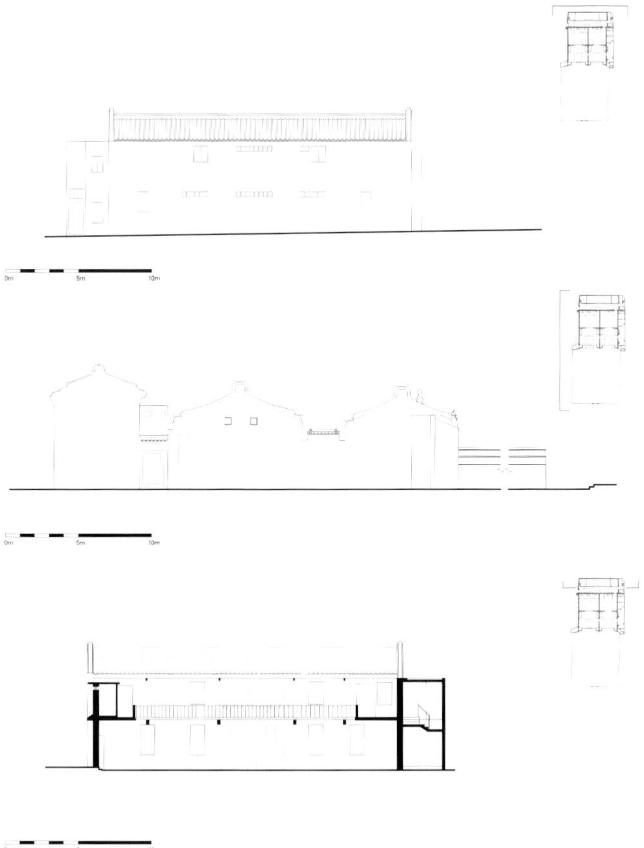

Fig. 4.43.

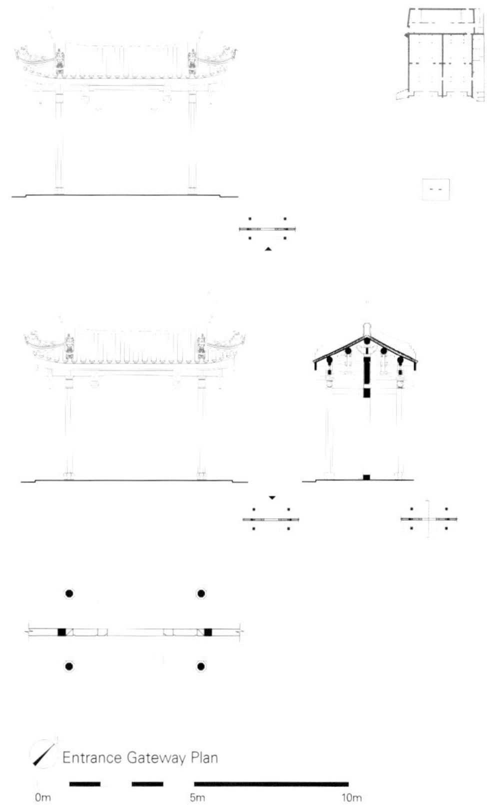

Fig. 4.4.

Fig. 4.43. Rear elevation and side elevation of Wak Hai Cheng Bio, as well as front elevation of Wak Hai Cheng Bio's rear block.
Source: Illustrated by Hsieh Mei-En; base illustration adapted from restoration drawings by Shāntóu Jì Chuányīng Ancient Construction and Decoration Designing Co. Ltd (山頭市紀傳英古建築裝飾設計有限公司); author's collection.

Fig. 4.44. Entrance gateway of Wak Hai Cheng Bio.
Source: Illustrated by Hsieh Mei-En; base illustration adapted from restoration drawings by Shāntóu Jì Chuányīng Ancient Construction and Decoration Designing Co. Ltd (山頭市紀傳英古建築裝飾設計有限公司); author's collection.

CHAPTER 5

Conclusion

Although Wak Hai Cheng Bio (粵海清廟) is without doubt Singapore's oldest Teochew temple and a prime representative example of Teochew architecture, its history has remained murky, with limited documentary evidence of its foundation and early history. Its prime location in the city centre, close to the Singapore River, hints at its resilience throughout history. As Singapore's oldest Teochew and possibly the oldest Chinese religious site in the city, how did it shape the community at large? As has been seen in the preceding chapters, the temple was more than just a religious site. It was the community's centre of activities.

In the 19th century, the colonial town was broadly planned along ethnic lines. The Chinese were allocated land south of the Singapore River as seen in Jackson's 1822 Town Plan. But within that broad area demarcated as the "Chinese Campong", smaller and finer divisions physically separated the Chinese by their dialect groupings. The Teochew community occupied the area immediately south of the Singapore River. Further south (geographically southwestwards), the Cantonese and the Hakka communities occupied the relatively small area bounded by Church Street and Cross Street. The Hokkiens occupied the relatively larger space after Cross Street, in the Telok Ayer Basin area.[1] This phenomenon reflects the heterogeneous nature of the Chinese diaspora in Singapore.[2]

The Chinese religious buildings of 19th-century Singapore directly reflect two particular aspects of the life of the community. The first of these was the conscious effort to assert the community's power and status within their broader social and political milieus vis-à-vis the power of their respective deities. The second was the pursuit of an impressive architectural form befitting the status of these deities and, by extension, their communities of worshippers. Both of these were played out within temples as sites of power.[3] Wak Hai Cheng Bio is no exception. As has been demonstrated in this book, the temple played both a religious and, perhaps more significantly, secular role for Singapore's Teochew community. In many ways, key temples and buildings became the proud symbols of their respective communities. This was why all dialect communities took great pains to distinguish themselves through the uniqueness of their architecture, which in turn conferred them with distinct identities.

This raises a troubling question: Why has there been the widespread and longstanding assumption in Singapore that all traditional Chinese architecture is uniform and unchanged? Given that China is vast, the form and spatial structures of its architecture should logically be markedly different in different regions. Is the perceived sameness of Chinese architecture in Singapore's urban landscape an unintended result of its post-colonial government language policy in promoting Mandarin and sidelining and marginalising dialects,[4] or simply the result of a lack of knowledge? This question remains but it is beyond the scope of this book to answer.

At the start of the 2010 restoration project, when the restoration team was attempting to reconstruct the architecture of the 1895 temple building, it quickly became apparent that there was a dearth of historical accounts regarding the early history of the temple. Unlike other historic Chinese temples in Singapore, Wak Hai Cheng Bio has no historical stele, and no surviving historical documents on its origins or date of establishment. These lacunae became the impetus for this work, to answer critical questions regarding the temple's raison d'être and its relationship with Singapore's Teochew community.

I began with what I knew best – architecture: its construction methods, techniques, materials, etc. This was carried out through an in-depth examination of the building's material culture during the 2010 to 2014 restoration process. The interrelated social research questions, such as who the owners and builders of the temple were, what the building was constructed of and the reason for its location, emerged naturally. Historical knowledge relies on the construction of documentary narratives, and involves "investigation from something that does not quite fit, something odd that needs to be explained",[5] as advocated by Ginzburg and Levi.[6] In the words of Levi:

> The unifying principle of all microhistorical research is the belief that microscopic observation will reveal factors previously unobserved ... [P]henomena previously considered to be sufficiently described and understood assume completely new meanings by altering the scale of observation. It is then possible to use these results to draw far wider generalizations although the initial observations were made within relatively narrow dimensions and as experiments rather than examples.[7]

A close focus on even an individual building thus provides us a powerful lens for historical inquiry. Indeed, it is from these seemingly micro-observations "on this reduced scale, and probably only on this scale, that we can understand, without deterministic reduction, the relationships between systems of beliefs, of values and representations on the one hand, and social affiliations on the another".[8] The careful examination of the building's physical fabric with the 1895 building plan in hand raised many useful questions. The realisation that social and cultural histories amalgamate in the micro-processes of everyday life provided the necessary direction for further inquiry, and made it possible for us to unearth a remarkable volume of information "hidden" in land transaction records, court files, and the meeting minutes of various associations. This rich variety of sources made it possible for us to establish the dynamic interconnections of the social roles played by the temple and the people behind the building.

One such strand of interconnectedness discussed in the preceding chapters was the strategic repositioning of the Teochew community in relation to other dialect communities from Guangdong province, namely the Cantonese and Hakkas, as well as the Hainanese, to counter the influence of the Hokkien community. This, too, demonstrated the heterogeneous nature of Chinese diaspora. The discovery in 2013 of a metal plaque of the Kwangtung Hui Kuan from 1962 in the storeroom of Wak Hai Cheng Bio led to the realisation that the Hui Kuan's founding leader in 1937 was a prominent Teochew, Lee Wee Nam (李偉南), and that the Hui Kuan's administrative office was located in Wak Hai Cheng Bio's rear building from 1937 to 1960 and from 1984 to 1994. From this, it became evident that the strategic partnership of the Teochew and Cantonese dialect groups persisted till the late 20th century. The Chinese community in Singapore has continued to be shaped by dialect groupings. It was only in 2010 that the most influential Chinese business body, the Singapore Chinese Chamber of Commerce and Industry (SCCCI), voted to change their constitution to scrap voting of council members along dialect or clan lines.[9]

Strategic alliances also meant that the Teochew leadership was conscious of the need to affirm, reinforce and consolidate their legitimacy in the eyes of other Guangdong province dialect communities in Singapore. Rituals, ceremonies and festivals were major vehicles through which the Teochews enhanced their authority within this alliance and perpetuated patterns of influence. The scale and expense of these events were a direct reflection of the influence of the temple and the wealth of the community. The size of the crowds these events drew was yet another indication of the community's broader influence. At the centre stage of these activities was the impressive architecture of Wak Hai Cheng Bio, decorated with allegorical narratives.

A large portion of this book is devoted to the understanding of architectural material culture. It attempts to give agency meaning, and power to the narratives and ideas embedded in the built landscape that provided a setting for both everyday life and major festivals. The temple, as both building and institution, was the centre of community life. In the 21st century, however, the contours of this community continue to change.

In contemporary Singapore, many traditional and cultural practices morph and transform in response to the modern condition. Many practices have been scaled down, altered in the name of "modernisation", or done away with altogether. Rituals and ceremonies developed their own visual cues and were reinforced by the allegorical stories found in the programmatic architecture of the temple built for the benefit of a community that was often historically illiterate. These, however, have little meaning for today's Chinese Singaporean.

What then does the restored Wak Hai Cheng Bio mean today? The answer seems fairly clear. The building is a physical reminder of Teochew identity in Singapore. Religious significance aside, the fine craftsmanship of the temple's myriad architectural components and its aesthetic principles are undeniably Teochew. A nation and its people need visual signposts, and though the exact circumstances of its establishment are impossible to confirm, Wak Hai Cheng Bio is the earliest manifestation of Teochew architecture and identity in Singapore. It remains one that everyone can access. In the capricious and fast-changing heart of Singapore's financial district, it has earned its keep, anchoring the city with an enduring reminder of its history. This book can be seen as an effort to understand what is in danger of being lost, or overwritten. It remains to be seen what value the traces of the past may possess, and what part they may yet come to play in contemporary Singapore.

富
長命

CHAPTER 6

Bibliographical Appreciation

Over the past century, there have been many studies and writings on traditional Chinese buildings in Singapore including places of worship, clan associations and residences. These have ranged from scholarly works to popular trade publications, mostly in Chinese and English. The earliest Chinese language works in this genre continue Chinese literary traditions with a focus on three main areas of studies or genres.

The first of these is the documentation and study of epigraphic materials within or related to buildings; this continues to be used as a source of historical information. The systematic collection and study of inscriptions as a distinct field of scholarship dates to the 11th century during the Song dynasty.[1] This field of scholarship is known as *jīnshí xué* (金石學) or the study of bronze and stone inscriptions, even though it encompasses inscriptions on other materials too.[2] As explained by Zhào Míngchéng (趙明誠) in the 12th century, epigraphic materials are valued as a source of historical information as they "are made at the time the events take place and can be trusted without reservation (而刻詞當時所立，可信不疑)".[3] The first collection of stone and bronze rubbings was published in 1063 in China.[4] In Singapore, this scholarly tradition was first taken up in the 1960s and 1970s. The two most important Chinese epigraphic works published during this time were *A Chronological Survey on Chinese Inscriptions in Singapore and Malaya* by Jao Tsung-I (饒宗頤), and *A Collection of Singapore Chinese Inscriptions* compiled by Chen Chingho (陳荊和) and Tan Yeok Seong (陳育崧).[5] They inspired and set the tone for subsequent Chinese epigraphic works in Southeast Asia. The efforts of these early scholars were continued by David K. Y. Chng (莊欽永) in the 1980s and 1990s, as well as Kenneth Dean (丁荷生) and Hue Guan Thye (許源泰) in the 2010s.[6] Similar works were also carried out in Malaysia and Indonesia in the 1980s and 2010s, notably by Wolfgang Franke (傅吾康) and Chen Tieh Fan (陳鐵凡), as well as Teoh Shiaw Kuan (張少寬).[7]

The second area of study focuses on the historical identities and other aspects of the deities worshipped in Chinese temples locally. Most deities worshipped in the Taoist tradition were actual historical figures. In the 1940s to early 1960s, scholars writing in the Chinese language such as Han Wai Toon (韓槐準), Hsu Yun-ts'iao (許雲樵), Wèi Jùxián (衛聚賢), Jao Tsung-I (饒宗頤) and Tiān Guānfú (天官福) were primarily concerned with the historical identities of Tua Pek Kong or Dàbógōng (大伯公) and Ji Pek Kong or Èrbógōng (二伯公).[8] The two deities are widely worshipped in Singapore and Malaysia. By the 1970s, fewer studies on deities were being conducted, and those that were published tended to be more temple-specific. An example is the study of the deities in the Singapore Hong San See Temple by Xiè Yúnshēng (謝雲聲).[9]

The third, less scholarly, form of writing in the Chinese literary tradition surveyed here is the genre of *yóujì* (遊記) or travellers' accounts. This genre has a long history, beginning in the third and fourth centuries during the Wei and Jin dynasties (魏晉) of China.[10] Its development reached a peak during the Song dynasty (宋代) with the works of famous scholar-officials such as Fàn Zhòngyān (范仲淹), Ōuyáng Xiū (歐陽脩), Wáng Anshí (王安石) and Sū Shì (蘇軾).[11] The first *yóujì* account containing descriptions of traditional Chinese buildings in Singapore and the region is the 1933 *An Account of Three Months in Nanyang* by Cheng Kin Lo (鄭健廬). A section of the travelogue describes the location, origins, spatial layout, deities, and the religious inhabitants of some of the temples in Singapore and Penang.[12] This tradition was continued by Phua Chay Long (潘醒農) in the 1940s and 1950s, albeit adapted to focus only on places of historical, cultural and natural significance.[13] Besides Singapore, Phua covered places in Malaya, Indonesia, Borneo, Thailand, Myanmar, Indochina and the Philippines. Phua's books differs from earlier *yóujì* accounts in that it was written from a third-person instead of first-person point of view. His writings blurred the lines between the traditional *yóujì* genre and the guidebooks on places of interest more commonly found today. In the 1960s, other travel guides covering Chinese temples with a similar writing style include the work of Zéng Tiěchén (曾鐵忱).[14]

From the late 1960s, the urban landscape of Singapore underwent rapid changes. Many old buildings were torn down to make way for development. There were concerns that historically significant buildings would also be demolished. The enactment of the Preservation of Monuments Act in 1970 and the gazetting of eight buildings as National Monuments in 1973 was the first step towards conserving Singapore's built heritage. The rapid changes in the built environment and the nascent efforts at building conservation spurred a heightened consciousness of the built heritage. Historical Chinese temples in Singapore became increasingly seen not only as places of worship and centres of dialect-based communities but also as important heritage sites. This is especially evident in books published since the 1970s, beginning with the 1975 *Shílè gǔjī* 《石叻古蹟》, a compilation of Chinese language articles on the historical buildings of Singapore.[15] These articles were written by a group of scholars and heritage enthusiasts based on their observations during site visits and extant literature on the subject. Subsequent works that treated historical Chinese temples as part of the broader category of built heritage of Singapore include the works of Chen Yun Yong (陳漢榮) in the late 1970s, Christopher Hooi and Gretchen Liu in the 1980s, Edwin Lee, Dhoraisingam S. Samuel, Goh Ngan Hong (吳彥鴻), Gretchen Liu and Pugalenthi Sr. in the 1990s as well as Lee Geok Boi, Wan Menghao and Jacqueline Lau in the 2000s.[16]

Since the 1980s, the increased consciousness of heritage in Singapore has led to a greater appreciation of traditional Chinese buildings from an art historical and iconographic perspective. The 1985 book by Jane Beamish and Jane Ferguson contains a section about Chinese temples and sought to understand the buildings from the perspective of art history.[17] After a gap of about 25 years, further works focusing specifically on the iconography and art history of traditional Chinese architecture in Southeast Asia and Singapore have been penned by Ronald G. Knapp, Kang Ger-wen and a group comprising of Foo Su Ling, Lim Chen Sian, Wee Sheau Theng and Yeo Kang Shua (楊茳善).[18]

The first serious attempt to study traditional Chinese architecture in Singapore from a western architectural perspective began in the 1980s with Evelyn Lip Mong Har, a lecturer at the National University of Singapore, and David G. Kohl.[19] In the 2000s, Liú Xiānjué (劉先覺) and Lee Coo (李谷) attempted to trace the development of Buddhist architecture in Singapore.[20] These works treated Chinese or southern Chinese architecture as homogenous, and failed to recognise the different regional forms and architectural styles peculiar to the various dialect groups. This issue was addressed in 2006 in a journal article by Yeo Kang Shua.[21]

Burgeoning interest in Singapore's architectural heritage saw the conservation and restoration of historical buildings, including traditional Chinese ones. One of the earliest buildings that underwent conservation and restoration works was Thian Hock Keng (天福宮) along Telok Ayer Street from the mid-1970s onwards. The conservation and restoration measures undertaken at the Hokkien temple were documented in an article in the July and August 1980 issue of the *Journal of the Singapore Institute of Architects*.[22] This was a significant start to the actual conservation and documentation of historical buildings in Singapore. Unfortunately, there have been very few works on the conservation and restoration works carried out to specific historical buildings in Singapore written since then. One of the few examples of this genre is the 2003 book on Teochew-style architecture and the conservation of the House of Tan Yeok Nee (資政第) written by Chan Yew Lih, Heng Chye Kiang and Gretchen Liu.[23] Since then, there have been only two other books touching briefly on the restoration of traditional Chinese buildings in Singapore. One book, edited by Ho Phang Phow (何炳彪), includes recommendations for the restoration and conservation of the Fook Tet Soo Khek Temple (客屬八邑福德祠, also known as 望海大伯公廟), in addition to brief information on its origins, social history and architectural features.[24] The other book, edited by Toh Lam Huat (杜南發), covers a much broader range of perspectives. Aside from a brief description of the restoration of Thian Hock Keng beginning in 1995, it touches on the religious rituals, epigraphic materials, iconography, social history and architectural layout and features.[25] In 2018, Toh Lam Huat and Yeo Kang Shua edited a two-volume commemorative book set entitled *Lian Shan Shuang Lin Monastery 120th Anniversary Compendium* (Social History Volume and Architecture Volume) where the latter attempted to provide a more comprehensive understanding on the monastery's architectural evolution.[26]

In neighbouring Malaysia, there have been a few books concerning restoration of traditional Chinese buildings published, particularly in Penang.[27] The most significant and holistic of these are the works of Tan Yeow Wooi (陳耀威), a Penang-based heritage conservation architect. His books cover the epigraphic materials and artefacts within the buildings, as well as their architectural features, social history and restoration.

There has also been myriad works published pertaining entirely to Chinese temples in Singapore and the region. The earliest of these writings were general surveys of Chinese temples in Singapore. They usually provide a brief description of the origins, location, and main deities worshipped, as well as the social and architectural histories of each temple. In the 1950s, this work was mainly undertaken by Xiè Míngfēi (謝鳴非) and Leon Comber.[28] Their works remain important today as a record of the architectural features, locations and state of the temples at the time. In the 21st century, a more comprehensive survey of Chinese temples in Singapore was undertaken and published in four volumes alongside other smaller books providing a general overview on historical Singapore Chinese temples.[29] Similar books on Chinese temples in Malaysia and Indonesia were also published in the 1970s, 2000s and 2010s.[30] Of particular importance is the work of Claudine Salmon and Denys Lombard first published in 1977 on the Chinese temples of Jakarta.[31] Their work is significant in being one of the earliest holistic studies of Chinese temples in the region. It encompasses a historical survey of the Chinese temples in Jakarta, organised according to the century in which they were constructed, and situates these buildings within their broader historical context alongside a study of the deities worshipped, the epigraphic materials and historical records in the temples, their social organisations, and the religious festivals celebrated, as well as the architectural layout and furnishings of temples.

Besides general surveys of Chinese temples, there have been numerous publications focusing on specific temples. The bulk of these publications take the form of souvenir magazines and anniversary publications issued by various Chinese temples; these works have been published since at least the 1960s. From the 2000s, there has been a rise in popularity of dialect community histories, temple-specific religious histories and social histories often commissioned by or written in collaboration with the various temple management committees. These writings provide a description of the main deities and religious practices of the temples, their social and religious histories, historical artefacts and, in some instances, land history.[32]

Through a review of the existing literature on traditional Chinese buildings and Chinese temples in Singapore, Malaysia and Indonesia, it is clear that there have been few books on the restoration and conservation of these buildings in Singapore and the region. Most works focus on the social, religious, epigraphic and iconographic aspects of the buildings. The very few works that mainly consider the architectural aspects treat Chinese or southern Chinese architecture as homogeneous, without recognising the regional and dialect-specific architectural traditions underpinning the construction of these buildings. Moreover, little attention has been paid to material culture and to the extant physical fabric of these historical buildings. Few technical details and little information about the decision-making process behind conservation works have been included. This book attempts to address this gap by elaborating in detail the entire conservation and restoration process of a traditional Chinese building, grounded in a sound understanding of the specific architectural style, traditional crafts, historical construction techniques, and building materials, while being sensitive to the history and the needs of the stakeholders of the place. It provides an example of architectural conservation in Asia that reinforces the importance of historical research and technical surveys to the restoration process.

Endnotes

Note on Translation, Transliteration and Traditional Chinese Script

1 "*Tán hànzì de jiǎnhuà* 談漢字的簡化 [A Discussion on the Simplification of Chinese Text]," *Nányáng Shāngbào* 《南洋商報》 [Nanyang Siang Pau], 21 September 1955; "*Luètán hànzì gǎigé* 略談漢字改革 [An Overview Discussion on the Chinese Text Reform]," *Nányáng Shāngbào* 《南洋商報》 [Nanyang Siang Pau], 16 June 1956; "*Guānyú hànzì zhī tǎolùn hànzì nányì yǔ luómǎhuà jí jiǎntǐzì píngyì* 關於漢字之討論漢字難易與羅馬化及簡體字平議 [About the Difficulties and Ease of Learning Chinese, as well as the Romanisation of Chinese Text and Simplification of Chinese Text]," *Nányáng Shāngbào* 《南洋商報》 [Nanyang Siang Pau], 9 October 1957; "*Hànzì jiǎnhuà de gōngyòng jiūjìng rúhé* 漢字簡化的功用究竟如何 [What are the Uses of the Simplification of Chinese Text]," *Nányáng Shāngbào* 《南洋商報》 [Nanyang Siang Pau], 1 January 1958.

2 "2-Language Schools", *The Straits Times*, 19 November 1968; "*Dièr yǔwén (huáyǔ) jiàoxué yántǎohuì nǎi yīngxiào jiāqiáng huáwén jiàoxué lǐchéngbēi zhǐzài tígāo yīngxiào huáwén shuǐzhǔn jiàocháng xuānbù shè wěiyuánhuì yánjiū hànzì jiǎnhuà wèntí zài xuéxiào zhōng zhèngshì shǐyòng jiǎntǐzì yǐ kèbù rónghuǎn* 第二語文(華語)教學研討會乃英校加强華文教學里程碑旨在提高英校華文水準教長宣佈設委員會研究漢字簡化問題在學校中正式使用簡體字已刻不容緩 [Second Language (Chinese) Pedagogy Symposium: Raising the Standards of Chinese in English-medium Schools is a milestone for such Schools; The Director of Education announced that a Committee to study the Challenges in the Simplification of Chinese Text will be setup and the use of Simplified Chinese Text will be Inevitable]," *Nányáng Shāngbào* 《南洋商報》 [Nanyang Siang Pau], 19 November 1968.

3 "*Jiàobù chūbǎn huáwén jiǎntǐzì xiǎocè jǐngtàn zài wǔjiān shūdiàn sōuchū yīpī fānyìnběn jǐngfāng jīngcǎi xíngdòng duìfù diàndōng* 教部出版華文簡體字小册警探在五間書店搜出一批翻印本警方經採行動對付店東 [The Ministry of Education published Simplified Chinese Booklet; The Police found Counterfeits Booklets in Five Bookshops and will be Taking Actions against the Owners]," *Nányáng Shāngbào* 《南洋商報》 [Nanyang Siang Pau], 16 October 1969; "*Běnbào jīnrì kāishǐ kānzài wǔbǎi língèr gè jiǎntǐzì* 本報今日開始刊載五百零二個簡體字 [Our Newspapers will start to use Five Hundred and Two Simplified Chinese Characters from Today]," *Nányáng Shāngbào* 《南洋商報》 [Nanyang Siang Pau], 28 August 1969.

4 "*Hànyǔ pīnyīn fāngàn* 漢語拼音方案 [The *Hànyǔ pīnyīn* Romanisation System of Chinese Text]," *Nányáng Shāngbào* 《南洋商報》 [Nanyang Siang Pau], 1 February 1971.

5 "*Lǐ Zhāomíng bùcháng hūxū bàoguǎn chūbǎnjiè jí diànshìtái děng xiézhù tuīxíng huáwén jiǎntǐzì bìng cǎiyòng yóuzuǒ dàoyòu héngpái fāngshì yìnshuā jiàoyù chūbǎnshè míngnián qǐ jiàokēshū zhújiàn gǎiyòng jiǎntǐzì biānyìn* 李昭銘部長呼吁報館出版界及電視台等協助推行華文簡體字并採用由左到右横排方式印刷教育出版社明年起教科書逐漸改用簡體字編印 [Lee Chiaw Meng, Minister of Education, urged the Press, Publishing and Media Sectors to work together to Popularise the Usage of Simplified Chinese Text; With effect from the Next Year, Chinese Educational Materials will be Laid Out from Left to Right with the Gradual Change into Simplified Chinese Text]," *Nányáng Shāngbào* 《南洋商報》 [Nanyang Siang Pau], 16 March 1974.

6 "*Míngnián yīnián jí huáwén cǎiyòng jiǎntǐzì jiàoshòu* 明年一年級華文采用簡體字教授 [Simplified Chinese Text will be Adopted in Teaching of Primary One from Next Year],"

Xīngzhōu Rìbào 《星洲日報》 [Sin Chew Jit Poh], 24 July 1982; "*Wénhuàbù tōnghán yǐshēn zuòzé guānfāng jīgòu zài sānnián nèi quánmiàn cǎiyòng jiǎntǐ hànzì* 文化部通函以身作則官方機構在三年內全面采用簡體漢字 [Ministry of Culture issued a Letter stating that the Government will lead by example to adopt Simplified Chinese Text fully within Three Years]," *Liánhé Zǎobào* 《聯合早報》 [Lianhe Zaobao], 20 December 1983; "*Quánmiàn cǎiyòng jiǎntǐzì wǔnián nèi kěwàng shíxiàn* 全面采用簡體字五年內可望實現 [Full Utilisation of Simplified Chinese Text is expected to be Realised within Five Years]," *Liánhé Zǎobào* 《聯合早報》 [Lianhe Zaobao], 25 April 1984; "*Huáwén jiǎntǐzì wǔnián nèi kě quánmiàn cǎiyòng* 華文簡體字五年內可全面采用 [Full Utilisation of Simplified Chinese Text within Five Years]," *Liánhé Zǎobào* 《聯合早報》 [Lianhe Zaobao], 25 April 1984; "*Jiǎntǐzì yīngyònglǜ qùniándǐ chuàngjìlù* 簡體字應用率 去年底創記錄 [The Usage of Simplified Chinese Text breaks New Records in the Past Year]," *Liánhé Wǎnbào* 《聯合晚報》 [Lianhe Wanbao], 7 January 1989.

Introduction

1 *Singapore in Figures 2018* (Singapore: Department of Statistics, 2018), accessed 1 June 2019, https://www.singstat.gov.sg/-/media/files/publications/reference/sif2018.pdf
2 Kwa, Chong Guan, et al., *Seven Hundred Years: A History of Singapore* (Singapore: National Library Board; Singapore: Marshall Cavendish Editions, 2019), 19–49.
3 Ibid., 181–188.
4 Ibid., 215.
5 Yeo, Kang Shua, "Homogenously Heterogenous?: The Diversity of Traditional Chinese Architecture in Singapore," *Journal of Southeast Asian Architecture* 9 (2006): 87–106.
6 Sinologist Victor Mair proposed that topolect is more appropriate than dialect to refer to *fāngyán* 方言 as dialect failed in the linguists' test of "mutual intelligibility". However, for the purpose of this work, the commonly used term "dialect" is used. Mair, Victor, "What Is a Chinese "Dialect/Topolect"? Reflections on Some Key Sino-English Linguistic Terms," *Sino-Platonic Papers*, vol. 29 (September, 1991): 1–31.
7 Akashi, Yoji, "Japanese Policy Towards the Malayan Chinese 1941–1945," *Journal of Southeast Asian Studies* 1, no. 2 (1970): 61–89; Fatt, Yong Ching, "Leadership and Power in the Chinese Community of Singapore during the 1930s," *Journal of Southeast Asian Studies* 8, no. 2 (1977): 195–209; Blackburn, Kevin, "The Collective Memory of the Sook Ching Massacre and the Creation of the Civilian War Memorial of Singapore," *Journal of the Malaysian Branch of the Royal Asiatic Society* 73, no. 2 (279) (2000): 71–90.

Chapter One

1 Phua, Chay Long 潘醒農, "*Mǎláiyà cháoqiáo nánlái fāzhǎn shǐ* 馬來亞潮僑南來發展史 [The Southward Migration History of the Teochews in Malaya]," in *Mǎláiyà cháoqiáo tōngjiàn* 《馬來亞潮僑通鑑》 [A History of Overseas Teochew in Malaya], ed. Phua Chay Long 潘醒農 (Singapore: The Nantao Publishing House, 1950), 29; Phua, Chay Long 潘醒農, "*Xīnjiāpō cháoqiáo gàikuàng* 新嘉坡潮僑概況 [An Overview of the Teochews in Singapore]," in *Mǎláiyà cháoqiáo tōngjiàn* 《馬來亞潮僑通鑑》 [A History of Overseas Teochew in Malaya], 39–40; Phua, Chay Long 潘醒農, "*Huígù xīnróu cháorén gānmì shǐ* 回顾新柔潮人甘蜜史 [A Retrospective Gambier History of the Teochews in Singapore and Johor]," in *Xīnjiāpō cháozhōu bāyì huìguǎn chénglì qīshí zhōunián jìniàn tèkān* 《新嘉坡潮州八邑會館成立七十週年紀念特刊》 [Singapore Teochew Poit Ip Huay Kuan 70th Anniversary Magazine], ed. Teochew Poit Ip Huay Kuan (Singapore: Singapore Teochew

Poit Ip Huay Kuan, 2000), 209.

2 Trocki, Carl A., "Rise and Fall of the Ngee Heng Kongsi in Singapore," in *"Secret Societies" Reconsidered: Perspectives on the Social History of Modern South China and Southeast Asia*, eds. David Ownby and Mary Somers Heidhues (Armonk, N.Y.: M.E. Sharpe, 1993), 98.

3 Franke, Wolfgang 傅吾康, *Yìndùníxīyà huáwén míngkè huìbiān*《印度尼西亞華文銘刻編》 *Chinese Epigraphic Materials in Indonesia*, vol. 1 (Singapore: South Seas Society, 1988), 354–357.

4 According to the Bugis-Malay chronicle *Tuhfat al-Nafis* [The Precious Gift], gambier and pepper cultivation was started by the Bugis and Malays in the 1740s: "The Bugis and Malays planted the gambier, establishing several hundred holdings. The labourers who processed it were Chinese from China and with the cultivation of gambier, Riau became even more populous." It was also suggested that "Riau benefited from the exodus of Batavian Chinese after the 1740 riots".
Ali al-Haji Riau, Raja, *The Precious Gift: Tuhfat al-nafis,* annotated trans. Virginia Matheson and Barbara Watson Andaya (Kuala Lumpur; New York: Oxford University Press, 1982), 90 and 340; Trocki, Carl A., *Prince of Pirates: The Temenggongs and the Development of Johor and Singapore, 1784–1885* (Singapore: NUS Press, 2007), 34.

5 Trocki, Carl A., "Singapore as a Nineteenth Century Migration Node," in *Connecting Seas and Connected Ocean Rims: Indian, Atlantic, and Pacific Oceans and China Seas Migrations from the 1830s to the 1930s*, eds. Donna R. Gabaccia and Dirk Hoerder (Leiden; Boston: Brill, 2011), 212.

6 "... and there was no one left in Riau except the Chinese in the jungle. They acted as coolies for the Malays and Bugis who cultivated gambier and pepper." And "in March 1787 Ruhde [David Ruhde, first Dutch Resident in Riau based in Tanjung Pinang, 1785–1788] reported that there were 5,000 Chinese on Riau, 4,000 from Canton and 1,000 from Amoy." Canton Chinese should be understood as people from Canton (modern-day Guǎngdōng) and Amoy Chinese as people from Amoy (modern-day Xiàmén). The latter is easier to identify as Hokkien while the Cantonese and the Teochew were from Guangdong. Scholars are of the view that the "Canton" Chinese referred by Ruhde in Riau were Teochew. Ali al-Haji Riau, *The Precious Gift: Tuhfat al-nafis,* 186, 373; Yen, Ching-Hwang, *Ethnicities, Personalities and Politics in the Ethnic Chinese Worlds* (Singapore: World Scientific Publishing, 2016), 45–94.

7 Trocki, *Prince of Pirates*, 40.

8 Ibid., 41; Tagliacozzo, Eric, and Chang, Wen-Chin, *Chinese Circulations: Capital, Commodities, and Networks in Southeast Asia* (Durham: Duke University Press), 93.

9 Yen, Ching-Hwang, *A Social History of the Chinese in Singapore and Malaya, 1800–1911* (Singapore: Oxford University Press, 1986), 120; Trocki, *Prince of Pirates*, 42–43.

10 Kwa, Chong Guan, et al., *Seven Hundred Years: A History of Singapore* (Singapore: National Library Board; Singapore: Marshall Cavendish Editions, 2019), 152–158.

11 Trocki, *Prince of Pirates,* 42–43; Bartley, W., "The Population of Singapore in 1819," *Journal of the Malayan Branch of the Royal Asiatic Society* 11, no. 2 (1933): 177; Winstedt, R. O., "A History of Johore (1365–1895 A.D.)," *Journal of the Malayan Branch of the Royal Asiatic Society* 10, no. 3 (115) (1932): 81, 86–90.

12 Trocki, *Prince of Pirates,* 43. Also see Lee Poh Ping's account of the conflicts between the "older society", comprising mainly Malacca Chinese and Teochew gambier-pepper financiers, and a newer "free trade" society and claimed that the former was already established in Singapore before 1819. Lee asserted that "the slow means of Chinese and native communication ... it would take many more years for a population to settle in response to British policy". Lee's claim has been

refuted by John Bastin who said that "European sources confirm the rapid influx of thousands of Asians, mainly Chinese, during the first eighteen months of British settlement, as does Munsyi Abdullah in his *Hikayat*". Lee, Poh Ping, *Chinese Society in Ninetheenth Century Singapore* (Kuala Lumpur; New York: Oxford University Press, 1978); Bastin, John, "Reviews," *Bulletin of the School of Oriental and African Studies, University of London* 43, no. 3 (1980): 632.

13 Trocki, *Prince of Pirates,* 104–107; Trocki, Carl A., "The Origins of the Kangchu System 1740–1860," *Journal of the Malaysian Branch of the Royal Asiatic Society* 49, no. 2 (1976): 139–140; Turnbull, Constance Mary, *A History of Modern Singapore, 1819–2005* (Singapore: NUS Press, 2009), 32; Mizuno, Kosuke, et al., eds., *Catastrophe & Regeneration in Indonesia's Peatlands: Ecology, Economy & Society* (Singapore: NUS Press in association with Kyoto University Press, 2016), 157–158.

14 Kuo, Huei-Ying, *Transnational Business Networks and Sub-Ethnic Nationalism: Chinese Business and Nationalist Activities in Interwar Hong Kong and Singapore, 1919–1941* (PhD Thesis, New York: State University of New York at Binghamton, 2007), 57–58.

15 The earliest landward map of Singapore is known as the Bute Map. The map is named after the archives in which it is deposited, that is, the Bute Collection at Mount Stuart, Isle of Bute, Scotland. A reproduction of the map can be found in Bastin, John, *The Founding of Singapore 1819: Based on the Private Letters of Sir Stamford Raffles to the Governor-General and Commander-in-Chief in India, the Marguess of Hastings, Preserved in the Bute Collection at Mount Stuart, Isle of Bute, Scotland* (Singapore: National Library Board, 2012).

16 Most of these accounts refer to the works of Phua Chay Long (潘醒農 1904–1987) and Ngow Wah (吴華 1933–2018) published between 1950 and the mid-1970s. See Phua, Chay Long 潘醒農, "*Yuèhǎiqīngmiào* 粤海清廟 [Wak Hai Cheng Bio]," in *Mǎláiyà cháoqiáo tōngjiàn* 《馬來亞潮僑通鑑》 [A History of Overseas Teochew in Malaya], 351; Phua, Chay Long 潘醒農, "*Xīnjiāpō huárén gǔ shénmiào yuèhǎiqīngmiào* 新嘉坡華人古神廟 粤海清廟 [Historic Chinese Temple of Singapore: Wak Hai Cheng Bio]," *Nányáng Shāngbào* 《南洋商報》 [Nanyang Siang Pau], 26 July 1976; Ngow, Wah 吴華, "*Yuèhǎiqīngmiào huàjiù* 粤海清廟話舊 [Reminiscences of Wak Hai Cheng Bio]," in *Fānglín jīnxī* 《芳林今昔》 [Hong Lim: Past and Present], ed. Ong Geok Seng 王玉成 (Singapore: Hong Lim Citizens' Consultative Committee, 1977), 36–39; Ngow, Wah 吴華, "*Yuèhǎiqīngmiào huàjiù* 粤海清廟話舊 [Reminiscences of Wak Hai Cheng Bio]," in *Shílè gǔjī* 《石叻古蹟》 [Monuments of Singapore], ed. Lim How Seng 林孝勝 (Singapore: South Seas Society, 1975), 145–149. Although their writings shed some light on the temple's history, it is unfortunate that neither Phua nor Ngow cited their sources of information. As Phua was the Secretary of both Ngee Ann Kongsi and Teochew Poit Ip Huay Kuan, for 55 years and 54 years respectively from 1930, he presumably had access to the archives of both organisations when writing about the temple. The Kongsi is the owner of Wak Hai Cheng Bio, while the Huay Kuan is a sister organisation that was officially established in 1929. See more discussions on the Ngee Ann Kongsi and the Teochew Poit Ip Huay Kuan in the Chapter 2 section on "Reforming the Society's Management Style and the 1933 Incorporation Ordinance".

17 Ngow, Wah 吴華, "*Yuèhǎiqīngmiào huàjiù* 粤海清廟話舊 [Reminiscences of Wak Hai Cheng Bio]," 145–149; Phua, Chay Long 潘醒農, "*Yuèhǎiqīngmiào* 粤海清廟 [Wak Hai Cheng Bio]," in *Mǎláiyà cháoqiáo tōngjiàn* 《馬來亞潮僑通鑑》 [A History

of Overseas Teochew in Malaya], 351. Subsequent writers such as Ning Ngui Ngi (林緯毅), Xiè Yòuzhāi (謝又齋), Han Tan Juan (韓山元), Issei Tanaka (田仲一成), Sumiko Tan (陳澄子) and Chia Yei Yei (謝燕燕) have followed this assertion. See Ning, Ngui Ngi 林緯毅, "*Wànshìshùn gōngsī yǔ xīnjiāpō cháorén de māzǔ jìsì* 萬世順公司與新嘉坡潮人的媽祖祭祀 [Ban See Soon Kongsi and the Worship of the Goddess of the Sea by Singaporeans]," in *Bǎinián huímóu: mǎhuá shèhuì yǔ zhèngzhì* 《百年回眸：馬華社會與政治》[100 Years of Malaysian Chinese Society and Politics: Review and Prognosis], ed. Hé Guózhōng 何國忠 (Kuala Lumpur: *Huáshè yánjiū zhōngxīn* 華社研究中心, 2005), 139–153; Han, Tan Juan 韓山元, "*Cháozhōu xiānxián chuàng yuèhǎiqīngmiào nóngsuō 180 nián huárén fèndǒu shǐ* 潮州先賢創粵海清廟濃縮 180年華人奮斗史 [The Establishment of Wak Hai Cheng Bio by Teochew Pioneers: Condensing 180 Years History of the Chinese in Singapore]," in *Xīnjiāpō cháozhōu wénhuà zhǎn tèkān* 《新嘉坡潮州文化展特刊》[Exhibition on the Heritage of the Teochew Community in Singapore], eds. Hóng Yúnshēng 洪雲生 and Xǔ Xuěqīng 許雪卿 (Singapore: Singapore Teochew Poit Ip Huay Kuan, 2002), 80–83; Xiè, Yòuzhāi 謝又齋, "*Cháozhōu mínzú sùyuán* 潮州民族溯源 [Origins of the Teochew Community]," in *Xīnjiāpō cháozhōu wénhuà zhǎn tèkān* 《新嘉坡潮州文化展特刊》[Exhibition on the Heritage of the Teochew Community in Singapore], 31; Tanaka, Issei 田仲一成, "*Shíjiǔ shìjì mòqī yǔ èrshí shìjì xīnjiāpō cháorén zǔzhī yǔ yǎnjù huódòng* 十九世紀末期與二十世紀新嘉坡潮人組織與演劇活動 [Late 19th-Century and 20th-Century Singapore Teochew Organisations and Opera Performances]," trans. Tan Huifang 譚惠芳, *Asian Culture* 16 (Jun 1992): 97; Tan, Sumiko 陳澄子, *Yì'ān gōngsī: kuàrù lìng yīgè qiānxǐ nián* 《義安公司：跨入另一個千禧年》*Ngee Ann Kongsi: Into the Next Millennium* (Singapore: Ngee Ann Kongsi, 2005), 89; Chia, Yei Yei 謝燕燕, "*Yuèhǎiqīngmiào shǔhǎi xiángyún* 粵海清廟 曙海祥雲 [Wak Hai Cheng Bio: Light of the Seas and Auspicious Clouds]," in *Miàoyǔ wénhuà: xīnjiāpō mínsú dǎolǎn dì'èr běn* 《廟宇文化：新嘉坡民俗導覽第二本》[Temple Culture: A Guide to Singapore's Folk Customs, vol. 2], ed. Chia Yei Yei 謝燕燕 (Singapore: Focus Publishing Ltd, 2007), 33.

18 Phua, Chay Long 潘醒農, "*Mǎláiyà cháoqiáo nánlái fāzhǎn shǐ* 馬來亞潮僑南來發展史 [The Southward Migration History of the Teochews in Malaya]," 29; Phua, Chay Long 潘醒農, "*Cháorén nánlái fāzhǎn shǐ* 潮人南來發展史 [The Southward Migration History of the Teochew People]," in *Cháoqiáo sùyuán jí* 《潮僑溯源集》[Origins of Overseas Teochew] (Singapore: Global Publishing, 1993), 10; Phua, Chay Long 潘醒農, "*Cháorén nánlái fāzhǎn shǐ* 潮人南來發展史 [The Southward Migration History of the Teochew People]," in *Xīnjiāpō cháozhōu wénhuà zhǎn tèkān* 《新嘉坡潮州文化展特刊》[Exhibition on the Heritage of the Teochew Community in Singapore], 35.

19 This was the same date that Raffles signed the 1819 Singapore Treaty with Temenggong Abdu'r Rahman and Sultan Admad Husain Muazzam Shah giving the British East India Company the right to set up a trading post in Singapore. How plausible it is that the plantation was founded on the same date remains debatable.

20 Attap is the frond of the nipah palm (*Nypa fruticans*) which was used as thatching for roofs. The fronds of the palm are commonly used as roofing materials in vernacular dwellings in Southeast Asia. The terms *shéntáng* (神堂) and *shéntán* (神壇) are used here to denote a shrine of a smaller scale and more private nature, as opposed to a temple (廟), which is usually of a larger scale and open to the public. Goh, Ngan Hong 吳彥鴻, "*Yuèhǎiqīngmiào:*

cháojírén de bǎinián "lǎoyégōng"《粵海清庙：潮籍人的百年"老爷宫"》[Wak Hai Cheng Bio: Century-old Temple of the Teochews]," in *Xīnjiāpō fēngtǔ zhì*《新嘉坡風土志》[A Gazatteer of Singapore] (Singapore: Singapore Teochew Poit Ip Huay Kuan, 1997), 86–87. Han Tan Juan agreed with Goh's claims but he was less specific about the dates. See Han, Tan Juan 韓山元, 80.

21 Ibid., 86.

22 Ning, Ngui Ngi 林緯毅, "*Wànshìshùn gōngsī yǔ xīnjiāpō cháorén de māzǔ jìsì* 萬世順公司與新嘉坡潮人的媽祖祭祀 [Ban See Soon Kongsi and the Worship of the Goddess of the Sea by Singaporeans]," 139–153; Teochew Poit Ip Huay Kuan, *Cháoyǒng: xīnjiāpō cháozhōu bāyì huìguǎn bāshí zhōunián jìniàn tèkān* 《潮涌: 新嘉坡潮州八邑會館八十週年紀念特刊》[Singapore Teochew Poit Ip Huay Kuan 80th Anniversary Magazine] (Singapore: Singapore Teochew Poit Ip Huay Kuan, 2009), 43. Xiè Yòuzhāi 謝又齋 made the slightly different assertion that Lín Pàn built the attap shrine, which was then later reconstructed as an architecturally distinguished Chinese temple; Wáng Fēngshùn subsequently established Ban See Soon Kongsi to manage the shrine of Māzǔ. See Xiè, Yòuzhāi 謝又齋, 31.

23 Ngow, 145; Han, 80; Chia, 33; Tan, 89. However, Phua's later writing also claims that Wáng Fēngshùn and others established the Ban See Soon Kongsi to manage affairs pertaining to the worship of Māzǔ. See Phua, Chay Long 潘醒農, "*Xīnjiāpō huárén gǔ shénmiào: Yuèhǎiqīngmiào* 新嘉坡華人古神廟: 粵海清廟 [Historic Chinese Temple of Singapore: Wak Hai Cheng Bio]," in *Fānglín jīnxī*《芳林今昔》[Hong Lim: Past and Present], 34; Phua, Chay Long 潘醒農, "*Yuèhǎiqīngmiào – xīnjiāpō huárén gǔshénmiào* 粵海清廟 – 新嘉坡華人古神廟 [Wak Hai Cheng Bio – Historic Chinese Temple of Singapore]," in *Xīnjiāpō cháozhōu bāyì huìguǎn chénglì qīshí zhōunián jìniàn tèkān*《新嘉坡潮州八邑會館成立七十週年紀念特刊》[Singapore Teochew Poit Ip Huay Kuan 70th Anniversary Magazine], ed. Teochew Poit Ip Huay Kuan (Singapore: Singapore Teochew Poit Ip Huay Kuan, 2000), 248; Phua, Chay Long 潘醒農, "*Yuèhǎiqīngmiào – xīnjiāpō huárén gǔshénmiào* 粵海清廟 – 新嘉坡華人古神廟 [Wak Hai Cheng Bio – Historic Chinese Temple of Singapore]," in *Cháoqiáo sùyuán jí*《潮僑溯源集》[Origins of Overseas Teochew] , 72. Ning agrees with Phua that Wáng Qīn and Wáng Fēngshùn were the founders of Ban See Soon Kongsi, an organisation established to manage the shrine of Māzǔ, even though Lín Pàn first built the attap shrine. See Ning, "*Wànshìshùn gōngsī yǔ xīnjiāpō cháorén de māzǔ jìsì* 萬世順公司與新嘉坡潮人的媽祖祭祀 [Ban See Soon Kongsi and the Worship of the Goddess of the Sea by Singaporeans]," 140.

24 Some online blog entries mention that Wáng Qīn was a trader from a village in the Ampou (Ān Bù 庵埠) township of the Teo Ann (Cháo Ān 潮安) district. He and Wáng Fēngshùn plied the seas to trade, arrived in Singapore in the late 18th to early 19th century and founded Wak Hai Cheng Bio and Ngee Ann Kun (義安郡). Wáng Qīn subsequently returned to his home village in China, was conferred the title of fourth rank official, and passed away in 1850. The writers of these entries did not cite the sources of their information and this information remains to be corroborated against primary sources. See "*Wáng, Qīn* 王欽," 20 April 2009, accessed 17 August 2016, http://wangqin.ren.hqcr.com/.

25 "From Kim Seng and 14 other Chinese Merchants, 15 February, Enclosing Petition addressed to the most noble the Marquis of Dalhousie K. T. Governor General of British India, relating to the reestablishment of the Pork Farm for the support of the Pauper Hospital at this station," 15 February 1850, Governor: Miscellaneous Letters (In), W15, folder 61, Raffles Museum and

Library, National Archives of Singapore. This petition was one of the three petitions written in Chinese asking for the reestablishment of the Pork Farm to support the Pauper Hospital. The content of the petitions were: "... Amongst the numerous natives comprising the inhabitants of this highly privileged island, especially of our own countrymen, there are many who are unfortunately disabled by sickness and various causes from maintaining themselves by honest labour and thereby obliged to wander in the principal thoroughfares for alms. Although we sincerely acknowledge with deep thankfulness that a charitable institution has been built for their accommodation, yet the want of funds renders the necessity of raising a monthly subscription contributed by the shopkeepers, but this gratuitous undertaking, we beg to respectfully apprize your Honour is not an easy expedient. About three years ago, we had submitted a petition praying for the restoration of the Pork Farm and suggesting the appropriation of its revenue for the relief of the distressed patients of the Pauper Hospital, through your Honour for transmission to the Supreme Government of Bengal, but as yet we humbly remind your Honour that no reply has been vouchsafed to us. We view our settlement as highly favoured by the condescending visit of the Most Noble the Governor-General. We have prized this most favourable opportunity of renewing our humble supplication for the gracious bestowal of the charitable object aforementioned summed up in the accompanying petition addressed to the Most Noble Marquis of Dalhousie, which we humbly and earnestly request may be submitted to his Lordship and supported by your Honour's powerful recommendation. The gratitude to which your Honour shall be entitled from both of ourselves and the afflicted will truly be inexpressible, should our humble effort be crowned with success..." c.f. Lee, Yong Kiat, "The Pauper Hospital in Early Singapore (Part IV) (1850–1859) – Section 1," *Singapore Medical Journal* 16, no. 4 (1975): 269.

26 "Collections 10. Certificates of Naturalization Granted, March, 1857," Governor's Diary: Narrative, X27, folder 71, Raffles Museum and Library, National Archives of Singapore.

27 Phua, Chay Long 潘醒農, "*Yuèhǎiqīngmiào – xīnjiāpō huárén gǔshénmiào* 粵海清廟 – 新嘉坡華人古神廟 [Wak Hai Cheng Bio – Historic Chinese Temple of Singapore]," in *Cháoqiáo sùyuán jí*《潮僑溯源集》[Origins of Overseas Teochew], 71. The Teochew Poit Ip Huay Kuan's 80th-anniversary publication follows Phua's arguments that the temple was already in existence during the reign of the Emperor Qianlong (乾隆) (r. 1736–1795). See Teochew Poit Ip Huay Kuan, *Cháoyǒng*, 43.

28 Phua made typographical errors in his article "*Yuèhǎiqīngmiào – xīnjiāpō huárén gǔshénmiào* 粵海清廟 – 新嘉坡華人古神廟 [Wak Hai Cheng Bio – Historic Chinese Temple of Singapore]". He wrote "清道光二十六年(1836年)再重建" [Reconstructed again in the 26th year of Emperor Daoguang's reign (1836)] when he meant "清道光六年(1826年)再重建" [Reconstructed again in the sixth year of Emperor Daoguang's reign (1826)] when referring to the date on the couplets "道本真通總摄靈源歸静穆" and "魔憑武伏還将生氣寓威嚴". The 26th year of Emperor Daoguang's reign does not correspond to the year 1836; it is the year 1846. This gave rise to subsequent confusion that there were possible construction works in 1846 and 1836. See Phua, Chay Long 潘醒農, "*Yuèhǎiqīngmiào – xīnjiāpō huárén gǔshénmiào* 粵海清廟 – 新嘉坡華人古神廟 [Wak Hai Cheng Bio – Historic Chinese Temple of Singapore]," in *Cháoqiáo sùyuán jí*《潮僑溯源集》[Origins of Overseas Teochew], 71; Phua, Chay Long 潘醒農, "*Yuèhǎiqīngmiào – xīnjiāpō huárén gǔshénmiào* 粵海清廟 – 新嘉坡華人古神廟 [Wak

Hai Cheng Bio – Historic Chinese Temple of Singapore],” in *Xīnjiāpō cháozhōu bāyì huìguǎn chénglì qīshí zhōunián jìniàn tèkān* 《新嘉坡潮州八邑會館成立七十週年紀念特刊》 [Singapore Teochew Poit Ip Huay Kuan 70th Anniversary Magazine], 248; Phua, Chay Long 潘醒農, “*Xīnjiāpō huárén gǔshénmiào: Yuèhǎiqīngmiào* 新嘉坡華人古神廟: 粵海清廟 [Historic Chinese Temple of Singapore: Wak Hai Cheng Bio],” in *Fānglín jīnxī* 《芳林今昔》 [Hong Lim: Past and Present], 33.

29 Xiè, 31; Han, 80; Ning, “*Wànshìshùn gōngsī yǔ xīnjiāpō cháorén de māzǔ jìsì* 萬世順公司與新嘉坡潮人的媽祖祭祀 [Ban See Soon Kongsi and the Worship of the Goddess of the Sea by Singaporeans],” 140; Ngow, 145; Tanaka, 97.

30 Ning, “*Wànshìshùn gōngsī yǔ xīnjiāpō cháorén de māzǔ jìsì* 萬世順公司與新嘉坡潮人的媽祖祭祀 [Ban See Soon Kongsi and the Worship of the Goddess of the Sea by Singaporeans],” 140; Ning, Ngui Ngi 林緯毅, “*Cóng yuèhǎiqīngmiào de wénwù kàn xīnjiāpō cháorén duì xuántiān shàngdì de xìnyǎng* 從粵海清廟的文物看新嘉坡潮人對玄天上帝的信仰 [A Study of Teochew Singaporeans' Xuantian Shangdi Belief through the Artefacts of Wak Hai Cheng Bio],” in *Hǎiwài cháorén de yímín jīngyàn* 《海外潮人的移民經驗》 [The Migration Experience of the Overseas Teochews], ed. Lee Chee Hiang 李志賢 (Singapore: Singapore Teochew Poit Ip Huay Kuan and Global Publishing, 2003), 214.

31 Many other writers have repeated the claim that the temple was established in or around 1826. See Comber, Leon, *Chinese Temples in Singapore* (Singapore: Eastern Universities Press, 1958), 61; Edwards, Norman, and Keys, Peter, *Singapore: A Guide to Buildings, Streets, Places* (Singapore: Times Books International, 1988), 417; Liu, Gretchen, and Lim, Albert K. S., *In Granite and Chunam: The National Monuments of Singapore* (Singapore: Landmark Books and Preservation of Monuments Board, 1996), 155; Lee, Geok Boi, *The Religious Monuments of Singapore: Faiths of Our Forefathers* (Singapore: Landmark Books, 2002), 22.

32 Chia, 32.

33 See Chapter 1 section on “Land Titles of Wak Hai Cheng Bio”.

34 “TS” stands for “Town Subdivision”. The whole island of Singapore was divided into mukims, and the area within town limits was Mukim I. To distinguish between the different parts of town, Mukim I was further divided into 30 subdivisions. Wak Hai Cheng Bio is located within Town Subdivision 4.

35 “Lot Particulars, TS4-624L,” 2016, Singapore Land Authority.

36 “Watt-Hai Cheng Beo Temple A Piece of Land at Phillip Street as Lot No. 428-1 of T.S. IV An Area is 13,273 sq. ft.,” unpublished minutes of meeting, Ngee Ann Kongsi; Phua, Chay Long 潘醒農, “*Yuèhǎiqīngmiào – xīnjiāpō huárén gǔshénmiào* 粵海清廟 – 新嘉坡華人古神廟 [Wak Hai Cheng Bio – Historic Chinese Temple of Singapore],” in *Cháoqiáo sùyuán jí* 《潮僑溯源集》 [Origins of Overseas Teochew], 73; Ngow, 145; Han, 80–81; Goh, 87; Chia, 33–34. Phua, Ngow, Han, Goh and Chia all listed Chan Wai Chua's name as 曾匯泉 instead of 曾懷泉; only Ngee Ann Kongsi's internal records list the latter as Chan's name in Chinese.

37 In some records, his name is spelt as Seah Lian Seah.

38 Quek Num Seng 郭南盛 is the name of a business. Its owner was Quek Kee Jin and the business had failed by 1929. See Singapore Land Authority, “Index to Land,” book 120, page 387, Singapore Land Authority; Singapore Improvement Trust, “Backlane – Phillip St. 33, Phillip St,” 1929–1933, SIT T9/29, HDB 1013, National Archives of Singapore.

39 Ghee Ann Koon was also known as Ghee Ann Society, Ghee Ann Koon Society, Gee Ann Society, Ghee Ann Koon Association, Ngee Ann

Kun and Guee Ahn Congsee. Throughout the book, the name Ghee Ann Koon will be used to refer to the society before it was incorporated in 1933, except when citing historical documents, where original spellings will be retained in quotation marks.

40 "Straits Settlements No. 2674," Indenture of Land, 18 April 1909, Singapore Land Authority; also see Chapter 2 sections on "'Public Property' of the Teochew Community", "Management of Wak Hai Cheng Bio prior to 1916", and "The 1914 'Ghee Ann Society' Lawsuit".

41 Lornie, James, "Land Tenure," in *One Hundred Years of Singapore: Being Some Account of the Capital of the Straits Settlements from Its Foundation by Sir Stamford Raffles on the 6th February 1819 to the 6th February 1919,* vol. 1, eds. Walter Makepeace, Gilbert E. Brooke and Roland St. J. Braddell (London: John Murray, 1921), 301–312.

42 "Edward Presgrave to Walter Sewell Cracroft, 25 August 1826," Papers regarding land tenures and quit rents at Singapore, vol. 2, 191–201, India Office Records and Private Papers, IOR/F/4/1042/28678, British Library.

43 Lornie, 303.

44 "Presgrave to Cracroft"; Lornie, 304.

45 "Extract Singapore Diary, 9 January 1827," Papers regarding land tenures and quit rents at Singapore, vol. 2, 237–239, India Office Records and Private Papers, IOR/F/4/1042/28678, British Library.

46 "John Prince to Phillip Jackson, January 9, 1827," Papers regarding land tenures and quit rents at Singapore, vol. 2, 242–244, India Office Records and Private Papers, IOR/F/4/1042/28678, British Library.

47 Lornie, 303–304.

48 Lornie, 304.

49 "No. 2 Register of Lands held on Grants of the New Form Established by Mr. Crawfurd," Papers regarding land tenures and quit rents at Singapore, vol. 2, 407, India Office Records and Private Papers, IOR/F/4/1042/28678, British Library.

50 Ibid.

51 Thomson, John Turnbull, "Plan of Singapore Town and Adjoining Districts from Actual Survey by John Turnbull Thomson, Govt Surveyor, Singapore (London: J.M. Richardson, 1846)".

52 "Lot No. 1 of Lease No. 473 for 999 Years," Indenture of Land, 25 August 1848, Singapore Land Authority.

53 "Land Division at Philip Street, c. 1830–1890, SP000178," Survey Department, National Archives of Singapore.

54 Left of the temple from the perspective of the deities but to the right when facing the temple. "Plan of the Town of Singapore and Its Environs Surveyed in 1842 by Government Surveyor Singapore, March 1854", Surveyor-General, Federated Malay States (F.M.S.) and Straits Settlements (S.S.). Surveyed in 1842 by government surveyor (F.M.S. Surveys No. 275, 1922). Survey Department, Singapore Collection. National Archives of Singapore (20050000698 - AccNo981).

55 "Lot No. 1 of Lease No. 473 for 999 Years."

56 Ibid.

57 Ibid.

58 Thomson, "Plan of Singapore Town".

59 "Plan of the Town of Singapore and Its Environs Surveyed in 1842 by Government Surveyor Singapore, March 1854."

60 Phua wrote in Chinese that the land was occupied with permission from "*Yuán míng guǒ sūdān* 圓明果蘇丹". While "*sūdān* 蘇丹" is the recognised transliteration for "Sultan", it is unclear who "*Yuánmíng guǒ* 圓明果" or "Sultan *Yuánmíng guǒ*" was. The Teochew pronunciation of "*Yuánmíng guǒ* 圓明果" is "*in*^{5} *mêng*^{5} *guê*^{2}", which does not seem to correspond to the names or titles of the native chiefs. Despite it being unclear who Phua was particularly referring to, it

is evident that he was alluding to the native chiefs instead of the British. See Phua, "*Yuèhǎiqīngmiào – xīnjiāpō huárén gǔshénmiào* 粵海清廟 – 新嘉坡華人古神廟 [Wak Hai Cheng Bio – Historic Chinese Temple of Singapore]," in *Cháoqiáo sùyuán jí* 《潮僑溯源集》 [Origins of Overseas Teochew], 73; Phua, "*Yuèhǎiqīngmiào* 粵海清廟 [Wak Hai Cheng Bio]," in *Mǎláiyà cháoqiáo tōngjiàn* 《馬來亞潮僑通鑑》 [A History of Overseas Teochew in Malaya], 351.

61 Goh, 87. Han made a similar assertion that the temple was originally located within a plantation. However, Han's arguments differ from that of Goh in stating that the temple moved from its original plantation site near the Singapore River to its present location between 1852 and 1855. Han is the only writer to have mentioned that the temple's present location is not its original site. See Han, 80.

62 Phua, Chay Long 潘醒農, "*Yuèhǎiqīngmiào – xīnjiāpō huárén gǔshénmiào* 粵海清廟 – 新嘉坡華人古神廟 [Wak Hai Cheng Bio – Historic Chinese Temple of Singapore]," in *Cháoqiáo sùyuán jí* 《潮僑溯源集》 [Origins of Overseas Teochew], 73; Phua, Chay Long 潘醒農, "*Yuèhǎiqīngmiào* 粵海清廟 [Wak Hai Cheng Bio]," in *Mǎláiyà cháoqiáo tōngjiàn* 《馬來亞潮僑通鑑》 [A History of Overseas Teochew in Malaya], 351. This claim is also made by Ngow. See Ngow, 146.

63 "To Lieutt L. Nelson Hull, Actg Secy to the Lt Governor," 28 December 1822, Letters to and from Raffles, L11, folder 151, Raffles Museum and Library, National Archives of Singapore.

64 Ibid.

65 The Bute Map was publicly exhibited for the first time in 2012 world premiere at the National Library of Singapore during the exhibition, "Raffles Letters: The Intrigues behind the Founding of Singapore".

66 Lim, Chen Sian, "The Earliest Landward Map of Singapore Preserved in the The Bute Collection at Mount Stuart, Isle of Bute, Scotland," in Bastin, John, *The Founding of Singapore 1819*, 203–204.

67 Ibid., 204.

68 I am grateful to Mok Ly Yng, a notable Singapore map researcher, for pointing out the cartographic conventions denoting agriculture land.

69 Chew, Ernest C.T., "The Foundation of a British Settlement," in *A History of Singapore*, eds. Ernest C.T. Chew and Edwin Lee (Singapore: Oxford University Press, 1991), 38–39; Kwa, Chong Guan, et al., *Singapore: A 700-Year History: From Early Emporium to World City* (Singapore: National Archives of Singapore, 2009), 94.

70 "No. 1 Register of Lands Held on Grants Signed by T.S. Raffles," December 1823 to June 1827, Papers regarding land tenures and quit rents at Singapore, vol. 2, 399–402, India Office Records and Private Papers, IOR/F/4/1042/28678, British Library.

71 Raffles, Thomas S., "Johore Document of 26 June, 1819: Raffles' First Memo on the Administration of Singapore," in *A Collection of Treaties and Other Documents Affecting the States of Malaysia 1761–1963*, Volume I, eds. J. de V. Allen, A.J. Stockwell and L.R. Wright (London; New York: Oceana Publications, 1981), 33.

72 Ibid.

73 Ibid.

74 "Part of Singapore Island, June 18, 1825," India Office Records and Private Papers, IOR/X/3346, British Library.

75 Siah, U Chin, "The Chinese in Singapore: General Sketch of the Numbers, Tribes and Avocations of the Chinese in Singapore," *Journal of Indian Archipelago and Eastern Asia* II (1848): 290.

76 Phua, Chay Long 潘醒農, "*Huígù xīnróu cháorén gānmì shǐ* 回顧新柔潮人甘蜜史 [The Singapore and Johor Teochew Gambier History in Retrospect]," in *Xīnjiāpō cháozhōu bāyì huìguǎn chénglì qīshí zhōunián jìniàn tèkān* 《新嘉坡潮州八邑會館成立七十週年紀念特刊》 [Singapore Teochew Poit Ip Huay Kuan

70th Anniversary Magazine], 208–214.

77 "Part of Singapore Island, June 18, 1825". The 1825 British Library Manuscript Map shows building footprints all over the "Campong China" area, which includes the area marked out as "Coleased Grounds" on the Bute Map. These building footprints do not correspond to actual buildings; instead they serve as an indication that the area was built-up.

78 "Thomas Stamford Raffles to Captain C.E. Davis, George Bonham and Alex. L. Johnston, November 4, 1822," in "Notices of Singapore," *The Journal of the Indian Archipelago and Eastern Seas* 8 (1854): 102.

79 "Thomas Stamford Raffles to Land Allotment Committee, October 17, 1823," in "Notices of Singapore," *The Journal of the Indian Archipelago and Eastern Seas* 8 (1854): 405–406. The three-person Land Allotment Committee consists of James Lumsdaine, Nathaniel Wallich and Captain Francis Salmond.

80 "Raffles to Davis, Bonham and Johnston," 105.

81 Ibid., 104.

82 Ibid.

83 "Raffles to Land Allotment Committee," 407.

84 Ibid.

85 "Raffles to Davis, Bonham and Johnston," 106.

86 "Singapore. Reproduced from a map of 1862," 1862, XXXX-02126, National Museum of Singapore.

87 This is based on the assumption that the rate of ground rent for first-class roads was $3 per fathom, and that the length of the temple's frontage in the early to mid-19th century was the same as that of 1895.

88 "Plan of the Town of Singapore and Its Environs Surveyed in 1842 by Government Surveyor Singapore, March 1854".

89 "Raffles to Davis, Bonham and Johnston," 106.

90 The word "shophouse" is etymologically based on the literal translation of the term *diàn cuò* (店厝) in Teochew or Hokkien, *diem*^{3} *cu*^{3} or *tiàm chhù*. It is more commonly known today as *diàn wū* (店屋) in Mandarin. The latter term literally means *shop* and *house*, that is, a place of business and residence within a single building. According to the Oxford English Dictionary (1979), the term "shophouse" became common from the 1950s.

91 Hall-Jones, John, and Hooi, Christopher, *An Early Surveyor in Singapore: John Turnbull Thomson in Singapore, 1841–1853* (Singapore: National Museum, 1979); Hall-Jones, John, and Thomson, John Turnbull, *The Thomson Paintings: Mid-Nineteenth Century Paintings of the Straits Settlements and Malaya* (Singapore: Oxford University Press, 1983).

92 August Sachtler, a German photographer, ran a photographic studio (Sachtler & Co.) on High Street approximately between 1864 to 1873. This albumen print of the Singapore Town is in the collection of the National Museum of Singapore (2009-01632).

93 The Town Planning Committee and Land Allotment Committee are believed to have laid out land blocks based on instructions given by Raffles in 1822 and 1823. The garrison engineer, Lieutenant Phillip Jackson, depicted Raffles' plans in 1822 in what is now known as the Jackson Plan. The Jackson Plan was to have a profound influence on the future development of the colonial town of Singapore. Slight deviations in urban development from the Jackson Plan resulted from the Town Planning Committee's lack of statutory powers for the implementation the Plan.

94 "Plan of the Town of Singapore and Its Environs Surveyed in 1842 by Government Surveyor Singapore, March 1854".

95 "Jewish Synagogue Ordinance, Ordinance I of 1878," *Straits Settlements Government Gazette*, 5 April 1878, 445–447.

96 Nathan, Eze, *The History of Jews in Singapore 1830–1945* (Singapore: HERBILU Editorial & Marketing Services), 11–13.

97 “Municipal Notice,” *The Straits Times*, 1 August 1921.

98 Haughton, H.T., “Native Names of Streets in Singapore,” *Journal of the Straits Branch of the Royal Asiatic Society* 23 (June 1891): 57.

Toponymics: Temple (p. 11)

1 Buckley, Charles Burton, *An Anecdotal History of Old Times in Singapore, from the Foundation of the Settlement under the Honourable the East India Company, on Feb. 6th, 1819, to the Transfer to the Colonial Office as Part of the Colonial Possessions of the Crown on April 1st, 1867*, vol. 1 (Singapore: Fraser & Neave, 1902), 88.

Toponymics: Environs (pp. 16–17)

1 Dunlop, Peter K. G., *Street Names of Singapore* (Singapore: Who's Who Pub., 2000), 242. According to some writers, Phillip Street was named after Charles Phillips, Superintendent of the Sailors' Home. See Savage, Victor R., and Yeoh, Brenda S. A., *Singapore Street Names: A Study of Toponymics* (Singapore: Marshall Cavendish Editions, 2013), 295–296. It is, however, highly unlikely that Phillip Street was named after Charles Phillips. Charles Phillips was born in 1834 and became the Superintendent of the Sailors' Home in Singapore in 1866. However, by 1826, well before Charles Phillips was born, the street was already named “Phillip's Street”. See "No. 2 Register of Lands held on Grants of the New Form Established by Mr. Crawfurd,” Papers regarding land tenures and quit rents at Singapore, vol. 2, 407, India Office Records and Private Papers, IOR/F/4/1042/28678, British Library; Knowles, Owen, “Introduction – Sources,” in Joseph Conrad, *The Shadow-Line: A Confession*, eds. J. H. Stape and Allan H. Simmons (New York: Cambridge University Press, 2013); Lau, Earnest, *From Mission to Church: The Evolution of the Methodist Church in Singapore and Malaysia: 1885–1976* (Singapore: Genesis Books, 2008), 9.

2 See “Map of the Town and Environs of Singapore, Drawn by J. B. Tassin, from an Actual Survey by G. D. Coleman (Calcutta: J. B. Tassin's Lith' Press, 1836)”. National Archives of Singapore 20140000101-0003-TM000037).

3 Haughton, H. T., “Native Names of Streets in Singapore,” *Journal of the Straits Branch of the Royal Asiatic Society* 23 (June 1891): 60.

4 Ibid.

5 Firmstone, H. W., “Chinese Names of Streets and Places in Singapore and the Malay Peninsula,” *Journal of the Straits Branch of the Royal Asiatic Society* 42 (February 1905): 78–79.

6 Haughton: 53.

7 Ibid.

8 It appears that Teochews in Singapore commonly refer to this place by its Hokkien name rather than its Teochew name. In particular, *Keng* is used instead of *Goin*[1].

9 Firmstone: 132–133. Both 玻璃後 (*Bō Lí Hòu*) and 保黎後 (*Bǎo Lí Hòu*) have similar pronunciations in the three dialects and were used interchangeably. 玻璃後 (*Bō Lí Hòu*) should not be understood literally as “behind the glass”. Instead, the term meant “behind the police station”, 玻璃 (*Bō Lí*) being the Chinese transliteration of the English word “police”. The police station was known as *Po Lê Chhù* (玻璃厝) in Hokkien. See Douglas, Carstairs, *Chinese–English Dictionary of the Vernacular or Spoken Language of Amoy, with the Principal Variations of the Chang-chew and Chin-chew Dialects* (London: Trübner & Co., 1873), 175. The police station was in the area bounded by George Street, South Bridge Road, South Canal Road and Pickering Street (formerly Macao Street). Synagogue Street, being one street away from George Street, was thus known as “behind the police station”.

10 Kling Street was officially renamed Chulia Street from 1 January 1922 by order of the Acting Municipal Secretary H. L. Manchester. See

"Municipal Notice," *The Straits Times,* 1 August 1921.

11 Although Kling Street was the official name used before 1922, the Chinese equivalence of the name, 吉寧街 (*Jí Níng Jiē*), was used mainly to refer to Cross Street instead of Kling/Chulia Street. See Hsu, Yun Tsiao 許雲樵, *Nányáng huáyǔ lǐsú cídiǎn* 《南洋華語俚俗辭典》 [A Dictionary of Nanyang Vernacular Chinese] (Singapore: *Shìjiè shūjú* 世界書局, 1961), 72; Mydin, Iskander, *Pioneers of the Streets* (Singapore: Art, Antiques and Antiquities, 1989), 24.

12 Firmstone: 102–103; Buckley, Charles Burton, *An Anecdotal History of Old Times in Singapore, from the Foundation of the Settlement under the Honourable the East India Company, on Feb. 6th, 1819, to the Transfer to the Colonial Office as Part of the Colonial Possessions of the Crown on April 1st, 1867*, vol. 1 (Singapore: Fraser & Neave, 1902), 88.

13 According to Phua Chay Long, 山仔頂 (Shān Zái Dǐng) was also known as 萬順街 (Wàn Shùn Jiē). The Chinese divided the area in the temple's district into segments to fundraise for temple festivities. Each segment was known as a *jiē* (街) or "street", though these may not necessarily correspond to the entire length of an official street. See Phua, Chay Long 潘醒農, *Cháoqiáo sùyuán jí* 《潮僑溯源集》 [Origins of Overseas Teochew] (Singapore: Global Publishing, 1993), 73.

14 Haughton: 57; the two shophouses at the junction of Phillip and Chulia streets were owned by Mr. M. Meyer in 1891 and subsequently by the Sze Hai Tong Banking and Insurance Company. The addresses of these houses were 57 and 58 Chulia Street. The buildings have since been demolished. See "Plan of Two Shophouses to be Erected on Site of Nos. 56 & 57 Kling Street Singapore," 128/1891, CBS331, National Archives of Singapore; "Designs for Proposed Brackets to Girders at Nos. 56 & 57 Kling Street, Singapore," 127/1892, CBS332, National Archives of Singapore; "Sze Hai Tong Banking and Insurance Company Corporation Nos. 57 & 58 Chulia Street," 8791/1907, CBS1130, National Archives of Singapore.

15 Firmstone: 102–103.

16 Haughton: 63.

17 Ibid.: 63–64. "Theruvu" means street in Tamil. "Sadakku" could be a corrupted word from "Sadak" which means street in Hindi.

Overview of the Early Land Administration System in Singapore (pp. 24–25)

1 I am grateful to Mok Ly Yng, a notable Singapore map researcher, for sharing his expert knowledge on this subject.

2 Mok, Ly Yng, "Mapping Singapore: 1819–2014," in *Visualizing Space: Maps of Singapore and the Region* (Singapore: National Library Board, 2015), 93.

3 Lornie, James, "Land Tenure," in *One Hundred Years of Singapore: Being Some Account of the Capital of the Straits Settlements from Its Foundation by Sir Stamford Raffles on the 6th February 1819 to the 6th February 1919*, vol. 1, eds. Walter Makepeace, Gilbert E. Brooke and Roland St. J. Braddell (London: John Murray, 1921), 301–305.

4 Mok, 97.

5 Ibid.

6 Ng, Mayers, and Choy, Chan Pong, *Land Framework of Singapore: Building a Sound Land Administration and Management System* (Singapore: Centre for Liveable Cities, 2018), 7–19.

7 Ibid.

8 Koh, T. T. B., and Lim, William S. W., "Planning Law and Processes in Singapore," *Malaya Law Review*, vol. 11, no. 2 (National University of Singapore, 1969), 315.

9 Ibid.

10 Ng, Mayers, and Choy, Chan Pong, *Land Framework of Singapore*, 7–19; Lornie, 301–305; Lo, Wai Ping, and Lim, Jen Hui, "The Development of Land Registration in Singapore," in *Essays in Singapore Legal History*, ed. Kevin Y. L. Tan (Singapore: Singapore Academy of Law & Marshall Cavendish Academic, 2005), 218.

Chapter Two

1 Although DeBernadi researched and wrote on the Chinese community in Penang, Malaysia, the establishment of temples and their social roles there is similar to the situation in Singapore. See DeBernardi, Jean, *Rites of Belonging: Memory, Modernity and Identity in a Malaysian Chinese Community* (Stanford: Stanford University Press, 2004).

2 Wee, Vivienne, *Religion and Ritual among the Chinese of Singapore: An Ethnographic Study* (Unpublished Master's Thesis, Singapore: University of Singapore, 1977), 40–41.

3 The management committee of the Ngee Ann Kongsi, led by the president, pay their respects to the deities at the temple on four occasions annually: the birthday of the Mysterious Supreme Emperor of Heaven on the third day of the third lunar month is marked with an opera performance on the third and fourth days of the third lunar month; the birthday of the Goddess of the Sea on the 23rd day of the third lunar month is marked with an opera performance on the 23rd and 24th days of the third lunar month; the Hungry Ghost Festival, which spans the entire seventh lunar month, is marked by prayers held on the 15th day of the seventh lunar month; and Thanksgiving on the 23rd and 24th day of the tenth lunar month. The trustees of the Ban See Soon Kongsi pay their respects to the deities at the temple once a year during the birthday of the Goddess of the Sea on the 24th day of the third lunar month (the Ngee Ann Kongsi's prayer event is held one day before the Ban See Soon Kongsi's).

4 Woo, Nelson 余義源, personal communication (e-mail) with author, 8 August 2017. Mr. Nelson Woo is the manager of Teochew Funeral Parlour, which is under the management of the Ngee Ann Kongsi. He is also a master of rites at Seu Teck Sean Tong Yiang Sin Sia (修德善堂養心社) at No. 335 Bedok North Avenue 3, Singapore 469718.

5 Ban See Soon Kongsi Accounts, 3 and 4 May 1937, Ban See Soon Kongsi, Singapore; Ban See Soon Kongsi Accounts, 23 and 24 April 1938, Ban See Soon Kongsi, Singapore; Ban See Soon Kongsi Accounts, 12 and 13 May, 1939, Ban See Soon Kongsi, Singapore; Ban See Soon Kongsi Accounts, 30 April and 1 May 1940, Ban See Soon Kongsi, Singapore; Ban See Soon Kongsi Accounts, 19 and 20 April 1941, Ban See Soon Kongsi, Singapore; Ban See Soon Kongsi Accounts, 7 and 8 May 1942, Ban See Soon Kongsi, Singapore; Ban See Soon Kongsi Accounts, 27 and 28 May 1943, Ban See Soon Kongsi, Singapore; Ban See Soon Kongsi Accounts, 15 and 16 April 1944, Ban See Soon Kongsi, Singapore; Ban See Soon Kongsi Accounts, 4 and 5 May 1945, Ban See Soon Kongsi, Singapore.

6 Chong, Terence, "Chinese Opera in Singapore: Negotiating Globalisation, Consumerism and National Culture," *Journal of Southeast Asian Studies* 34, no. 3 (2003): 454.

7 Kuah-Pearce, Khun Eng, *State, Society and Religious Engineering: Towards a Reformist Buddhism in Singapore*, 2nd ed. (Singapore: Institute of Southeast Asian Studies, 2009), 67.

8 "Friday, 1st September," *Straits Times Overland Journal*, 9 September 1871.

9 Such practices are still carried out in parts of mainland China and Taiwan. In the case of Taiwan, the public can usually help themselves to the offerings on the last day of the seventh lunar month. There have been a few master's theses written on this topic. Unfortunately, there is a dearth of literature on such practices in Singapore

and Malaysia. See Wáng, Àiwén 王愛雯, *Ānpíng língjìdiàn 'gūpéng jì' yánjiū*《安平靈濟殿「孤棚祭」研究》[Study on "solitary shed worship" at Anping Ling Chi Temple] (Master's Thesis, Taiwan: National University of Tainan, 2017), accessed 28 July 2017, http://handle.ncl.edu.tw/11296/ndltd/40991615394713449027; Hsu, Tzer-Yaw 許澤耀, *Cóng shénshèng dào shìsú – yǐ tóuchéng qiǎnggū wéilì*《從神聖到世俗 – 以頭城搶孤為例》[From Sacred to Profane: A Study on Ghost's Festival in Touchen] (Master's Thesis, Taiwan: National Taiwan Normal University, 2010), accessed 28 July 2017, http://handle.ncl.edu.tw/11296/ndltd/01410701752595734231.

10 "Friday, 1st September," *Straits Times Overland Journal*, 9 September 1871.

11 Phua, Chay Long 潘醒農, 2 July 1931, *Xīnjiāpō yì'ān gōngsī yīng 1930 nián mínguó shíjiǔnián sìyuè shíèrrì lì yì'ànbù* 新嘉坡義安公司 英1930年民國十九年四月十二日立 議案簿 [Singapore Ngee Ann Kongsi A.D. 1930 12 April in the 19th year of the Chinese Republic Minutes of Meeting Folder], Ngee Ann Kongsi (hereinafter cited as Phua, Ngee Ann Kongsi Minutes 1930). The minutes of meeting stated that "主席[林義順]云關於陰曆七月份普度事我之意思擬將歷年所搭之孤棚及孤山取消另將做孤山之款由公司買辦品物以祭之未稔諸位之意如何楊纘文君附議將孤山取消用以購買品物 通過".

12 Ibid. It was stated in the minutes that "李偉南君提議普度用費總共酌為一千元之譜楊書典君附議 通過".

13 Ibid., 1 August 1932. It was stated in the minutes of meeting as follows: "楊纘文君報告云前日据粵海廟祝云孤棚之大木柱已多毀壞今年如須搭孤棚宜多購百餘元之木料否則不能搭孤棚弟意無搭孤棚似不雅观然因搭孤棚而費百餘元則又嫌不合經濟故折充办法為戲枱高些便可未譜如何主席（李偉南）云孤棚應如何辦理交由該四委員措議之周瑞麟君提議普渡之辦理委員可照去年所舉之楊纘文君陳秋槎君劉正興君吳竹村君四人任之郭斯高君附議众贊成 通過".

14 Ibid.

15 Ibid.

16 Ibid.

17 *Ang ku kueh* and *tau ki* are the commonly used spellings for the two types of food. Their spelling, as per the general transliteration standard used in this book, would be *ang*[5] *gu*[1] *guê*[2] and *dao*[7] *gi*[1] respectively.

18 Wee in her master's thesis detailed the rituals of the seventh lunar month rites for "the home, the temple, and the locality". The rituals appear to be largely similar, with some minute differences. Wee, Vivienne, *Religion and Ritual among the Chinese of Singapore: An Ethnographic Study*, 295–300.

19 Between 1872 and 1906, there were numerous newspaper articles on the Chingay processions. 1 December 1872 Procession: "Untitled," *The Straits Times*, 30 November 1872. 16 December 1881 Procession: "Thursday, 15th December," *Straits Times Overland Journal*, 19 December 1881. 14 December 1887 Procession (農歷十月三十日出巡); 30 January 1888 Return Procession (農歷十二月十九回鑾): "*Sàishén dìngqī* 賽神定期 [Dates of Religious Processions]," *Lat Pau*《叻報》, 1 December 1887; "*Pàichà dànyā* 派差彈壓 [Activation of Police]," *Lat Pau*《叻報》, 14 December 1887; "*Huǒchē tínggōng* 火車停工 [Halting of Train Services]," *Lat Pau*《叻報》, 14 December 1887; "Untitled," *Straits Times Weekly Issue*, 19 December 1887. 5 December 1890 Procession (農歷十月廿四日); 19 January 1891 Return Procession (農歷十二月十日回鑾): "*Sàishén dìngqī* 賽神定期 [Dates of Religious Processions]," *Lat Pau*《叻報》, 29 November 1890; "*Yíngshén zhìlüè* 迎神誌略 [An Account of Religious Procession]," *Lat Pau*《叻報》, 8 December 1890. 17 December 1892 Procession; 30 January

1893 Return Procession: "Local and General," *Daily Advertiser*, 17 December 1892; "Local and General," *Daily Advertiser*, 30 January 1893. 24 November 1894 Procession (農歷十月廿七日); 14 January 1895 Return Procession (農歷十二月十九日): "*Mǐnyuè sàishén dìngqī* 閩粵賽神定期 [Fujian and Guangdong Religious Processions Dates]," *Lat Pau*《叻報》, 13 November 1894; "Untitled," *The Singapore Free Press and Mercantile Advertiser (Weekly)*, 27 November 1894; "*Sàishén jìlüè* 賽神紀略 [An Account of Religious Procession]," *Lat Pau*《叻報》, 26 November 1894; "*Huíluán zhìlüè* 回鑾誌畧 [An Account of Religious Returning Procession]," *Lat Pau*《叻報》, 16 January 1895. 7 December 1895 Procession (農歷十月廿一日); 24 January 1896 Return Procession (農歷十二月初十日): "*Yuèshāng yíngshén zhìlüè* 粵商迎神誌畧 [An Account of Guangdong Merchants' Religious Procession]," *Lat Pau*《叻報》, 9 December 1895; "*Tínggōng bùgào* 停工佈告 [One Day Holiday Notice]," *Lat Pau*《叻報》, 23 January 1896; "*Mǐnyuè sòngshén zhìlüè* 閩粵送神誌畧 [An Account of Fujian and Guangdong Religious Processions]," *Lat Pau*《叻報》, 25 January 1896. 2 December 1896 Procession (農歷十月廿八日); 14 January 1897 Return Procession (農歷十二月十二日): "*Sàishén dìngqī* 賽神定期 [Dates of Religious Processions]," *Lat Pau*《叻報》, 20 November 1896; "Untitled," *The Singapore Free Press and Mercantile Advertiser*, 27 November 1896; "*Yíngshén rǎnzhì* 迎神冉誌 [An Account of Religious Procession]," *Lat Pau*《叻報》, 2 December 1896; "The Chingay," *The Straits Times*, 2 December 1896; "The 'Chingay'," *The Straits Times*, 14 January 1897; "Untitled," *The Singapore Free Press and Mercantile Advertiser*, 14 January 1897; "*Sòngshén zhìlüè* 送神誌畧 [An Account of Religious Returning Procession]," *Lat Pau*《叻報》, 15 January 1897. 22 November 1897 Procession (農歷十月廿八日): "*Chóushén bǔdìng* 酬神卜定 [Determination of Religious Dates]," *Lat Pau*《叻報》, 10 November 1897; "*Sàishén lùchéng*賽神路程 [The Route of Religious Procession]," *Lat Pau*《叻報》, 22 November 1897; "A Huge Chinese Procession," *Mid-Day Herald and Daily*, 22 November 1897; "The Chingay," *The Straits Times*, 22 November 1897; "The Chingay and Prices," *The Straits Times*, 23 November 1897; "*Yíngshén jìshì* 迎神紀事 [An Account of Religious Procession]," *Lat Pau*《叻報》, 23 November 1897. 6 December 1898 Procession (農歷十月廿三日); 26 January 1899 Return Procession (農歷十二月十五日): "*Yuèshāng sàishén dìngqī* 粵商賽神定期 [Dates of Guangdong Merchants' Religious Procession]," *Lat Pau*《叻報》, 29 November 1898; "*Sàishén qījiè* 賽神期屆 [Religious Procession]," *Lat Pau*《叻報》, 6 December 1898; "*Sàishén jìlüè* 賽神紀畧 [An Account of Religious Procession]," *Lat Pau*《叻報》, 7 December 1898; "*Huíluán jiāngjiè* 回鑾將屆 [Religious Returning Procession]," *Lat Pau*《叻報》, 14 January 1899; "*Yǔshī bàixīng* 雨師敗興 [Rain Dampened Spirits]," *Lat Pau*《叻報》, 27 January 1899. 12 January 1900 Return Procession: "Untitled," *The Straits Times*, 12 January 1900. 18 December 1900 Procession; 8 February 1901 Return Procession: "Untitled," *The Straits Times*, 17 December 1900; "Untitled," *The Straits Times*, 29 January 1901. 4 December 1901 Procession: "Untitled," *The Straits Times*, 27 November 1901. 25 November 1902 Procession: "Untitled," *The Straits Times*, 24 November 1902; "The Chinese Procession," *The Straits Times*, 25 November 1902. 12 December 1903 Procession; 1 February 1904 Return Procession: "Untitled," *The Straits Times*, 12 December 1903; "Untitled," *The Straits Times*, 29 January 1904; "The Chingay Festival," *The Straits Times*, 1 February 1904. 1 December 1904 Procession: "Untitled," *The Straits Times*, 30 November 1904. 11 January 1906 Return Procession: "Untitled," *The Straits Times*,

11 January 1906. 9 December 1906 Procession: "Untitled," *The Straits Times*, 8 December 1906.

20 "News of the Week," *Straits Times Weekly Issue*, 3 November 1883.

21 "The great annual religious procession commonly called Chingay...," *Straits Times Weekly Issue*, 19 December 1887.

22 Ibid.

23 "Thursday, 15th December," *Straits Times Overland Journal*, 19 December 1881. There were slight alterations to the procession routes over the years. The route published by *Lat Pau* on 22 November 1897 was: "賽神路程 本日為寓叻粵商迎神賽會之期茲承董事寄來路徑單一紙囑登本報用特照錄以供眾覽 瓊州社由小坡來大坡合社路引自海墘 (Beach Road) 起行轉入爪亞街 (Java Road) 出大火車路直至福音館 (Chinese Gospel Hall) 十字路鼓樂暫止到纏綸影像館 (G.R. Lambert & Co. Studio: No. 1 High Street) 前再奏鼓樂過鐵吊橋 (Elgin Bridge) 落十八間後 (Circular Road) 上山仔頂 (Chulia Street) 鼓樂復正轉至粵海廟 (Wak Hai Cheng Bio) 會齊 潮州廣府客籍瓊州一齊起行路引 自粵海廟前起行過五代天宮前 (Church Street) 落賭間口 (China Street) 灣落豆腐街 (Upper Chin Chew Street) 出大火車站直上牛車水 (Kreta Ayer) 到丹絨巴葛 (Tanjong Pagar) 就原路回大火車路至吉甯廟 (Sri Mariamman Temple) 前鼓樂暫停直落漆木街 (South Bridge Road) 灣入戲館街 (Carpenter Street) 再奏鼓樂出柴吊橋 (Read Bridge) 鼓樂復止灣過怡園 (Ee Hng: Merchant Road) 前出新巴虱 (Ellenborough Market) 直街 (Read Street) 海墘灣落柴吊橋 (Read Bridge) 直街 (Read Street) 鼓樂復止入馬車街出大火車路過鐵吊橋 (Elgin Bridge) 落海墘過雪廠 (Whampoa's Ice House) 直到打鐵廠 (possibly Riley Hargreaves Iron Foundry: Ord Road – expunged) 灣回王家山 (Fort Canning) 後行落雙井 (foot of Fort Canning along Hill Street, facing High Street) 鼓樂復止灣入雙井橫街出大火車路過鐵吊橋 (Elgin Bridge) 落十八間墘 (Boat Quay) 入茄萣街鼓樂復止出山仔頂 (Chulia Street) 鼓樂亦止落十八間後 (Circular Road) 出大火車街到玻璃角 (Corner of Police Courts) 鼓樂又止 灣過溝仔邊中街 (Market Street) 到直落亞送實得力(Telok Ayer Street)入媽祖宮街後 (Amoy Street) 過五代天宮 (Church Street) 復回粵海廟 (Wak Hai Cheng Bio) 各股拜社". [... the Hainanese started from Beach Road, turned into Java Road, passed the junction near Chinese Gospel Hall, Lambert & Co. Studio, Elgin Bridge, Circular Road, Chulia Street and reached Wak Hai Cheng Bio... The Teochews, Cantonese, Hakkas and Hainanese then started from Wak Hai Cheng Bio and proceeded to Church Street, China Street, Upper Chin Chew Street, Kreta Ayer, and Tanjong Pagar before returning. Passed Sri Mariamman Temple, South Bridge Road, Carpenter Street, Coleman Bridge, Merchant Road, Ellenborough Market, Read Street, crossed Read Bridge, and continued along Read Street, Elgin Bridge, Whampoa's Ice House, Fort Canning, Hill Street, Elgin Bridge, Boat Quay, ..., Chulia Street, Circular Road, corner of Police Courts, Market Street, Telok Ayer Street, Amoy Street, Church Street, before returning back to Wak Hai Cheng Bio.] "*Sàishén lùchéng* 賽神路程 [The Route of Religious Procession]," *Lat Pau* 《叻報》, 22 November 1897.

24 The Hokkien did away with Chingay processions and "Sembayang Hantu" in 1931. Although it is unknown when the Teochew discontinued their Chingay practices, it is generally believed to be around the same time as the Hokkien. "Chinese Topics in Malaya." *The Straits Times*, 10 December 1931.

25 Durkheim, Emile, *The Elementary Forms of Religious Life* (New York: Free Press, 1965).

26 Mak, Lau Fong, *The Dynamics of Chinese Dialect Groups in Early Malaya* (Singapore: Singapore Society of Asian Studies, 1995), 169; Lim, How Seng 林孝勝, *Xīnjiāpō huáshè yǔ huáshāng*

《新加坡華社與華商》[Singapore's Chinese Community and Chinese Traders] (Singapore: Singapore Society of Asian Studies, 1999), 30–43.

27 Yeo, Kang Shua, "Homogenously Heterogenous?: The Diversity of Traditional Chinese Architecture in Singapore," *Journal of Southeast Asian Architecture* 9 (2006): 87–106.

28 Mak, Lau Fong, *The Dynamics of Chinese Dialect Groups in Early Malaya*, 3–4.

29 In 1891, 1901 and 1911, Hakkas made up approximately 6.1%, 5.2% and 8.5% of the Chinese population in Singapore respectively, while Cantonese represented 19.2%, 18.7% and 21.1% and Teochews comprised 19.5%, 16.8% and 15.8%. Superintendent of Census, *Report on the Census of the Straits Settlements, taken on 5th April 1891* (Singapore: Straits Settlements, 1891); Superintendent of Census, *Report on the Census of the Straits Settlements, taken on 1st March 1901* (Singapore: Straits Settlements, 1901); Superintendent of Census, *Report on the Census of the Straits Settlements, taken on 10th March 1911* (Singapore: Straits Settlements, 1911).

30 In 1891, 1901 and 1911, the percentage of Hokkiens among the Chinese population in Singapore was approximately 37.6%, 36.0% and 44.2% respectively. If we combine the population of Cantonese and Hakkas with the Teochews, the percentage distribution in 1891, 1901 and 1911 was approximately 44.7%, 40.7% and 45.5% respectively. Ibid.

31 During the Qing dynasty, Hainan Island was part of Guangdong Province. It was only in 1988 that it became a province of its own.

32 Dean, Kenneth 丁荷生, and Hue, Guan Thye 許源泰, *Xīnjiāpō huáwén míngkè huìbiān* 《新加坡華文銘刻彙編》 *Chinese Epigraphy in Singapore 1819–1911* (Singapore: NUS Press; Guilin: Guangxi Normal University, 2017), vol. 1, 2–34.

33 Ngow, Wah 吳華, "*Yuèhǎiqīngmiào huàjiù* 粵海清廟話舊 [Reminiscences of Wak Hai Cheng Bio]," in *Shílè gǔjì* 《石叻古蹟》 [Monuments of Singapore], ed. Lim How Seng 林孝勝 (Singapore: South Seas Society, 1975), 149.

34 Lao, Chee Hean, "Plan of Temple to be Rebuilt in Phillip Street," 27 February 1895, 86/1895, CBS334, National Archives of Singapore; "Additions and Alterations to a Chinese Temple, situated in Teluk Ayer Street. Property of Eng Wah Quan," 1898, 203/1898, CBS337, National Archives of Singapore.

35 Ghee Hok Society (also known as Ghee Hok Kongsi) was a Teochew triad headed by Choa Moh Choon (蔡茂春).

36 "Seh Tan" (姓陳) refers to the people with the surname of Tan or the Tan clan. "Samseng" (三牲) refers to the three sacrificial offerings of pork, duck, and chicken. The word also developed connotations of bully, hooligan or gangster. Here, it meant gangster from the Tan clan. Wilkinson, R.J., *A Malay-English Dictionary (Romanised)*, Part 2 (London: Macmillan, 1955), 1013.

37 The discord between Seh Tan and Ghee Hok was historic. As early as 1861, the two groups had been fighting one another. "Untitled," *The Straits Times*, 6 April 1861.

38 "Friday, 1st September," *Straits Times Overland Journal*, 9 September 1871.

39 "From the Daily Times, October 23rd. The Riots," *Straits Times Overland Journal*, 25 October 1871; "Fortnight's Summary," *Straits Times Overland Journal*, 16 January 1873.

40 Song, Ong Siang, *One Hundred Years' History of the Chinese in Singapore* (Singapore: University Malaya Press, 1967), 166.

41 For more on spectacular punishment, see Foucault, Michel, "The Spectacle of the Scaffold," in Michel Foucault, *Discipline and Punish: The Birth of the Prison* (New York: Vintage Books, 1995), 32–69.

42 After the war, the Chinese Charitable Institutions Union (中華慈善機構聯合會) was known

varyingly as the Blue Cross Chinese Charitable Institutions Union (藍十字中華善堂救濟總會) or the Blue Cross Charitable Institution (中華善堂藍十救濟總會). Today, it is known by the latter name. "2,500 Get More Relief," *The Straits Times*, 13 August 1951; "Disaster fund to be held in reserve," *The Straits Times*, 30 August 1951.

43 "Free Food Centres Being Opened to Give Succour to Syonan's Destitute: Blue Cross Workers' Laudable Scheme," *Syonan Shimbun*, 28 March 1945; "Mass Feeding of Poor People Starts in Syonan: 2,100 Blue Cross Workers Giving Good Service," *Syonan Shimbun*, 3 April 1945.

44 "Blue Cross To Treat Lepers," *Syonan Shimbun*, 28 April 1945; "Syonan's Great Fortune," *Syonan Shimbun Fortnightly*, 20 June 1945.

45 "Relief & Charity," *Syonan Shimbun*, 27 January 1945.

46 "Chinese Forming Strong Body to Provide Assistance to Air Raid Victims Fully Supported by Authorities," *Syonan Shimbun*, 19 January 1945.

47 "Chinese Forming Strong Body"; "Charitable Institutions Union Holding Big Confab Tomorrow," *Syonan Shimbun*, 5 February 1945; "As Long As There Is Food In Syonan, None Shall Go Hungry, Suffer Distress," *Syonan Shimbun*, 7 February 1945.

48 The headquarters of the Black Cross Society was opened in April 1945 at No. 76 Club Street of the Chinese Weekly Entertainment Club (威基利俱樂部). "Black Cross Association To Hold Inaugural Meeting," *Syonan Shimbun*, 13 March 1945; "Black Cross H.Q. Opened In Syonan," *Syonan Shimbun*, 24 & 25 April 1945.

49 "Three Chinese Relief Bodies Amalgamate," *Syonan Shimbun*, 2 April 1945; "Syonan's Charitable Bodies Pooling Resources for More Effective Relief," *Syonan Shimbun*, 11 April 1945.

50 "Free Food Centres Being Opened to Give Succour to Syonan's Destitute: Blue Cross Workers' Laudable Scheme."

51 For more information about the Blue Cross Charitable Institution, refer to Lee, Chee Hiang 李志賢, *Lánshí chūnqiū: xīnjiāpō cháorén shàntáng kǎo*《藍十春秋: 新加坡潮人善堂考》[A History of the Blue Cross: A Study of Singapore Teochew Charitable Institutions] (Singapore: Blue Cross Charitable Institution, 2017), 24–39.

52 "Chinese Forming Strong Body."

53 Oversea Chinese Association, "Notice: Re: Invitation to Gunpo (Auxiliary Servicemen) for the Second Term in Syonan," *Syonan Shimbun*, 20 September 1943.

54 Syonan Tokubetu Si Tyo, "Tokubetu-Si Notice No. 265," *Syonan Simbun*, 18 September 1943.

55 Oversea Chinese Association, "Notice: Re: Invitation."

56 Oversea Chinese Association, "Endau Development Scheme," *Syonan Shimbun*, 2 December 1943; "Registration Centres for Settlers Opened," *Syonan Shimbun*, 3 December 1943.

57 Oversea Chinese Association, "Recruitment of Chinese Policemen," *Syonan Shimbun*, 10 May 1944.

58 "Chinese Police Will Not Be Sent Outside Syonan," *Syonan Shimbun*, 26 July 1944.

59 "Chua Kian Thye, interview by Lee Beng Beng, 31 May 1999," Reel 2 of 3, Accession Number 002138, Oral History Interviews, National Archives of Singapore.

60 *Ngoh hiang* and *tau pok* are the common spellings used for the two types of food. Their spelling, according to the general transliteration standard used in this book, would be *ngou*^{5} *hiang*^{1} and *dao*^{7} *bog*^{4} respectively.

61 "Chua Kian Thye, interview by Lee Beng Beng," 31 May 1999," Reel 2 of 3.

62 Also spelt "Wan Tien Seang Tee", "Wan Tsin Seang Tee", or "Wun Yien Seang Tie".

63 Also spelt "Hin Tean Sang Te".

64 "Suit No. 430 of 1914, In the Matter of the Trustee Ordinance 1914 and In the Matter of the 'Ghee Ann Society'," 8 February 1916, Settlement of Singapore Registry of Deed, volume CDXXXVI, 505, no. 142; Seah Euching was also known as Seah Eu Chin, Seah U Chin and Seah Yoochin, while Sim Ah Kie was also known as Sim Ah Kai, Sim Ah Khai, Sim Ah Khay and Sym Ah Kai. See Appendix for more details of these trustees.

65 This is a rough estimation based on the death dates of some of the trustees, and the years during which they were active.

66 Singapore Improvement Trust, "Backlane – Phillip St. 33, Phillip St," 1929–1933, SIT T9/29, HDB 1013, National Archives of Singapore.

67 The addresses of Nos. 32 Circular Road and 48 South Boat Quay remain the same. The burial ground in the "District of Amokiah" was part of Kwong Ngee Suah, also known as Kwang Nee Suah Teochew Cemetery (廣義山), located along Upper Serangoon Road. It was exhumed in phases in 1982 and 1985–86; See map by Singapore Survey Department, "Singapore. Mukim No. XVIII_Ang Mo Kio, Mukim No. XVII_Toa Payoh, Mukim No. XXIV_Kalang," 1956, SP001719, National Archives of Singapore; "No. 5 of 1933 An Ordinance to Incorporate the Ngee Ann Kongsi," *Straits Settlements Government Gazette,* 10 March 1933, 384; "Suit No. 430 of 1914."

68 Ning, Ngui Ngi 林緯毅, "*Wànshìshùn gōngsī yǔ xīnjiāpō cháorén de māzǔ jìsì* 萬世順公司與新嘉坡潮人的媽祖祭祀 [Ban See Soon Kongsi and the Worship of the Goddess of the Sea by Singaporeans]," *Bǎinián huímóu: mǎhuá shèhuì yǔ zhèngzhì*《百年回眸：馬華社會與政治》[100 Years of Malaysian Chinese Society and Politics: Review and Prognosis], ed. Hé Guózhōng 何國忠 (Kuala Lumpur: *Huáshè yánjiū zhōngxīn* 華社研究中心, 2005), 140.

69 Ibid.

70 No primary sources have been found to date that corroborate this. Writers who mention 1845 as the year in which management of the temple was transferred to Ngee Ann Kun or Ngee Ann Kongsi includes Teochew Poit Ip Huay Kuan, *Cháoyǒng: xīnjiāpō cháozhōu bāyì huìguǎn bāshí zhōunián jìniàn tèkān*《潮涌：新嘉坡潮州八邑會館八十周年紀念特刊》[Singapore Teochew Poit Ip Huay Kuan 80th Anniversary Magazine] (Singapore: Singapore Teochew Poit Ip Huay Kuan, 2009), 46; Phua, Chay Long 潘醒農, "*Xīnjiāpō cháozhōu bāyì huìguǎn jiǎnshǐ* 新嘉坡潮州八邑會館簡史 [A Brief History of the Singapore Teochew Poit Ip Huay Kuan]," in Teochew Poit Ip Huay Kuan, *Xīnjiāpō cháozhōu bāyì huìguǎn chénglì qīshí zhōunián jìniàn*《新嘉坡潮州八邑會館成立七十周年紀念特刊》[Singapore Teochew Poit Ip Huay Kuan 70th Anniversary Magazine] (Singapore: Singapore Teochew Poit Ip Huay Kuan, 2000), 132; Ngow, Wah 吳華, "*Yuèhǎiqīngmiào huàjiù* 粵海清廟話舊 [Reminiscences of Wak Hai Cheng Bio]," in *Shílè gǔjì*《石叻古蹟》[Monuments of Singapore], 146; Ngow, Wah 吳華, "*Yuèhǎiqīngmiào huàjiù* 粵海清廟話舊 [Reminiscences of Wak Hai Cheng Bio]," in *Fānglín jīnxī*《芳林今昔》[Hong Lim: Past and Present], ed. Ong Geok Seng 王玉成 (Singapore: Hong Lim Citizens' Consultative Committee, 1977), 37.

71 "Report on an Ordinance to Incorporate the Ngee Ann Kongsi (No. 5 of 1933)," 1933, Straits Settlements Dispatches to the Secretary of State 1933 No. 151, GD100, NL6139, National Archives of Singapore.

72 "Suit No. 430 of 1914."

73 See Chapter 1 endnote 38.

74 "Suit No. 430 of 1914."

75 Chose is a term used in English common law to refer to rights in property. Here, "chose in action" refers to rights that can be recovered in a lawsuit.

76 "Suit No. 430 of 1914."
77 Ibid.
78 Ibid.; "Copy of a Conveyance to be Registered on Behalf of Seah Liang Seah of No. 14 North Boat Quay, Singapore, Merchant," Settlement of Singapore Registry of Deeds, Volume CCCLX, 712, No. 200."
79 "Suit No. 430 of 1914." The "Poh Seng Tye Tee" temple was situated along Johore Road while the "Choh Soo Kong Temple" was located along Jalan Besar (Town Subdivision XVII Lot No. 14). The latter temple's land was first bought by Seah Liang Seah in his capacity as trustee of the "Choh Soo Kong Temple" on 23 October 1894. This land was later acquired by the Singapore Improvement Trust between 1928 and 1932 for the construction of a back lane. The Ghee Ann Kongsi was compensated $5,000 for this. See Singapore Improvement Trust, "Chinese Temple at Jalan Besar Lot 14 T S D XVII – Ngee Ann Kongsi," 1928–1936, SIT 871/28, HDB1011, National Archives of Singapore.
80 "No. 103 – Ordinance No. 116 (Societies)," *Straits Settlements Government Gazette*, 19 January 1934, 142; There is a lot of confusion regarding what the society's name was at different points in time. Some writers inaccurately claim that Ghee Ann Koon (義安郡), the predecessor of Ngee Ann Kongsi, was formed by Seah Eu Chin and members of 12 other clans in or around 1830, while Ngee Ann Kongsi was formally formed in 1845. See Ngow, Wah 吴華, *Xīnjiāpō huázú huìguǎn zhì*《新嘉坡華族會館志》[Gazetteer of Singapore's Chinese Clans] (Singapore: South Seas Society, 1975), 62–63; the only official use of the name "Ngee Ann Kongsi" before 1933 was in the 1895 Wak Hai Cheng Bio building plan submitted to municipal authorities. It was spelt as "Ngee Ann Kongsee". See Lao, Chee Hean, "Plan of Temple to be Rebuilt in Phillip Street," February 27, 1895, 86/1895, CBS334, National Archives of Singapore.
81 The name, Yì'ān Jùn (義安郡), was the historical name of the Teochew prefecture in China between 413 and 487 CE, as well as between 557 and 621 CE.
82 The term, if spelt according to the general transliteration standard used in this book, would have been *ngi*[6] *ang*[1] *gung*[6] instead.
83 It was erroneously listed in the "Suit No. 430 of 1914" that Lot No. 9-1 of Town Subdivision XXIX is in the District of Amokiah. "Suit No. 430 of 1914."; the four shophouses are no longer in existence. The old land lot number of the land on which the four shophouses were situated was Lot No. 116-12 of Town Subdivision VII, and the new lot number is TS07-99548T. It currently forms part of Eu Tong Sen Street, near its junction with Tew Chew Street.
84 "Copy of a Conveyance to be Registered on Behalf of Seah Liang Seah."
85 Phua, Chay Long 潘醒農, "*Yì'ān gōngsī* 義安公司 [The Ngee Ann Kongsi]," in *Mǎláiyà cháoqiáo tōngjiàn*《馬來亞潮僑通鑑》[A History of Overseas Teochew in Malaya], ed. Phua Chay Long 潘醒農 (Singapore: The Nantao Publishing House, 1950), 331.
86 "No. 36," Indenture of Land, 20 October 1845, District of Claymore, Singapore Land Authority.
87 "Ordinance No. I of 1889," *Straits Settlements Government Gazette*, 22 February 1889, 188.
88 "Government Notification No. 753," *Straits Settlements Government Gazette*, 20 December 1889, 2542.
89 "Government Notification No. 486," *Straits Settlements Government Gazette*, 29 August 1890, 1839.
90 "No. 962 – Ordinance No. 116 (Societies)," *Straits Settlements Government Gazette*, 12 May 1933, 967.
91 "F.M.S. Loan," *The Straits Times*, 17 May 1916.
92 "An Aged Defendant!," *The Singapore Free Press and Mercantile Advertiser*, 14 December 1922.
93 "Report on an Ordinance to Incorporate the

Ngee Ann Kongsi."

94 Ibid.

95 Ibid.

96 "No. 5 of 1933 An Ordinance to Incorporate the Ngee Ann Kongsi," 384; "Ngee Ann Kongsi (Incorporation) Ordinance, (Chapter 370)," revised edition 1985, accessed 28 July 2017, https://sso.agc.gov.sg/Act/NAKIO1933.

97 The leadership role held by Seah Liang Seah and Seah Eng Tong were certain. Seah Eu Chin was trustee of Heang Tiang Siang Tee Kongsi, Wun Yien Seang Tie Kongsi, 32 Circular Road, 48 South Boat Quay, burial grounds in the "District of Amokiah", i.e. Kwong Ngee Suah (廣義山), and Tye Swah Teng (泰山亭), while Seah Cheo Seah was trustee of Ghee Ann Koon as seen in the land documents for Kwong Eng Suah (廣恩山) and the New Bridge Road properties. It is unclear if they held specific leadership roles, but it can be assumed that the Seahs were the de facto leaders of the society due to their influence and prominence within the community. See Appendix.

98 The end dates of the presidencies are based on the year of death of each individual except Seah Eng Tong, and might not reflect the exact period during which each individual had effective control over the Ghee Ann Koon.

99 "No. 858 – Ordinance No. 116 (Societies)," *Straits Settlements Government Gazette*, 3 May 1929, 1066.

100 "No. 5 of 1933," 374.

101 "*Yīngzhōng xiānshēng yì'ān jùn zhū zhíshì* 應忠先生 義安郡諸執事 [Mr. Eng Tong and the Various Trustees of Ngee Ann Kun]," *Lat Pau* 《叻報》, 29 December 1927; "*Dàiyóu* 代郵 [Posted on behalf of]," *Nányáng Shāngbào* 《南洋商報》 [Nanyang Siang Pau], 29 December 1927.

102 Yen Ching-Hwang notes that Lim Nee Soon's group of Teochews did not raise the issue of Ghee Ann Koon's mismanagement earlier out of respect for Seah Liang Seah. See Yen, Ching-Hwang, *Ethnicities, Personalities and Politics in the Ethnic Chinese Worlds* (Singapore: World Scientific Publishing, 2016), 125. It was highly probable that Seah Liang Seah knew the problems of Ghee Ann Koon and, in his old age, sought to rectify it through an ordinance incorporating the society.

103 "Lim Nee Soon to Arthur M. Goodman, 4 January 1928," Ngee Ann Kongsi, Singapore; Phua, Chay Long 潘醒農, "*Yì'ān gōngsī shǐmò jì* 《義安公司始末記》 [Historical Changes of the Ngee Ann Kongsi]," Ngee Ann Kongsi, 18 April 1931, NA539, National Archives of Singapore. The latter document was approved by the society's Committee of Management on 25 May 1931.

104 "Lim to Goodman".

105 Ibid.

106 Ibid.

107 It was Seah Eng Kun (佘應謹) who led the attempt by other members of the Seah family in disrupting the handover of power to Lim's group. He was the son of Seah Cheo Seah. Two other Teochews, Cài Juéqiū (蔡蕚秋) and Teo Keong Meng (張恭銘) in turn engaged a lawyer to challenge his claims. See Phua, "*Yì'ān gōngsī shǐmò jì* 《義安公司始末記》 [Historical Changes of the Ngee Ann Kongsi] ".

108 Ibid.; Ngow, *Xīnjiāpō huázú huìguǎn zhì* 《新嘉坡華族會館志》 [Gazetteer of Singapore's Chinese Clans], 62–63.

109 Ibid.

110 Ibid.

111 "*Chóushè xīnjiāpō cháozhōu huìguǎn yuánqǐ* 籌設新嘉坡潮州會館緣起 [Origins of the Establishment of the Singapore Teochew Huay Kuan]," *Nányáng Shāngbào* 《南洋商報》 [Nanyang Siang Pau], 10 September 1928, 8; this proposal to form a Teochew Huay Kuan was also reprinted in *Xīnjiāpō cháozhōu bāyì huìguǎn jīnxǐ jìniànkān* 《新加坡潮州八邑會館金禧紀念刊》. Phua, Chay Long 潘醒農, "*Xīnjiāpō cháozhōu bāyì huìguǎn jiǎnshǐ* 新加坡潮州八邑

會館簡史 [Brief History of Singapore Teochew Poit Ip Huay Kuan]," in *Xīnjiāpō cháozhōu bāyì huìguǎn jīnxǐ jìniànkān*《新加坡潮州八邑會館金禧紀念刊》[Singapore Teochew Poit Ip Huay Kuan 50th Anniversary Magazine], ed. Teochew Poit Ip Huay Kuan (Singapore: Singapore Teochew Poit Ip Huay Kuan, 1980), 293.

112 Ibid., 294.

113 "No. 732 – Ordinance No. 116 (Societies)," *Straits Settlements Government Gazette*, 19 April 1929, 969.

114 Phua, "*Xīnjiāpō cháozhōu bāyì huìguǎn jiǎnshǐ* 新加坡潮州八邑會館簡史 [Brief History of Singapore Teochew Poit Ip Huay Kuan]", 294.

115 Phua, "*Yì'ān gōngsī shǐmò jì*《義安公司始末記》 [Historical Changes of the Ngee Ann Kongsi]".

116 Ngow, *Xīnjiāpō huázú huìguǎn zhì* 《新嘉坡華族會館志》 [Gazetteer of Singapore's Chinese Clans], 62–63, 128–129; Liu, Hong, and Wong, Sin-Kiong, *Singapore Chinese Society in Transition: Business, Politics, & Socio-Economic Change, 1945–1965* (New York: Peter Lang, 2004), 32.

117 Phua, "*Yì'ān gōngsī shǐmò jì*《義安公司始末記》 [Historical Changes of the Ngee Ann Kongsi]".

118 "No. 5 of 1933," 375.

119 Ibid., 371.

120 Ibid., 370.

121 Ibid.

122 The 24 names listed in the 1933 Ordinance did not tally fully with the names listed in *Ngee Ann Kongsi: Into the Next Millennium*. Ibid. Also see Tan, Sumiko 陳澄子, *Yì'ān gōngsī: kuàrù lìng yīgè qiānxǐ nián*《義安公司:跨入另一個千禧年》*Ngee Ann Kongsi: Into the Next Millennium* (Singapore: Ngee Ann Kongsi, 2005), 115.

123 "Report on an Ordinance to Incorporate the Ngee Ann Kongsi."

124 Ibid.

125 Ibid.

126 Singapore Improvement Trust, "Backlane – Phillip St."

127 "Report on an Ordinance to Incorporate the Ngee Ann Kongsi."

128 Wee, Vivienne, *Religion and Ritual among the Chinese of Singapore: An Ethnographic Study*, 74–75.

129 Phua, 28 October 1930, Ngee Ann Kongsi Minutes 1930. The minutes stated "(四)各廟廟祝嗣後宜由眾投阄標之不得相傳沿襲".

130 Ibid.

131 Phua, 25 May 1931, Ngee Ann Kongsi Minutes 1930. It was stated in the minutes as follows:
"主席[林義順]云粵海廟廟祝每屆定若干年
請酌議之郭廷通君提議每屆定為三年
林雨巖君附議 通過
林雨巖君提議當登報端俾便週知計刊登華字日報二家各 一星期
陳秋槎君附議 通過"

132 Xiè, Xiánglóng 謝祥龍, "*Yàhuà chòngxīn huàzhǎn shì shénmiào zhǔchí yěshì míng huàjiā* 亞化重新畫展　是神廟主持也是名畫家 [The Alpha Revival Art Exhibition: Temple Caretaker is also an Artist]," *Xīnmíng Rìbào* 《新明日報》[Shin Min Daily News], 15 November 2000. During an interview, Wak Hai Cheng Bio's caretaker, Qwek Wee Chew (郭維洲), stated that, "粵海清廟主持的職位是從我的祖父開始，後來傳給了我的父親 [Kwek Yong Hock]，然後又由我接任這個職位。" Qwek Wee Chew was trained at the Nanyang Academy of Fine Arts by Cheong Soo Pieng (鐘四賓).

133 Phua, 11 June 1931, Ngee Ann Kongsi Minutes 1930. It was stated in the minutes as follows:
"主席 [林義順] 云第三條議程係解決粵海廟廟祝事此次投來之鬮共有九張內有一人投兩張取消一張後寔存八張計廣雨八百一十元郭岳成六百六十元陳木拱六百元楊成永五百五十元傅蓮師五百元霖手四百五十五元能見四百弍十弍元舊廟祝郭君永福此次無投鬮只來一信謂彼當粵海廟祝十有餘

年近來神權衰落給廟祝費若干全憑裁奪等語統請討論之
李金賜君云請先解決是否准和尚加入後再表決其他
劉炳先君提議和尚不准為粵海廟之廟祝
陳秋槎君附議 通過
楊纘文君云永福君已有來函可着彼面詢能出值若干若較他人更多理應仍予彼任之庶乎駕輕就熟□示優待結果永福君願年出六百七十元承受粵海廟祝"

134 Ibid.

135 Phua, 16 July 1931, Ngee Ann Kongsi Minutes 1930. The meeting minutes stated:
"主席［林義順］報告粵海廟祝前被郭永福君標得本議定以半年之值為底壓費郭君要求準其將每月繳納之廟祝費作為半年繳交一次似此已變成無壓底矣茲為折衷起見改為每三個月繳交一次未知可否
楊纘文君附議 通過";
Phua, 1 July 1932, Ngee Ann Kongsi Minutes 1930. The minutes recorded the following:
"粵海清廟廟祝郭永福君來函謂神權日落市況不景懇每月減二十元案
李金賜君提議準其每年減壹佰元
陳立植君附議众賛成 通過";
Phua, 28 April 1934, Ngee Ann Kongsi Minutes 1930. The following was recorded in the meeting minutes:
"粵海清廟廟祝滿期案
主席[李偉南]云粵海清廟廟祝郭永福君係於本年陰曆四月滿期茲欲另承人標押仍由郭永福君照前期源價續租其壓底銀得酌降減為弍佰八十五元嗣後每個月應清還一次但所有前欠租金應於陰曆四月內完清以清手續
郭斯高君附議众賛成通過
林樹林君提議本届粵海廟租期仍訂為三年嗣後無論投標與否概定為期二年以符董事之選舉期
楊纘文君附議众賛成通過";
Phua, 6 July 1935, Ngee Ann Kongsi Minutes 1930. The minutes stated:
"粵海廟租壓底續繼案
林錦成君報告查賬員謂前議決粵海廟祝郭永福原有壓底弍百八十五元現無壓底銀存在欲否須另討論議決粵海廟祝郭永福其壓底銀仍為弍佰八十五元至租金則繼續催討";
Phua, 23 March 1937, Ngee Ann Kongsi Minutes 1930. The minutes of the meeting reported the following:
"粵海廟祝續定案
主席(楊纘文)云粵海清廟廟祝之租期至本年陰曆四月滿期如何請決定之
陳秋槎君提議粵海清廟廟祝仍予郭永福君繼租租價照舊每年五百七十元（壓底如前）一期二年由本年陰曆五月起算
李偉南君附議众賛成通過";
Phua, 19 August 1942, Ngee Ann Kongsi Minutes 1930. The minutes stated the following:
"粵海廟祝請求豁免宮租案
通過对粵海廟祝郭永福函以去年十月至本年四月因戰事影响香火□然輪虧不少請求豁免宮租應准其免繳去年十月至本年三月共半年租金"

136 Phua, 23 March 1937, Ngee Ann Kongsi Minutes 1930.

137 Qwek, Wee Chew 郭維洲, personal communication with author, Wak Hai Cheng Bio, 12 May 2010.

138 Tan, Siew Eng 陳秀英, personal communication with author, Wak Hai Cheng Bio, Singapore, 8 December 2016. Ms Tan is an administrator of the Ngee Ann Kongsi.

139 Ibid.

140 Phua, "*Xīnjiāpō cháozhōu bāyì huìguǎn jiǎnshǐ* 新加坡潮州八邑會館簡史 [Brief History of Singapore Teochew Poit Ip Huay Kuan]", 294; "No. 858 – Ordinance No. 116 (Societies)," *Straits Settlements Government Gazette*, 3 May 1929, 1075.

141 "No. 1064 – The Societies Ordinance (Chapter 217)," *Straits Settlements Government Gazette*, 2 May 1941, 963. By 1937, the Teochew Poit Ip

Huay Kuan's office was located at the rear building of Wak Hai Cheng Bio. The address of the newly formed Kwangtung Hui Kuan in 1937 was "c/o Teochew Poit Ip Huay Kuan, Church Street". See "List of Existing Societies Exempted from Registration in the Settlement of Singapore," *Straits Settlements Government Gazette*, 12 August 1938, 2201.

142 "No. 858 – Ordinance No. 116 (Societies)," 1066; "No. 913 – Ordinance No. 116 (Societies)," *Straits Settlements Government Gazette*, 8 May 1930, 787; "No. 928 – Ordinance No. 116 (Societies)," *Straits Settlements Government Gazette*, 8 May 1931, 879.

143 The official address of Yit Hai Hoe Kuan listed in the "List of Existing Societies Exempted from Registration in the Settlement of Singapore" was "Temple, Phillip Street". This remains the case all the way till the outbreak of the Second World War. See "No. 928 – Ordinance No. 116 (Societies)," 879; "No. 1064 – The Societies Ordinance (Chapter 217)," 959; Lee, Sean Wah 李先華, personal communication with author, Ngee Ann City Civic Plaza, Singapore, 17 April 2016. According to Lee Sean Wah, a member of Ngee Ann Kongsi's Committee of Management and the Chairman of Temple and Prayer Subcommittee (酬神與宮廟管理小組委員會主席) in 2016, Yit Hai Hoe Kuan's Chinese name is 粵海會館 (Yuèhǎi huìguǎn). He added that there were many interrelated societies based in the temple. Unfortunately, he does not know how Yit Hai Hoe Kuan is related to Wak Hai Cheng Bio.

144 When Kwangtung Hui Kuan's first executive council was formed in 1939, two years after its official registration in 1937, Phua served as its secretary. He held this post until 1949.

The First Chinese Imperial Plaque in Singapore (pp. 38–40)

1 Phua, Chay Long 潘醒農, *Cháoqiáo sùyuán jí* 《潮僑溯源集》 [Origins of Overseas Teochew] (Singapore: Global Publishing, 1993), 71–74.

2 Liu, Gretchen, and Lim, Albert K. S., *In Granite and Chunam: The National Monuments of Singapore* (Singapore: Landmark Books and Preservation of Monuments Board, 1996), 155; Lee, Geok Boi, *The Religious Monuments of Singapore: Faiths of Our Forefathers* (Singapore: Landmark Books and Preservation of Monuments Board, 2002), 22.

3 Toh, Lam Huat 杜南發, "*Guāngxù yùcì biǎn'é bōjìng nánmíng* 光緒御賜匾額《波靖南溟》 [Guāngxù royally bestowed plaque "calm the waves of the Southern Seas"]," in *Nánhǎi míngzhū: tiānfúgōng* 《南海明珠: 天福宮》 [Pearl of the South Seas: Thian Hock Keng Temple], ed. Toh Lam Huat 杜南發 (Singapore: Singapore Hokkien Huay Kuan, 2010), 212–215.

4 Ning, Ngui Ngi 林緯毅, "*Wànshìshùn gōngsī yǔ xīnjiāpō cháorén de māzǔ jìsì* 萬世順公司與新嘉坡潮人的媽祖祭祀 [Ban See Soon Kongsi and the Worship of the Goddess of the Sea by Singaporeans]," in *Bǎinián huímóu: mǎhuá shèhuì yǔ zhèngzhì* 《百年回眸: 馬華社會與政治》 [100 Years of Malaysian Chinese Society and Politics: Review And Prognosis], ed. Hé Guózhōng 何國忠 (Kuala Lumpur: *Huáshè yánjiū zhōngxīn* 華社研究中心, 2005), 139–153.

5 Han, Tan Juan 韓山元, "*Cháozhōu xiānxián chuàng yuèhǎiqīngmiào nóngsuō 180 nián huárén fèndǒu shǐ* 潮州先賢創粵海清廟濃縮180年華人奮斗史 [The Establishment of Wak Hai Cheng Bio by Teochew Pioneers: Condensing 180 Years History of the Chinese in Singapore]," in *Xīnjiāpō cháozhōu wénhuà zhǎn tèkān* 《新嘉坡潮州文化展特刊》 [Exhibition on the Heritage of the Teochew Community in Singapore], eds. Hóng Yúnshēng 洪雲生, and Xǔ Xuěqīng 許雪卿 (Singapore: Singapore Teochew Poit Ip Huay Kuan, 2002), 80–83.

6 Tan, Sumiko 陳澄子, *Yì'ān gōngsī: kuàrù lìng yīgè qiānxǐ nián* 《義安公司: 跨入另一個千禧年》 *Ngee Ann Kongsi: Into the Next Millennium* (Singapore: Ngee Ann Kongsi, 2005),

84; Teochew Poit Ip Huay Kuan, *Cháoyǒng: xīnjiāpō cháozhōu bāyì huìguǎn bāshí zhōunián jìniàn tèkān* 《潮涌：新嘉坡潮州八邑會館八十周年紀念特刊》 [Singapore Teochew Poit Ip Huay Kuan 80th Anniversary Magazine] (Singapore: Singapore Teochew Poit Ip Huay Kuan, 2009), 49.

7 Dézōng Jǐnghuángdì is the posthumous title of Emperor Guāngxù. In the *Factual Record of Qing Emperor Dézōng*, for the 4th lunar month of 1899, the bestowment of the imperial plaque to Wak Hai Cheng Bio was recorded as follows, "丙午 以潮洲（州）僑民捐助東賑，頒新加坡天后廟扁額曰：曙海祥雲". See *Dézōng jǐnghuángdì shílù* 《德宗景皇帝實錄》 [Factual Record of Qing Emperor Dézōng], Volume 443, 4th lunar month, 1899, quoted in Jao, Tsung-I 饒宗頤, *Xīnjiāpō gǔshì jì* 《新加坡古事記》 [The Chinese Sources for the History of Singapore before 1912] (Hong Kong: Chinese University Press, 1994), 6.

8 Wáng, Míngguāng 王明光, "*Yuèhǎiqīng miào cháobāng liùgǔ yǔ fúbāng sīhuìdǎng bāgǔ* 《粵海清廟潮幫六股與福幫私會黨八股》 [Yueh Hai Ching Temple Teochew clan's six shares and Hokkien clan's eight shares]," accessed on 19 December 2016, http://blog.sina.com.cn/s/blog_50e8ed7e0102ejnk.html.

9 Ibid.

10 Jiǎng, Wéitán 蔣維錟, and Yáng, Yǒngzhān 楊永佔, *Qīngdài māzǔ dàng'àn shǐliào huìbiān* 《清代媽祖檔案史料匯編》 [Qing Dynasty's Goddess of the Sea Historical Records] (Beijing: China Archives Press, 2003), 407–409; Jiǎng, Wéitán 蔣維錟, "*Qīngdài yùcì tiānhòugōng biǎn'é jí qí lìshǐ bèijǐng* 清代御賜天后宮匾額及其歷史背景 [Qing Dynasty Imperial Plaques Bestowed upon Temples of the Goddess of the Sea and their Historical Backgrounds]," *Pútián xuéyuàn xuébào* 《莆田學院學報》 [Journal of Putian University] , no. 4 (July–August 2005): 79–86. Jiǎng mentions that the imperial plaque is currently kept at the Singapore Teochew [Poit Ip] Huay Kuan, and that the accompanying documents (such as the original imperial scroll) have not been found. It is worth noting, however, that while the accompanying documents are indeed missing, the imperial plaque is currently installed at Wak Hai Cheng Bio and not at the Huay Kuan as Jiǎng mentioned.

11 Wáng erroneously stated the Emperor approved the petition on 25 June 1899 (农历己亥年五月十八日). See Wáng, "*Yuèhǎiqīng miào cháobāng liùgǔ yǔ fúbāng sīhuìdǎng bāgǔ* 《粵海清廟潮幫六股與福幫私會黨八股》 [Yueh Hai Ching Temple Teochew clan's six shares and Hokkien clan's eight shares]"; Jiǎng and Yáng, *Qīngdài māzǔ dàng'àn shǐliào huìbiān* 《清代媽祖檔案史料匯編》 [Qing Dynasty's Goddess of the Sea Historical Records], 407–409.

12 Wáng, "*Yuèhǎiqīng miào cháobāng liùgǔ yǔ fúbāng sīhuìdǎng bāgǔ* 《粵海清廟潮幫六股與福幫私會黨八股》 [Yueh Hai Ching Temple Teochew clan's six shares and Hokkien clan's eight shares]".

13 Ibid.

14 *Jiǎng* and *Yáng*, *Qīngdài māzǔ dàng'àn shǐliào huìbiān* 《清代媽祖檔案史料匯編》 [Qing Dynasty's Goddess of the Sea Historical Records], 407–409.

Kwangtung Hui Kuan (pp. 52–53)

1 In 1988, Hǎinán Island became a province in its own right.

2 Tan, Yeow Wooi 陳耀威, *Yuèdōng kǎo* 《粵東考》 [A Study Into the Origins of *Yuèdōng*], unpublished manuscript 未出版, 2005.

3 Singapore Kwangtung Hui Kuan, *Xīnjiāpō guǎngdōng huìguǎn jīnxǐ tèkān* 《新加坡廣東會館金禧特刊》 [Singapore Kwangtung Hui Kuan Golden Jubilee Souvenir Magazine] (Singapore: Kwangtung Hui Kuan, 1989), 68; Singapore Kwangtung Hui Kuan, *Guǎngdōng huìguǎn qìngzhù liùshí zhōunián jìniàn tèkān, 1937–1997*

《廣東會館慶祝六十周年紀念特刊，1937–1997》 [Kwangtung Hui Kuan 60th Anniversary Publication] (Singapore: Kwangtung Hui Kuan, 1997), 92–93.

4 Ibid.

5 The membership in 1997 comprised of 69 associations, 61 companies, 417 Cantonese, 377 Teochews, 133 Hakkas and 47 Hainanese forming a total of 1,104 members.
Singapore Kwangtung Hui Kuan, *Guǎngdōng huìguǎn qìngzhù liùshí zhōunián jìniàn tèkān, 1937–1997*《廣東會館慶祝六十周年紀念特刊, 1937–1997》[Kwangtung Hui Kuan 60th Anniversary Publication], 92.

6 Ibid.

7 "List of Existing Societies Exempted from Registration in the Settlement of Singapore," *Straits Settlements Government Gazette*, 12 August 1938, 2201.

8 Singapore Kwangtung Hui Kuan, *Xīnjiāpō guǎngdōng huìguǎn jīnxǐ tèkān*《新加坡廣東會館金禧特刊》[Singapore Kwangtung Hui Kuan Golden Jubilee Souvenir Magazine], 1989, 68; Singapore Kwangtung Hui Kuan, *Guǎngdōng huìguǎn qìngzhù liùshí zhōunián jìniàn tèkān, 1937–1997*《廣東會館慶祝六十周年紀念特刊, 1937–1997》[Kwangtung Hui Kuan 60th Anniversary Publication] 1997, 93.

9 Singapore Kwangtung Hui Kuan, Xīnjiāpō guǎngdōng huìguǎn jīnxǐ tèkān《新加坡廣東會館金禧特刊》[Singapore Kwangtung Hui Kuan Golden Jubilee Souvenir Magazine] 1989, 69.

10 Ngow, Wah 吳華, *Xīnjiāpō huázú huìguǎn zhì*《新嘉坡華族會館志》[Gazetteer of Singapore's Chinese Clans] (Singapore: South Seas Society, 1975), 145–146.

11 "*Jiǎn shǐ* 簡史 [Brief History]," Singapore Kwangtung Hui Kuan, accessed 15 December 2016, http://www.8path.com.sg/kwangtungclan/.

Chapter Three

1 "A Chinese Citizen Complains of the Condition of a Chinese Temple," *Straits Times Weekly Issue*, 4 March 1890.

2 Refer to the Chapter 1 section on "Founding Wak Hai Cheng Bio".

3 It is speculated that the temple might have been affected by the 1830 fire that "broke out in a blacksmith's shop in Circular Road, burned down Philip Street and one side of Market Street, and nearly got to Commercial Square...." This could have possibly necessitated renovation to be carried out. Buckley, Charles Burton, *An Anecdotal History of Old Times in Singapore, from the Foundation of the Settlement under the Honourable the East India Company, on Feb. 6th, 1819, to the Transfer to the Colonial Office as Part of the Colonial Possessions of the Crown on April 1st, 1867*, vol. 1 (Singapore: Fraser & Neave, 1902), 209–210.

4 The 1837 bronze bell is inscribed with the text "清道光十七年 陳仁合敬奉 天后宮 [Presented by *Dang*[5] *Ring*[5] *Hah*[8] in the 17th year of Emperor Daoguang's reign to Tiānhòugōng]" and the 1838 bronze bell with the words "清道光十八年 洽峰敬奉 上帝宮 [Presented by *Zieb*[8] *Hong*[1] in the 18th year of Emperor Daoguang's reign to Shàngdìgōng]".

5 Phua, Chay Long 潘醒農, "*Yuèhǎiqīngmiào – xīnjiāpō huárén gǔshénmiào* 粵海清廟 – 新嘉坡華人古神廟 [Wak Hai Cheng Bio – Historic Chinese Temple of Singapore]," in *Cháoqiáo sùyuán jí*《潮僑溯源集》[Origins of Overseas Teochew] (Singapore: Global Publishing, 1993), 72; Ngow, Wah 吳華, "*Yuèhǎiqīngmiào huàjiù* 粵海清廟話舊 [Reminiscences of Wak Hai Cheng Bio]," in *Shílè gǔjì*《石叻古蹟》[Monuments of Singapore], ed. Lim How Seng 林孝勝 (Singapore: South Seas Society, 1975), 145 and 148; Comber, Leon, *Chinese Temples in Singapore* (Singapore: Eastern Universities Press, 1958), 61; Edwards, Norman, and Keys, Peter,

Singapore: A Guide to Buildings, Streets, Places (Singapore: Times Books International, 1988), 417; Liu, Gretchen, and Lim, Albert K. S., *In Granite and Chunam: The National Monuments of Singapore* (Singapore: Landmark Books and Preservation of Monuments Board, 1996), 155; Goh, Ngan Hong 吴彦鴻, "*Yuèhǎiqīngmiào – cháojírén de bǎinián 'lǎoyégōng'* 粵海清廟 – 潮籍人的百年"老爺宮" [Wak Hai Cheng Bio – The Teochew's Hundred-year-old 'Palace of the Deity']," in *Xīnjiāpō fēngtǔ zhì* 《新加坡風土志》 [A Gazetteer of Singapore] (Singapore: Singapore Teochew Poit Ip Huay Kuan, 1997), 87; Lee, Geok Boi, *The Religious Monuments of Singapore: Faiths of Our Forefathers* (Singapore: Landmark Books, 2002), 22; Han, Tan Juan 韓山元, "*Cháozhōu xiānxián chuàng yuèhǎiqīngmiào nóngsuō 180 nián huárén fèndǒu shǐ* 潮州先賢創粵海清廟濃縮 180年華人奮斗史 [The Establishment of Wak Hai Cheng Bio by Teochew Pioneers: Condensing 180 Years History of the Chinese in Singapore]," in *Xīnjiāpō cháozhōu wénhuà zhǎn tèkān* 《新嘉坡潮州文化展特刊》 [Exhibition on the Heritage of the Teochew Community in Singapore], eds. Hóng Yúnshēng 洪雲生 and Xǔ Xuěqīng 許雪卿 (Singapore: Singapore Teochew Poit Ip Huay Kuan, 2002), 80; Tan, Sumiko 陳澄子, *Yì'ān gōngsī: kuàrù lìng yīgè qiānxǐ nián* 《義安公司: 跨入另一個千禧年》 *Ngee Ann Kongsi: Into the Next Millennium* (Singapore: Ngee Ann Kongsi, 2005), 89; Ning, Ngui Ngi 林緯毅, "*Wànshìshùn gōngsī yǔ xīnjiāpō cháorén de māzǔ jìsì* 萬世順公司與新加坡潮人的媽祖祭祀 [Ban See Soon Kongsi and the Worship of the Goddess of the Sea by Singaporeans]," in *Bǎinián huímóu: mǎhuá shèhuì yǔ zhèngzhì* 《百年回眸:馬華社會與政治》 [100 Years of Malaysian Chinese Society and Politics: Review and Prognosis], ed. Hé Guózhōng 何國忠 (Kuala Lumpur: *Huáshè yánjiū zhōngxīn* 華社研究中心, 2005), 140.

6 Lee, *The Religious Monuments*, 22.

7 "A Chinese Citizen Complains of the Condition of a Chinese Temple."

8 Lao, Chee Hean, "Plan of Temple to be Rebuilt in Phillip Street," 27 February 1895, 86/1895, CBS334, National Archives of Singapore.

9 On 26 April 1895 (Friday) the municipal engineer, James MacRitchie, passed away. The plan of Wak Hai Cheng Bio might be one of the first plans approved by Howard Newton on 29 April 1895 (Monday) in his capacity as acting municipal engineer.

10 Billion wood (*Eusideroxylon zwageri*) is also known as belian, balian, billian or Borneo ironwood. This timber is no longer available commercially as the primary producer, Indonesia, has imposed a total prohibition on the export of this timber. See "ULIN (*Eusideroxylon zwageri*)," accessed 8 December 2016, http://www.tropicaltimber.info/specie/ulin-eusideroxylon-zwageri/#lower-content; Tempanis (*Streblus elongates*) is also known as tempinis. This tree gives Tampines New Town its name. "TEMPINIS (*Streblus elongatus*)," accessed 8 December 2016, http://www.tropicaltimber.info/specie/tempinis-streblus-elongatus/; Tampines Constituency Sports Association, *30 Years of Tampines* (Singapore: Tampines Constituency Sports Association, 1988), 9–10; Darroo is also known as dedaru, bedaru or daru-daru. Its scientific name is *Cantleya corniculata (Becc.) Howard*, *Cantleya johorica Ridl.*, *Platea corniculata Becc.*, *Stemonurus corniculatus (Becc.) Ridl.* or *Urandra corniculata (Becc.) Foxw.* See Foxworthy, F. W., "Tree Names – A Few Changes," *Journal of the Malayan Branch of the Royal Asiatic Studies* 5, no. 2 (Nov 1927): 339; "DEDARU (*Cantleya corniculata*)," accessed 8 December 2016, http://www.tropicaltimber.info/specie/dedaru-cantleya-corniculata/; "*Cantleya corniculata (Becc.) Howard*," accessed 8 December 2016, http://www.gbif.org/species/3596897.

11 Besides the prayer area and rear building (ancillary religious uses area), the approved areas in the 2013 restoration also include an ancillary related uses area (comprising caretaker's room, lounge and kitchen) measuring 75.78 m^2; information on the various approved areas was taken from the following unpublished building plans submitted to the authorities: Raymond Woo & Associates Architects, "1st Storey Plan," Proposed Amendment to Approved Restoration and Additions/Alternations to the Existing Yueh Hai Ching Temple (National Monument) on Lot 98989L, 98988X, 00624L, TS 04, No. 30B Phillip Street, Singapore 048696, February 2013.

12 Based on Ning Ngui Ngi's interpretation, only the boundary walls, the roof, the granite courtyard and perhaps the entrance gateway were rebuilt; the main structures of the two shrines remain untouched. However, the 1895 building plan of the temple proves otherwise. The main structures of the shrines were new, while most parts of the boundary wall were retained. See Ning, "*Wànshìshùn gōngsī yǔ xīnjiāpō cháorén de māzǔ jìsì* 萬世順公司與新嘉坡潮人的媽祖祭祀 [Ban See Soon Kongsi and the Worship of the Goddess of the Sea by Singaporeans]," 140.

13 Ang Kheng Leng & Associates, "Proposed Reconstruction of Existing Brick Boundary Wall on Lots 428-1 & 428-2 T.S. IV at Phillip Street for M/S The Ngee Ann Kongsi," 12 November 1979, 3299/1979, Collection of the Ngee Ann Kongsi.

14 The claim that most building materials were imported from China has been repeated by many writers. See Phua, "*Yuèhǎiqīngmiào – xīnjiāpō huárén gǔshénmiào* 粵海清廟 – 新嘉坡華人古神廟 [Wak Hai Cheng Bio – Historic Chinese Temple of Singapore]," in *Cháoqiáo sùyuán jí* 《潮僑溯源集》 [Origins of Overseas Teochew], 73; Ngow, "*Yuèhǎiqīngmiào huàjiù* 粵海清廟話舊 [Reminiscences of Wak Hai Cheng Bio]," 146; Goh, "*Yuèhǎiqīngmiào – cháojírén de bǎinián "lǎoyégōng"* 粵海清廟 – 潮籍人的百年"老爺宮 [Wak Hai Cheng Bio – The Teochew's Hundred-year-old 'Palace of the Deity']," 87.

15 Other historical Chinese temples in Singapore use tropical hardwood too. The 1906 stele in Thian Hock Keng, located along Telok Ayer Street, listed "噶智柴" (Hokkien pronunciation: *jiá-tì chhâ*) or teak as a building material of the temple. *Jiá-tì* is from the Malay word, *jati*, meaning teak, while *chhâ* simply means wood. Teak was also listed in the historical accounts books of Hong San See as one of the building materials used in the reconstruction of the temple, which was completed in 1913. Other tropical timber used in Hong San See include kapur (氷片; officially known as 山樟木), balau (油抄; officially known as 重娑羅雙木), merbau (扣叻母; officially known as 菠蘿格木) and bintangor (文桐梧; officially known as 海棠木). See Yeo, Kang Shua 楊茳善, "*Tiānfúgōng dìlǐ jí jiànzhù yángéshǐ* 天福宮地理及建筑沿革史 [A Geographical and Architectural History of Thian Hock Keng Temple]," in *Nánhǎi míngzhū: Tiānfúgōng* 《南海明珠：天福宮》 [Pearl of the South Seas: Thian Hock Keng Temple], ed. Toh Lam Huat 杜南發 (Singapore: Singapore Hokkien Huay Kuan, 2010), 322–339.

16 In late 19th-century Singapore, darroo was also used as a building material for posts, girders, floor joists, plates, collar beams, and door and window frames.

17 It is commonly believed that the granite used in the construction of Chinese temples in Singapore came from China as shipping ballast. See "Thian Hock Keng Temple," in *GuideGecko, Singapore Travel Guide* (New Jersey: BookBaby, 2011). It is highly unlikely, however, that all the granite used in Singapore's Chinese temples came from China. Firstly, a petrographic analysis of the granite used in several historic Chinese temples in Singapore, including Hong San See, Thian Hock Keng and Wak Hai Cheng Bio shows that locally quarried granite was used alongside imported stone.

Secondly, the stone used as shipping ballast was typically crushed stone rather than slabs as this was easier to load, conformed better to the curvature of a ship's hull, thus maximising hull space. Thirdly, long stone slabs, such as those used as beams or columns, were unlikely to have been used as shipping ballast as they tend to break more easily due to poor tension. In cases where the granite used was not locally quarried, it is more likely that this granite was specially imported as a building material.

18 Lee Kim Woon graduated from the University of Malaya in 1972 with a bachelor's degree in applied geology. He has more than 30 years of local experience as a geologist, including 27 years in the Public Works Department Chief Civil Engineer's Office from 1972 to 1999. He played a key role in the production of the first Geological Map of Singapore in 1976, and the 2009 update of the map. He has also cowritten a book on Singapore's geology. See Lee, Kim Woon, and Zhou, Yingxin, *Geology of Singapore* (Singapore: Defence Science and Technology Agency, 2009).

19 There is a 1907 construction tender notice for Hong San See published in *Lat Pau* that specified Pulau Ubin granite as one of its building materials ("筑造宫地四圍浮羅宇敏石岸"). Specifically, "浮羅宇敏" refers to Pulau Ubin. See "*Fèngshānsì zhāogōng guǎnggào* 鳳山寺招工廣告 [Hong San See Tender Notice]," *Lat Pau* 《叻報》, 9 December 1907.

20 Phua, "*Yuèhǎiqīngmiào – xīnjiāpō huárén gǔshénmiào* 粵海清廟 – 新嘉坡華人古神廟 [Wak Hai Cheng Bio – Historic Chinese Temple of Singapore]," in *Cháoqiáo sùyuán jí* 《潮僑溯源集》 [Origins of Overseas Teochew], 72; Ngow, "*Yuèhǎiqīngmiào huàjiù* 粵海清廟話舊 [Reminiscences of Wak Hai Cheng Bio]," 145. No other written evidence has yet been found to corroborate the claim that Chén Miánjié oversaw the 1895 reconstruction works. According to Walter Lim (林志強), Chén Miánjié was a gambier trader and father of Tan Swee Kee (陳瑞麟), an early director of Sze Hai Tong Banking and Insurance Company. See Lim, Walter 林志強, "*Chén Ruìlín – sìhǎitōng yínháng fāqǐrén* 陳瑞麟 – 四海通銀行發起人 [Tan Swee Kee – Founder of Sze Hai Tong Banking and Insurance Company]," 24 November 2012, accessed 25 April 2017, http://bukitbrowntomb.blogspot.sg/2012/11/blog-post_24.html.

21 Ning, "*Wànshìshùn gōngsī yǔ xīnjiāpō cháorén de māzǔ jìsì* 萬世順公司與新加坡潮人的媽祖祭祀 [Ban See Soon Kongsi and the Worship of the Goddess of the Sea by Singaporeans]," 140.

22 Tan, Yeow Wooi 陳耀威, *Yuèdōng kǎo* 《粵東考》 [A Study into the Origins of *Yuèdōng*], unpublished manuscript 未出版, 2005.

23 "*Tóngshēn qìnghè* 同申慶賀 [Universal Celebration]," *Lat Pau* 《叻報》, 24 September 1896.

24 Ibid.

25 Ibid.

26 "*Sàishén dìngqī* 賽神定期 [Dates of Religious Processions]," *Lat Pau* 《叻報》, 20 November 1896.

27 "*Wànshùnjiē tíjuān chóngxiū yuèhǎiqīngmiào fāngmíng lièzuǒ* 萬順街題捐重修粵海清廟芳名列左 [List of Wànshùn Street (Chulia Street) Donors for the Reconstruction of Wak Hai Cheng Bio]," *Lat Pau* 《叻報》, 19 March 1896; "*Juānlù zhàodēng* 捐錄照登 [List of Donations Published Accordingly]," *Lat Pau* 《叻報》, 10 August 1896; "*Juānlù zhàodēng* 捐錄照登 [List of Donations Published Accordingly]," *Lat Pau* 《叻報》, 11 August 1896; "*Zījiāng guǎngfǔjí xǐjuān chóngxiū yuèhǎiqīngmiào fāngmíng liè* 茲將廣府籍喜捐重修粵海清廟芳名列 [The Names of Delightful Cantonese Donors for the Cause of Reconstructing Wak Hai Cheng Bio are hereby Listed]," *Lat Pau* 《叻報》, 24 August 1896; "*Zījiāng qióngzhōu fǔjí xǐjuān chóngxiū yuèhǎiqīngmiào fāngmíng liè* 茲將瓊州府籍喜捐重修粵海清廟芳名

列 [The Names of Delightful Hainanese Donors for the Cause of Reconstructing Wak Hai Cheng Bio are hereby Listed]," *Lat Pau*《叻報》, 25 August 1896; "*Zījiāng shùnxīngjiē xǐjuān chóngxiū yuèhǎiqīngmiào fāngmíng liè* 茲將順興街喜捐重修粵海清廟芳名列 [The Names of Delightful Shùnxīng Street (Boat Quay) Donors for the Cause of Reconstructing Wak Hai Cheng Bio are hereby Listed]," *Lat Pau*《叻報》, 29 August 1896; "*Zījiāng xiǎopō zhèngxīngjiē xǐjuān chóngxiū yuèhǎiqīngmiào fāngmíng lièzuǒ* 茲將小坡正興街喜捐重修粵海清廟芳名列左 [The Names of Delightful Small Town's Zhèngxīng Street (possibly the expunged Chin Hin Street which is normally known in Chinese as *Zhènxīngjiē* 振興街) Donors for the Cause of Reconstructing Wak Hai Cheng Bio are hereby Listed on the Left]," *Lat Pau*《叻報》, 29 October 1896; "*Zījiāng chángxīngjiē xǐjuān chóngxiū yuèhǎiqīngmiào fāngmíng liè* 茲將長興街喜捐重修粵海清廟芳名列 [The Names of Delightful Chángxīng Street (Circular Road) Donors for the Cause of Reconstructing Wak Hai Cheng Bio are hereby Listed]," *Lat Pau*《叻報》, 26 November 1896; "*Zījiāng cháyángjí xǐjuān chóngxiū yuèhǎiqīngmiào fāngmíng liè* 茲將茶陽籍喜捐重修粵海清廟芳名列 [The Names of Delightful Cháyáng Donors for the Cause of Reconstructing Wak Hai Cheng Bio are hereby Listed]," *Lat Pau*《叻報》, 25 January 1897; "*Zījiāng xǐjuān chóngxiū yuèhǎiqīngmiào fāngmíng kānzuǒ* 茲將喜捐重修粵海清廟芳名刊左 [The Names of Delightful Donors for the Cause of Reconstructing Wak Hai Cheng Bio are hereby Published on the Left]," *Lat Pau*《叻報》, 9 March 1897; "*Zījiāng shàngxīngjiē xǐjuān chóngxiū yuèhǎiqīngmiào fāngmíng liè* 茲將上興街喜捐重修粵海清廟芳名列 [The Names of Delightful Shàngxīng Street Donors for the Cause of Reconstructing Wak Hai Cheng Bio are hereby Listed]," *Lat Pau*《叻報》, 6 April 1897.

28 Ibid.

29 Ceramic ornamentation is also known as ceramic shards ornamentation, or *qiàncí* 嵌瓷 which is pronounced as *kam*^{2} *ce*^{5} in Teochew. It is known as *jiǎncí* 剪瓷 or *jiǎnnián* 剪黏 in Hokkien architecture.

30 Fascia board or *yánbǎn* 檐板 is pronounced as *siem*^{5} *bang*^{2} in Teochew. It is generally known as *fēng yánbǎn* 封檐板.

31 This void or gap between two beams or lintels above the entrance gateway and the main entrance, or *tiāndì zǐsūn fèng* 天地子孫縫 is pronounced as *tiêng*^{1} *di*^{7} *ze*^{2} *sung*^{1} *hong*^{5} in Teochew. This is one of the characteristic features of Teochew architecture.

32 The door seals or *fáyuè* 閥閱 is pronounced as *huêg*^{8} *luêg*^{4} in Teochew. It is generally known as *ménzānyìn* 門簪印.

33 Teochew fascia board or *yánbǎn* 檐板 can be divided into two categories: *ruǎn* 軟 and *yìng* 硬 [literally: "soft" and "hard"]. *Yìng yánbǎn* 硬檐板 is similar to an eave purlin and could support loads, while *ruǎn yánbǎn* 軟檐板 is a plank or board. Wak Hai Cheng Bio's fascia boards belong to the former.

34 The recessed entranceway or *āodù mén* 凹肚門 is pronounced as *ao*^{1} *dou*^{6} *mung*^{5} in Teochew. The recessed space is known as *āodù* 凹肚. This space is known as *āoshòu* 凹壽 in Hokkien architecture.

35 This characteristic beam has a carved dragon head on the cantilevered end and is known specifically as *jītóu fāngzǎi* 屐頭方樴 or as *jītóu* 屐頭. It is pronounced as *giah*^{8} *tao*^{5} *bang*^{1} *zai*^{3} or *giah*^{8} *tao*^{5} in Teochew respectively.

36 Fresco work refers to a mural painting technique in which coloured pigments are applied to the plaster before it dries.

37 Screen doors or *píngyè* 屏頁 is pronounced as *ping*^{5} *hiêh*^{8} in Teochew. It is known as *géshan* 隔扇 or *géshan* 格扇 in Hokkien architecture.

38 The "工-shape" can also be found in Teochew temples in China built or rebuilt around the same time as Wak Hai Cheng Bio. The Lǎomāgōng

(老媽宮(天后宮、關帝廟)) temple rebuilt in 1879 and Cúnxīn shàntáng (存心善堂) built in 1895 in Swatow both have a similar "工-shape" plan. Lǎomāgōng is also a twin shrine temple like Wak Hai Cheng Bio. See "*6, Cúnxīn shàntáng (shuǐlóng jú)* 六、存心善堂 (水龍局)" and "*7, Lǎomāgōng (Tiānhòugōng, Guāndìmiào)* 七、老媽宮 (天后宮、關帝廟)," in "*Lǎobù wénhuà lǚyóu jǐngdiǎn* 老埠文化旅遊景點 [Cultural Tourist Attractions of the Old Port]," accessed 27 April 2017, http://www.stly.gov.cn/article/detail/301172.

39 The span of three bays or *sānjiān guò* 三間過 is pronounced as *san*^{1} *goin*^{1} *guê*^{3} in Teochew. It is generally known as *sān kāijiān* 三開間.

40 Kim, Young Jae, and Park, Sungjin, "Tectonic Traditions in Ancient Chinese Architecture, and Their Development," *Journal of Asian Architecture and Building Engineering* 38, no. 1 (January 2017): 32.

41 This characteristic Teochew timber truss known as *sānzài wǔguā shí'èr kuài* 三檝五瓜十二塊 or *wǔzàng nèi shí'èr kuài huāpī* 五臟內十二塊花坯 is pronounced as *san*^{1} *zai*^{3} *ngou*^{6} *guê*^{1} *zab*^{8} *ri*^{6} *go*^{3} and *ngou*^{6} *zang*^{6} *lai*^{6} *zab*^{8} *ri*^{6} *go*^{3} *huê*^{1} *puê*^{1} in Teochew respectively.

42 Pseudo-beam panel or *zǎifù* 檝腹 is pronounced as *zai*^{3} *bag*^{4} in Teochew. It is known as *yuánguāng* 圓光 or *tōngsuí* 通隨 in Hokkien architecture.

43 Chua, Ai Hua, *Pilot Timber Consolidation Research Project: Technical Report for Yueh Hai Ching Temple (National Monument) at 30B Phillip Street, Singapore 048696* (Singapore: 2010).

44 The round-ridged roof construction or *chóngcuò* 重厝 is also known as *fǎnguāng* 反光. They are pronounced as *cong*^{5} *cu*^{3} or *huêng*^{2} *guang*^{1} in Teochew respectively. It is known as *juànpéng* 卷棚 in Hokkien architecture.

45 The phrases "思無邪" and "志於道" originates from the *Analects*: 《論語·為政第二》載："子曰：《詩》三百，一言以蔽之，曰'思無邪'" and 《論語·述而》載："子曰：志於道，據於德，依於仁，游於藝。"

46 *Wānbǎn* 彎板 is a lateral bracing timber member. It can also be understood to be like a short beam. It is typically camber-shaped but some are straight. Apart from *wānbǎn* 彎板, it is known varyingly as *wānbiǎn* 彎匾, *gǒng bǎn* 拱板, or in the case of straight member, *píngbǎn* 平板. It is pronounced as *uêng*^{1} *bang*^{2}, *uêng*^{1} *biêng*^{2}, *giong*^{2} *bang*^{2} and *bên*^{5} *bang*^{2} respectively. It is known as *shùmù* 束木 in Hokkien architecture.

47 See Chapter 2 section on "Reforming the Society's Management Style and the 1933 Incorporation Ordinance".

48 Gable roof or *pí* 埤 is pronounced as *bi*^{1} in Teochew. It is generally known as *shānqiáng* 山牆.

49 "Inverted hull" or *fǎnbèi chuán* 反背船 is also known varyingly as *dàozhì lóngchuán* 倒置龍船 or *dàogài chuán* 倒蓋船. It is pronounced as *huêng*^{2} *bê*^{3} *zung*^{5}, *dao*^{2} *di*^{3} *lêng*^{5} *zung*^{5} and *dao*^{2} *gai*^{3} *zung*^{5} respectively.

50 Rain gutter or *liūmǔcáo* 霤母槽 is pronounced as *lao*^{3} *bho*^{2} *zo*^{5} in Teochew. It is generally known as *tiāngōu* 天溝.

51 Apart from the Teochew colloquial term for this "inverted hull" roof *huêng*^{2} *buê*^{3} *zung*^{5} 反背船, it is also known as *zǎohéxíng tiāngōu* 棗核形天溝, literally meaning, "Jujube pit-shaped roof gutter". There is another similar roof construction, known as *guībèi* 龜背 or "tortoiseshell roof" in northern China or *xièké ding* 蟹殼頂 or "crab-shell roof" in southern China. The difference between the former and latter is that the ridge of this roof is parallel to the ridges of the two gabled roofs, while the latter's ridge is perpendicular to the ridges of the two gabled roofs.

52 Tegula roof tiles or *wǎbǎn* 瓦板 is pronounced as *hia*^{6} *bang*^{2} in Teochew. It is generally known as *bǎnwǎ* 板瓦.

53 Phua, Chay Long 潘醒農, 6 June 1930, *Xīnjiāpō yì'ān gōngsī yīng 1930 nián mínguó shíjiǔ nián*

sìyuè shí'èr rì lì yì'àn bù 新嘉坡義安公司 英1930年民國十九年四月十二日立 議案簿 [Singapore Ngee Ann Kongsi A.D. 1930 12 April in the 19th year of the Chinese Republic Minutes of Meeting Folder], Ngee Ann Kongsi (hereinafter cited as Phua, Ngee Ann Kongsi Minutes 1930). It was stated as follows in the minutes of meeting, "主席[林義順]云修整粵海清廟後座作義安公司辦事處并購置傢俬應用文具等事宜可交由林君雨岩及佘乙任君共同辦理 通過".

54 Ibid., 6 June 1930 and 13 November 1930. It was stated in the minutes of meeting as follows, "主席[林義順]云潮州八邑會館係潮人共有之機關辦事處前設端蒙本公司則附寄於會館之辦事處現本公司即修整完竣為便利办事人起見應附設於本公司內未知諸位贊成否 郭斯高君附議 通過".

55 Ibid., 17 March 1933. It was stated in the minutes of the meeting as follows, "李君又云本公司办事廳破漏須要修葺眾議舉楊纘文君李金賜君與匠人接洽办理".

56 It was reported in the *Nanyang Siang Pau*《南洋商報》that the repainting of door gods was completed by May 1963 and the total expenditure was $1,650. According to the anecdotal accounts given by the temple's caretaker, Qwek Wee Chew (郭維洲), the two pairs of lacquered wooden doors at the shrines' entranceways depicting the Tang dynasty generals turned door gods were purportedly refurbished in 1962 by Liáng Zhōng (梁忠), a Swatow Sia (汕頭社) carpenter and lacquer craftsman. Swatow Sia, a Teochew temple otherwise known as Swatow Sia Mazu Temple (汕頭社天后廟), is currently located at 5 Lorong 40 Geylang. Two members of Swatow Sia, Quek Nang Kwang (郭南光) and Ng Ngiap Khiang (黄業強), reveal on separate occasions that they were unaware of the existence of a person named Liáng Zhōng. The temple's caretaker added that other works of Liáng Zhōng can be found in the residence of Yeo Khee Lim (楊启霖) at 63 Emerald Hill Road. The residence has been owned by the Yeo family since the early 20th century. It was restored in the early 2000s and won the URA Architectural Heritage Award (AHA) in 2005. Based on a personal communication with Yeo Eng Koon (楊應群), the son of Yeo Khee Lim, the former does not know of the presence of any Liáng Zhōng works in the family's residence. According to Tan Yeow Wooi, a certain Liáng Zhōng left a signature during the restoration of a mural in Cheng Hoon Teng (青雲亭) in Malacca, Malaysia. This mural is located at the Entrance Gateway of Cheng Hoon Teng. The work is entitled *Fú Lù Shòu* "福祿壽" [The Three Stars: Fortune, Prosperity and Longevity] with the colophon "新嘉坡合順梁忠作 寫于 歲立庚子年冬月" [Drawn by Liáng Zhōng of Hé Shùn, Singapore in the Winter Months of 1960]. "*Yì'ān gōngsī zhàokāi dàhuì fābiǎo chángnián yàoshì jiǎnbào zhǔxí Lián Yíngzhōu chēng cháozhōu dàshà luòchéng jì yì'ān xuéyuàn kāixué zuì zhídé jìniàn* 義安公司召開大會發表常年要事簡報主席連瀛洲稱潮州大廈落成暨義安學院開學最值得紀念 [Lien Ying Chow, President of The Ngee Ann Kongsi reported at its Annual General Meeting that the Completion of the Teochew Building and the Commencement of Term of Ngee Ann College were worthy of Commemoration]," *Nányáng Shāngbào*《南洋商報》[Nanyang Siang Pau], 31 May 1963, 17; Qwek, Wee Chew 郭維洲, personal communication with author, Wak Hai Cheng Bio, 12 May 2010; Quek, Nang Kwang 郭南光, personal communication with author, 5 Lorong 40 Geylang, 9 August 2014; Ng, Ngiap Khiang 黄業強, personal communication with Ng Ching Huei 吳慶輝, 5 Lorong 40 Geylang, 20 September 2014; Yeo, Eng Koon 楊應群, personal communication with author, 50 Chin Swee Road, 15 August 2016; Tan, Yeow Wooi 陳耀威, personal communication with author, Georgetown, Penang, 7 August 2018; Urban Redevelopment Authority, "Nos. 63 & 65

Emerald Hill Road: Two Distinct Personalities" (Singapore: Urban Redevelopment Authority, 2005), accessed 28 April 2017, https://www.ura.gov.sg/uol/publications/corporate/aha/2005/63-65-Emerald-Hill-Road.

57 The 1933 Ngee Ann Kongsi meeting minutes also reported the replacement of a small window with a bigger one on the front courtyard's left boundary wall. This was done without the knowledge and approval of the Kongsi's committee of management, who were the trustees of the temple. See Phua, 17 March 1933, Ngee Ann Kongsi Minutes 1930. It was stated in the minutes that "李金賜君報告云粵海清廟前左傍牆壁昔時虽有窗係為狹小者今竟有人開鑿大窗似此恐有妨碍所以弟與律師相商行字質問惟尚未□如何答復窃思昔時已有小窗今開大窗若□其□為誠恐駸駸不已若欲交涉制止应根據何種理由方樑勝算鄙意再□问律師是否合法以定進止众贊成通過".

58 Ang Kheng Leng was a former reporter of the Chinese daily, *Sin Chew Jit Poh* (星洲日報). He subsequently pursued his architectural studies at the University of Manitoba, Winnipeg, and graduated with a Bachelor of Architecture. Throughout his architectural career, Ang designed numerous architecture projects for Ngee Ann Kongsi and Teochew Poit Ip Huay Kuan. "S'pore Newsman Wins Degree in Architecture," *Singapore Standard*, 25 June 1952, 1 & 4; "*Cháozhōu huìguǎn nǐ chuàngbàn bìnyíguǎn túshì yǐ cǎojiù jiāo yì'ān gōngsī shěnhé* 潮州會館擬創辦殯儀館圖式已草就交義安公司審核 [Teochew Huay Kuan's Plans for a Funeral Palour have been submitted to The Ngee Ann Kongsi for Approval]," *Nányáng Shāngbào* 《南洋商報》 [Nanyang Siang Pau], 6 August 1959, 7; "*Cháozhōu bāyì huìguǎn zhàokāi dǒngshì huìyì* 潮州八邑會館召開董事會議 [Teochew Poit Ip Huay Kuan called for a Directors' Meeting]," *Nányáng Shāngbào* 《南洋商報》 [Nanyang Siang Pau], 17 October 1959, 6; "*Cháozhōu bāyì huìguǎn niánhuì tōngguò zài hòugǎng chuàngbàn bìnyíguǎn* 潮州八邑會館年會通過在後港創辦殯儀館 [Teochew Poit Ip Huay Kuan's Annual Meeting Approved the Setting up of a Funeral Palour in Hougang]," *Nányáng Shāngbào* 《南洋商報》 [Nanyang Siang Pau], 27 February 1960, 6; "*Yì'ān xuéyuàn gōngyìbù xīn xiàoshè gōngchéng jìnzhǎn xùnsù sìyuè jíkě yīngyòng quánbù dìngyú jīnnián bāyuè jùngōng* 義安學院工藝部新校舍工程進展迅速四月卽可應用全部定於今年八月竣工 [The Ngee Ann College's Technical College Campus Project Proceeds at a Rapid Pace; User can start using Portion of the Campus in April and Full Completion expected by August]," *Nányáng Shāngbào* 《南洋商報》 [Nanyang Siang Pau], 7 March 1966, 5.

59 "Index of Land," book 54, 348, Singapore Land Authority; "Index of Land," book 120, 387, Singapore Land Authority.

60 Lao, "Plan of Temple".

61 Ang, "Proposed Reconstruction".

62 Ibid.

63 "Index of Land," book 117, 32, Singapore Land Authority. The wall abutting 31 Phillip Street was probably only partially demolished and rendered with plaster during the demolition of shophouses and construction of OCBC East Centre between 1992 to 1996. See "OCBC Revives Plan to Build Office Block," *The Straits Times*, 9 May 1992; "OCBC Goes Ahead with 15-Storey Office Building – after 10 Years," *The Business Times*, 19 October 1994; "ABN AMRO to Lease 70–80% of Unfinished OCBC Centre East," *The Business Times*, 16 February 1996.

64 Yeo, Kang Shua, and Chen, Yu, "Building a Modern Chinese Identity in Singapore: From Orientalism to Chinese 'Traditional Eclectic Style' Renaissance," in *International Conference on East Asian Architectural Culture, Tainan, Taiwan 2009: Whose East Asia? The East Asian Architecture and Urbanism Under Occidentalism*,

ed. Xu Mingfu 徐明福 (Tainan: Society of Architectural Historians of Taiwan and College of Planning and Design, National Cheng Kung University, 2009).

65 Urban Redevelopment Authority, *Changing the Face of Singapore: Through the URA Sale of Sites* (Singapore: Urban Redevelopment Authority, 1995), 68.

66 Chia & Associates Architects, "Wak Hai Cheng Bio Chinese Temple: Measured and Record Drawings of Existing Structure," September, 1992, Collection of the Ngee Ann Kongsi.

67 Dating of this photographic survey to 1994 is based on the time stamps on the photographs.

68 Lú, Zhīgāo 盧芝高, personal communication with author, Cháo'ān xiàn jīnhú jiànzhù gōngchéng yǒuxiàn gōngsī 潮安縣金湖建築工程有限公司 (currently Cháozhōushì jīnhú jiànzhù gōngchéng yǒuxiàn gōngsī 潮州市金湖建筑工程有限公司), Guǎngdōngshěng cháo'ān xiàn cháozhōushì dàdào 廣東省潮安縣潮州市大道, 20 January 2011. The author spoke to Lú Zhīgāo during a trip to the Teochew region of China (Chaozhou and Shantou) undertaken by the Ngee Ann Kongsi Temple Restoration Committee and Consultants from 19 to 22 January 2011. Lu's account was corroborated by the temple's caretaker, Qwek Wee Chew. For more information on master craftsman, Lú Zhīgāo, see "*Cháozhōu qiàncí yìshù chuánchéngrén Lú Zhīgāo: suìcípiàn qiàntiē qǐlì shìjiè* 潮州嵌瓷藝術傳承人盧芝高：碎瓷片嵌貼綺麗世界 [Successor of Teochew Ceramic Ornamentation, Lú Zhīgāo: Composing a Beautiful World with Ceramic Shards]," *Huánqiú cháorén wǎng* 环球潮人网 [Global Teochew webpage], *Cháozhōu rìbào* 《潮州日報》 [Chaozhou Daily], 7 July 2014, accessed 18 May 2017, http://news.hqcr.com/projects/news/view.aspx?nid=420625.

69 Ibid.

70 On 17 March 1997, *Shin Min Daily News* carried an article on the completion of works for Wak Hai Cheng Bio. In the article, it was claimed that the works by Malacca (Wah Kee) Handicraft Co. commenced in November 1995 and took a total of 14 months [... 这间耗资超过200万元装修的神庙，将在4月9日举行落成酬神仪式。... 1995年11月间开始进行工程浩大的装修。今年初终告完工。...整个工程预定14个月完成。目前经已提前完工。...]. Based on the date inscribed on two secondary ridge beams in the two front halls (旹次甲戌年九月廿八日午時重修 公元一九九四年十一月一號 [Temple (commenced) restoration on 1 November 1994]), and Raymond Woo & Associates Architects, Chin Jian Ping and Lee Zhi Gao's report of June 1994, the commencement date of the works should be as inscribed on the beam, i.e. November 1994, as opposed to November 1995. One possible explanation for this discrepancy in the dates may be that Malacca (Wah Kee) Handicraft Co. only came on board the project in November 1995. Chén, Kūngāng 陳坤綱, "*Wèiyú shānzǎidǐng 170 nián gǔmiào huàn xīnzhuāng: měitiān shàngbǎi lǚkè yóu yuèhǎiqīngmiào* 位於山仔頂 170年古廟換新裝：每天上百旅客游粵海清廟 [170 Year Old Historic Temple at Shānzáidǐng gets a New Look: Over a Hundred Tourists Visit Wak Hai Cheng Bio Every Day]," *Xīnmíng Rìbào* 《新明日報》 [Shin Min Daily News], 17 March 1997; Raymond Woo & Associates Architects, Chin, Jian Ping and Lee, Zhi Gao, "Proposed Additions & Alterations and Preservation to the Existing Yueh Hai Ching Temple on Lot 428-1 and 428-2 TS 4 at 30B Phillip Street," (Raymond Woo & Associates Architects; Construction and Planning Institute, Guangdong Province, Teochew City, June 1994).

71 Chén, Kūngāng 陳坤綱, "*Qǐng dàoshì tōngxiāo niànjīng, shòuyàn yòupìn gētái zhùxīng shāngrén qìngshēngrì biékāi shēngmiàn* 請道士通宵念經，壽宴又聘歌台助興 商人慶生日別開生面 [Taoist Priests invited to Chant Overnight, Gētái Singers were engaged to sing for the

Birthday Banquet, Merchant celebrates Birthday in an Unconventional Way],” *Xīnmíng Rìbào* 《新明日報》[Shin Min Daily News], 22 January 1997.

72 Chén, Kūngāng 陳坤綱, “*Tóngdé shàntáng niànxīnshè 30 wàn dàzhuāngxiū 300 wàn zhāng jīnbó wéi shénxiàng tiējīn* 同德善堂念心社·30萬大裝修 300萬張金箔為神像貼金 [Thong Teck Sian Tong Lian Sin Sia. $300,000 Extensive Renovation, 3,000,000 Sheets of Gold Leaf for Gilding Statues of Deities],” *Xīnmíng Rìbào* 《新明日報》[Shin Min Daily News], 8 June 1999.

73 Urban Redevelopment Authority, *Yueh Hai Ching Temple Preservation Guidelines*, vol. 1, September 1997, Preservation of Monuments Board.

74 The 5 x 5-inch tile measures 127 x 127 mm. The light maroon tile is commonly known as the 18 x 18-inch tile even though the actual dimensions is slightly smaller, measuring 450 x 450 mm (17.7 x 17.7 inches).

75 The Suzhou style is polychromatic and is more stylised and less formal than the monochromatic gold-on-black Teochew style. The Suzhou style was popularised during the Qing dynasty by the imperial family, who used it in their summer palaces.

76 A possible explanation for the temple’s rising damp problem after 2005 is that it was caused by a rise in the water table. The construction of the Marina Barrage between January 2005 and December 2007 may have contributed to this rise. The temple is situated near the mouth of the Singapore River, where the water was brackish. With the construction of the Barrage, water in the mouth of the Singapore River, and indeed the entire Marina Bay, was converted into freshwater. With higher mineral content, brackish water is denser and has a higher water pressure than freshwater. The conversion into freshwater meant a change in water pressure and, as a result, may have led to a rise in the level of the water table. That the water table around the temple has risen has yet to be substantiated by scientific studies (for example, water isotope analysis). If proven, it would explain the relatively sudden appearance of rising damp in the temple.

Teochew Architecture in Singapore (pp. 68–72)

1 Li, Xiaodong 李曉東 and Yeo, Kang Shua 楊茳善, *Zhōngguó kōngjiān* 《中國空間》*Chinese Conception of Space* (Beijing: China Architecture & Building Press, 2007).

2 Yeo, Kang Shua, “Homogenously Heterogenous?: The Diversity of Traditional Chinese Architecture in Singapore,” *Journal of Southeast Asian Architecture* 9 (2006): 87–106.

3 Song, Ong Siang, *One Hundred Years’ History of the Chinese in Singapore* (London: John Murray, 1923), 335.

4 The radio broadcast took place on 18 January 1961 and the transcript was published in *Nanyang Siang Pau* the following day. Hsu, Yun Ts’iao 許云樵, “*Mǎláiyà cóngtán zhī niànsān liǎngshuāngbàn wà sìdàcuò* 馬來亞叢談之廿三兩雙半襪四大厝 [Essays on Malaya 23: Two Half Pairs of Socks and the Four Grand Mansions],” *Nányáng Shāngbào* 《南洋商報》 [Nanyang Siang Pau], 19 January 1961, 6.

5 For a detailed discussion on the *si*^{3} *dua*^{7} *cu*^{3} or four grand mansions, please refer to: Yeo, Huijun Martina, and Yeo, Kang Shua, “‘Typical’ Chinese Residences of Late Nineteenth-Century Singapore: A Case Study of the Four Grand Mansions (四大厝),” *EAAC 2017: International Conference on East Asian Architectural Culture: East Asian Architecture in Globalization: Values, Inheritance and Dissemination* (People’s Republic of China: Tianjin University, 2017).

6 Yeo, Huijun Martina, and Yeo, Kang Shua, “The House of Ripples,” *BiblioAsia*, vol. 14, issue 3 (2018): 40–45.

7 The historic building plans of Kwan Im Thong Hood Cho Temple could not be located. There

is no 19th-century stele in the temple either. According to the two 1984 steles 《觀音堂佛祖廟頌德碑記》 and 《擴建觀音堂佛祖廟功德碑記》, the temple underwent reconstruction in 1895 and a rear hall was added. In 1981, work on the current temple building commenced and the construction was completed in 1984. Dean, Kenneth 丁荷生, and Hue, Guan Thye 許源泰, *Xīnjiāpō huáwén míngkè huìbiān* 《新加坡華文銘刻彙編》 *Chinese Epigraphy in Singapore 1819–1911* (Singapore: NUS Press; Guilin: Guangxi Normal University, 2017), vol. 2, 738–748. Also see Sim, Arthur, "Kwan Im Temple now a historic site," *The Straits Times*, 29 September 2001, 8–9.

8 Tong Sian Tng also underwent works in 1902. "Plan of Proposed Extension. Temple at Devonshire Road for Trustee Bay Soon Cheng," 1897, 141/1897, CBS336, National Archives of Singapore; "Plan of a Chinese Temple Proposed to be erected at Devonshire Road Singapore Property of Mr. Bay Soon Cheng," 1897, 304/1897, CBS336, National Archives of Singapore; "Plan of Alterations and Additions Buddhism Temple at Devonshire Road MC No. 1-C for Bay Soon Cheng (Trustee)," 1902, 5101/1902, CBS1139, National Archives of Singapore.

9 According to the 1894 《同善堂碑》 stele, the original building was constructed in 1894. Another stele dated 1898 《同善堂眾善信喜捐緣碑》 recorded the contributions to works and marks the completion of the 1897 works. Although there was another repair recorded on the 1919 stele 《重修同善堂碑記》, the extant structure retains much of the features seen on the 1897 building plan. Dean, Kenneth 丁荷生, and Hue, Guan Thye 許源泰, *Xīnjiāpō huáwén míngkè huìbiān* 《新加坡華文銘刻彙編》 *Chinese Epigraphy in Singapore 1819–1911*, vol. 2, 957–980. Also see, Chen, Chingho 陳荊和, and Tan, Yeok Seong 陳育崧, *Xīnjiāpō huáwén bēimíng jílù* 《新嘉坡華文碑銘集錄》 [A Collection of Singapore Chinese Inscriptions] (Hong Kong: The Chinese University Press, 1970), 148–151.

10 Unfortunately, there is no historic stele in the temple. "Plan of a New Chinese Temple to be Erected at Peak Seah Street for the Priest (Swee Ooh)," 1907, 8861/1907, CBS1130, National Archives of Singapore.

11 "Plan of Additions and Alterations at Temple of Peck Seah Street for Cheng Siew Ho Site Plan 1," 1917, 399/1917, CBS1108, National Archives of Singapore; "Plan of Additions and Alterations at Temple of Peck Seah Street for Cheng Siew Ho Site Plan 2," 1917, 399/1917, CBS1108, National Archives of Singapore; "Plan of Additions and Alterations at Temple of Peck Seah Street for Cheng Siew Ho," 1917, 399/1917, CBS1108, National Archives of Singapore; "Amended Passed Plan No. 339 Dated 13-7-17 at Temple of Peck Seah Street for Cheng Siew Ho," 1917, 399A/1917, CBS1108, National Archives of Singapore.

12 According to a timber stele of 1892 《皇清光緒六年新建萬壽山觀音堂壬辰年重修共兩次碑記》 Ban Siew San Temple was originally constructed in 1880 and underwent reconstruction in 1892. Dean, Kenneth 丁荷生, and Hue, Guan Thye 許源泰, *Xīnjiāpō huáwén míngkè huìbiān* 《新加坡華文銘刻彙編》 *Chinese Epigraphy in Singapore 1819–1911*, vol. 2, 726–736. Also see, Chen, Chingho 陳荊和, and Tan, Yeok Seong 陳育崧, *Xīnjiāpō huáwén bēimíng jílù* 《新嘉坡華文碑銘集錄》 [A Collection of Singapore Chinese Inscriptions], 144–148.

13 According to Dean and Hue, the builder of this hall in 1905 was Zhèng Jiéyì (鄭節義) from Chaozhou. His name was inscribed in the 1905 timber stele 《大清光緒六年創建堃成堂乙巳年平基重建》 although it does not specifically state that he was the builder. Dean, Kenneth 丁荷生, and Hue, Guan Thye 許源泰,

Xīnjiāpō huáwén míngkè huìbiān《新加坡華文銘刻彙編》 *Chinese Epigraphy in Singapore 1819–1911*, vol. 2, 1310–1322.

14 "Plan of Proposed Additions and Alterations. A Buddhist Temple at Alexandra Road for Bea Hock," 1906, 8167/1906, CBS1131, National Archives of Singapore.

15 "Plan of a Chinese Temple to be Rebuilt at the 4th Mile off Telok Blangah Rd. Trustee Mr. Ong Whye Teck," 1906, 8217/1906, CBS1131, National Archives of Singapore; "Proposed Plan Shewing Chinese Vegetarian Temple to be Erected at Telok Blanga Road for Ong Guan Teck," 1919, 72/1919, CBS1094, National Archives of Singapore; "Alterations of Passed Plan No. 70 Dated 25.3.1919 for Chinese Vegetarian Temple to be Erected at Telok Blangah Road," 1922, 72A/1919, CBS1094, National Archives of Singapore; "Re-alterations of Passed Plan No. 72A-22 Dated 29.4.22 for Vegetarian Temple at Telok Blangah Rd," 1923, 72B/1919, CBS1094, National Archives of Singapore; "Amended 1st Floor Plans Shewing Rooms as per Notice No. 129 for Temple at Telok Blangah Rd," 1923, 72C/1919, CBS1094, National Archives of Singapore; "Proposed Additions and Alterations to Chinese Vegetarian Temple M.C. No. 436 Telok Blangah Road Drawing 1," 1932, 72D/1919, CBS1094, National Archives of Singapore; "Proposed Additions and Alterations to Chinese Vegetarian Temple M.C. No. 436 Telok Blangah Road Drawing 2," 1931, 72D/1919, CBS1094, National Archives of Singapore; "Proposed Addition to Worshipping Portico on Open Terrace Etc. Sheet No. 1 (Being Amendment to Passed Plan No. 72D 19)," 1932, 72F/1919, CBS1094, National Archives of Singapore; "Proposed Addition to Worshipping Portico on Open Terrace Etc. Sheet No. 2 (Being Amendment to Passed Plan No. 72D 19)," 1932, 72F/1919, CBS1094, National Archives of Singapore; "Half Inch Details of R.C. Beams and Slabs for Additions and Alterations to Temple at 578 Telok Blangah Road Sheet No. 1," 1932, 72E/1919, CBS1094, National Archives of Singapore; "Half Inch Details of R.C. Beams for Additions and Alterations to Temple at 578 Telok Blangah Road Sheet No. 2," 1932, 72E/1919, CBS1094, National Archives of Singapore; "Half Inch Details of R.C. Slab Columns etc. for Additions and Alterations to Temple at 578 Telok Blangah Road Sheet No. 3," 1932, 72E/1919, CBS1094, National Archives of Singapore.

16 According to the 1844 《重建應和館碑》, 1875《建修應和會館碑記(五城福地)》 and 1898《重修應和館碑記》 steles in the building, the original building was constructed in 1823 and works were carried out in 1844, 1875 and 1898. The extant building essentially retained the 1898 structure with the exception of the façade ornamentation, where the traditional Teochew pargetting with fresco painting was replaced with Shanghai plasterwork. Dean, Kenneth 丁荷生, and Hue, Guan Thye 許源泰, *Xīnjiāpō huáwén míngkè huìbiān*《新加坡華文銘刻彙編》 *Chinese Epigraphy in Singapore 1819–1911*, vol. 1, 200–224. Also see Chen, Chingho 陳荊和, and Tan, Yeok Seong 陳育崧, *Xīnjiāpō huáwén bēimíng jílù* 《新嘉坡華文碑銘集錄》 [A Collection of Singapore Chinese Inscriptions], 171–184.

17 According to the 1861 《重修□□吧嗝大伯公祠宇碑》 stele in the temple, the temple was reconstructed in 1861. Dean, Kenneth 丁荷生, and Hue, Guan Thye 許源泰, *Xīnjiāpō huáwén míngkè huìbiān* 《新加坡華文銘刻彙編》 *Chinese Epigraphy in Singapore 1819–1911*, vol. 1, 226–245. Also see Chen, Chingho 陳荊和, and Tan, Yeok Seong 陳育崧, *Xīnjiāpō huáwén bēimíng jílù* 《新嘉坡華文碑銘集錄》 [A Collection of Singapore Chinese Inscriptions], 94–98; Tan, Yeow Wooi 陳耀威, "Tanjong Pagar Fu De Ci Temple: Architectural Features and Recommendations for Restoration/Conservation [丹戎巴葛福德

祠建築特色與修復建議]", in *Bǎinián gōngdé bèi nánbāng: Wànghǎi Dàbógōng miào jìshì* 《百年公德被南邦：望海大伯公庙纪事》 *The Living Heritage: Stories of Fook Tet Soo Khek*, ed. Ho Phang Phow 何炳彪 (Singapore: Char Yong (Dabu) Association, 2006), 19–29; Yeo, Kang Shua 楊茳善, "Preliminary Observations of Fook Tet Soo Khek Temple: Case for Conservation and Preservation [丹戎巴葛福德祠的初步觀察: 論建築的保護與保存], in *Bǎinián gōngdé bèi nánbāng: Wànghǎi Dàbógōng miào jìshì* 《百年公德被南邦：望海大伯公庙纪事》 *The Living Heritage: Stories of Fook Tet Soo Khek*, 30–64.

18 "Additions and Alterations to a Chinese Temple, situated in Teluk Ayer Street. Property of Eng Wah Quan," 1898, 203/1898, CBS 337, National Archives of Singapore.

The Land Acquisition of No. 33 Phillip Street (pp. 86–87)

1 Fraser, J. M., *The Work of the Singapore Improvement Trust, 1927–1947* (Singapore: Authority of Singapore Improvement Trust), 1; "Singapore Improvement Ordinance (No. 10 of 1927)," Ordinances enacted by the governor of the Straits Settlements with the advice and consent of the Legislative Council thereof in the year 1927 (Straits Settlements, 1927).

2 "Singapore Sanitation Commission," *The Straits Times*, 16 June 1906, 5; Simpson, W. J., *Report on the Sanitary Condition of Singapore* (London: Waterlow & Sons, 1907).

3 Yeoh, Brenda S. A., *Contesting Space in Colonial Singapore: Power Relations and the Urban Built Environment* (Singapore: Singapore University Press, 2003), 94 & 102.

4 Singapore Improvement Trust, "Backlane – Phillip St. 33, Phillip St," 1929–1933, SIT T9/29, HDB 1013, National Archives of Singapore.

5 "Suit No. 430 of 1914, In the Matter of the Trustee Ordinance 1914 and In the Matter of the 'Ghee Ann Society'," 8 February 1916, Settlement of Singapore Registry of Deed, vol. CDXXXVI, 505, no. 142.

6 Singapore Improvement Trust, "Backlane – Phillip St. 33, Phillip St".

7 "No. 5 of 1933 An Ordinance to Incorporate the Ngee Ann Kongsi," *Straits Settlements Government Gazette,* 10 March 1933; "Ngee Ann Kongsi (Incorporation) Ordinance, (Chapter 370)," Revised Edition 1985, accessed 28 July 2017, https://sso.agc.gov.sg/Act/NAKIO1933.

8 Singapore Improvement Trust, "Backlane – Phillip St. 33, Phillip St".

Chapter Four

1 Chua, Ai Hua, *Pilot Timber Consolidation Research Project: Technical Report for Yueh Hai Ching Temple (National Monument) at 30B Phillip Street, Singapore 048696* (Singapore: 2010).

2 Rafter or *jué* 桷 is pronounced as *gag*[4] in Teochew. It is generally known as *chuán zǐ* 椽子.

3 *Purlin* or *yíng* 楹 is pronounced as *ên*[5] in Teochew. It is generally known as *héng* 桁.

4 Lee Ee Khim (李燕琴) was the Ngee Ann Kongsi staff member who handled the administrative affairs of the temple.

5 Australia ICOMOS *The Burra Charter*:

4.1 *Conservation* should make use of all the knowledge, skills and disciplines which can contribute to the study and care of the *place.*

4.2 Traditional techniques and materials are preferred for the *conservation* of significant *fabric.* In some circumstances modern techniques and materials which offer substantial conservation benefits may be appropriate.

15.2 Changes which reduce *cultural significance* should be reversible, and be reversed when circumstances permit.

21.1 *Adaptation* is acceptable only where the adaptation has minimal impact on the *cultural significance* of the *place*.

21.2 *Adaptation* should involve minimal change

to significant *fabric*, achieved only after considering alternatives.
22.1 New work such as additions or other changes to the *place* may be acceptable where it respects and does not distort or obscure the *cultural significance* of the place, or detract from its *interpretation* and appreciation.
22.2 New work should be readily identifiable as such, but must respect and have minimal impact on the *cultural significance* of the *place.*
ICOMOS, Australia, *The Burra Charter: The Australia ICOMOS Charter for Places of Cultural Significance 1999* (Burwood: Australia ICOMOS, 2000), revised in 2013, accessed 5 October 2017, https://australia.icomos.org/wp-content/uploads/The-Burra-Charter-2013-Adopted-31.10.2013.pdf.

6 2004 Principles for the Conservation of Heritage Sites in China:
Article 19: Intervention should be minimal. Apart from routine maintenance, there should be no intervention on parts of a building or site that are not at imminent risk of serious damage. Intervention should only be undertaken when absolutely necessary and then should be kept to a minimum. The main goals of conservation and management measures are to preserve the site's existing condition and to slow deterioration.
Commentary 4.4.3: Physical interventions should not result in permanent structures and should be reversible, allowing a site to be restored to its historic condition when necessary.
Commentary 12.3: Major restoration constitutes the greatest intervention on the physical remains. Survey and design work must be done with great attention to detail; the historical information inherent in the existing condition of a site must be carefully considered; and procedures for evaluation by experts and for approval must be strictly followed.
Commentary 12.3.1: Major restoration through complete disassembly of a structure should be avoided as far as possible; instead, other types of intervention should be used to make the entire structure stable and safe.
Commentary 12.3.2: Partial or complete disassembly is permitted only when the main structure is seriously deformed or its main components have been badly damaged and reinstatement to a safe and stable condition is not possible without disassembly. Restoration through disassembly should result in the removal of all unsafe elements and should ensure that no further treatment is needed for a long time.
Commentary 12.3.3: During major restoration, it is permitted to reinforce a structure, to use strengthening substances, and to replace damaged components. Additions to original structures should be in places that are hidden from view, and replaced components should be marked with the date of replacement.
Commentary 12.3.4: In principle, remaining vestiges and traces of fabric or components from different periods should be retained. If these cannot be retained in total, those of most significance should be preserved. Samples should be kept of elements that are removed, and their removal should be recorded in the site archives.
Commentary 12.4: Major restoration allows for the reinstatement of lost parts of a site, where appropriate, in order to return it to historic condition.
Commentary 12.4.1: Restoration to historic condition must be based on indisputable extant physical remains. Conjecture, based solely on documentary records, is not permitted.
Commentary 12.4.2: On the determination of experts, it is permissible to reinstate a small number of missing components by referencing examples of the same period, type, and regional origin and by using the same materials. The added fabric must be labelled with the date of replacement.
Commentary 12.4.3: Damaged carvings, clay

sculptures, mural paintings, rare and valuable decorative paintings, and other artworks must be protected in their existing condition to guard against deterioration. It is not necessary to restore such works to their original completeness.

Note that this document has been substantially revised in 2015. ICOMOS, China, *Principles for the Conservation of Heritage Sites in China*, ed. Neville Agnew and Martha Demas, trans. Peter Barker (Los Angeles: Getty Conservation Institute, 2004), 63, 74, 84–85.

7 Some of these findings were mentioned in Chapter 3.

8 See Chapter 3 endnote 74.

9 See Chapter 3 endnote 75.

10 The floor level of the rear courtyard before the 2010 to 2014 restoration was higher than the original floor level, and the bases of two granite columns were partially concealed.

11 Nelson Woo (余義源), Manager of the Ngee Ann Kongsi's Teochew Funeral Parlour, was tasked with facilitating a visit to prospective specialist contractors in China.

12 Members of the restoration team who went on the China trip were Jamie Teo Miang Yeow (Chairman of the Ngee Ann Kongsi Restoration Sub-committee), Richard Lee Sew-Iam (Deputy Chairman of the Ngee Ann Kongsi Restoration Sub-committee), Raymond Woo (architect), Lee Foh Sang (civil and structural engineer from Chong & Lee Consultants), Yeo Kang Shua, Tan Siew Eng and Nelson Woo.

13 *Qiàncí* (嵌瓷) master craftsman, Xǔ Shàoxióng (許少雄), hails from a family of *qiàncí* craftsmen. Xǔ's great grandfather Xǔ Shíquán (許石泉), grandfather Xǔ Méicūn (許梅村) and father Xǔ Zhìbiāo (許志标) were *qiàncí* master craftsmen. Xǔ learnt the craft at a young age from his grandfather and inherited the mastery of *qiàncí* crafts. According to the local gazetteer, Dàliáo village (大寮村) where Xǔ is from is famous for their *qiàncí* crafts and among the villagers, the Xǔ family is considered the best. *Cháoyángshì dìfāngzhì biānzuǎn wěiyuánhuì* 潮陽市地方志編纂委員會, *Cháoyáng xiànzhì*《潮陽縣志》[Cháoyáng Gazetteer] (Guangzhou: *Guǎngdōng rénmín chūbǎnshè* 廣東人民出版社, 1997), 450 and 1111.

14 The three members who climbed the scaffolding to observe the *qiàncí* were Nelson Woo, Jamie Teo and Yeo Kang Shua.

15 Suzhou tiles or *sūzhōu wǎ* 蘇州瓦 consists of both *tegula* and *imbrex* or *wǎbǎn* 瓦板 and *wǎtóng* 瓦瓴. They are pronounced as *hia*[6] *bang*[2] and *hia*[6] *dang*[6] respectively. They are generally known as *bǎnwǎ* 板瓦 and *tǒngwǎ* 筒瓦.

16 In Singapore, it is a safety requirement for all workers to wear safety boots onsite. This increases the risk of damaging the thin Teochew clay tiles if one is untrained. Traditionally in China, roofers wore cloth shoes to avoid breaking the tiles while standing on the roof.

17 The other three famous regional timber carving styles of China are Dōngyáng woodcarving (東陽木雕), Huángyáng woodcarving (黄楊木雕) and Lóngyǎn woodcarving (龍眼木雕).

18 Lion-shaped strut or *shīzuò* 獅座 is pronounced as *sai*[1] *zo*[7] in Teochew.

19 The "hanging basket" strut or *huātǒng* 花筒 is pronounced as *huê*[1] *dang*[6] in Teochew. It is generally known as *chuíhuātǒng* 垂花筒.

20 When exposed to high heat, the calcium carbonate in the shell collapses into calcium oxide or "quicklime". This is then slaked with water to form slaked lime (hydrated lime or calcium hydroxide). This is then ground, sieved, and packed as oyster lime (貝灰).

21 The reversible protective coating is dissolvable in alcohol. Either acetone or ethanol can be used to remove the protective coating.

22 Hide or colloid glue is typically made by boiling down the collagen from the skin of cattle today.

23 The addition of a small amount of Portland cement makes the lime hydraulic.

24 Clay figurines or *nídīng* (泥丁) is pronounced as *ni*[5] *dêng*[1] in Teochew.

25 Qwek, Wee Chew 郭維洲, personal communication with author, Wak Hai Cheng Bio, 17 October 2009.

26 The positions of the *qiàncí*, especially those on the roofs, were measured relative to a minimum of three points.

27 "Administrative Report of the Singapore Municipality 1906," NL3408, 36, National Archives of Singapore.

Competitive Timberwork Construction in Wak Hai Cheng Bio (pp. 134–136)

1 Lǐ, Zhéyáng 李哲揚, *Cháozhōu chuántǒng jiànzhù: Dàmù gòujià* 《潮州傳統建築：大木構架》 [Traditional Teochew Architecture: Structural Timber Frame] (Guangdong: *Guǎngdōng rénmín chūbǎnshè* 廣東人民出版社, 2009), 254–257. Also see Lee, Ch'ian-Lang 李乾朗, "*Wáng Yìshùn jiàngshī zài táiwān zhī miàoyǔ jiànzhù zhī yánjiū* 王益順匠師在台灣之廟宇建築之研究" [Temple Architecture Works of Wáng Yìshùn in Taiwan], in *Táiwān chuántǒng jiànzhù jiàngyì – dìyī jí* 《台灣傳統建築匠藝 – 第一輯》 [Taiwan Traditional Architecture Crafts – First Volume] (Taipei: *Yànlóu gǔjiànzhù* 燕樓古建築, 1995), 123.

2 Lee, Ch'ian-Lang 李乾朗, "*Duìcháng yíngzào* 對場營造" [Competitive Team Construction], *Zhōnghuá shǒugōng* 《中華手工》 [Chinese Craftsmanship], no. 1 (2005): 68–73.

3 Ibid.

4 The phoenix cantilever arm or *fèngtuō* 鳳托 is pronounced as *hong*[6] *toh*[4] in Teochew. This component is characteristic of Teochew architecture.

Chapter Five

1 Yeo, Kang Shua, "Homogenously Heterogenous?: The Diversity of Traditional Chinese Architecture in Singapore," *Journal of Southeast Asian Architecture* 9 (2006): 87–106.

2 Skeldon, Ronald, "The Chinese Diaspora or the Migration of Chinese Peoples?," in *The Chinese Diaspora: Space, Place, Mobility, and Identity*, eds. Laurence J. C. Ma and Carolyn Cartier (Lanham: Rowman & Littlefield, 2003), 51–68; Salaff, Janet W., "Cluster Introduction: Subethnicity in the Chinese Diaspora," *International Migration*, vol. 43, issue 3 (2005), 3–7.

3 Wee, Vivienne, *Religion and Ritual among the Chinese of Singapore: An Ethnographic Study* (Unpublished Master's Thesis, Singapore: University of Singapore, 1977), 40–41.

4 Wee, Lionel, "'Burdens' and 'Handicaps' in Singapore's Language Policy: On the Limits of Language Management," *Language Policy*, vol. 9, no. 2 (2010): 97–114; Wee, Lionel, and Bokhorst-Heng, Wendy D., "Language Policy and Nationalist Ideology: Statal Narratives in Singapore," *Journal of Cross-Cultural and Interlanguage Communication*, vol. 24, issue 3 (2005): 159–183. Also see Kong, Lily, and Yeoh, Brenda, "Nation, Ethnicity, and Identity: Singapore and the Dynamics and Discourses of Chinese Migration," in *The Chinese Diaspora: Space, Place, Mobility, and Identity*, 193–220.

5 Peltonen, Matti, "Clues, Margins, and Monads: The Micro-Macro Link in Historical Research," *History and Theory* 40, no. 3 (2001): 349.

6 Ginzburg, Carlo, "Microhistory: Two or Three Things That I Know About It," *Critical Inquiry* 20, no. 1 (1993): 10–35; Levi, Giovanni, "On Microhistory," in *New Perspectives on Historical Writing*, ed. Peter Burke, (Cambridge: Polity Press, 1991), 93–113.

7 Levi, Giovanni, "On Microhistory," 97–98.

8 Chartier, Roger, "Intellectual History or Sociocultural History?," in *Modern European Intellectual History: Reappraisals & New Perspectives*, eds. Dominick LaCapra and Steven L. Kaplan (Ithaca: Cornell University Press,

1981), 32.

9 "Sources say that as the Hokkiens and Teochews form the two largest dialect groups which founded the chamber, their elders do not want to lose their grip over Singapore's most influential and prestigious business body.... So entrenched is the dialect-based system that several attempts at reform in the past decades failed. It was only in 1993 that changes were finally made to its Constitution", which removed the dialect proportional representation system and seven seats on SCCCI's council have been reserved for each of its seven founding dialect groups, namely Hokkien, Teochew, Cantonese, Hainanese, Sānjiāng (三江), Méixiàn (梅縣), and Dàbù (大埔). Leong, Weng Kam, "Is the end of the clan system in sight?" *The Straits Times*, 24 April 2010. Also see Chan, Fiona, "SCCCI to do away with dialect representation," *The Straits Times*, 30 March 2010; Chay, Felda, "'Dialect representation' is out at SCCCI," *The Business Times*, 28 May 2010; Leong, Weng Kam, "Group opts to scrap clan-based voting," *The Straits Times*, 28 May 2010.

Chapter Six

1 Franke, Wolfgang 傅吾康 and Chen, Tieh Fan 陳鐵凡, *Mǎláixīyà huáwén míngkè cuìbiān* 《馬來西亞華文銘刻萃編》 *Chinese Epigraphic Materials in Malaysia*, vol. 1 (Kuala Lumpur: University of Malaya Press, 1983), 1.

2 Ibid.

3 Rudolph, R. C., "Preliminary Notes on Sung Archaeology," *The Journal of Asian Studies* 22, no. 2 (February 1963): 170; Zhào, Míngchéng 趙明誠, "*Jīn shí lù* 金石錄" [A Collection of Inscriptions], in *Qīndìng sìkù quánshū* 《欽定四庫全書》 [Complete Library in Four Sections], vol. 14 of *Shǐbù* 史部 [History Section], accessed 30 November 2017, http://ctext.org/library.pl?if=gb&file=2017&page=11&remap=gb.

4 Ōuyáng, Xiū 歐陽脩, *Jígǔ lù báwěi* 《集古錄拔尾》 [A Postscript of A Compilation of Ancient Inscriptions], accessed 30 November 2017, http://ctext.org/wiki.pl?if=gb&res=865633.

5 Jao, Tsung-I 饒宗頤, "*Xīng mǎ huáwén bēikè xìnián (jìluè)* 星馬華文碑刻繫年(紀畧) [A Chronological Survey on Chinese Inscriptions in Singapore and Malaya]," *Xīnjiāpō dàxué zhōngwén xuéhuì xuébào* 《新加坡大學中文學會學報》 *Journal of the Chinese Society, University of Singapore* 10 (December 1969): 1–51; Chen, Chingho 陳荊和, and Tan, Yeok Seong 陳育崧, *Xīnjiāpō huáwén bēimíng jílù* 《新嘉坡華文碑銘集錄》 [A Collection of Singapore Chinese Inscriptions] (Hong Kong: The Chinese University Press, 1970). Another epigraphic work carried out in the 1960s was "*Fúdécí bēijì huìjí* 福德祠碑記彙集 [A Collection of Hok Tek Chi Inscriptions]," in *Fúdécí lǜyětíng yángé shǐ tèkān* 《福德祠綠野亭沿革史特刊》 [A Special Publication on the History of Hok Tek Chi Loke Yah Teng] (Singapore: Hok Tek Chi Loke Yah Teng Association, 1963), 7–27. Other epigraphy related works from the 1970s include Yì, Zhì 奕志, "*Yījiān shénmì de cítáng – shègōngmiào* 一間神祕的祠堂 – 社公廟 [A Mysterious Shrine: Shegong Temple]," *Nányáng wénzhāi* 《南洋文摘》 *Nanyang Digest* 14, no. 8 (August 1973): 527–528.

6 Chng, David K. Y. 莊欽永, "*Xīnjiāpō huáwén míngkè jìlù chūbiān* 新加坡華文銘刻記錄初編 [A Preliminary Documentation of Singapore Chinese Inscriptions]," in *Xīnjiāpō huárénshǐ lùncóng* 《新加坡華人史論叢》 [Collected Essays on Chinese in 19th-century Singapore] (Singapore: South Seas Society, 1986), 154–161; Chng, David K. Y. 莊欽永, "*Tiānfúgōng qiānlóng gǔzhōng xiǎozhì* 天福宮乾隆古鐘小誌 [An Account of the Thian Hock Keng Temple Qianlong Ancient Bell]," in *Xīnjiāpō huárénshǐ lùncóng* 《新加坡華人史論叢》 [Collected Essays on Chinese in 19th-Century Singapore], 151–153; Chng, David K. Y. 莊欽

永, "*Mǎliùjiǎ、Xīnjiāpō huáwén bēiwén jílù* 馬六甲、新加坡華文碑文輯錄 [A Collection of Chinese Inscriptions in Malacca and Singapore]," *Mínzú xué yánjiū suǒ zīliào huìbiān* 《民族學研究所資料彙編》, Field Materials, Institute of Ethnology, Academia Sinica, vol. 12 (Taipei: Institute of Ethnology, Academia Sinica, 1998); Chng, David K. Y. 莊欽永, *Heroic Images of Ming Loyalists: A Study of the Spirit Tablets of the Ghee Hin Kongsi Leaders in Singapore* (Singapore: Singapore Society for Asian Studies, 1999); Dean, Kenneth 丁荷生, and Hue, Guan Thye 許源泰, *Xīnjiāpō huáwén míngkè huìbiān* 《新加坡華文銘刻彙編》 *Chinese Epigraphy in Singapore 1819–1911* (Singapore: NUS Press; Guilin: Guangxi Normal University, 2017).

7 Franke, Wolfgang 傅吾康, and Chen, Tieh Fan 陳鐵凡, *Mǎláixīyà huáwén míngkè cuìbiān* 《馬來西亞華文銘刻萃編》 *Chinese Epigraphic Materials in Malaysia*, vols. 1–3 (Kuala Lumpur: University of Malaya Press, 1982–1987); Franke, Wolfgang 傅吾康, *Yìndùníxīyà huáwén míngkè huìbiān* 《印度尼西亞華文銘刻彙編》 *Chinese Epigraphic Materials in Indonesia*, vols. 1–3 (Singapore: South Seas Society, 1988–1997); Teoh, Shiaw Kuan 張少寬, *Bīnlángyǔ huárén sìmiào bēimíng jílù* 《檳榔嶼華人寺廟碑銘集錄》 [Collection of Epigraphy from Buddhist and Taoist Temples in Penang] (Penang: *Nányáng tiányě yánjiūshì* 南洋田野研究室, 2013).

8 Han, Wai Toon 韓槐準, "*Dàbógōng kǎo* 大伯公考 [A Study of the Dabogong Deity]," *Nányáng xuébào* 《南洋學報》 *Journal of the South Seas Society* 1, no. 2 (December 1940): 18–26; Hsu, Yun-ts'iao 許雲樵, "*Dàbógōng, èrbógōng yǔ běntóugōng* 大伯公, 二伯公與本頭公 [The Deities Dabogong, Erbogong and Bentougong]," *Nányáng xuébào* 《南洋學報》 *Journal of the South Seas Society* 7, no. 2 (November 1951): 6–10; Hsu, Yun-ts'iao 許雲樵, "*Zàitán Dàbógōng yánjiū* 再談大伯公研究 [A Further Discussion on the Study of Dabogong]," *Nányáng xuébào* 《南洋學報》 *Journal of the South Seas Society* 8, no. 2 (December 1952): 19–24; Wèi, Jùxián 衛聚賢, "*[Èrbógōng] de yǒuwúshuō* [二伯公]的有無說 [A Discussion of the Existence of Erbogong]," *Nányáng xuébào* 《南洋學報》 *Journal of the South Seas Society* 8, no. 2 (December 1952): 25–26; Jao, Tsung-I 饒宗頤, "*Tán Bógōng* 談伯公 [A Discussion of the Bogong Deities]," *Nányáng xuébào* 《南洋學報》 *Journal of the South Seas Society* 8, no. 2 (December 1952): 27–28; Tiān, Guānfú 天官福, "*Dàbógōng shì héfāng shénshèng* 大伯公是何方神聖 [Who is the Dabogong Deity?], *Nányáng wénzhāi* 《南洋文摘》 *Nanyang Digest* 4, no. 1 (January 1963): 25–28.

9 Xiè, Yúnshēng 謝雲聲, "*Xīnjiāpō fèngshānsì gōngfèng shénkǎo* 新加坡鳳山寺供奉神考 [A Study of the Deities in the Singapore Hong San See Temple]," in *Xīnjiāpō nán'ān huìguǎn jīnxǐ jìniàn tèkān* 《新加坡南安會館金禧紀念特刊》 [Singapore Lam Ann Association Golden Jubilee Special Publication] (Singapore: Singapore Lam Ann Association, 1977), 25.

10 Méi, Xīnlín 梅新林, and Yú, Zhānghuá 俞樟華, eds., *Zhōngguó yóujì wénxuéshǐ* 《中國遊記文學史》 [A Literary History of Travellers' Accounts in China] (Shanghai: *Xuélín chūbǎnshè* 學林出版社, 2004), 7–8.

11 Ibid., 9–10.

12 Cheng, Kin Lo 鄭健廬, *Nányáng sānyuè jì* 《南洋三月記》 [An Account of Three Months in Nanyang] (Hong Kong: *Zhōnghuá shūjú* 中華書局, 1933), 71–75, 121–122, 157; Cheng, Kin Lo, *Three Months in Nanyang*, trans. from *Nányáng sānyuè jì* 《南洋三月記》 [An Account of Three Months in Nanyang] (Shanghai: Chung Hwa Book Store, 1935).

13 Phua, Chay Long 潘醒農, *Xīnjiāpō yóulǎn zhǐnán* 《新嘉坡游覽指南》 [Travellers' Guide to Singapore] (Singapore: The Nantao Publishing House, 1946); Phua, Chay Long 潘醒農, *Dōngnányà míngshèng* 《東南亞名勝》

[Celebrated Places in Southeast Asia] (Singapore: The Nantao Publishing House, 1954).

14 Zéng, Tiěchén 曾鐵忱, *Xīnjiāpō lǚyóu biànlǎn* 《新加坡旅遊便覽》 [A Brief Tourist Guide of Singapore] (Singapore: *Xīn qǐyè chūbǎnshè* 新企業出版社, 1966).

15 Lim, How Seng 林孝勝, ed., *Shílè gǔjī* 《石叻古蹟》 [Monuments of Singapore] (Singapore: South Seas Society, 1975).

16 Chen, Yun Yong 陳漢榮, *Xīnjiāpō gǔjī* 《新加坡古蹟》 [Singapore Historical Sights] (Singapore: Educational Publications Bureau, 1978); Hooi, Christopher, *National Monuments of Singapore* (Singapore: National Museum, Singapore, 1982); Liu, Gretchen, *Pastel Portraits: Singapore's Architectural Heritage* (Singapore: Singapore Coordinating Committee, 1984); Lee, Edwin, *Historic Buildings of Singapore* (Singapore: Preservation of Monuments Board, 1990); Samuel, Dhoraisingam S., *Singapore's Heritage Through Places of Historical Interest* (Singapore: Elixir Consultancy Service, 1991); Goh, Ngan Hong 吳彥鴻, *Xīnjiāpō fēngtǔ zhì* 《新嘉坡風土志》 [A Gazetteer of Singapore] (Singapore: Singapore Teochew Poit Ip Huay Kuan, 1997); Liu, Gretchen, and Lim, Albert K. S., *In Granite and Chunam: The National Monuments of Singapore* (Singapore: Landmark Books and Preservation of Monuments Board, 1996); Pugalenthi, Sr., *Singapore Landmarks: Monuments, Memorials, Statues & Historic Sites* (Singapore: VJ Times International, 1999); Lee, Geok Boi, *The Religious Monuments of Singapore: Faiths of Our Forefathers* (Singapore: Landmark Books and Preservation of Monuments Board, 2002); Wan, Meng Hao, and Lau, Jacqueline, *Heritage Places of Singapore* (Singapore: Marshall Cavendish Editions, 2009).

17 Beamish, Jane, and Ferguson, Jane, *A History of Singapore Architecture: The Making of a City* (Singapore: Graham Brash, 1985).

18 Knapp, Ronald G., *Chinese Houses of Southeast Asia: The Eclectic Architecture of Sojourners and Settlers* (Clarendon, Vermont: Tuttle, 2010); Kang, Ger-wen, *Decoration and Symbolism in Chinese Architecture: Understanding Singapore's Historic Chinese Buildings* (Singapore: Preservation of Sites and Monuments, 2013); Foo, Su Ling, et al., *NUS Baba House: Architecture and Artefacts of a Straits Chinese Home* (Singapore: NUS Baba House; Editions Didier Millet, 2016).

19 Lip, Mong Har Evelyn, *Chinese Temples and Deities* (Singapore: Times Book International, 1981); Lip, Mong Har Evelyn, *Chinese Temple Architecture in Singapore* (Singapore: Singapore University Press, 1983); Kohl, David G., *Chinese Architecture in the Straits Settlements and Western Malaya: Temples, Kongsis and Houses* (Kuala Lumpur: Heinemann Asia, 1984).

20 Liú, Xiānjué 劉先覺, and Lee, Coo 李谷, *Xīnjiāpō fójiào jiànzhú yìshù* 《新加坡佛教建築藝術》 [Buddhist Architecture in Singapore] (Singapore: Kepmedia International, 2007).

21 Yeo, Kang Shua, "Homogenously Heterogenous?: The Diversity of Traditional Chinese Architecture in Singapore," *Journal of Southeast Asian Architecture* 9 (2006): 87–106.

22 "Restoration of Thian Hock Keng Temple at Telok Ayer Street," *Journal of the Singapore Institute of Architects* 101 (July/August 1980): 3–7.

23 Chan, Yew Lih, et al., *The House of Tan Yeok Nee: The Conservation of a National Monument* (Singapore: Winpeak Investment and Wingem Investment, 2003).

24 Ho, Phang Phow 何炳彪, ed., *Bǎinián gōngdé bèi nánbāng: Wànghǎi Dàbógōng miào jìshì* 《百年公德被南邦：望海大伯公廟紀事》 *The Living Heritage: Stories of Fook Tet Soo Khek Temple* (Singapore: Char Yong (Dabu) Association, 2006).

25 Toh, Lam Huat 杜南發, ed., *Nánhǎi míngzhū: tiānfúgōng* 《南海明珠: 天福宮》 [Pearl of the South Seas: Thian Hock Keng Temple] (Singapore: Singapore Hokkien Huay Kuan, 2010).

26 Toh, Lam Huat 杜南發, ed., *Liánshān shuānglín: Xīnjiāpō liánshān shuānglín chánsì yībǎi èrshí zhōunián wénjí: wénshǐ jí*《蓮山雙林：新加坡蓮山雙林禪寺一百二十周年文集：文史集》[Lian Shan Shuang Lin Monastery 120th Anniversary Compendium (Social History)] (Singapore: Singapore Lianshan Shuanglin Monastery, 2018); Yeo Kang Shua 楊茳善, ed., *Liánshān shuānglín: Xīnjiāpō liánshān shuānglín chánsì yībǎi èrshí zhōunián wénjí: jiànzhú jí*《蓮山雙林：新加坡蓮山雙林禪寺一百二十周年文集：建築集》[Lian Shan Shuang Lin Monastery 120th Anniversary Compendium (Architecture)] (Singapore: Singapore Lianshan Shuanglin Monastery, 2018).

27 Tan, Yeow Wooi 陳耀威, *Bīnchéng lóngshāntáng qiū gōngsī : lìshǐ yǔ jiànzhú*《檳城龍山堂邱公司：歷史與建築》[Leong San Tong Khoo Kongsi: The History and Architecture] (Penang: Trustees of Leong San Tong Khoo Kongsi, 2003); Tan, Yeow Wooi 陳耀威, *Fúbì zhòngshēng: xiūfù jùngōng jìniàn tèkān*《福庇眾生：修復竣工紀念特刊》[Bestowing Luck & Prosperity on All: Commemorative Publication] (Penang: Hock Teik Cheng Sin Temple, 2007); Tan, Yeow Wooi 陳耀威, *Jiǎbìdān zhèng jǐngguì de shèn zhī jiāshú yǔ hǎijìzhàn*《甲必丹鄭景貴的慎之家塾與海記棧》[Kapitan Chung Keng Kwee's Shen Zhi Jia Shu and Hai Ji Zhan] (Penang: Pinang Peranakan Museum, 2013).

28 Xiè, Míngfēi 謝鳴非, *Xīnjiāpō miàoyǔ gàilǎn*《新加坡廟宇概覽》[An Overview of Temples in Singapore] (Singapore: *Nánfēng shāngyè chūbǎnshè yǐngyìn* 南風商業出版社影印, 1951); Comber, Leon, *Chinese Temples in Singapore* (Singapore: Eastern Universities Press, 1958).

29 Chia, Yei Yei 謝燕燕, et al., eds., *Xīnjiāpō mínsú dǎolǎn: miàoyǔ wénhuà*《新加坡民俗導覽：廟宇文化》[A Guide to Singapore Folk Customs: The Cultures of Temples], vols. 1–4 (Singapore: Focus Publishing, 2005–2014); Mò, Měiyán 莫美顏, *Shīchéng gǔmiào zǒu yīhuí*《獅城古廟走一回》[A Walk Through Historic Temples in Singapore], vol. 3, *Huázú wénhuà cóngshū* 華族文化叢書 [Chinese Cultural Series] (Singapore: SNP Panpac and Singapore Federation of Chinese Clan Associations, 2005).

30 Salmon, Claudine, and Lombard, Denys, *Les Chinois de Jakarta: Temples et Vie Collective* [The Chinese of Jakarta: Temples and Communal Life], vol. 6, Cahier d'Archipel (Guéret: SECMI, 1977); Atmodjo, Junus Satrio, and Witanto, Eddy Prabowo, eds., *Kelenteng Kuno di DKI Jakarta dan Jawa Barat* [Old Temples in Jakarta and West Java] (Jakarta: Departemen Pendidikan Nasional, 2000); Hú, Jǐnchāng 胡錦昌, ed., *Róufó miàoyǔ wénhuà*《柔佛廟宇文化》[Johor Temple] (Petaling Jaya, Selangor: *Shēnghuó chūbǎnshè* 生活出版社, 2008); Kleinsteuber, Asti, and Maharadjo, Syafri M., *Kelenteng-kelenteng Kuno di Indonesia, Yìnní gǔdài de sìmiào*《印尼古代的寺廟》[The Old Chinese Temples in Indonesia] (Jakarta: Genta Kreasi Nusantara, 2010).

31 Salmon, and Lombard, *Les Chinois de Jakarta*.

32 Xú, Lǐyǐng 徐李穎, *Jiǔhuáng shèngjī: hòugǎng dǒumǔgōng*《九皇聖蹟：後港斗母宮》[Sacred Site of the Nine Emperor Gods: The Hougang Dou Mu Temple] (Singapore: Hougang Tou Mu Temple, 2006); Xú, Lǐyǐng 徐李穎, *Jiǔshí chūnqiū: Xīnjiāpō jiǔcàibā chénghuáng miào shǐjì*《九十春秋：新加坡韭菜芭城隍廟史記》[A 90 Year History of Lorong Koo Chye Sheng Hong (City-God) Temple] (Singapore: Lorong Koo Chye Sheng Hong Temple Association, 2007); Loo, Say Chong 呂世聰, and Ang, Yik Han 洪毅瀚, *Tóutáo zhī bào: Wànshāngǎng fúdécí lìshǐ sùyuán*《投桃之報：萬山港福德祠歷史溯源》[A Boon Returned: The History of Mun San Fook Tuck Chee] (Singapore: Selat Society, 2008); Ang, Yik Han 洪毅瀚, *Xiāngqíng cíyùn: Shāgāng cūn hé wànshān gang fúdécí de liúbiàn*

yǔ chuánchéng《鄉情祠韵: 沙岡村和萬山港福德祠的流變與傳承》 [A Kampong and its Temple: Change and Tradition in Kampong Sar Kong and the Mun San Fook Tuck Chee] (Singapore: Mun San Fook Tuck Chee, 2016); Tan, Gia Lim, *An Introduction to the Culture and History of the Teochews in Singapore* (Singapore: World Scientific, 2018); Leong, Ching, and Tan, Lye Huat, eds., *The Story of Singapore Teochews* 《新加坡潮人故事》(Singapore: Teochew Poit Ip Huay Kuan, 2019; 新加坡: 新加坡潮州八邑会馆, 2018).

Appendix

Trustees of Wak Hai Cheng Bio[1]

Year	Land Document	Organisation		Trustees	
late 1820s	Lease No. 174 (now T.S. IV lots 428-1)	Twa Law Yaw Kiong	大老爺宮		
circa 1848 or later	Lot No. 1 of Lease No. 473 (now T.S. IV lots 428-2)	Heang Tiang Siang Tee Kongsi	玄天上帝公司	Seah Euching [Eu Chin] Laow Soon Heng Sim Ah Kie Weng Moh Thang	佘有進 (1805–1883) □□□ 沈亞開 (沈開合) □□□
1850		Wun Yien Seang Tie Kongsi[2]	元天上帝公司	Seah Eu Chin Sim Ah Kie Tay Ah Bock Wan Mong Sun	佘有進 (1805–1883) 沈亞開 (沈開合) 鄭□□ 袁茂春
1909	Lease No. 2674 (now T.S. IV lots 428-1)	Wan Tein Siang Tie Kongsi	元天上帝公司	Seah Liang Seah Teo Wee Choi Kwek Tye Hak	佘連城 (1850–1925) 張為千 郭泰合
1914 (1916)[3]	T.S. IV lots 428-1 and 428-2	Ghee Ann Koon	義安郡	Seah Liang Seah Quek Num Seng Lim Chew Kwang Low Teng Pheow Chan Wai Chua Goh Teck Chue [Goh Tek Chng/Goh Tek Cher] Teo Wee Choi Heng Pang Kiat Yeo Swee Keong Tan Seow Kwang Ng Yeow Quee Sim Lye Choon Seah Chin Moey [Seah Chin Mui] Chua Sok Chew	佘連城 (1850–1925) 郭南盛 林秋光 劉廷標 曾懷泉 吳竹村 (1876–1935) 張為千 王邦傑 (1856–1930) 楊瑞恭 陳紹光 (unknown–1925) 黃耀奎 沈來春 佘振美 蔡雪舟
Before 1933	T.S. IV lots 428-1 and 428-2	Ghee Ann Koon	義安郡	Seah Eng Tong Seah Chin Mui [Seah Chin Moey] Kwek Liang Choon [Quek Liang Choon] Low Peng Soy Chan Kim Seng	佘應忠 (1880–1940) 佘振美 郭兩存 劉炳先 (1886–1938) 曾金昇

1 The "Heang Tiang Siang Tee" group were the earlier trustees, active from at least 1850 up till about the late 1870s and early 1880s, while the "Wun Yien Seang Tie" and "Wan Tein Siang Tie" trustees were active from the 1880s to the late 1910s. These dates are a rough estimation based on the death dates of some of the trustees and the years that they were active. The two groups of trustees should be understood simply as trustees of the Mysterious Supreme Emperor of Heaven. They were not separate organisations, but trustees at different points in time.

2 As Trustees of 33 Phillip Street

3 "Suit No. 430 of 1914, In the Matter of the Trustee Ordinance 1914 and In the Matter of the 'Ghee Ann Society'," 8 February 1916, Settlement of Singapore Registry of Deed, vol. CDXXXVI, page 505, no. 142.

Year	Land Document	Organisation		Trustees	
				Goh Tek Chng [Goh Tek Cher/ Goh Teck Chue]	吳竹村 (1876–1935)
				Teo Keong Meng	張恭銘
				Heng Pang Keat	王邦傑 (1856–1930)
				Yeo Huang Kok	楊芳國
				Tan Miang Long	陳綿隆
				Ng Chok Sam	黃祝三
				Sim Ka Siew	沈教授
				Chua Ngak Chew	蔡咢秋
				Lim Hak Khiam	林學謙
After 1933[4]	T.S. IV lots 428-1 and 428-2	The Ngee Ann Kongsi	義安公司	Lim Nee Soon	林義順 (1879–1936)
				Low Peng Soy	劉炳先 (1886–1938)
				Lee Wee Nam	李偉南 (1880–1964)
				Tan Lip Sek	陳立植
				Lim Woo Ngam	林雨岩 (1880–1972)
				Yeo Choo Tian	楊書典
				Kwek Liang Choon [Quek Liang Choon]	郭兩存
				Liau Chia Heng	廖正興 (1874–1934)
				Yeo Chan Boon	楊纘文 (1881–1967)
				Tan Chew Char	陳秋槎 (1893–1942)
				Goh Teck Chng [Goh Tek Cher/ Goh Teck Chue]	吳竹村 (1876–1935)
				Tan Miang Long	陳綿隆
				Sim Ka Siew	沈教授
				Goh Yang Pheng	吳揚屏
				Kwek Soo Kow	郭斯高 (1895–1952)
				Low Chia Heng	劉正興 (1871–1941)
				Lim Soo Siam	林樹森 (1887–1947)
				Chew Swee Lin	周瑞麟 (unknown–1939)
				Nah Wee Liat	藍偉烈 (unknown–1968)
				Kwek [Quek] Teng Thong	郭廷通
				Low Peng Soo	劉炳思 (1898–1973)
				Lee Kim Soo	李金賜 (1888–1933)
				Lim Chong Pang	林忠邦 (1904–1956)
				Seah Eng Tong	佘應忠 (1880–1940)

Trustees of 32 Circular Road and 48 South Boat Quay

Year	Land Document	Organisation		Trustees	
Before 1916		Hin Tean Sang Te	玄天上帝	Seah Eu Chin	佘有進 (1805–1883)
				Sim Ah Kie	沈亞開 (沈開合)
				Wun Mong Soon	袁茂春
				Laow Soon Heng	□□□

4 The names of the committee members listed here are taken from the 1933 Ordinance. It is to note that the 24 names listed in the 1933 Ordinance did not tally fully with the names listed in *Ngee Ann Kongsi: Into the Next Millennium*.
"No. 5 of 1933 An Ordinance to Incorporate the Ngee Ann Kongsi," *Straits Settlements Government Gazette*, 10 March 1933, 384 and "Ngee Ann Kongsi (Incorporation) Ordinance, (Chapter 370)," Revised Edition 1985, accessed 28 July 2017, https://sso.agc.gov.sg/Act/NAKIO1933. Also see Tan, Sumiko 陳澄子, *Yì'ān gōngsī: kuàrù lìng yīgè qiānxǐ nián* 《義安公司: 跨入另一個千禧年》 *Ngee Ann Kongsi: Into the Next Millennium* (Singapore: Ngee Ann Kongsi, 2005), 115.

Trustees of Tye Swah Teng (泰山亭)

Year	Land Document	Organisation		Trustees	
1845		Chinese Burial Ground "Tie Swah"	泰山	Seah Eu Chin Choa Po Choo	佘有進 (1805–1883) 蔡報之
1916		Ghee Ann Koon	義安郡		

Trustees of Kwong Ngee Suah (廣義山)

Year	Land Document	Organisation	Trustees	
1857	Grant No. 14 Mukim 24		Seah Eu Chin Sim Ah Khie Wan Mong Choon Low Tan Hee	佘有進 (1805–1883) 沈亞開 (沈開合) 袁茂春 劉同喜
1866	Grant No. 40 Mukim 24		Tan Seng Poh Lim Chub Hee	陳成寶 (1828–1879) 林捶喜
1890	Statutory Land Grant No. 2305 Mukim 17		Seah Liang Seah Sun Keng Hoo Goh Hup Tee	佘連城 (1850–1925) □□□ 吴□□

Trustees of Kwong Siu Suah (廣壽山)

Year	Land Document	Organisation	Trustees	
1860	Grant No. 14 Mukim 5	Tew Chew Chinese Burial Ground	Seah Eu Chin Heng Ban Soon Sim Ah Njah	佘有進 (1805–1883) 王萬順 沈亞岳
1901	Statutory Land Grant No. 13072 Mukim 5	Teo Chew Burial Ground	Seah Peck Seah Lau Chiang Yi Heng Koan Chiap Tui Ui Choi	佘柏城 (unknown–1939) 劉□□ 王□□ □□□

Trustees of Kwong Eng Suah (廣恩山)

Year	Land Document	Organisation		Trustees	
1866	T.S. XXIX lot 9-1			Tan Seng Poh Lim Cheap Hee	陳成寶 (1828–1879) 林捶喜
1872	T.S. XXIX lot 9-1	Ghee Ann Congsee; Ghee Ann Koon	義安公司; 義安郡	Tan Seng Poh Heng Tek Heng Seah Cheok Sia Ung Ah Watt	陳成寶 (1828–1879) 王得興 佘石城 (1846–1885) 黄亞發

Trustees of Nos. 197, 198, 199 and 200 New Bridge Road

Year	Land Document	Organisation		Trustees	
Before 1916	T.S. VII lot 116-12	Ghee Ann Society	義安郡	Tan Seng Poh Wee Ah Watt Seah Cheo Seah Goh Teck Tee	陳成寶 (1828–1879) 黄亞發 佘石城 (1846–1885) 吴□□

Trustees of 29 Phillip Street

Year	Land Document	Organisation		Trustees	
Before 1916				Tan Seng Poh Seah Ciek Seah	陳成寶 (1828–1879) 佘石城 (1846–1885)

Trustees of Choh Soo Kong Temple (祖師公廟)

Year	Land Document	Organisation		Trustees	
1914	Lease No. 5467 (T.S. XVII lot 14)	Choh Soo Kong Temple	祖師公廟	Seah Liang Seah	佘連城 (1850–1925)

Trustees of Poh Seng Tye Tee (保生大帝)

Year	Land Document	Organisation		Trustees	
Before 1916	Lease No. 1434 (T.S. XIII lot 357)	Poh Seng Tye Tee	保生大帝	Tan Kian Cheap Tan Seok Ann Koh Meng Kim Seah Leang Seah	陳□□ 陳□□ □□□ 佘連城 (1850–1925)

List of Figures

Toponymics: Environs

Chapter 2

Fig. 2.12. Lim Nee Soon and 13 other individuals' public letter to Seah Eng Tong and trustees of Ngee Ann Kun published in *Lat Pau* on 29 December 1927, p. 51.

The First Chinese Imperial Plaque in Singapore Fig. BS04.1. The imperial plaque blackened by incense soot. This photograph was taken on 22 March 1994 in preparation for the 1994 to 1997 renovation works, p. 39.

The First Chinese Imperial Plaque

Fig. BS04.1. The imperial plaque blackened by incense soot. This photograph was taken on 22 March 1994 in preparation for the 1994 to 1997 renovation works. Note the gaps in between characters of the date inscription: *Guāngxù ... shíwǔ ... wǔ ... rì* 光緒 ... 十五 ... 五 ... 日.

Fig. BS04.2. The imperial plaque with the inscription date of *Guāngxù èrshíwǔ nián sìyuè jílì* 光緒二十五年四月吉立 [The 4th lunar month of the 25th year of Emperor Guāngxù's reign], p. 39.

Kwangtung Hui Kuan

Fig. BS05.1. Metal plaque entitled "新嘉坡廣東會館 購置會所募捐事畧" [An account of fundraising efforts to purchase premises for Singapore Kwangtung Hui Kuan] dated 1962, p. 53.

Chapter 3

Opener: Restoration of a fresco depicting a story from "Generals of the Yang family" where the centenarian matriarch prepares to lead a battle, p. 58.

Source: Photographed by Lim Shao Bin.

Fig. 3.1. Building Plan of Wak Hai Cheng Bio submitted to the municipal engineer in 1895, p. 60.

Fig. 3.2. Photograph of locally quarried granite with inclusion, p. 63.

Fig. 3.3. *Lat Pau* (叻報) article reported that Wak Hai Cheng Bio's beam-raising ceremony took place on 24 September 1896. This date is different from the date, 7 May 1896, inscribed on three secondary ridge beams (*zǐsūn liáng* 子孫樑) in the main halls of the two shrines and in the rear building. Hence, 7 May 1896 ought to be understood as the date for commencement of works, p. 64.

Fig. 3.4. Secondary ridge beams (*zǐsūn liáng* 子孫樑) in the front hall of Shàngdìgōng. The secondary ridge beams in the front halls of the two shrines have the same two sets of inscriptions that bear the dates of the 1994 and 2014 works: "旹次甲戌年九月廿八日午時重修 公元一九九四年十一月一號" [Temple (commenced) restoration on 1 November 1994] and "旹次甲午年三月初一 公元二零一四年竣修 義安公司主持大修" [Full restoration of temple by The Ngee Ann Kongsi was completed on 31 March 2014], p. 65.

Fig. 3.5. Donation notices published in 1896 for the rebuilding of Wak Hai Cheng Bio: 19 March; 1, 11, 24, 25, and 29 August; 29 October; and 26 November, p. 66.

Fig. 3.6. Donation notices published in 1897 for the rebuilding of Wak Hai Cheng Bio: 25 January; 9 March and 6 April, p. 67.

Fig. 3.7. Plaques presented to Wak Hai Cheng Bio: Hèzhuó shēnglíng 赫濯聲靈 [(The god's) dynamic influence and supernatural power are well known and widespread] presented by Char Yong Association (潮郡茶陽會館衆信商敬酬) in 1897 (光緒弍十三年丁酉冬月吉旦); Nìyuán tiānxià 溺援天下 [(All) those drowning in suffering will be aided (by the goddess)] presented by Ying Fo Kun (應和館衆等仝敬) in 1898 (光緒戊戌歲冬月吉旦); and Shǔhǎi xiángyún 曙海祥雲 [Auspicious clouds above the sea at dawn] bestowed by Emperor Guāngxù in 1899 (光緒二十五年四月吉旦) (*left to right*), p. 73.

Fig. 3.8. Entrance gateway of Wak Hai Cheng Bio. The temple's gilded name "粵海清廟" is inscribed on the granite plaque. The void below this plaque is known as *tiāndì zǐsūn fèng* (天地子孫縫), p. 75.

Competitive Timberwork Construction

Chapter 5

Chapter 6

Bibliography

Books

Allen, J. de V., et al., eds, *A Collection of Treaties and Other Documents Affecting the States of Malaysia 1761–1963,* vol. I (London; New York: Oceana Publications, 1981).

Ang, Yik Han 洪毅瀚, *Xiāngqíng cíyùn: Shāgāng cūn hé wànshān gang fúdécí de liúbiàn yǔ chuánchéng* 《鄉情祠韵:沙岡村和萬山港福德祠的流變與傳承》 [A Kampong and its Temple: Change and Tradition in Kampong Sar Kong and the Mun San Fook Tuck Chee] (Singapore: Mun San Fook Tuck Chee, 2016).

Ali al-Haji Riau, Raja, *The Precious Gift: Tuhfat al-nafis,* annotated trans. Virginia Matheson and Barbara Watson Andaya (Kuala Lumpur; New York: Oxford University Press, 1982)

Atmodjo, Junus Satrio, and Witanto, Eddy Prabowo, eds., *Kelenteng Kuno di DKI Jakarta dan Jawa Barat* [Old Temples in Jakarta and West Java] (Jakarta: Departemen Pendidikan Nasional, 2000).

Bastin, John, *The Founding of Singapore 1819: Based on the Private Letters of Sir Stamford Raffles to the Governor-General and Commander-in-Chief in India, the Marguess of Hastings, Preserved in the Bute Collection at Mount Stuart, Isle of Bute, Scotland* (Singapore: National Library Board, 2012).

Beamish, Jane, and Ferguson, Jane, *A History of Singapore Architecture: The Making of a City* (Singapore: Graham Brash, 1985).

Buckley, Charles Burton, *An Anecdotal History of Old Times in Singapore, from the Foundation of the Settlement under the Honourable the East India Company, on Feb. 6th, 1819, to the Transfer to the Colonial Office as Part of the Colonial Possessions of the Crown on April 1st, 1867*, vol. 1 (Singapore: Fraser & Neave, 1902).

Burke, Peter, ed., *New Perspectives on Historical Writing* (Cambridge: Polity Press, 1991).

Chan, Yew Lih, et al., *The House of Tan Yeok Nee: The Conservation of a National Monument* (Singapore: Winpeak Investment and Wingem Investment, 2003).

Cháoyángshì dìfāngzhì biānzuǎn wěiyuánhuì 潮陽市地方志編纂委員會, *Cháoyáng xiànzhì* 《潮陽縣志》 [Cháoyáng Gazetteer] (*Guangzhou: Guǎngdōng rénmín chūbǎnshè* 廣東人民出版社, 1997).

Chapters on Asia: A Selection of Papers from the Lee Kong Chian Research Fellowship (2014–2016) (Singapore: National Library Board Singapore, 2018).

Chen, Chingho 陳荊和, and Tan, Yeok Seong 陳育崧, *Xīnjiāpō huáwén bēimíng jílù* 《新嘉坡華文碑銘集錄》 [A Collection of Singapore Chinese Inscriptions] (Hong Kong: The Chinese University Press, 1970).

Chen, Yun Yong 陳漢榮, *Xīnjiāpō gǔjī* 《新加坡古蹟》 [Singapore Historical Sights] (Singapore: Educational Publications Bureau, 1978).

Cheng, Kin Lo, *Three Months in Nanyang*, trans. from *Nányáng sānyuè jì* 《南洋三月記》 [An Account of Three Months in Nanyang] (Shanghai: Chung Hwa Book Store, 1935).

Cheng, Kin Lo 鄭健廬, *Nányáng sānyuè jì* 《南洋三月記》 [An Account of Three Months in Nanyang] (Hong Kong: *Zhōnghuá shūjú* 中華書局, 1933.

Chew, Ernest C.T., and Lee, Edwin, eds., *A History of Singapore* (Singapore: Oxford University Press, 1991).

Chia, Yei Yei 謝燕燕, et al., eds., *Xīnjiāpō mínsú dǎolǎn: miàoyǔ wénhuà* 《新加坡民俗導覽: 廟宇文化》 [A Guide To Singapore Folk Customs: The Cultures of Temples], vols. 1–4 (Singapore: Focus Publishing, 2005–2014).

Chng, David K. Y. 莊欽永, *Heroic Images of Ming Loyalists: A Study of the Spirit Tablets of the Ghee Hin Kongsi Leaders in Singapore* (Singapore: Singapore Society for Asian Studies, 1999).

Chng, David K. Y. 莊欽永, *Xīnjiāpō huárénshǐ*

lùncóng《新加坡華人史論叢》[Collected Essays on Chinese in 19th-century Singapore] (Singapore: South Seas Society, 1986).

Comber, Leon, *Chinese Temples in Singapore* (Singapore: Eastern Universities Press, 1958).

Conrad, Joseph, *The Shadow-Line: A Confession*, eds. J.H. Stape and Allan H. Simmons (New York: Cambridge University Press, 2013).

Dean, Kenneth 丁荷生, and Hue, Guan Thye 許源泰, *Xīnjiāpō huáwén míngkè huìbiān*《新加坡華文銘刻彙編》*Chinese Epigraphy in Singapore 1819–1911* (Singapore: NUS Press; Guilin: Guangxi Normal University, 2017).

DeBernardi, Jean, *Rites of Belonging: Memory, Modernity and Identity in a Malaysian Chinese Community* (Stanford: Stanford University Press, 2004).

Douglas, Carstairs, *Chinese-English Dictionary of the Vernacular or Spoken Language of Amoy, with the Principal Variations of the Chang-chew and Chin-chew Dialects* (London: Trübner & Co., 1873).

Dunlop, Peter K.G., *Street Names of Singapore* (Singapore: Who's Who Pub., 2000).

Durkheim, Emile, *The Elementary Forms of Religious Life* (New York: Free Press, 1965).

Edwards, Norman, and Keys, Peter, *Singapore: A Guide to Buildings, Streets, Places* (Singapore: Times Books International, 1988).

Foucault, Michel, *Discipline and Punish: The Birth of the Prison* (New York: Vintage Books, 1995).

Franke, Wolfgang 傅吾康, *Yìndùníxīyà huáwén míngkè huìbiān*《印度尼西亞華文銘刻編》*Chinese Epigraphic Materials in Indonesia*, vols. 1–3 (Singapore: South Seas Society, 1988–1997).

Franke, Wolfgang 傅吾康, and Chen, Tieh Fan 陳鐵凡, *Mǎláixīyà huáwén míngkè cuìbiān*《馬來西亞華文銘刻萃編》*Chinese Epigraphic Materials in Malaysia*, vols. 1–3 (Kuala Lumpur: University of Malaya Press, 1982–1987).

Fraser, J. M., *The Work of the Singapore Improvement Trust, 1927–1947* (Singapore: Authority of Singapore Improvement Trust).

Foo, Su Ling, Lim, Chen Sian, Wee, Sheau Theng, and Yeo, Kang Shua, *NUS Baba House: Architecture and Artefacts of a Straits Chinese Home* (Singapore: NUS Baba House; Editions Didier Millet, 2016).

Gabaccia, Donna R., and Hoerder, Dirk, eds., *Connecting Seas and Connected Ocean Rims: Indian, Atlantic, and Pacific Oceans and China Seas Migrations from the 1830s to the 1930s* (Leiden; Boston: Brill, 2011).

Goh, Ngan Hong 吳彥鴻, *Xīnjiāpō fēngtǔ zhì*《新嘉坡風土志》[A Gazetteer of Singapore] (Singapore: Singapore Teochew Poit Ip Huay Kuan, 1997).

GuideGecko, Singapore Travel Guide (New Jersey: BookBaby, 2011).

Hall-Jones, John, and Hooi, Christopher, *An Early Surveyor in Singapore: John Turnbull Thomson in Singapore, 1841–1853* (Singapore: National Museum, 1979).

Hall-Jones, John, and Thomson, John Turnbull, *The Thomson Paintings: Mid-Nineteenth Century Paintings of the Straits Settlements and Malaya* (Singapore: Oxford University Press, 1983).

Hé, Guózhōng 何國忠, ed., *Bǎinián huímóu: mǎhuá shèhuì yǔ zhèngzhì*《百年回眸: 馬華社會與政治》[100 Years of Malaysian Chinese Society and Politics: Review And Prognosis] (Kuala Lumpur: *Huáshè yánjiū zhōngxīn* 華社研究中心, 2005).

Ho, Phang Phow 何炳彪, ed., *Bǎinián gōngdé bèi nánbāng: Wànghǎi Dàbógōng miào jìshì*《百年公德被南邦: 望海大伯公廟紀事》*The Living Heritage: Stories of Fook Tet Soo Khek Temple* (Singapore: Char Yong (Dabu) Association, 2006).

Hok Tek Chi Loke Yah Teng Association, *Fúdécí lüyětíng yángé shǐ tèkān*《福德祠綠野亭沿革史特刊》[A Special Publication on the History of Hok Tek Chi Loke Yah Teng] (Singapore: Hok Tek Chi Loke Yah Teng Association, 1963).

Hóng, Yúnshēng 洪雲生, and Xǔ, Xuěqīng 許雪卿, eds., *Xīnjiāpō cháozhōu wénhuà zhǎn tèkān*《新嘉坡潮州文化展特刊》[Exhibition on the Heritage of the Teochew Community in

Singapore] (Singapore: Singapore Teochew Poit Ip Huay Kuan, 2002).

Hooi, Christopher, *National Monuments of Singapore* (Singapore: National Museum, Singapore, 1982).

Hsu, Yun Tsiao 許雲樵, *Nányáng huáyǔ lǐsú cídiǎn* 《南洋華語俚俗辭典》 [A Dictionary of Nanyang Vernacular Chinese] (Singapore: *Shìjiè shūjú* 世界書局, 1961).

Hú, Jǐnchāng 胡錦昌, ed., *Róufó miàoyǔ wénhuà* 《柔佛廟宇文化》 [Johor Temple] (Petaling Jaya, Selangor: *Shēnghuó chūbǎnshè* 生活出版社, 2008).

Jao, Tsung-I 饒宗頤, *Xīnjiāpō gǔshì jì* 《新加坡古事記》 [The Chinese Sources for the History of Singapore before 1912] (Hong Kong: Chinese University Press, 1994).

Jiǎng, Wéitán 蔣維錟, and Yáng, Yǒngzhān 楊永佔, *Qīngdài māzǔ dàng'àn shǐliào huìbiān* 《清代媽祖檔案史料匯編》 [Qing Dynasty's Goddess of the Sea Historical Records] (Beijing: China Archives Press, 2003).

Kang, Ger-wen, *Decoration and Symbolism in Chinese Architecture: Understanding Singapore's Historic Chinese Buildings* (Singapore: Preservation of Sites and Monuments, 2013).

Kleinsteuber, Asti, and Maharadjo, Syafri M., *Kelenteng-kelenteng Kuno di Indonesia, Yìnní gǔdài de sìmiào* 《印尼古代的寺廟》 [The Old Chinese Temples in Indonesia] (Jakarta: Genta Kreasi Nusantara, 2010).

Knapp, Ronald G., *Chinese Houses of Southeast Asia: The Eclectic Architecture of Sojourners and Settlers* (Clarendon, Vermont: Tuttle, 2010).

Kohl, David G., *Chinese Architecture in the Straits Settlements and Western Malaya: Temples, Kongsis and Houses* (Kuala Lumpur: Heinemann Asia, 1984).

Kuah-Pearce, Khun Eng, *State, Society and Religious Engineering: Towards a Reformist Buddhism in Singapore*, 2nd ed. (Singapore: Institute of Southeast Asian Studies, 2009).

Kwa, Chong Guan, et al., *Seven Hundred Years: A History of Singapore* (Singapore: National Library Board; Singapore: Marshall Cavendish Editions, 2019).

Kwa, Chong Guan, et al., *Singapore: A 700-Year History: From Early Emporium to World City* (Singapore: National Archives of Singapore, 2009).

LaCapra, Dominick, and Kaplan, Steven L., eds., *Modern European Intellectual History: Reappraisals & New Perspectives* (Ithaca: Cornell University Press, 1981).

Lau, Earnest, *From Mission to Church: The Evolution of the Methodist Church in Singapore and Malaysia: 1885–1976* (Singapore: Genesis Books, 2008).

Lee, Chee Hiang 李志賢, ed., *Hǎiwài cháorén de yímín jīngyàn* 《海外潮人的移民經驗》 [The Migration Experience of the Overseas Teochews] (Singapore: Singapore Teochew Poit Ip Huay Kuan and Global Publishing, 2003).

Lee, Chee Hiang 李志賢, *Lánshí chūnqiū: xīnjiāpō cháorén shàntáng kǎo* 《藍十春秋: 新加坡潮人善堂考》 [A History of the Blue Cross: A Study of Singapore Teochew Charitable Institutions] (Singapore: Blue Cross Charitable Institution, 2017).

Lee, Ch'ian-Lang 李乾朗, *Táiwān chuántǒng jiànzhù jiàngyì – dìyī jí* 《台灣傳統建築匠藝 – 第一輯》 [Taiwan Traditional Architecture Crafts – First Volume] (Taipei: *Yànlóu gǔjiànzhù* 燕樓古建築, 1995).

Lee, Edwin, *Historic Buildings of Singapore* (Singapore: Preservation of Monuments Board, 1990).

Lee, Geok Boi, *The Religious Monuments of Singapore: Faiths of Our Forefathers* (Singapore: Landmark Books and Preservation of Monuments Board, 2002).

Lee, Kim Woon, and Zhou, Yingxin, *Geology of Singapore* (Singapore: Defence Science and Technology Agency, 2009).

Lee, Poh Ping, *Chinese Society in Ninetheenth Century Singapore* (Kuala Lumpur; New York: Oxford

University Press, 1978).

Leong, Ching, and Tan, Lye Huat, eds., *The Story of Singapore Teochews*《新加坡潮人故事》(Singapore: Teochew Poit Ip Huay Kuan, 2019; 新加坡: 新加坡潮州八邑会馆, 2018).

Li, Xiaodong 李曉東, and Yeo, Kang Shua 楊茳善, *Zhōngguó kōngjiān*《中國空間》*Chinese Conception of Space* (Beijing: China Architecture & Building Press, 2007).

Lǐ, Zhéyáng 李哲揚, *Cháozhōu chuántǒng jiànzhù: Dàmù gòujià*《潮州傳統建築: 大木構架》[Traditional Teochew Architecture: Structural Timber Frame] (*Guangdong: Guǎngdōng rénmín chūbǎnshè* 廣東人民出版社, 2009).

Lim, How Seng 林孝勝, *Xīnjiāpō huáshè yǔ huáshāng*《新加坡華社與華商》[Singapore's Chinese Community and Chinese Traders] (Singapore: Singapore Society of Asian Studies, 1999).

Lim, How Seng 林孝勝, ed., *Shílè gǔjī*《石叻古蹟》[Monuments of Singapore] (Singapore: South Seas Society, 1975).

Lip, Mong Har Evelyn, *Chinese Temple Architecture in Singapore* (Singapore: Singapore University Press, 1983).

Lip, Mong Har Evelyn, *Chinese Temples and Deities* (Singapore: Times Book International, 1981).

Liu, Gretchen, and Lim, Albert K. S., *In Granite and Chunam: The National Monuments of Singapore* (Singapore: Landmark Books and Preservation of Monuments Board, 1996).

Liu, Gretchen, *Pastel Portraits: Singapore's Architectural Heritage* (Singapore: Singapore Coordinating Committee, 1984).

Liu, Hong, and Wong, Sin-Kiong, *Singapore Chinese Society in Transition: Business, Politics, & Socio-Economic Change, 1945–1965* (New York: Peter Lang, 2004).

Liú, Xiānjué 劉先覺, and Lee, Coo 李谷, *Xīnjiāpō fójiào jiànzhú yìshù*《新加坡佛教建築藝術》[Buddhist Architecture in Singapore] (Singapore: Kepmedia International, 2007).

Loo, Say Chong 呂世聰, and Ang, Yik Han 洪毅瀚, *Tóutáo zhī bào: Wànshāngǎng fúdécí lìshǐ sùyuán*《投桃之報:萬山港福德祠歷史溯源》[A Boon Returned: The History of Mun San Fook Tuck Chee] (Singapore: Selat Society, 2008).

Ma, Laurence J.C., and Cartier, Carolyn, eds., *The Chinese Diaspora: Space, Place, Mobility, and Identity* (Lanham: Rowman & Littlefield, 2003).

Mak, Lau Fong, *The Dynamics of Chinese Dialect Groups in Early Malaya* (Singapore: Singapore Society of Asian Studies, 1995).

Makepeace, Walter, et al., eds., *One Hundred Years of Singapore: Being Some Account of the Capital of the Straits Settlements from Its Foundation by Sir Stamford Raffles on the 6th February 1819 to the 6th February 1919*, vol. 1, (London: John Murray, 1921).

Méi, Xīnlín 梅新林, and Yú, Zhānghuá 俞樟華, eds., *Zhōngguó yóujì wénxuéshǐ*《中國遊記文學史》[A Literary History of Travellers' Accounts in China] (Shanghai: *Xuélín chūbǎnshè* 學林出版社, 2004).

Mizuno, Kosuke, et al., eds., *Catastrophe & Regeneration in Indonesia's Peatlands: Ecology, Economy & Society* (Singapore: NUS Press in association with Kyoto University Press, 2016).

Mò, Měiyán 莫美顏, *Shīchéng gǔmiào zǒu yīhuí*《獅城古廟走一回》[A Walk Through Historic Temples in Singapore], vol. 3, *Huázú wénhuà cóngshū* 華族文化叢書 [Chinese Cultural Series] (Singapore: SNP Panpac and Singapore Federation of Chinese Clan Associations, 2005).

Mydin, Iskander, *Pioneers of the Streets* (Singapore: Art, Antiques and Antiquities, 1989).

Nathan, Eze, *The History of Jews in Singapore 1830–1945* (Singapore: HERBILU Editorial & Marketing Services).

National Library Board, *Visualizing Space: Maps of Singapore and the Region* (Singapore: National Library Board, 2015).

Ng, Mayers, and Choy, Chan Pong, *Land Framework of*

Singapore: Building a Sound Land Administration and Management System (Singapore: Centre for Liveable Cities, 2018).

Ngow, Wah 吴華, *Xīnjiāpō huázú huìguǎn zhì* 《新嘉坡華族會館志》 [Gazetteer of Singapore's Chinese Clans] (Singapore: South Seas Society, 1975).

Ong, Geok Seng 王玉成, ed., *Fānglín jīnxī* 《芳林今昔》 [Hong Lim: Past and Present] (Singapore: Hong Lim Citizens' Consultative Committee, 1977).

Ownby, David, and Heidhues, Mary Somers, eds., *"Secret Societies" Reconsidered: Perspectives on the Social History of Modern South China and Southeast Asia* (Armonk, N.Y.: M.E. Sharpe, 1993).

Phua, Chay Long 潘醒農, *Cháoqiáo sùyuán jí* 《潮僑溯源集》 [Origins of Overseas Teochew] (Singapore: Global Publishing, 1993).

Phua, Chay Long 潘醒農, *Dōngnányà míngshèng* 《東南亞名勝》 [Celebrated Places in Southeast Asia] (Singapore: The Nantao Publishing House, 1954).

Phua, Chay Long 潘醒農, *Xīnjiāpō yóulǎn zhǐnán* 《新嘉坡游覽指南》 [Travellers' Guide to Singapore] (Singapore: The Nantao Publishing House, 1946).

Phua, Chay Long 潘醒農, ed., *Mǎláiyà cháoqiáo tōngjiàn* 《馬來亞潮僑通鑑》 [A History of Overseas Teochew in Malaya] (Singapore: The Nantao Publishing House, 1950).

Pugalenthi, Sr., *Singapore Landmarks: Monuments, Memorials, Statues & Historic Sites* (Singapore: VJ Times International, 1999).

Raffles, Sophia, ed., *Memoir of the Life and Public Services of Sir Stamford Raffles, F.R.S. & c. Particularly in the Government of Java, 1811–1816, and of Bencoolen and its Dependencies, 1817–1824; with Details of the Commerce and Resources of the Eastern Archipelago and Selections from His Correspondence* (London John Murray, 1830).

Salmon, Claudine, and Lombard, Denys, *Les Chinois de Jakarta: Temples et Vie Collective [The Chinese of Jakarta: Temples and Communal Life]*, vol. 6, Cahier d'Archipel (Guéret: SECMI, 1977).

Samuel, Dhoraisingam S., *Singapore's Heritage Through Places of Historical Interest* (Singapore: Elixir Consultancy Service, 1991).

Savage, Victor R., and Yeoh, Brenda S. A., *Singapore Street Names: A Study of Toponymics* (Singapore: Marshall Cavendish Editions, 2013).

Simpson, W. J., *Report on the Sanitary Condition of Singapore* (London: Waterlow & Sons, 1907).

Singapore Kwangtung Hui Kuan, *Xīnjiāpō guǎngdōng huìguǎn jīnxǐ tèkān* 《新加坡廣東會館金禧特刊》 [Singapore Kwangtung Hui Kuan Golden Jubilee Souvenir Magazine] (Singapore: Kwangtung Hui Kuan, 1989).

Singapore Kwangtung Hui Kuan, *Guǎngdōng huìguǎn qìngzhù liùshí zhōunián jìniàn tèkān, 1937–1997* 《廣東會館慶祝六十周年紀念特刊，1937–1997》 [Kwangtung Hui Kuan 60th Anniversary Publication] (Singapore: Kwangtung Hui Kuan, 1997).

Singapore Lam Ann Association, *Xīnjiāpō nán'ān huìguǎn jīnxǐ jìniàn tèkān* 《新加坡南安會館金禧紀念特刊》 [Singapore Lam Ann Association Golden Jubilee Special Publication] (Singapore: Singapore Lam Ann Association, 1977).

Song, Ong Siang, *One Hundred Years' History of the Chinese in Singapore* (London: John Murray, 1923).

Song, Ong Siang, *One Hundred Years' History of the Chinese in Singapore* (Singapore: University Malaya Press, 1967).

Tagliacozzo, Eric, and Chang, Wen-Chin, *Chinese Circulations: Capital, Commodities, and Networks in Southeast Asia* (Durham: Duke University Press).

Tampines Constituency Sports Association, *30 Years of Tampines* (Singapore: Tampines Constituency Sports Association, 1988).

Tan, Gia Lim, *An Introduction to the Culture and History of the Teochews in Singapore* (Singapore:

World Scientific, 2018).

Tan, Kevin Y. L., ed., *Essays in Singapore Legal History* (Singapore: Singapore Academy of Law & Marshall Cavendish Academic, 2005).

Tan, Sumiko 陳澄子, *Yì'ān gōngsī: kuàrù lìng yīgè qiānxǐ nián*《義安公司: 跨入另一個千禧年》*Ngee Ann Kongsi: Into the Next Millennium* (Singapore: Ngee Ann Kongsi, 2005).

Tan, Yeow Wooi 陳耀威, *Jiǎbìdān zhèng jǐngguì de shèn zhī jiāshú yǔ hǎijìzhàn*《甲必丹鄭景貴的慎之家塾與海記棧》[Kapitan Chung Keng Kwee's Shen Zhi Jia Shu and Hai Ji Zhan] (Penang: Pinang Peranakan Museum, 2013).

Tan, Yeow Wooi 陳耀威, *Bīnchéng lóngshāntáng qiū gōngsī: lìshǐ yǔ jiànzhú*《檳城龍山堂邱公司: 歷史與建築》[Leong San Tong Khoo Kongsi: The History and Architecture] (Penang: Trustees of Leong San Tong Khoo Kongsi, 2003).

Tan, Yeow Wooi 陳耀威, *Fúbì zhòngshēng: xiūfù jùngōng jìniàn tèkān*《福庇眾生: 修復竣工紀念特刊》[Bestowing Luck & Prosperity on All: Commemorative Publication] (Penang: Hock Teik Cheng Sin Temple, 2007).

Teochew Poit Ip Huay Kuan, *Cháoyǒng: xīnjiāpō cháozhōu bāyì huìguǎn bāshí zhōunián jìniàn tèkān*《潮涌: 新嘉坡潮州八邑會館八十周年紀念特刊》[Singapore Teochew Poit Ip Huay Kuan 80th Anniversary Magazine] (Singapore: Singapore Teochew Poit Ip Huay Kuan, 2009).

Teochew Poit Ip Huay Kuan, ed., *Xīnjiāpō cháozhōu bāyì huìguǎn chénglì qīshí zhōunián jìniàn tèkān*《新嘉坡潮州八邑會館成立七十週年紀念特刊》[Singapore Teochew Poit Ip Huay Kuan 70th Anniversary Magazine] (Singapore: Singapore Teochew Poit Ip Huay Kuan, 2000).

Teochew Poit Ip Huay Kuan, ed., *Xīnjiāpō cháozhōu bāyì huìguǎn jīnxǐ jìniànkān*《新加坡潮州八邑會館金禧紀念刊》[Singapore Teochew Poit Ip Huay Kuan 50th Anniversary Magazine] (Singapore: Singapore Teochew Poit Ip Huay Kuan, 1980).

Teoh, Shiaw Kuan 張少寬, *Bīnlángyǔ huárén sìmiào bēimíng jílù*《檳榔嶼華人寺廟碑銘集錄》[Collection of Epigraphy from Buddhist and Taoist Temples in Penang] (Penang: *Nányáng tiányě yánjiūshì* 南洋田野研究室, 2013).

Toh, Lam Huat 杜南發, ed., *Liánshān shuānglín: Xīnjiāpō liánshān shuānglín chánsì yībǎi èrshí zhōunián wénjí: wénshǐ jí*《蓮山雙林: 新加坡蓮山雙林禪寺一百二十周年文集 : 文史集》[Lian Shan Shuang Lin Monastery 120th Anniversary Compendium (Social History)] (Singapore: Singapore Lianshan Shuanglin Monastery, 2018).

Toh, Lam Huat 杜南發, ed., *Nánhǎi míngzhū: tiānfúgōng*《南海明珠: 天福宮》[Pearl of the South Seas: Thian Hock Keng Temple] (Singapore: Singapore Hokkien Huay Kuan, 2010).

Trocki, Carl A., *Prince of Pirates: The Temenggongs and the Development of Johor and Singapore, 1784–1885* (Singapore: NUS Press, 2007).

Turnbull, Constance Mary, *A History of Modern Singapore, 1819–2005* (Singapore: NUS Press, 2009).

Urban Redevelopment Authority, *Changing the Face of Singapore: Through the URA Sale of Sites* (Singapore: Urban Redevelopment Authority, 1995).

Urban Redevelopment Authority, *Yueh Hai Ching Temple Preservation Guidelines*, vol. 1 & 2, September, 1997, Preservation of Monuments Board.

Wan, Meng Hao, and Lau, Jacqueline, *Heritage Places of Singapore* (Singapore: Marshall Cavendish Editions, 2009).

Wilkinson, R.J., *A Malay-English Dictionary (Romanised)*, Part 2 (London: Macmillan, 1955).

Xiè, Míngfēi 謝鳴非, *Xīnjiāpō miàoyǔ gàilǎn*《新加坡廟宇概覽》[An Overview of Temples in Singapore] (Singapore: *Nánfēng shāngyè chūbǎnshè yǐngyìn* 南風商業出版社影印, 1951).

Xú, Lǐyǐng 徐李穎, *Jiǔhuáng shèngjī: hòugǎng*

dǒumǔgōng《九皇聖蹟：後港斗母宮》[*Sacred Site of the Nine Emperor Gods: The Hougang Dou Mu Temple*] (Singapore: Hougang Tou Mu Temple, 2006).

Xú, Lǐyǐng 徐李穎, *Jiǔshí chūnqiū: Xīnjiāpō jiǔcàibā chénghuáng miào shǐjì*《九十春秋:新加坡韭菜芭城隍廟史記》[A 90 Year History of Lorong Koo Chye Sheng Hong (City-God) Temple] (Singapore: Lorong Koo Chye Sheng Hong Temple Association, 2007).

Yen, Ching-Hwang, *A Social History of the Chinese in Singapore and Malaya, 1800–1911* (Singapore: Oxford University Press, 1986).

Yen, Ching-Hwang, *Ethnicities, Personalities and Politics in the Ethnic Chinese Worlds* (Singapore: World Scientific Publishing, 2016).

Yeo, Kang Shua 楊茳善, ed., *Liánshān shuānglín: Xīnjiāpō liánshān shuānglín chánsì yībǎi èrshí zhōunián wénjí: jiànzhú jí*《蓮山雙林：新加坡蓮山雙林禪寺一百二十周年文集：建築集》[Lian Shan Shuang Lin Monastery 120th Anniversary Compendium (Architecture)] (Singapore: Singapore Lianshan Shuanglin Monastery, 2018).

Yeoh, Brenda S. A., *Contesting Space in Colonial Singapore: Power Relations and the Urban Built Environment* (Singapore: Singapore University Press, 2003).

Zéng, Tiěchén 曾鐵忱, *Xīnjiāpō lǚyóu biànlǎn*《新加坡旅遊便覽》[A Brief Tourist Guide of Singapore] (Singapore: *Xīn qǐyè chūbǎnshè* 新企業出版社, 1966).

Journal Articles

"Restoration of Thian Hock Keng Temple at Telok Ayer Street," *Journal of the Singapore Institute of Architects* 101 (July/August 1980): 3–7.

"Thomas Stamford Raffles to Captain C.E. Davis, George Bonham and Alex. L. Johnston, November 4, 1822," in "Notices of Singapore," *The Journal of the Indian Archipelago and Eastern Seas* 8 (1854): 102–109.

"Thomas Stamford Raffles to Land Allotment Committee, October 17, 1823," in "Notices of Singapore," *The Journal of the Indian Archipelago and Eastern Seas* 8 (1854): 405–407.

Akashi, Yoji, "Japanese Policy Towards the Malayan Chinese 1941–1945," *Journal of Southeast Asian Studies* 1, no. 2 (1970): 61–89.

Bartley, W., "The Population of Singapore in 1819," *Journal of the Malayan Branch of the Royal Asiatic Society* 11, no. 2 (1933): 177.

Bastin, John, "Reviews," *Bulletin of the School of Oriental and African Studies, University of London* 43, no. 3 (1980): 632.

Blackburn, Kevin, "The Collective Memory of the Sook Ching Massacre and the Creation of the Civilian War Memorial of Singapore," *Journal of the Malaysian Branch of the Royal Asiatic Society* 73, no. 2 (279) (2000): 71–90.

Chng, David K.Y. 莊欽永, "*Mǎliùjiǎ*、*Xīnjiāpō huáwén bēiwén jílù* 馬六甲、新加坡華文碑文輯錄 [A Collection of Chinese Inscriptions in Malacca and Singapore]," *Mínzú xué yánjiū suǒ zīliào huìbiān*《民族學研究所資料彙編》Field Materials, Institute of Ethnology, Academia Sinica, vol. 12 (Taipei: Institute of Ethnology, Academia Sinica, 1998): 34–197.

Chong, Terence, "Chinese Opera in Singapore: Negotiating Globalisation, Consumerism and National Culture," *Journal of Southeast Asian Studies* 34, no. 3 (2003): 449–471.

Fatt, Yong Ching, "Leadership and Power in the Chinese Community of Singapore during the 1930s," *Journal of Southeast Asian Studies* 8, no. 2 (1977): 195–209.

Firmstone, H.W., "Chinese Names of Streets and Places in Singapore and the Malay Peninsula," *Journal of the Straits Branch of the Royal Asiatic Society* 42 (February 1905): 53–208.

Foxworthy, F.W., "Tree Names – A Few Changes," *Journal of the Malayan Branch of the Royal Asiatic Studies* 5, no. 2 (Nov 1927): 339–341.

Ginzburg, Carlo, "Microhistory: Two or Three Things

That I Know About It," *Critical Inquiry* 20, no. 1 (1993): 10–35.

Han, Wai Toon 韓槐準, "*Dàbógōng kǎo* 大伯公考 [A Study of the Dabogong Deity]," *Nányáng xuébào* 《南洋學報》 *Journal of the South Seas Society* 1, no. 2 (December 1940): 18–26.

Haughton, H.T., "Native Names of Streets in Singapore," *Journal of the Straits Branch of the Royal Asiatic Society* 23 (June 1891): 49–65.

Hsu, Yun-ts'iao 許雲樵, "*Dàbógōng, èrbógōng yǔ běntóugōng* 大伯公, 二伯公與本頭公 [The Deities Dabogong, Erbogong and Bentougong]," *Nányáng xuébào* 《南洋學報》 *Journal of the South Seas Society* 7, no. 2 (November 1951): 6–10.

Hsu, Yun-ts'iao 許雲樵, "*Zàitán Dàbógōng yánjiū* 再談大伯公研究 [A Further Discussion on the Study of Dabogong]," *Nányáng xuébào* 《南洋學報》 *Journal of the South Seas Society* 8, no. 2 (December 1952): 19–24.

ICOMOS, Australia, *The Burra Charter: The Australia ICOMOS Charter for Places of Cultural Significance 1999* (Burwood: Australia ICOMOS, 2000), revised in 2013, accessed 5 October 2017, https://australia.icomos.org/wp-content/uploads/The-Burra-Charter-2013-Adopted-31.10.2013.pdf.

ICOMOS, China, *Principles for the Conservation of Heritage Sites in China*, ed. Neville Agnew and Martha Demas, trans. Peter Barker (Los Angeles: Getty Conservation Institute, 2004).

Jao, Tsung-I 饒宗頤, "*Xīng mǎ huáwén bēikè xìnián (jìluè)* 星馬華文碑刻繫年(紀畧) [A Chronological Survey on Chinese Inscriptions in Singapore and Malaya]," *Xīnjiāpō dàxué zhōngwén xuéhuì xuébào* 《新加坡大學中文學會學報》 *Journal of the Chinese Society, University of Singapore* 10 (December 1969): 1–51.

Jao, Tsung-I 饒宗頤, "*Tán Bógōng* 談伯公 [A Discussion of the Bogong Deities]," *Nányáng xuébào* 《南洋學報》 *Journal of the South Seas Society* 8, no. 2 (December 1952): 27–28.

Jiǎng, Wéitán 蔣維錟, "*Qīngdài yùcì tiānhòugōng biǎn'é jí qí lìshǐ bèijǐng* 清代御賜天后宮匾額及其歷史背景 [Qing Dynasty Imperial Plaques Bestowed upon Temples of the Goddess of the Sea and their Historical Backgrounds]," *Pútián xuéyuàn xuébào* 《莆田學院學報》 [Journal of Putian University], no. 4 (July–August 2005): 79–86.

Kim, Young Jae, and Park, Sungjin, "Tectonic Traditions in Ancient Chinese Architecture, and Their Development," *Journal of Asian Architecture and Building Engineering* 38, no. 1 (January 2017): 31–38.

Koh, T. T. B., and Lim, William S. W., "Planning Law and Processes in Singapore," *Malaya Law Review*, vol. 11, no. 2 (National University of Singapore, 1969), 315–344.

Lee, Ch'ian-Lang 李乾朗, "*Duìcháng yíngzào* 對場營造" [Competitive Team Construction], *Zhōnghuá shǒugōng* 《中華手工》 [Chinese Craftsmanship], no. 1 (2005): 68–73.

Lee, Yong Kiat, "The Pauper Hospital in Early Singapore (Part IV) (1850–1859) – Section 1," *Singapore Medical Journal* 16, no. 4 (1975): 269–289.

Mair, Victor, "What Is a Chinese "Dialect/Topolect"? Reflections on Some Key Sino-English Linguistic Terms," *Sino-Platonic Papers*, vol. 29 (September 1991): 1–31.

Peltonen, Matti, "Clues, Margins, and Monads: The Micro-Macro Link in Historical Research," *History and Theory* 40, no. 3 (2001): 347–359.

Rudolph, R.C., "Preliminary Notes on Sung Archaeology," *The Journal of Asian Studies* 22, no. 2 (February 1963): 169–177.

Salaff, Janet W., "Cluster Introduction: Subethnicity in the Chinese Diaspora," *International Migration*, vol. 43, issue 3 (2005): 3–7.

Siah, U Chin, "The Chinese in Singapore: General Sketch of the Numbers, Tribes and Avocations of the Chinese in Singapore," *Journal of Indian Archipelago and Eastern Asia* II (1848): 283–290.

Tanaka, Issei 田仲一成, "*Shíjiǔ shìjì mòqī yǔ èrshí shìjì xīnjiāpō cháorén zǔzhī yǔ yǎnjù huódòng* 十

九世紀末期與二十世紀新嘉坡潮人組織與演劇活動 [Late 19th-Century and 20th-Century Singapore Teochew Organisations and Opera Performances]," trans. Tan Huifang 譚惠芳, *Asian Culture* 16 (Jun 1992): 95–114.

Tiān, Guānfú 天官福, "*Dàbógōng shì héfāng shénshèng* 大伯公是何方神聖 [Who is the Dabogong Deity?]," *Nányáng wénzhāi* 《南洋文摘》 *Nanyang Digest* 4, no. 1 (January 1963): 25–28.

Trocki, Carl A., "The Origins of the Kangchu System 1740–1860," *Journal of the Malaysian Branch of the Royal Asiatic Society* 49, no. 2 (1976): 132–155.

Wee, Lionel, "'Burdens' and 'Handicaps' in Singapore's Language Policy: On the Limits of Language Management," *Language Policy*, vol. 9, no. 2 (2010): 97–114.

Wee, Lionel, and Bokhorst-Heng, Wendy D., "Language Policy and Nationalist Ideology: Statal Narratives in Singapore," *Journal of Cross-Cultural and Interlanguage Communication*, vol. 24, issue 3 (2005): 159–183.

Wèi, Jùxián 衛聚賢, "*[Èrbógōng] de yǒuwúshuō* [二伯公]的有無說 [A Discussion of the Existence of Erbogong]," *Nányáng xuébào* 《南洋學報》 *Journal of the South Seas Society* 8, no. 2 (December 1952): 25–26.

Winstedt, R. O., "A History of Johore (1365–1895 A.D.)," *Journal of the Malayan Branch of the Royal Asiatic Society* 10, no. 3 (115) (1932): 1–167.

Yeo, Huijun Martina, and Yeo, Kang Shua, "The House of Ripples," *BiblioAsia*, vol. 14, issue 3 (2018): 40–45.

Yeo, Kang Shua, "Homogenously Heterogenous?: The Diversity of Traditional Chinese Architecture in Singapore," *Journal of Southeast Asian Architecture* 9 (2006): 87–106.

Yì Zhì 奕志, "*Yījiān shénmì de cítáng – shègōngmiào* 一間神祕的祠堂 – 社公廟 [A Mysterious Shrine: Shegong Temple]," *Nányáng wénzhāi* 《南洋文摘》 *Nanyang Digest* 14, no. 8 (August 1973): 527–528.

Conference Papers

Yeo, Huijun Martina, and Yeo, Kang Shua, "'Typical' Chinese Residences of Late Nineteenth-Century Singapore: A Case Study of the Four Grand Mansions (四大厝)," *EAAC 2017: International Conference on East Asian Architectural Culture: East Asian Architecture in Globalization: Values, Inheritance and Dissemination* (People's Republic of China: Tianjin University, 2017).

Yeo, Kang Shua, "The Flux of Chinese Architectural Diaspora in 19th Century through an Architectural Comparative Study of the Oldest Teochew Temple in Senggarang, Tanjung Pinang, Indonesia and Singapore," *International Conference On Chinese Indonesian Studies – Chinese Diaspora Tradition In Indonesia Nation Building: Challenges And Opportunities* (Indonesia: Maranatha Christian University Indonesia, 2015)

Yeo, Kang Shua, and Chen, Yu, "Building a Modern Chinese Identity in Singapore: From Orientalism to Chinese 'Traditional Eclectic Style' Renaissance," *International Conference on East Asian Architectural Culture, Tainan, Taiwan 2009: Whose East Asia? The East Asian Architecture and Urbanism Under Occidentalism*, ed. Xu Mingfu 徐明福 (Tainan: Society of Architectural Historians of Taiwan and College of Planning and Design, National Cheng Kung University, 2009).

E-books and Websites

"6, *Cúnxīn shàntáng (shuǐlóng jú)* 六、存心善堂（水龍局）" and "7, *Lǎomāgōng (Tiānhòugōng, Guāndìmiào)* 七、老妈宫（天后宫、關帝廟）," in "*Lǎobù wénhuà lüyóu jǐngdiǎn* 老埠文化旅遊景點 [Cultural Tourist Attractions of the Old Port]," accessed 27 April 2017, http://www.stly.gov.cn/article/detail/301172.

"*Cantleya corniculata (Becc.) Howard*," accessed 8 December 2016, http://www.gbif.org/species/3596897.

"DEDARU (*Cantleya corniculata*)," accessed 8 December 2016, http://www.tropicaltimber.

info/specie/dedaru-cantleya-corniculata/.
"TEMPINIS (*Streblus elongatus*)," accessed 8 December 2016, http://www.tropicaltimber.info/specie/tempinis-streblus-elongatus/.
"ULIN (*Eusideroxylon zwageri*)," accessed 8 December 2016, http://www.tropicaltimber.info/specie/ulin-eusideroxylon-zwageri/#lower-content.
"Wáng, Qīn 王欽," 20 April 2009, accessed 17 August 2016, http://wangqin.ren.hqcr.com/.
Lim, Walter 林志強, "*Chén Ruìlín – sìhǎitōng yínháng fāqǐrén* 陳瑞麟 – 四海通銀行發起人 [Tan Swee Kee – Founder of Sze Hai Tong Banking and Insurance Company]," 24 November 2012, accessed 25 April 2017, http://bukitbrowntomb.blogspot.sg/2012/11/blog-post_24.html.
Ōuyáng, Xiū 歐陽脩, *Jígǔ lù báwěi*《集古錄拔尾》[A Postscript of A Compilation of Ancient Inscriptions], accessed 30 November 2017, http://ctext.org/wiki.pl?if=gb&res=865633.
Singapore in Figures 2018 (Singapore: Department of Statistics, 2018), accessed 1 June 2019, https://www.singstat.gov.sg/-/media/files/publications/reference/sif2018.pdf
Singapore Kwangtung Hui Kuan, accessed 15 December 2016, http://www.8path.com.sg/kwangtungclan/
Urban Redevelopment Authority, "Nos. 63 & 65 Emerald Hill Road: Two Distinct Personalities" (Singapore: Urban Redevelopment Authority, 2005), accessed 28 April 2017, https://www.ura.gov.sg/uol/publications/corporate/aha/2005/63-65-Emerald-Hill-Road.
Wáng, Míngguāng 王明光, "*Yuèhǎiqīng miào cháobāng liùgǔ yǔ fúbāng sīhuìdǎng bāgǔ*《粵海清廟潮幫六股與福幫私會黨八股》[Yueh Hai Ching Temple Teochew clan's six shares and Hokkien clan's eight shares]," accessed on 19 December 2016, http://blog.sina.com.cn/s/blog_50e8ed7e0102ejnk.html.
Zhào, Míngchéng 趙明誠, "*Jīn shí lù* 金石錄" [A Collection of Inscriptions], in *Qīndìng sìkù quánshū*《欽定四庫全書》[Complete Library in Four Sections], vol. 14 of *Shǐbù* 史部 [History Section], accessed 30 November 2017, http://ctext.org/library.pl?if=gb&file=2017&page=11&remap=gb.

Theses and Unpublished Manuscripts

Hsu, Tzer-Yaw 許澤耀, *Cóng shénshèng dào shìsú – yǐ tóuchéng qiǎnggū wéilì*《從神聖到世俗 – 以頭城搶孤為例》[From Sacred to Profane: A Study on Ghost's Festival in Touchen] (Master's Thesis, Taiwan: National Taiwan Normal University, 2010), accessed 28 July 2017, http://handle.ncl.edu.tw/11296/ndltd/01410701752595734231.
Kuo, Huei-Ying, *Transnational Business Networks and Sub-Ethnic Nationalism: Chinese Business and Nationalist Activities in Interwar Hong Kong and Singapore, 1919—1941*, (PhD Thesis, New York: State University of New York at Binghamton, 2007).
Tan, Yeow Wooi 陳耀威, *Yuèdōng kǎo*《粵東考》[A Study Into the Origins of *Yuèdōng*], Unpublished Manuscript, 2005.
Wáng, Àiwén 王愛雯, *Ānpíng língjìdiàn 'gūpéng jì' yánjiū*《安平靈濟殿「孤棚祭」研究》[Study on "solitary shed worship" at Anping Ling Chi Temple] (Master's Thesis, Taiwan: National University of Tainan, 2017), accessed 28 July 2017, http://handle.ncl.edu.tw/11296/ndltd/40991615394713449027.
Wee, Vivienne, *Religion and Ritual among the Chinese of Singapore: An Ethnographic Study* (Unpublished Master's Thesis, Singapore: University of Singapore, 1977).

Newspapers

- *Chaozhou Daily*《潮州日報》
- *Daily Advertiser*
- *Lat Pau*《叻報》
- *Liánhé Wǎnbào*《聯合晚報》
- *Liánhé Zǎobào*《聯合早報》
- *Mid-Day Herald and Daily*

- *Nanyang Siang Pau*《南洋商報》
- *Shin Min Daily News*《新明日報》
- *Sin Chew Jit Poh*《星洲日報》
- *Singapore Standard*
- *Straits Times Overland Journal*
- *Straits Times Weekly Issue*
- *Syonan Shimbun*
- *Syonan Shimbun Fortnightly*
- *The Business Times*
- *The Singapore Free Press and Mercantile Advertiser*
- *The Singapore Free Press and Mercantile Advertiser (Weekly)*
- *The Straits Times*

Chaozhou Daily

"*Cháozhōu qiàncí yìshù chuánchéngrén Lú Zhīgāo: suìcípiàn qiàntiē qǐlì shìjiè* 潮州嵌瓷藝術傳承人盧芝高：碎瓷片嵌貼綺麗世界 [Successor of Teochew Ceramic Ornamentation, Lú Zhīgāo: Composing a Beautiful World with Ceramic Shards]," *Huánqiú cháorén wǎng* 环球潮人网 [Global Teochew webpage], *Cháozhōu rìbào*《潮州日報》[Chaozhou Daily], July 7, 2014, accessed 18 May 2017, http://news.hqcr.com/projects/news/view.aspx?nid=420625.

Daily Advertiser

"Local and General," *Daily Advertiser*, 17 December 1892.

"Local and General," *Daily Advertiser*, 30 January 1893.

Lat Pau《叻報》

"*Chóushén bǔdìng* 酬神卜定 [Determination of Religious Dates]," *Lat Pau*《叻報》, 10 November 1897.

"*Fèngshānsì zhāogōng guǎnggào* 鳳山寺招工廣告 [Hong San See Tender Notice]," *Lat Pau*《叻報》, 9 December 1907.

"*Huíluán jiāngjiè* 回鑾將屆 [Religious Returning Procession]," *Lat Pau*《叻報》, 14 January 1899.

"*Huíluán zhìlüè* 回鑾誌畧 [An Account of Religious Returning Procession]," *Lat Pau*《叻報》, 16 January 1895.

"*Huǒchē tínggōng* 火車停工 [Halting of Train Services]," *Lat Pau*《叻報》, 14 December 1887.

"*Juānlù zhàodēng* 捐錄照登 [List of Donations Published Accordingly]," *Lat Pau*《叻報》, 10 August 1896.

"*Juānlù zhàodēng* 捐錄照登 [List of Donations Published Accordingly]," *Lat Pau*《叻報》, 11 August 1896.

"*Mǐnyuè sàishén dìngqī* 閩粵賽神定期 [Fujian and Guangdong Religious Processions Dates]," *Lat Pau*《叻報》, 13 November 1894.

"*Mǐnyuè sòngshén zhìlüè* 閩粵送神誌畧 [An Account of Fujian and Guangdong Religious Processions]," *Lat Pau*《叻報》, 25 January 1896.

"*Pàichà dànyā* 派差彈壓 [Activation of Police]," *Lat Pau*《叻報》, 14 December 1887.

"*Sàishén dìngqī* 賽神定期 [Dates of Religious Processions]," *Lat Pau*《叻報》, 1 December 1887.

"*Sàishén dìngqī* 賽神定期 [Dates of Religious Processions]," *Lat Pau*《叻報》, 29 November 1890.

"*Sàishén dìngqī* 賽神定期 [Dates of Religious Processions]," *Lat Pau*《叻報》, 20 November 1896.

"*Sàishén dìngqī* 賽神定期 [Dates of Religious Processions]," *Lat Pau*《叻報》, 20 November 1896.

"*Sàishén jìlüè* 賽神紀略 [An Account of Religious Procession]," *Lat Pau*《叻報》, 26 November 1894.

"*Sàishén jìlüè* 賽神紀畧 [An Account of Religious Procession]," *Lat Pau*《叻報》, 7 December 1898.

"*Sàishén lùchéng* 賽神路程 [The Route of Religious Procession]," *Lat Pau*《叻報》, 22 November 1897.

"*Sàishén qījiè* 賽神期屆 [Religious Procession]," *Lat Pau*《叻報》, 6 December 1898.

"*Sòngshén zhìlüè* 送神誌畧 [An Account of Religious

Returning Procession],” *Lat Pau*《叻報》, 15 January 1897.

“*Tínggōng bùgào* 停工佈告 [One Day Holiday Notice],” *Lat Pau*《叻報》, 23 January 1896.

“*Tóngshēn qìnghè* 同申慶賀 [Universal Celebration],” *Lat Pau*《叻報》, 24 September 1896.

“*Wànshùnjiē tíjuān chóngxiū yuèhǎiqīngmiào fāngmíng lièzuǒ* 萬順街題捐重修粵海清廟芳名列左 [List of Wànshùn Street (Chulia Street) Donors for the Reconstruction of Wak Hai Cheng Bio],” *Lat Pau*《叻報》, 19 March 1896.

“*Yíngshén jìshì* 迎神紀事 [An Account of Religious Procession],” *Lat Pau*《叻報》, 23 November 1897.

“*Yíngshén rǎnzhì* 迎神冉誌 [An Account of Religious Procession],” *Lat Pau*《叻報》, 2 December 1896.

“*Yíngshén zhìlüè* 迎神誌略 [An Account of Religious Procession],” *Lat Pau*《叻報》, 8 December 1890.

“*Yīngzhōng xiānshēng yì'ān jùn zhū zhíshì* 應忠先生義安郡諸執事 [Mr. Eng Tong and the Various Trustees of Ngee Ann Kun],” *Lat Pau*《叻報》, 29 December 1927.

“*Yuèshāng sàishén dìngqī* 粵商賽神定期 [Dates of Guangdong Merchants' Religious Procession],” *Lat Pau*《叻報》, 29 November 1898.

“*Yuèshāng yíngshén zhìlüè* 粵商迎神誌畧 [An Account of Guangdong Merchants' Religious Procession],” *Lat Pau*《叻報》, 9 December 1895.

“*Yǔshī bàixīng* 雨師敗興 [Rain Dampened Spirits],” *Lat Pau*《叻報》, 27 January 1899.

“*Zījiāng chángxīngjiē xǐjuān chóngxiū yuèhǎiqīngmiào fāngmíng liè* 茲將長興街喜捐重修粵海清廟芳名列 [The Names of Delightful Chángxīng Street (Circular Road) Donors for the Cause of Reconstructing Wak Hai Cheng Bio are hereby Listed],” *Lat Pau*《叻報》, 26 November 1896.

“*Zījiāng cháyángjí xǐjuān chóngxiū yuèhǎiqīngmiào fāngmíng liè* 茲將茶陽籍喜捐重修粵海清廟芳名列 [The Names of Delightful Cháyáng Donors for the Cause of Reconstructing Wak Hai Cheng Bio are hereby Listed],” *Lat Pau*《叻報》, 25 January 1897.

“*Zījiāng guǎngfǔjí xǐjuān chóngxiū yuèhǎiqīngmiào fāngmíng liè* 茲將廣府籍喜捐重修粵海清廟芳名列 [The Names of Delightful Cantonese Donors for the Cause of Reconstructing Wak Hai Cheng Bio are hereby Listed],” *Lat Pau*《叻報》, 24 August 1896.

“*Zījiāng qióngzhōu fǔjí xǐjuān chóngxiū yuèhǎiqīngmiào fāngmíng liè* 茲將瓊州府籍喜捐重修粵海清廟芳名列 [The Names of Delightful Hainanese Donors for the Cause of Reconstructing Wak Hai Cheng Bio are hereby Listed],” *Lat Pau*《叻報》, 25 August, 1896.

“*Zījiāng shàngxīngjiē xǐjuān chóngxiū yuèhǎiqīngmiào fāngmíng liè* 茲將上興街喜捐重修粵海清廟芳名列 [The Names of Delightful Shàngxīng Street Donors for the Cause of Reconstructing Wak Hai Cheng Bio are hereby Listed],” *Lat Pau*《叻報》, 6 April 1897.

“*Zījiāng shùnxīngjiē xǐjuān chóngxiū yuèhǎiqīngmiào fāngmíng liè* 茲將順興街喜捐重修粵海清廟芳名列 [The Names of Delightful Shùnxīng Street (Boat Quay) Donors for the Cause of Reconstructing Wak Hai Cheng Bio are hereby listed],” *Lat Pau*《叻報》, 29 August 1896.

“*Zījiāng xiǎopō zhèngxīngjiē xǐjuān chóngxiū yuèhǎiqīngmiào fāngmíng lièzuǒ* 茲將小坡正興街喜捐重修粵海清廟芳名列左 [The Names of Delightful Small Town's Zhèngxīng Street (possibly the expunged Chin Hin Street which is normally known in Chinese as *Zhènxīngjiē* 振興街) Donors for the Cause of Reconstructing Wak Hai Cheng Bio are hereby Listed on the Left],” *Lat Pau*《叻報》, 29 October 1896.

“*Zījiāng xǐjuān chóngxiū yuèhǎiqīngmiào fāngmíng kānzuǒ* 茲將喜捐重修粵海清廟芳名刊左 [The Names of Delightful Donors for the Cause of Reconstructing Wak Hai Cheng Bio are hereby Published on the Left],” *Lat Pau*《叻報》, 9 March 1897.

Liánhé Wǎnbào《聯合晚報》

"*Jiǎntǐzì yīngyònglǜ qùniándǐ chuàngjìlù* 簡體字應用率 去年底創記錄 [The Usage of Simplified Chinese Text breaks New Records in the Past Year]," *Liánhé Wǎnbào*《聯合晚報》[Lianhe Wanbao], 7 January 1989.

Liánhé Zǎobào《聯合早報》

"*Huáwén jiǎntǐzì wǔnián nèi kě quánmiàn cǎiyòng* 華文簡體字五年內可全面采用 [Full Utilisation of Simplified Chinese Text within Five Years]," *Liánhé Zǎobào*《聯合早報》[Lianhe Zaobao], 25 April 1984.

"*Quánmiàn cǎiyòng jiǎntǐzì wǔnián nèi kěwàng shíxiàn* 全面采用簡體字五年內可望實現 [Full Utilisation of Simplified Chinese Text is expected to be Realised within Five Years]," *Liánhé Zǎobào*《聯合早報》[Lianhe Zaobao], 25 April 1984.

"*Wénhuàbù tōnghán yǐshēn zuòzé guānfāng jīgòu zài sānnián nèi quánmiàn cǎiyòng jiǎntǐ hànzì* 文化部通函以身作則 官方機構在三年內全面采用簡體漢字 [Ministry of Culture issued a Letter stating that the Government will lead by example to adopt Simplified Chinese Text fully within Three Years]," *Liánhé Zǎobào*《聯合早報》[Lianhe Zaobao], 20 December 1983.

Mid-Day Herald and Daily

"A Huge Chinese Procession," *Mid-Day Herald and Daily*, 22 November 1897.

Nanyang Siang Pau《南洋商報》

"*Běnbào jīnrì kāishǐ kānzài wǔbǎi língèr gè jiǎntǐzì* 本報今日開始刊載五百零二個簡體字 [Our Newspapers will start to use Five Hundred and Two Simplified Chinese Characters from Today]," *Nányáng Shāngbào*《南洋商報》[Nanyang Siang Pau], 28 August 1969.

"*Cháozhōu bāyì huìguǎn niánhuì tōngguò zài hòugǎng chuàngbàn bìnyíguǎn* 潮州八邑會館年會通過在後港創辦殯儀館 [Teochew Poit Ip Huay Kuan's Annual Meeting Approved the Setting up of a Funeral Palour in Hougang]," *Nányáng Shāngbào*《南洋商報》[Nanyang Siang Pau], 27 February 1960.

"*Cháozhōu bāyì huìguǎn zhàokāi dǒngshì huìyì* 潮州八邑會館召開董事會議 [Teochew Poit Ip Huay Kuan called for a Directors' Meeting]," *Nányáng Shāngbào*《南洋商報》[Nanyang Siang Pau], 17 October 1959.

"*Cháozhōu huìguǎn nǐ chuàngbàn bìnyíguǎn túshì yǐ cǎojiù jiāo yì'ān gōngsī shěnhé* 潮州會館擬創辦殯儀館圖式已草就交義安公司審核 [Teochew Huay Kuan's Plans for a Funeral Palour have been submitted to The Ngee Ann Kongsi for Approval]," *Nányáng Shāngbào*《南洋商報》[Nanyang Siang Pau], 6 August 1959.

"*Chóushè xīnjiāpō cháozhōu huìguǎn yuánqǐ* 籌設新嘉坡潮州會館緣起 [Origins of the Establishment of the Singapore Teochew Huay Kuan]," *Nányáng Shāngbào*《南洋商報》[Nanyang Siang Pau], 10 September 1928.

"*Dàiyóu* 代郵 [Posted on behalf of]," *Nányáng Shāngbào*《南洋商報》[Nanyang Siang Pau], 29 December 1927.

"*Dìèr yǔwén (huáyǔ) jiàoxué yántǎohuì nǎi yīngxiào jiāqiáng huáwén jiàoxué lǐchéngbēi zhǐzài tígāo yīngxiào huáwén shuǐzhǔn jiàocháng xuānbù shè wěiyuánhuì yánjiū hànzì jiǎnhuà wèntí zài xuéxiào zhōng zhèngshì shǐyòng jiǎntǐzì yǐ kèbù rónghuǎn* 第二語文 (華語) 教學研討會乃英校加强華文教學里程碑旨在提高英校華文水準教長宣佈設委員會研究漢字簡化問題在學校中正式使用簡體字已刻不容緩 [Second Language (Chinese) Pedagogy Symposium: Raising the Standards of Chinese in English-medium Schools is a milestone for such Schools; The Director of Education announced that a Committee to study the Challenges in the Simplification of Chinese Text will be setup and the use of Simplified Chinese Text will be Inevitable]," *Nányáng Shāngbào*《南洋商報》[Nanyang Siang Pau], 19 November 1968.

"*Guānyú hànzì zhī tǎolùn hànzì nányì yǔ luómǎhuà jí jiǎntǐzì píngyì* 關於漢字之討論漢字難易與羅馬化及簡體字平議 [About the Difficulties and Ease of Learning Chinese, as well as the Romanisation of Chinese Text and Simplification of Chinese Text]," *Nányáng Shāngbào* 《南洋商報》 [Nanyang Siang Pau], 9 October 1957.

"*Hànyǔ pīnyīn fāngàn* 漢語拼音方案 [The *Hànyǔ pīnyīn* Romanisation System of Chinese Text]," *Nányáng Shāngbào* 《南洋商報》 [Nanyang Siang Pau], 1 February 1971.

"*Hànzì jiǎnhuà de gōngyòng jiūjìng rúhé* 漢字簡化的功用究竟如何 [What are the Uses of the Simplification of Chinese Text]," *Nányáng Shāngbào* 《南洋商報》 [Nanyang Siang Pau], 1 January 1958.

"*Jiàobù chūbǎn huáwén jiǎntǐzì xiǎocè jǐngtàn zài wǔjiān shūdiàn sōuchū yīpī fānyìnběn jǐngfāng jīngcǎi xíngdòng duìfù diàndōng* 教部出版華文簡體字小册警探在五間書店搜出一批翻印本警方經採行動對付店東 [The Ministry of Education published Simplified Chinese Booklet; The Police found Counterfeits Booklets in Five Bookshops and will be Taking Actions against the Owners]," *Nányáng Shāngbào* 《南洋商報》 [Nanyang Siang Pau], 16 October 1969.

"*Lǐ Zhāomíng bùcháng hūxū bàoguǎn chūbǎnjiè jí diànshìtái děng xiézhù tuīxíng huáwén jiǎntǐzì bìng cǎiyòng yóuzuǒ dàoyòu héngpái fāngshì yìnshuā jiàoyù chūbǎnshè míngnián qǐ jiàokēshū zhújiàn gǎiyòng jiǎntǐzì biānyìn* 李昭銘部長呼吁報館出版界及電視台等協助推行華文簡體字并採用由左到右橫排方式印刷教育出版社明年起教科書逐漸改用簡體字編印 [Lee Chiaw Meng, Minister of Education, urged the Press, Publishing and Media Sectors to work together to Popularise the Usage of Simplified Chinese Text; With effect from the Next Year, Chinese Educational Materials will be Laid Out from Left to Right with the Gradual Change into Simplified Chinese Text]," *Nányáng Shāngbào* 《南洋商報》 [Nanyang Siang Pau], 16 March 1974.

"*Luètán hànzì gǎigé* 略談漢字改革 [An Overview Discussion on the Chinese Text Reform]," *Nányáng Shāngbào* 《南洋商報》 [Nanyang Siang Pau], 16 June 1956.

"*Tán hànzì de jiǎnhuà* 談漢字的簡化 [A Discussion on the Simplification of Chinese Text]," *Nányáng Shāngbào* 《南洋商報》 [Nanyang Siang Pau], 21 September 1955.

"*Yì'ān gōngsī zhàokāi dàhuì fābiǎo chángnián yàoshì jiǎnbào zhǔxí Lián Yíngzhōu chēng cháozhōu dàshà luòchéng jì yì'ān xuéyuàn kāixué zuì zhídé jìniàn* 義安公司召開大會發表常年要事簡報主席連瀛洲稱潮州大廈落成暨義安學院開學最值得紀念 [Lien Ying Chow, President of The Ngee Ann Kongsi reported at its Annual General Meeting that the Completion of the Teochew Building and the Commencement of Term of Ngee Ann College were worthy of Commemoration]," *Nányáng Shāngbào* 《南洋商報》 [Nanyang Siang Pau], 31 May 1963.

"*Yì'ān xuéyuàn gōngyìbù xīn xiàoshè gōngchéng jìnzhǎn xùnsù sìyuè jíkě yīngyòng quánbù dìngyú jīnnián bāyuè jùngōng* 義安學院工藝部新校舍工程進展迅速四月卽可應用全部定於今年八月竣工 [The Ngee Ann College's Technical College Campus Project Proceeds at a Rapid Pace; User can start using Portion of the Campus in April and Full Completion expected by August]," *Nányáng Shāngbào* 《南洋商報》 [Nanyang Siang Pau], 7 March 1966.

Hsu, Yun Ts'iao 許云樵, "*Mǎláiyà cóngtán zhī niànsān liǎngshuāngbàn wà sìdàcuò* 馬來亞叢談之廿三兩雙半襪四大厝 [Essays on Malaya 23: Two Half Pairs of Socks and the Four Grand Mansions]," *Nányáng Shāngbào* 《南洋商報》 [Nanyang Siang Pau], 19 January 1961.

Phua, Chay Long 潘醒農, "*Xīnjiāpō huárén gǔ shénmiào yuèhǎiqīngmiào* 新嘉坡華人古神廟 粵海清廟 [Historic Chinese Temple of Singapore: Wak Hai Cheng Bio]," *Nányáng Shāngbào* 《南洋商報》 [Nanyang Siang Pau], 26 July 1976.

Shin Min Daily News《新明日報》

Chén, Kūngāng 陳坤綱, "*Qǐng dàoshì tōngxiāo niànjīng, shòuyàn yòupìn gētái zhùxīng shāngrén qìngshēngrì biékāi shēngmiàn* 請道士通宵念經，壽宴又聘歌台助興　商人慶生日別開生面 [Taoist Priests invited to Chant Overnight, Gētái Singers were engaged to sing for the Birthday Banquet, Merchant celebrates Birthday in an Unconventional Way]," *Xīnmíng Rìbào* 《新明日報》[Shin Min Daily News], 22 January 1997.

Chén, Kūngāng 陳坤綱, "*Tóngdé shàntáng niànxīnshè 30 wàn dàzhuāngxiū 300 wàn zhāng jīnbó wéi shénxiàng tiējīn* 同德善堂念心社·30萬大裝修 300萬張金箔為神像貼金 [Thong Teck Sian Tong Lian Sin Sia. $300,000 Extensive Renovation, 3,000,000 Sheets of Gold Leaf for Gilding Statues of Deities]," *Xīnmíng Rìbào*《新明日報》[Shin Min Daily News], 8 June 1999.

Chén, Kūngāng 陳坤綱, "*Wèiyú shānzǎidǐng 170 nián gǔmiào huàn xīnzhuāng: měitiān shàngbǎi lǚkè yóu yuèhǎiqīngmiào* 位於山仔頂 170年古廟換新裝：每天上百旅客游粵海清廟 [170 Year Old Historic Temple at Shānzáidǐng gets a New Look: Over a Hundred Tourists Visit Wak Hai Cheng Bio Every Day]," *Xīnmíng Rìbào*《新明日報》[Shin Min Daily News], 17 March 1997.

Xiè, Xiánglóng 謝祥龍, "*Yàhuà chòngxīn huàzhǎn shì shénmiào zhǔchí yěshì míng huàjiā* 亞化重新畫展 是神廟主持也是名畫家 [The Alpha Revival Art Exhibition: Temple Caretaker is also an Artist]," *Xīnmíng Rìbào*《新明日報》[Shin Min Daily News], 15 November 2000.

Sin Chew Jit Poh《星洲日報》

"*Míngnián yīnián jí huáwén cǎiyòng jiǎntǐzì jiàoshòu* 明年一年級華文采用簡體字教授 [Simplified Chinese Text will be Adopted in Teaching of Primary One from Next Year]," *Xīngzhōu Rìbào*《星洲日報》[Sin Chew Jit Poh], 24 July 1982.

Singapore Standard

"S'pore Newsman Wins Degree in Architecture," *Singapore Standard*, 25 June 1952.

Straits Times Overland Journal

"Fortnight's Summary," *Straits Times Overland Journal*, 16 January 1873.

"Friday, 1st September," *Straits Times Overland Journal*, 9 September 1871.

"From the Daily Times, October 23rd. The Riots," *Straits Times Overland Journal*, 25 October 1871.

"Thursday, 15th December," *Straits Times Overland Journal*, 19 December 1881.

Straits Times Weekly Issue

"A Chinese Citizen Complains of the Condition of a Chinese Temple," *Straits Times Weekly Issue*, 4 March 1890.

"News of the Week," *Straits Times Weekly Issue*, 3 November 1883.

"The great annual religious procession commonly called *Chingay*...," *Straits Times Weekly Issue*, 19 December 1887.

"Untitled," *Straits Times Weekly Issue*, 19 December 1887.

Syonan Shimbun

"As Long As There Is Food In Syonan, None Shall Go Hungry, Suffer Distress," *Syonan Shimbun*, 7 February 1945.

"Black Cross Association To Hold Inaugural Meeting," *Syonan Shimbun*, 13 March 1945.

"Black Cross H.Q. Opened In Syonan," *Syonan Shimbun*, 24 & 25 April 1945.

"Blue Cross To Treat Lepers," *Syonan Shimbun*, 28 April 1945.

"Charitable Institutions Union Holding Big Confab Tomorrow," *Syonan Shimbun*, 5 February 1945.

"Chinese Forming Strong Body to Provide Assistance to Air Raid Victims Fully Supported by Authorities," *Syonan Shimbun*, 19 January 1945.

"Chinese Police Will Not Be Sent Outside Syonan," *Syonan Shimbun*, 26 July 1944.

"Free Food Centres Being Opened to Give Succour to Syonan's Destitute: Blue Cross Workers' Laudable Scheme," *Syonan Shimbun*, 28 March 1945.

"Mass Feeding of Poor People Starts in Syonan: 2,100 Blue Cross Workers Giving Good Service," *Syonan Shimbun*, 3 April 1945.

"Registration Centres for Settlers Opened," *Syonan Shimbun*, 3 December 1943.

"Relief & Charity," *Syonan Shimbun*, 27 January 1945.

"Syonan's Charitable Bodies Pooling Resources for More Effective Relief," *Syonan Shimbun*, 11 April 1945.

"Three Chinese Relief Bodies Amalgamate," *Syonan Shimbun*, 2 April 1945.

Oversea Chinese Association, "Notice: Re: Invitation to Gunpo (Auxiliary Servicemen) for the Second Term in Syonan," *Syonan Shimbun*, 20 September 1943.

Oversea Chinese Association, "Endau Development Scheme," *Syonan Shimbun*, 2 December 1943.

Oversea Chinese Association, "Recruitment of Chinese Policemen," *Syonan Shimbun*, 10 May 1944.

Syonan Tokubetu Si Tyo, "Tokubetu-Si Notice No. 265," *Syonan Simbun*, 18 September 1943.

Syonan Shimbun Fortnightly

"Syonan's Great Fortune," *Syonan Shimbun Fortnightly*, 20 June 1945.

The Business Times

"ABN AMRO to Lease 70–80% of Unfinished OCBC Centre East," *The Business Times*, 16 February 1996.

"OCBC Goes Ahead with 15-Storey Office Building – after 10 Years," *The Business Times*, 19 October 1994.

Chay, Felda, "'Dialect representation' is out at SCCCI," *The Business Times*, 28 May 2010.

The Singapore Free Press and Mercantile Advertiser

"An Aged Defendant!," *The Singapore Free Press and Mercantile Advertiser*, 14 December 1922.

"Untitled," *The Singapore Free Press and Mercantile Advertiser*, 27 November 1896.

"Untitled," *The Singapore Free Press and Mercantile Advertiser*, 14 January 1897.

The Singapore Free Press and Mercantile Advertiser (Weekly)

"Untitled," *The Singapore Free Press and Mercantile Advertiser (Weekly)*, 27 November 1894.

The Straits Times

"2-Language Schools", *The Straits Times*, 19 November 1968.

"2,500 Get More Relief," *The Straits Times*, 13 August 1951.

"Chinese Topics in Malaya," *The Straits Times*, 10 December 1931.

"Disaster fund to be held in reserve," *The Straits Times*, 30 August 1951.

"F.M.S. Loan," *The Straits Times*, 17 May 1916.

"Municipal Notice," *The Straits Times,* 1 August 1921.

"OCBC Revives Plan to Build Office Block," *The Straits Times*, 9 May 1992.

"Singapore Sanitation Commission," *The Straits Times*, 16 June 1906.

"The 'Chingay'," *The Straits Times*, 14 January 1897.

"The Chinese Procession," *The Straits Times*, 25 November 1902.

"The Chingay and Prices," *The Straits Times*, 23 November 1897.

"The Chingay Festival," *The Straits Times*, 1 February 1904.

"The Chingay," *The Straits Times*, 2 December 1896.

"The Chingay," *The Straits Times*, 22 November 1897.

"Untitled," *The Straits Times*, 6 April 1861.

"Untitled," *The Straits Times*, 30 November, 1872.

"Untitled," *The Straits Times*, 12 January 1900.

"Untitled," *The Straits Times*, 17 December 1900.

"Untitled," *The Straits Times*, 29 January 1901.
"Untitled," *The Straits Times*, 27 November 1901.
"Untitled," *The Straits Times*, 24 November 1902.
"Untitled," *The Straits Times*, 12 December 1903.
"Untitled," *The Straits Times*, 29 January 1904.
"Untitled," *The Straits Times*, 30 November 1904.
"Untitled," *The Straits Times*, 11 January 1906.
"Untitled," *The Straits Times*, 8 December 1906.
Chan, Fiona, "SCCCI to do away with dialect representation," *The Straits Times*, 30 March 2010.
Leong, Weng Kam, "Group opts to scrap clan-based voting," *The Straits Times*, 28 May 2010.
Leong, Weng Kam, "Is the end of the clan system in sight?," *The Straits Times*, 24 April 2010.
Sim, Arthur, "Kwan Im Temple now a historic site," *The Straits Times*, 29 September 2001.

Government Records

"Administrative Report of the Singapore Municipality 1906," NL3408, page 36, National Archives of Singapore.
"Chua Kian Thye, interview by Lee Beng Beng, 31 May 1999," Reel 2 of 3, Accession Number 002138, Oral History Interviews, National Archives of Singapore.
"Collections 10. Certificates of Naturalization Granted, March, 1857," Governor's Diary: Narrative, X27, folder 71, Raffles Museum and Library, National Archives of Singapore.
"Copy of a Conveyance to be Registered on Behalf of Seah Liang Seah of No. 14 North Boat Quay, Singapore, Merchant," Settlement of Singapore Registry of Deeds, vol. CCCLX, page 712, no. 200.
"Edward Presgrave to Walter Sewell Cracroft, 25 August 1826," Papers regarding land tenures and quit rents at Singapore, vol. 2, 191–201, India Office Records and Private Papers, IOR/F/4/1042/28678, British Library.
"Extract Singapore Diary, 9 January 1827," Papers regarding land tenures and quit rents at Singapore, vol. 2, 237–239, India Office Records and Private Papers, IOR/F/4/1042/28678, British Library.
"From Kim Seng and 14 other Chinese Merchants, 15 February, Enclosing Petition addressed to the most noble the Marquis of Dalhousie K. T. Governor General of British India, relating to the reestablishment of the Pork Farm for the support of the Pauper Hospital at this station," 15 February 1850, Governor: Miscellaneous Letters (In), W15, folder 61, Raffles Museum and Library, National Archives of Singapore.
"Government Notification No. 486," *Straits Settlements Government Gazette*, 29 August 1890.
"Government Notification No. 753," *Straits Settlements Government Gazette*, 20 December 1889.
"Index of Land," book 54, page 348, Singapore Land Authority.
"Index of Land," book 117, page 32, Singapore Land Authority.
"Index of Land," book 120, page 387, Singapore Land Authority.
"Jewish Synagogue Ordinance, Ordinance I of 1878," *Straits Settlements Government Gazette*, 5 April 1878.
"John Prince to Phillip Jackson, January 9, 1827," Papers regarding land tenures and quit rents at Singapore, vol. 2, 242–244, India Office Records and Private Papers, IOR/F/4/1042/28678, British Library.
"List of Existing Societies Exempted from Registration in the Settlement of Singapore," *Straits Settlements Government Gazette,* 12 August 1938, 2201.
"Lot No. 1 of Lease No. 473 for 999 Years," Indenture of Land, 25 August 1848, Singapore Land Authority.
"Lot Particulars, TS4-624L," 2016, Singapore Land Authority.
"May 10, 1822, Singapore: Letters to Bencoolen," L6, folder 18, Raffles Museum and Library, National Archives of Singapore.
"Ngee Ann Kongsi (Incorporation) Ordinance, (Chapter 370)," revised edition 1985, accessed 28 July 2017, https://sso.agc.gov.sg/Act/NAKIO1933.
"No. 1 Register of Lands Held on Grants Signed by

T.S. Raffles," December 1823 to June 1827, Papers regarding land tenures and quit rents at Singapore, vol. 2, 399–402, India Office Records and Private Papers, IOR/F/4/1042/28678, British Library.

"No. 103 – Ordinance No. 116 (Societies)," *Straits Settlements Government Gazette*, 19 January 1934.

"No. 1064 – The Societies Ordinance (Chapter 217)," *Straits Settlements Government Gazette,* 2 May 1941.

"No. 2 Register of Lands held on Grants of the New Form Established by Mr. Crawfurd," Papers regarding land tenures and quit rents at Singapore, vol. 2, 407, India Office Records and Private Papers, IOR/F/4/1042/28678, British Library.

"No. 36," Indenture of Land, 20 October 1845, District of Claymore, Singapore Land Authority.

"No. 5 of 1933 An Ordinance to Incorporate the Ngee Ann Kongsi," *Straits Settlements Government Gazette,* 10 March 1933.

"No. 732 – Ordinance No. 116 (Societies)," *Straits Settlements Government Gazette*, 19 April 1929.

"No. 858 – Ordinance No. 116 (Societies)," *Straits Settlements Government Gazette*, 3 May 1929.

"No. 913 – Ordinance No. 116 (Societies)," *Straits Settlements Government Gazette*, 8 May 1930.

"No. 928 – Ordinance No. 116 (Societies)," *Straits Settlements Government Gazette*, 8 May 1931.

"No. 962 – Ordinance No. 116 (Societies)," *Straits Settlements Government Gazette*, 12 May 1933.

"Ordinance No. I of 1889," *Straits Settlements Government Gazette*, 22 February 1889.

"Part of Singapore Island, June 18, 1825," India Office Records and Private Papers, IOR/X/3346, British Library.

"Report on an Ordinance to Incorporate the Ngee Ann Kongsi (No. 5 of 1933)," 1933, Straits Settlements Dispatches to the Secretary of State 1933 No. 151, GD100, NL6139, National Archives of Singapore.

"Singapore Improvement Ordinance (No. 10 of 1927)," Ordinances enacted by the governor of the Straits Settlements with the advice and consent of the Legislative Council thereof in the year 1927 (Straits Settlements, 1927).

"Straits Settlements No. 2674," Indenture of Land, 18 April 1909, Singapore Land Authority.

"Suit No. 430 of 1914, In the Matter of the Trustee Ordinance 1914 and In the Matter of the 'Ghee Ann Society'," 8 February 1916, Settlement of Singapore Registry of Deed, vol. CDXXXVI, page 505, no. 142.

"To Lieutt L. Nelson Hull, Actg Secy to the Lt Governor," 28 December 1822, Letters to and from Raffles, L11, folder 151, Raffles Museum and Library, National Archives of Singapore.

"William Farquhar to L. Nelson Hull, 23 December 1822," Singapore: Letters to Bencoolen, L11, fols. 139–140, Raffles Museum and Library, National Archives of Singapore.

Phua, Chay Long 潘醒農, "*Yì'ān gōngsī shǐmò jì* 《義安公司始末記》 [Historical Changes of the Ngee Ann Kongsi]," Ngee Ann Kongsi, 18 April 1931, NA539, National Archives of Singapore.

Singapore Improvement Trust, "Backlane – Phillip St. 33, Phillip St," 1929–1933, SIT T9/29, HDB 1013, National Archives of Singapore.

Singapore Improvement Trust, "Chinese Temple at Jalan Besar Lot 14 T S D XVII – Ngee Ann Kongsi," 1928–1936, SIT 871/28, HDB1011, National Archives of Singapore.

Superintendent of Census, *Report on the Census of the Straits Settlements, taken on 5th April 1891* (Singapore: Straits Settlements, 1891).

Superintendent of Census, *Report on the Census of the Straits Settlements, taken on 1st March 1901* (Singapore: Straits Settlements, 1901).

Superintendent of Census, *Report on the Census of the Straits Settlements, taken on 10th March 1911* (Singapore: Straits Settlements, 1911).

Private Records and Reports

"Lim Nee Soon to Arthur M. Goodman, 4 January 1928," Ngee Ann Kongsi, Singapore.

"Watt-Hai Cheng Beo Temple A Piece of Land at

Phillip Street as Lot No. 428-1 of T.S. IV An Area is 13,273 sq. ft.," unpublished minutes of meeting, Ngee Ann Kongsi.

Ban See Soon Kongsi Accounts, 3 & 4 May 1937, Ban See Soon Kongsi, Singapore.

Ban See Soon Kongsi Accounts, 23 & 24 April 1938, Ban See Soon Kongsi, Singapore.

Ban See Soon Kongsi Accounts, 12 & 13 May 1939, Ban See Soon Kongsi, Singapore.

Ban See Soon Kongsi Accounts, 30 April & 1 May 1940, Ban See Soon Kongsi, Singapore.

Ban See Soon Kongsi Accounts, 19 & 20 April 1941, Ban See Soon Kongsi, Singapore.

Ban See Soon Kongsi Accounts, 7 & 8 May 1942, Ban See Soon Kongsi, Singapore.

Ban See Soon Kongsi Accounts, 27 & 28 May 1943, Ban See Soon Kongsi, Singapore.

Ban See Soon Kongsi Accounts, 15 & 16 April 1944, Ban See Soon Kongsi, Singapore.

Ban See Soon Kongsi Accounts, 4 & 5 May 1945, Ban See Soon Kongsi, Singapore.

Chua, Ai Hua, *Pilot Timber Consolidation Research Project: Technical Report for Yueh Hai Ching Temple (National Monument) at 30B Phillip Street, Singapore 048696* (Singapore: 2010).

Ngee Ann Kongsi, Pre-Restoration Photographic Records, The Ngee Ann Kongsi 1994, Singapore.

Phua, Chay Long 潘醒農, *Xīnjiāpō yì'ān gōngsī yīng 1930 nián mínguó shíjiǔnián sìyuè shíèrrì lì yì'ànbù* 新嘉坡義安公司 英1930年民國十九年四月十二日立 議案簿 [Singapore Ngee Ann Kongsi A.D. 1930 12 April in the 19th year of the Chinese Republic Minutes of Meeting Folder], Ngee Ann Kongsi.

Raymond Woo & Associates Architects, Chin, Jian Ping and Lee, Zhi Gao, "Proposed Additions & Alterations and Preservation to the Existing Yueh Hai Ching Temple on Lot 428-1 and 428-2 TS 4 at 30B Phillip Street," (Raymond Woo & Associates Architects; Construction and Planning Institute, Guangdong Province, Teochew City, June 1994).

Architectural Plans

"Additions and Alterations to a Chinese Temple, situated in Teluk Ayer Street. Property of Eng Wah Quan," 1898, 203/1898, CBS337, National Archives of Singapore.

"Alterations of Passed Plan No. 70 Dated 25.3.1919 for Chinese Vegetarian Temple to be Erected at Telok Blangah Road," 1922, 72A/1919, CBS1094, National Archives of Singapore.

"Amended 1st Floor Plans Shewing Rooms as per Notice No. 129 for Temple at Telok Blangah Rd," 1923, 72C/1919, CBS1094, National Archives of Singapore.

"Amended Passed Plan No. 339 Dated 13-7-17 at Temple of Peck Seah Street for Cheng Siew Ho," 1917, 399A/1917, CBS1108, National Archives of Singapore.

"Designs for Proposed Brackets to Girders at Nos. 56 & 57 Kling Street, Singapore," 127/1892, CBS332, National Archives of Singapore.

"Half Inch Details of R.C. Beams and Slabs for Additions and Alterations to Temple at 578 Telok Blangah Road Sheet No. 1," 1932, 72E/1919, CBS1094, National Archives of Singapore.

"Half Inch Details of R.C. Beams for Additions and Alterations to Temple at 578 Telok Blangah Road Sheet No. 2," 1932, 72E/1919, CBS1094, National Archives of Singapore.

"Half Inch Details of R.C. Slab Columns etc. for Additions and Alterations to Temple at 578 Telok Blangah Road Sheet No. 3," 1932, 72E/1919, CBS1094, National Archives of Singapore.

"Land Division at Philip Street, c. 1830–1890, SP000178," Survey Department, National Archives of Singapore.

"Plan of a Chinese Temple Proposed to be erected at Devonshire Road Singapore Property of Mr. Bay Soon Cheng," 1897, 304/1897, CBS336, National Archives of Singapore.

"Plan of a Chinese Temple to be Rebuilt at the 4th Mile off Telok Blangah Rd. Trustee Mr. Ong Whye Teck," 1906, 8217/1906, CBS1131, National

Archives of Singapore.

"Plan of a Dwelling House to be Built at River Valley Road. The Property of Seah Song Seah Esq.," 1896, 60/1896, CBS334, National Archives of Singapore.

"Plan of a New Chinese Temple to be Erected at Peck Seah Street for the Chinese Priest (Swee Ooh)," 1907, 8861/1907, CBS1130, National Archives of Singapore.

"Plan of a Temple at Jalan Besar for Toh Nghe What," 1886, 140/1896, CBS335, National Archives of Singapore.

"Plan of Additions and Alterations at Temple of Peck Seah Street for Cheng Siew Ho Site Plan 1," 1917, 399/1917, CBS1108, National Archives of Singapore.

"Plan of Additions and Alterations at Temple of Peck Seah Street for Cheng Siew Ho Site Plan 2," 1917, 399/1917, CBS1108, National Archives of Singapore.

"Plan of Additions and Alterations at Temple of Peck Seah Street for Cheng Siew Ho," 1917, 399/1917, CBS1108, National Archives of Singapore.

"Plan of Alterations and Additions Buddhism Temple at Devonshire Road MC No. 1-C for Bay Soon Cheng (Trustee)," 1902, 5101/1902, CBS1139, National Archives of Singapore.

"Plan of Proposed Additions and Alterations. A Buddhist Temple at Alexandra Road for Bea Hock," 1906, 8167/1906, CBS1131, National Archives of Singapore.

"Plan of Proposed Extension. Temple at Devonshire Road for Trustee Bay Soon Cheng," 1897, 141/1897, CBS336, National Archives of Singapore.

"Plan of Two Shophouses to be Erected on Site of Nos. 56 & 57 Kling Street Singapore," 128/1891, CBS331, National Archives of Singapore.

"Proposed Addition to Worshipping Portico on Open Terrace Etc. Sheet No. 1 (Being Amendment to Passed Plan No. 72D 19)," 1932, 72F/1919, CBS1094, National Archives of Singapore.

"Proposed Addition to Worshipping Portico on Open Terrace Etc. Sheet No. 2 (Being Amendment to Passed Plan No. 72D 19)," 1932, 72F/1919, CBS1094, National Archives of Singapore.

"Proposed Additions and Alterations to Chinese Vegetarian Temple M.C. No. 436 Telok Blangah Road Drawing 1," 1932, 72D/1919, CBS1094, National Archives of Singapore.

"Proposed Additions and Alterations to Chinese Vegetarian Temple M.C. No. 436 Telok Blangah Road Drawing 2," 1931, 72D/1919, CBS1094, National Archives of Singapore.

"Proposed Plan Shewing Chinese Vegetarian Temple to be Erected at Telok Blanga Road for Ong Guan Teck," 1919, 72/1919, CBS1094, National Archives of Singapore.

"Re-alterations of Passed Plan No. 72A-22 Dated 29.4.22 for Vegetarian Temple at Telok Blangah Rd," 1923, 72B/1919, CBS1094, National Archives of Singapore.

"Sze Hai Tong Banking and Insurance Company Corporation Nos. 57 & 58 Chulia Street," 8791/1907, CBS1130, National Archives of Singapore.

Ang Kheng Leng & Associates, "Proposed Reconstruction of Existing Brick Boundary Wall on Lots 428-1 & 428-2 T.S. IV at Phillip Street for M/S The Ngee Ann Kongsi," 12 November 1979, 3299/1979, Collection of the Ngee Ann Kongsi.

Chia & Associates Architects, "Wak Hai Cheng Bio Chinese Temple: Measured and Record Drawings of Existing Structure," September 1992, Collection of the Ngee Ann Kongsi.

Lao, Chee Hean, "Plan of Temple to be Rebuilt in Phillip Street," 27 February 1895, 86/1895, CBS334, National Archives of Singapore.

Raymond Woo & Associates Architects, "1st Storey Plan," Proposed Amendment to Approved Restoration and Additions/Alternations to the Existing Yueh Hai Ching Temple (National Monument) on Lot 98989L, 98988X, 00624L, TS 04, No. 30B Phillip Street, Singapore 048696,

February, 2013.

Singapore Survey Department, "Singapore. Mukim No. XVIII_Ang Mo Kio, Mukim No. XVII_ Toa Payoh, Mukim No. XXIV_Kalang," 1956, SP001719, National Archives of Singapore.

Maps and Plans

"Gazetteer of Singapore (Federated Malay States Surveys No. 54, 1935)". Courtesy of Mr Mok Ly Yng.

"Map of Singapore around 1819–20 (The Bute Map)". The Bute Collection at Mount Stuart, Isle of Bute, Scotland.

"Map of the Town and Environs of Singapore, Drawn by J.B. Tassin, from an Actual Survey by G.D. Coleman (Calcutta: J.B. Tassin's Lith' Press, 1836)". Courtesy of National Archives of Singapore 20140000101-0003-TM000037).

"Part of Singapore Island, June 18, 1825", India Office Records and Private Papers, IOR/X/3346. Courtesy of The British Library.

"Plan of Singapore Town and Adjoining Districts from Actual Survey by John Turnbull Thomson, Govt Surveyor, Singapore (London: J.M. Richardson, 1846)". Urban Redevelopment Authority Collection. Courtesy of National Archives of Singapore (20120001620-0005).

"Plan of Singapore Town Shewing Topographical Detail and Municipal Numbers. His Excellency Sir Cecil Clementi Smith, G.C.M.G. Governor of The Straits Settlements. Major H. E. McCallum, R.E.; C.M.G. Colonial Engineer and Surveyor General S.S. (1893)". Courtesy of Mr Mok Ly Yng.

"Plan of the Town of Singapore and Its Environs Surveyed in 1842 by Government Surveyor Singapore, March 1854", Surveyor-General, Federated Malay States (F.M.S.) and Straits Settlements (S.S.). Surveyed in 1842 by government surveyor (F.M.S. Surveys No. 275, 1922). Survey Department, Singapore Collection. Courtesy of the National Archives of Singapore (20050000698 - AccNo981).

"Plan of the Town of Singapore by Lieut. Jackson (London: Henry Colburn, 1822)". Courtesy of the National Museum of Singapore (XXXX-02072-002).

"Singapore. Reproduced from a map of 1862". Courtesy of the National Museum of Singapore (XXXX-02126).

"Singapore. Resurvey Town Sub-Division No. 4. Block No. 3". Courtesy of Lim Shao Bin.

"Singapore Town. Singapore Photomap, Sheet 16 (1950)". A Collection held by the National Archives of Singapore. Crown Copyright.

Personal Communications

Lee, Sean Wah 李先華, personal communication (interview) with author, Ngee Ann City Civic Plaza, Singapore, 17 April 2016.

Lú, Zhīgāo 盧芝高, personal communication with author, *Cháo'ān xiàn jīnhú jiànzhù gōngchéng yǒuxiàn gōngsī* 潮安縣金湖建築工程有限公司 (currently *Cháozhōushì jīnhú jiànzhù gōngchéng yǒuxiàn gōngsī* 潮州市金湖建筑工程有限公司), *Guǎngdōngshěng cháo'ān xiàn cháozhōushì dàdào* 廣東省潮安縣潮州市大道, 20 January 2011.

Ng, Ngiap Khiang 黄業強, personal communication with Ng Ching Huei 吳慶輝, 5 Lorong 40 Geylang, 20 September 2014.

Quek, Nang Kwang 郭南光, personal communication with author, 5 Lorong 40 Geylang, 9 August 2014.

Qwek, Wee Chew 郭維洲, personal communication with author, Wak Hai Cheng Bio, 17 October 2009 and 12 May 2010.

Tan, Siew Eng 陳秀英, personal communication with author, Wak Hai Cheng Bio, Singapore, 8 December 2016.

Tan, Yeow Wooi 陳耀威, personal communication with author, Georgetown, Penang, 7 August 2018.

Woo, Nelson 余義源, personal communication (e-mail) with author, 8 August 2017.

Yeo, Eng Koon 楊應群, personal communication with author, 50 Chin Swee Road, 15 August 2016.

Index

I

J

K

L

M

U

V

W